TAKEOVER

HITLER'S FINAL RISE TO POWER

Timothy W. Ryback

ALFRED A. KNOPF   NEW YORK   2024

THIS IS A BORZOI BOOK
PUBLISHED BY ALFRED A. KNOPF

Copyright © 2024 by Timothy W. Ryback

www.aaknopf.com

Knopf, Borzoi Books, and the colophon are
registered trademarks of Penguin Random House LLC.

Library of Congress Cataloging-in-Publication Data
Names: Ryback, Timothy W., author.
Title: Takeover : Hitler's final rise to power / Timothy W. Ryback.
Description: New York : Alfred A. Knopf, 2024. | Includes bibliographical
references and index.
Identifiers: LCCN 2023020412 (print) | LCCN 2023020413 (ebook) |
ISBN 9780593537428 (hardcover) | ISBN 9780593537435 (ebook)
Subjects: LCSH: Hitler, Adolf, 1889–1945. | Germany—History—1918–1933. |
Germany—History—1933–1945.
Classification: LCC DD247.H5 R946 2024 (print) | LCC DD247.H5 (ebook) |
DDC 943.086—dc23/eng/20230630
LC record available at https://lccn.loc.gov/2023020412
LC ebook record available at https://lccn.loc.gov/2023020413

Jacket image: Hitler shaking hands with President von Hindenburg,
Germany, 1933. Heritage Images/Getty Images
Jacket design by John Gall

Manufactured in the United States of America
First Edition

TAKEOVER

In memory of

Dr. Richard M. Hunt
1926–2020
Teacher, Mentor, Friend

When I walked into Adolf Hitler's room, I was
convinced that I was meeting the future dictator
of Germany. In something like fifty seconds, I
was quite sure that I was not. It took just about
that time to measure the startling insignificance
of this man who has set the world agog.

DOROTHY THOMPSON,
"I Saw Hitler!," JANUARY 1932

Contents

x   CONTENTS

TAKEOVER

STARGAZING

The world's greatest poker game is being played here.

—FREDERICK T. BIRCHALL, *The New York Times,*
DATELINE BERLIN, AUGUST 10, 1932

On a cloudless Tuesday night in mid-August 1932, Adolf Hitler sat on the veranda of Haus Wachenfeld, his alpine retreat on the Obersalzberg, just above the Bavarian town of Berchtesgaden, stargazing with Joseph Goebbels. The previous week had seen winds and rain of apocalyptic proportions. Hillsides collapsed, burying roads and railway lines with as much as four feet of mud. Some 50 percent of the Mosel Valley wine harvest was destroyed by hail. Brandenburg lost 75 percent of its cherry crop. The tobacco fields in Schwedt were obliterated. In Posen, a farmer and a female laborer were killed by lightning, and a woman and child hospitalized. The German newspaper *Vorwärts* reported in a headline, "Death Descends from the Clouds." Then the skies began to clear.

"With Hitler on the Obersalzberg. Wonderful sunshine," Goebbels wrote in his diary that Sunday. "Spirits high. And why not?" If all went according to plan, by week's end, Paul von Hindenburg, the Reich president, would have appointed

Hitler as Reich chancellor. In the Reichstag elections on July 31, 1932, the National Socialists had claimed thirteen million votes, more than 37 percent of the electorate, with 230 seats in the 600-member Reichstag, doubling their legislative mandate. "We have won a great victory!" Hitler proclaimed on election night. "There has never been anything like this in the history of our people."

Ten days later, Hitler and Goebbels sat beneath the star-studded sky on the Obersalzberg talking, planning, reminiscing, as Hitler was wont to do in close company. The previous evening, Hitler had strategized with Goebbels until four o'clock in the morning on their seemingly imminent "seizure of power." Goebbels was to serve as minister of culture and education. "I am getting schools, universities, film, radio, theatre, propaganda," he later wrote in his diary. "A vast portfolio. Enough to fill a lifetime." Goebbels vowed never to surrender power. He wrote, "They will have to drag us out as corpses."

Now on this mid-August Tuesday evening, Hitler and Goebbels mused, in a more subdued mood, on their respective childhoods. As a mid-level customs officer, Hitler's father, frustrated when sober and brutal when drunk, had demanded that his son follow in his own inglorious footsteps and pursue a career in the civil service. Hitler, as is known, wanted to be an artist. Not even the severest canings could deter his ambition. "My father refused to abandon his 'Never,' and I responded in kind," Hitler wrote in *Mein Kampf*. Hitler emerged from one thrashing proudly telling his mother, "Father beat me thirty-two times!" On another occasion, Hitler was beaten unconscious. His mother dragged him to safety, despite her husband's unrelenting blows. "Hitler had almost the same childhood as I did," Goebbels wrote in his diary. "The father a tyrant, the mother a source of goodness and love."

Hitler's artistic ambition eventually flagged then failed, but his tenacity, whether inherited or beaten into him by his father, remained as blinkered and unrelenting as ever. Following his failed bid for the Reich presidency in April 1932, Hitler went to court to have the election results annulled. "Hitler to Contest Validity of Election," *The New York Times* announced in a headline. The court dismissed the Hitler suit. Observing that Hindenburg had beaten Hitler by 5,941,582 votes, the court upheld the election results, ruling that the disparity was "so significant that it would make no sense for a national recount of the ballots." Hitler nevertheless declared victory, noting that his party had gained two million votes at the polls. "That is a feat that has never been equaled, and I have done this despite the unconstitutional ban placed on my broadcasting election appeals," Hitler said, denouncing the flood of "lies and slanders spread about me in the election campaign of the ten parties opposed to my candidature." Hitler looked ahead to the next Reichstag elections with equally fierce determination in his effort to destroy democracy through democratic process. Echoing Georges-Jacques Danton's revolutionary call for unrestrained and audacious action—"*l'audace, encore l'audace, toujours l'audace*"—that preceded and precipitated the first bloodshed of the Great Terror in France, Hitler offered his own triadic call to arms against his country's constitutional republic: "I shall continue as I have begun, I shall attack, attack, and attack again."

For thirteen years, since his first encounter with a handful of men in the back room of a Munich beer hall, in September 1919, Hitler had been driven by a single ambition: to destroy the political system that he held responsible for the myriad ills plaguing the German people. He vowed revenge on the politicians who "stabbed" the frontline soldiers in the back with the armistice, on the "traitors" who signed the Treaty of Versailles, saddling the German people with "war guilt" and crushing reparation payments. He said "heads will roll." He vowed to dismantle the multiparty political system that, he claimed, had fractured and polarized the German nation, pitting "individual against individual, city against the countryside, laborers against factory workers, Bavaria against Prussia, Catholics against Protestants, and Protestants against Catholics," as he said that July in advance of the Reichstag elections. Hitler's words are preserved on a two-disk recording titled "Appeal to the Nation." Hitler speaks with his distinctive cadence and stridency, but in a notably moderated tone. There is no ranting, no raving, no storms of applause, no Sieg heil choruses. One can hear, through the hissing and occasional snap of the shellac disks, traces of Bavarian and Austrian inflections—the *R*s are rolled and the *T*s are softer than the crisper, clipped consonants in the north. It is the sound of Hitler positioning himself as a political leader rather than as a revolutionary. As suggested by the brown record label, emblazoned with a swastika that spins into blur at seventy-eight revolutions per minute, this is an "appeal," not a tirade.

Harry Kessler, the son of a Hamburg banker and a British aristocrat, was a former diplomat, a pedestrian in national politics and peripatetic in lifestyle—Berlin, London, Paris, Cannes—who was one of the era's most astute observers of contemporary politics. While many observers saw Hitler as indecisive, fanatic, and occasionally unhinged, Kessler sensed that Hitler knew exactly what he was doing. Hitler's oratory style at political rallies—"trivial and bombastic rhetoric"—served to distract attention, Kessler argued, from Hitler's calculated and calibrated manipulation of the moment. What made Hitler so dangerous, Kessler believed, was his bluster, behind which lay "his intuition, lightning-fast ability to assess a situation, and ability to react with astonishing speed and effectiveness."

Hans Prinzhorn was a psychiatrist who wrote on art and politics. His landmark study on insanity and artistic expression remains a reference point for art historians. Prinzhorn had attended a Hitler rally in Weimar in spring 1930 and was struck by Hitler's mesmerizing effect on his listeners. Hitler raised his voice to a "demagogic register," then suddenly fell silent for a moment and continued in a "subdued" tone, "as if nothing had happened." Prinzhorn also noted that Hitler limited himself to a handful of tropes that he repeated over and over. "Jewish influence" and the "treason of Versailles" were favored phrases, as was "heads will roll." Prinzhorn suggested that listeners responded to Hitler's rhetoric devices—volume, rhythm, modulation, repetition—emotionally rather rationally, which rendered him impervious to attack by political opponents. "They keep thinking they've hit on a crucial point when they say Hitler's speeches are meaningless and empty," Prinzhorn wrote. "But intellectual judgments of the Hitler experience—*Hitler-Erlebnis*—miss the point entirely." With Hitler, the medium was the message. Bella Fromm, a journalist for the venerable *Vossische Zeitung*, observed, "Hitler knows his game."

One senses this same calculation and calibration in Hitler's "Appeal to the Nation," which was designed to reach beyond his fanatically loyal base and embrace the general voting public. Hitler dispenses with his most incendiary tropes. There is no threat that once he and his party are in power the heads of the signatories of the Versailles Treaty "will roll." There is no talk of vengeance on political enemies, no extended exegeses about Jewish conspiracies.

In fact, Hitler makes no mention of Jews. Instead, he talks about the astonishing rise of his political movement. "I began to work on reuniting Germans thirteen years ago with seven men, and today there are thirteen million in our ranks," Hitler says. At the time, the National Socialists were "mocked and ridiculed," Hitler recalls. "No one is laughing now."

Hitler enumerates the failings of representational democracy and multiparty rule. He talks about inflation and unemployment. Farmers have been "plunged into misery." The middle classes "ruined." One of every three working men and women is without a job. "The hopes of millions have been shattered." The government, at the federal, state, and municipal levels, is bankrupt. "The coffers are empty." One hears, as Prinzhorn noted, Hitler's uncanny ability "to hammer away" on a few key issues in a way "that the common man can comprehend and remember."

In anticipation of the July 31 Reichstag elections Hitler is clearly positioning himself as a future chancellor, reaching out to the nation, seeking to bridge divides of class and conscience, socialism and nationalism, with a special appeal to the large Catholic and Protestant voting constituencies that usually cast their ballots for the conservative centrist parties. "The Almighty who permitted a movement that began thirteen years ago with seven men to grow into thirteen million will further grant us the day when Germans again become a unified people," Hitler says to conclude his address. "If the nation fulfills its duty"—which meant voting National Socialist—"the day will come when we will again be granted a Reich of honor and freedom, work and bread."

The eight-and-a-half-minute address, available in a two-disk set, went on sale for 1.60 reichsmarks (or about $8 today) at bookstores and newspaper kiosks across the country in mid-July. It was marketed as "The First Adolf Hitler

Record!" Two weeks later, nearly fourteen million voters delivered Hitler his electoral triumph, with 37 percent of the electorate and 230 delegates in the six-hundred-seat assembly. The National Socialists were now the single most powerful political force in the country. Then, on August 4, Hitler received a phone call. Kurt von Schleicher was on the line.

*

Like everyone else, Hitler knew Schleicher was the ultimate Berlin power broker. As minister of defense, the fifty-year-old general commanded the *Reichswehr*, the country's military forces, but, equally important, he had the trust of Reich president Paul von Hindenburg, who possessed the constitutional authority to appoint and dismiss chancellors at will. In a reversal of the classic Clausewitz adage, Schleicher viewed power politics as war by other means. "You can do anything with bayonets except sit on them," Schleicher once told André François-Poncet, the French ambassador to Berlin. Impressed by Schleicher's *"réalisme"* and *"cynisme,"* François-Poncet called Schleicher a *"maître de l'intrigue politique."* Frederick T. Birchall, chief European correspondent of *The New York Times*, said that "everything which seems temporarily incomprehensible" in German politics could ultimately be traced to the "tall, spare, slightly stooped-shouldered" lieutenant general with "a shrewd rather than a hard visage."

Gottfried Treviranus, a former cabinet member, recalled that whenever he visited Schleicher in the defense ministry, he invariably found the general's desk vacant of files or paperwork. Instead, Schleicher had a dozen glass figurines in the shape of various animals. "He kept moving them around in and out of the light, like an impatient animal trainer, who treated his fellow human beings no differently than his glass menagerie," Treviranus recalled. Schleicher knew every-one who was anyone. He was on a first-name basis with the exiled kaiser's son and an intimate in the *Haus Hindenburg,* the Hindenburg family circle. He had been a fellow cadet with Hindenburg's only son, Oskar, and served with him in the 3rd Imperial Foot Guards, a regiment of the Royal Prus-sian Army. Schleicher attended gala events as frequently as military exercises, if not more, and liked to be photographed with pretty young women. Bella Fromm called Schleicher "a man of almost irresistible charm."

*

Hitler had been trying for several years to access Schleicher's rarefied circles, which also included Kurt von Hammerstein-Equord, the Reichswehr chief of staff whom Schleicher had known since their days, along with Oskar Hindenburg, in the same imperial regiment. Hitler was introduced to Ham-merstein in early 1924 at the villa of the piano manufacturer Edwin Bechstein, whose wife was a Hitler admirer. Hammer-stein was not impressed. He later described the thirty-five-year-old political leader as a *"Wirrkopf,"* or muddle head. A second meeting, in 1926 or 1927, at Hammerstein's apart-ment in the fashionable Hardenbergstrasse appeared to con-firm his initial assessment. "He talks too much and doesn't make much sense," Hammerstein said afterward. When Hammerstein called Schleicher, in September 1931, to say that the "the big man from Munich"—"*der grosse Mann aus München*"—wanted to meet, Schleicher declined. "Unfortu-nately, I'm not available," he said. Hammerstein subsequently met with Hitler, who spoke nonstop for the first hour of the meeting, until Hammerstein interrupted him. When briefed on Hitler's behavior, Schleicher asked, "What am I to do with that psychopath?"

Schleicher eventually agreed to meet Hitler, twice in October 1931, and again in May 1932, in the office of Werner von Alvensleben, a member of a Junker family with a lineage dating back to the twelfth century. Werner's younger brother Botho was co-founder and president of the influential *Herrenclub*, a private association of prominent businessmen and establishment politicians. Bella Fromm spoke of a "Junker clique" of Herrenclub intriguers. At the time, Schleicher was seeking to convince President Hindenburg to replace the chancellor, Heinrich Brüning, a centrist political leader, with Franz von Papen, a handsome but seemingly hapless aristocrat. Papen was generally viewed as a Schleicher puppet. Schleicher liked to say that Papen's head was made for carrying a top hat rather than brains, and referred to him as *"Fränzchen,"* or "my little Franz."

Alvensleben's office, situated in a leafy neighborhood, just down the street from the defense ministry, allowed for discreet meetings. Hitler agreed to support a Papen chancellorship if Schleicher agreed to convince Hindenburg to rescind a ban Brüning had imposed on the SA, or *Sturmabteilung*, Hitler's private army of 400,000 storm troopers, and to schedule new Reichstag elections. Hitler hoped to secure an absolute National Socialist majority in the Reichstag and with it a claim to the chancellorship. Schleicher readily agreed to Hitler's conditions. "Papen is isolated! His chancellorship will last no more than a few months," Hitler said afterward. But Hitler was wary. He didn't trust the look in Schleicher's eyes. "Dealing with Schleicher won't be easy," he said.

But Schleicher made good on his promises. Hindenburg dismissed Brüning on June 1 and appointed Papen, along with a new cabinet. Lutz Graf von Krosigk, a high-level government official, was made minister of finance. Schleicher became minister of defense. As promised, the ban on the SA was lifted on July 20, allowing the National Socialists to stage mass rallies in advance of the July 31 Reichstag elections, resulting in Hitler's landslide victory. Four days after the election, Hitler received Schleicher's call.

The phone call came as a welcome signal. Hitler had spent the previous day, August 3, in Tegernsee, at a lake in Bavaria, strategizing with Goebbels about how best to leverage their newly won Reichstag seats. Despite triumphal declarations in the National Socialist press, Hitler was in fact disappointed. He had hoped for a clear Reichstag majority that would give him an undisputed claim to the chancellorship. Instead, he was left with the choice of joining a coalition government or having his Reichstag delegates play obstructionist politics with the legislative process. As one of the leading hard-line radicals in Hitler's inner circle, Goebbels was inclined toward obstructionism and an "all or nothing"—*Alles oder nichts*— strategy, but Hitler wasn't so certain. Should the National Socialists in fact consider a coalition government? If so, with whom? Never with the Communists or the Social Democrats, of course, and certainly not with the Center Party, headed by Brüning, whose government had just been toppled. Which left the German National People's Party, financed significantly by Alfred Hugenberg, a cantankerous media mogul who was as intransigent on political matters as Hitler. "Difficult decisions," Goebbels wrote in his diary. "Enough to make you vomit." And yet Hitler had never been this close to attaining the chancellor position. The fact that the minister of defense was asking for a meeting was a good sign. After the call with Schleicher, Hitler telephoned Goebbels before calling back Schleicher to confirm the meeting. "Consulted briefly with Hitler again," Goebbels noted that evening. "He is driving to Schleicher to present our demands."

*

The circumstances of Hitler's August 5 meeting with Schleicher were so carefully guarded that even Hitler's closest associates, let alone the press, appear to have been left unaware of specifics. Fred Birchall of *The New York Times* heard that the meeting was either in Dresden or on the island of Rügen, three hours north of Berlin. *Vorwärts* situated the rendezvous in the town of Kyritz. Goebbels thought the meeting was in Berlin and assumed that Hitler would be accompanied by Ernst Röhm, the head of Hitler's storm troopers, who had joined Hitler in the May meeting with Schleicher, and Hermann Göring, who frequently accompanied Hitler. In fact, the rendezvous took place fifty miles north of Berlin, in the town of Fürstenberg, a clutch of red-roofed houses along a rail line that also serviced the adjacent community of Ravensbrück.* Hitler was joined by Gregor Strasser, officially the *Reichsorganisationsleiter*, the party administrator for the Reich, equivalent to the chief operating officer for the National Socialist movement.

Hitler had known Strasser since the earliest days of his political career, when he was still making the rounds on the radical fringe of Munich's beer-hall political scene, and Strasser was building his own right-wing movement in Augsburg. "He was a man of thirty-one, with regular features and a stubbly moustache," Strasser's younger brother, Otto, recalled of

---

* Ravensbrück became the site of a notorious concentration camp, where an estimated 132,000 women were imprisoned between 1939 and 1945, many of whom were forced into slave labor at a nearby factory affiliated with the Siemens corporation.

Hitler. "His face was not yet lined with thought." The synergies were evident to both Hitler and Strasser. Hitler was the fanatic nationalist, Strasser the committed socialist. Together, they gave truth to the National Socialist name. More important still was Strasser's pragmatism. "The visionary genius of this man is singular," Strasser said of Hitler. "But what good is genius that is not anchored in reality, whose brilliant ideas cannot be implemented in the real world." Strasser knew how to get things done.

Following the failed beer-hall putsch, while Hitler sat in Landsberg Prison, hoping for leniency, Strasser, who was also in prison on related charges, managed to get himself elected to the Bavarian state legislature, resulting in the suspension of his sentence. While Hitler waited, Strasser walked. As the chief party administrator, Strasser expanded party registrations from 27,000 in 1925 to 800,000 by 1931. Strasser also quadrupled the number of party chapters, from 71 to more than 270, and restructured the districts in a move that helped drive the stunning National Socialist victories in the Reichstag elections. In 1924, Strasser was among the first twelve National Socialist Reichstag delegates and, in June 1932, the first and only National Socialist allowed to address the nation on the radio, when he distilled a muddled political party agenda into a simple, clear message: "Germany, Germany, and only Germany!"

Strasser had also recruited some of the movement's top leaders, including Heinrich Himmler, Röhm, and Goebbels, who had served as Strasser's deputy for a time and joined him as one of the first Reichstag delegates, before shifting his loyalties to Hitler.

Goebbels had watched the ease with which Strasser engaged in cross-aisle dialogue with other political factions in the Reichstag. "It is curious how little resistance he finds here," Goebbels observed that May. "Of all of us he seems to be most favored by our opponents." Goebbels did not mean this as a compliment. But this was exactly the skill set Hitler wanted for his meeting with Schleicher.

*

On the morning of August 5, Hitler and Strasser traveled to Fürstenberg. Schleicher was accompanied by Wilhelm von Gayl, Papen's minister of the interior, a jurist who had headed the East Prussian delegation to the Treaty of Versailles. Hitler had met Gayl in June 1932 to facilitate the lifting of the ban on uniforms and public demonstrations. He found Gayl's attentiveness to legalities and bureaucratic foot-dragging infuriating. Goebbels called him "a pale aesthete unfit to ensure order and security in these wild times," and wrote, "He has to go. Otherwise the Reds will overwhelm him and us." Göring called the bespectacled interior minister "a weakling, hesitant, without initiative, afraid of responsibility." When Hitler railed against weak-kneed politicians and the traitors of Versailles, he was talking about people like Gayl and the other privileged aristocrats who filled Papen's "cabinet of monocles." Hitler spoke derisively of the "Kabinett von-von-von-von-von." He sniped, "If God wanted things to be the way they are, we'd all have been born with monocles." Goebbels was not with Hitler at the meeting and was wary of Schleicher's motives. He suspected Schleicher's intent was "to gradually lure the Führer away from the party." In fact, Schleicher had a strategy he called the *Zähmungsprozess*, or taming process, designed to marginalize the party "radicals" and bring the movement into the political mainstream. Schleicher praised Hitler as a "modest, orderly man who only wants what is best" and is committed to the rule of law. Schleicher had equally flattering words for Hitler's storm troopers. He saw them as a bulwark against left-wing radicalism and dismissed, against all evidence, the daily press reports of SA street violence as "malicious lies." Schleicher was being disingenuous, of course. He wanted to unleash Hitler's storm troopers on the Communist and Social Democratic paramilitaries, then have the Reichswehr crush the National Socialist army. Schleicher compared this strategy to navigating "between Scylla and Charybdis." It was the sort of elegant metaphor and political peril Schleicher relished.

With his meeting with Hitler on Friday, August 5, Schleicher was undertaking the ultimate step in his political adventurism: to lure the National Socialist leader away from the "all or nothing" faction of his movement with the offer of the Reich chancellorship. State Secretary Erwin Planck—son of physicist Max Planck—was present at the meeting and kept a record of the deliberations. The Planck protocol appears to have confirmed Goebbels's worst suspicions:

> Hitler stated that his party demanded that he now take over the management of the Reich's affairs. He said he wasn't very enthusiastic about this, but he also couldn't very well decline. If the Reich president asked him to state his opinion as party leader, he would propose that the Reich president entrust him with forming the cabinet. He would in any event not make any significant changes. Strasser would become minister of the interior. Papen would take over the Ministry of Foreign Affairs. The other ministers and state secretaries, including the state secretary in the Reich Chancellery, should remain in office.

Hitler said that he expected that the Reichstag would approve his cabinet. There was no reason to think that he intended to violate any legislation or amend the constitution. For his part, Strasser insisted that Hitler also be appointed prime minister of Prussia, whose state government had been suspended, and that he, Strasser, be assigned the Prussian Ministry of the Interior. The federal state of Prussia represented two-thirds of the country's landmass, and two-thirds of its population. It was common political wisdom that "whoever has Prussia has Germany." Strasser told Schleicher that his first move as interior minister would be to disband Röhm's army of storm troopers, which, Strasser said, "could be done without difficulty." Schleicher concluded the meeting by confirming that the time had come for Hitler to replace Papen as Reich chancellor. Schleicher would make sure that his "Fränzchen" was amenable. Hitler was so pleased with the deliberations that he proposed a plaque be installed on the site: "Here the memorable conference between Adolf Hitler and General von Schleicher took place."

News leaked of the meeting, as it inevitably did even in the most confidential of circumstances. Birchall parsed the Schleicher power play with flawless acuity for the reader of the *Times:* "The Hitlerites believe they hold the best cards, and undoubtedly they have an ace or two, but there is every reason to believe the big cards, the ones that will really decide the game, are still in the capable fists of Baron von Gayl, the minister of the interior, Chancellor von Papen, President von Hindenburg, and, above all, Lieut. Gen. von Schleicher, the minister of defense." Kessler happened to be in Berlin that week when word leaked of Papen's willingness to step aside to allow Hitler to become chancellor. "I have friends like him who are gamblers, and when it goes well, it goes well, but when it doesn't, they break their neck," Kessler wrote in his diary. "Except in the case of Papen, if things go wrong, he doesn't break his own neck but that of the country."

*

Hitler emerged from the Friday meeting with Schleicher confident enough to summon his key lieutenants to begin planning his chancellorship. Certainly, the most appropriate location to convene for Hitler's political endgame was the Hotel Kaiserhof, one of Berlin's finest hotels. Situated in a second-floor suite—sitting room, fireplace, en suite bathroom—Hitler could look out the window across the fashionable Wilhelmplatz to the stately façade of the Reich Chancellery, behind which lay the nation's center of political power. If geography determined destiny, as Hitler knew, then proximity signaled intentionality.

Or Hitler could have strategized at the Brown House in Munich, the headquarters of the National Socialist movement, at Briennerstrasse 34. The party's first office had been a single room in the Sterneckerbräu beer hall, rented for 50 reichsmarks, or $12, per month. "Slowly we got electric lighting, then more slowly a telephone, a table with a few borrowed chairs, and eventually a storage area, and somewhat later a filing cabinet," Hitler wrote in *Mein Kampf*. Just over a decade later, in January 1931, the party moved into the Barlow Palace, a neoclassical building purchased and renovated for 1.5 million reichsmarks ($6.5 million today), as the NSDAP administrative headquarters, with two SS guards positioned at the entrance, an enormous swastika flag fluttering over the mansard roof, and swaths of plush red carpet along the corridors protecting the parquet from hobnailed boots. "We were all proud of the Brown House, Hitler in particular," recalled Hans Frank, who ran the legal depart-

ment on the third floor. "He [Hitler] was continually making changes to the interior, beautifying, improving, making
sketches for bronze door handles, lamps, etc."

Hitler occupied a large second-floor corner salon whose
ceiling was decorated with stucco swastikas. On the walls
hung a portrait of Frederick the Great; a painting of Hitler's military unit, the 16th Bavarian Reserve Infantry Regiment, in action during the war; and a framed photograph of
Henry Ford. A German translation of Ford's anti-Semitic
treatise, *The International Jew: The World's Foremost Problem*,
sat on a table in the foyer. Never one to keep regular hours,
Hitler tended to arrive unannounced, make a phone call or
two, hold a few ad hoc meetings, then rush past his fellow
National Socialists with the parting words "Excuse me! But I
have to go! I'll be back tomorrow!"

But by August 1932, the Brown House was not the most
secure location for confidential deliberations. In March,
Goebbels overheard a "spy" tapping a telephone. "We have
the line checked," he noted. "Naturally nothing is found."
The following month, the Brown House was raided in a
coordinated crackdown on SA headquarters across the country. "The police searched not only the offices of the SA
and the SS, but every room in the building, especially the
archives," recalled Adolf Dresler, who worked in the fourth-
floor press section. "In several offices that had nothing to do
with the SA or the SS, files were confiscated and taken away."
An even larger raid followed in June, conducted by twelve
police vehicles and swarms of officers, armed with pistols and
rifles, who stormed the building. "The occupation lasted two
days and one overnight. Police were standing and lying in all
the corridors. Every telephone was put under watch," Philipp
Bouhler, the Brown House business manager, recalled. And
this was without knowledge that Schleicher had an intelli-

gence operative within the senior-most ranks of the Brown House administration.

Hitler tended to hold his most confidential—and consequential—discussions at Haus Wachenfeld. "It was here that I spent my most pleasant times and conceived all my great plans," he said. Situated on a hillside meadow, the rustic three-story house, heated with porcelain stoves, provided stunning vistas to the snowcapped Bavarian Alps and a distant view to the many-spired city of Salzburg, beyond which lay Hitler's native soil. Angela Raubal, Hitler's older half sister, who was widowed, kept house, cleaning, cooking, and providing familial comfort for him and his guests. "After meals we sit around the round table or on the long bench against the green porcelain oven," Otto Dietrich, NSDAP spokesperson, recalled of his frequent visits. A cage of parakeets and three dogs completed the scene of domestic tranquility.

Comfortably ensconced on the Obersalzberg, at a safe remove from intrusive reporters and disruptive police raids, not to mention the fierce summer heat, Hitler assembled his closest associates to strategize on what promised to be the most consequential moment of his thirteen-year political career. Virtually all the residents of the Brown House power corridor were there—Strasser, Goebbels, Röhm, Reichstag delegate Wilhelm Frick, and Hans Frank, Hitler's legal counsel at the time and the future governor-general of occupied Poland—along with Göring on the telephone from Berlin.

Hitler reprised his Friday deliberations with Schleicher, providing a version vastly more ambitious than the one preserved in the Planck protocol. "Göring will be minister of transport and Frick minister of finance," Goebbels noted. Richard Walther Darré, author of the National Socialist *Blut und Boden* doctrine—"blood and soil"—was to be minister of agriculture. Göring would serve as minister of transportation, and Goebbels as minister of culture and education. Strasser would assume the key position of minister of the interior, with control over the security forces and the secret police. "I found this an excellent choice, as a means of countering Himmler's violent conspiracies," Frank later recalled, referring to Heinrich Himmler, the head of the SS. Neither Hitler nor Strasser appears to have mentioned the discussion of disbanding the SA.

The only point of contention during the three days of deliberation came at the moment when Strasser hedged on making Hitler's appointment as chancellor a sine qua non to the negotiations. Strasser feared that taking a hard line could scuttle the entire process and, with it, the prospects of a National Socialist foothold on power. Why not consider having Hitler serve as vice chancellor under Papen, with the longer-term prospect of transitioning Hitler into the chancellor's seat once he had proven himself, as Papen himself had proposed? Like everyone, Strasser sensed that there was still more work to be done.

For all the public triumphalism over the July 31 election, the results had left Hitler 14 percentage points short of an absolute majority and an undisputed claim to political power. "We have won a pittance," Goebbels admitted privately. But expectations had been raised. Voters who had cast their ballot for the National Socialists were anxious to see political change. More unsettling, Röhm's army was clambering for a march on Berlin, be it to seize or celebrate or both, whether by democratic means or brute force. That left only two options: engineer a coalition of right-wing parties, as Strasser was proposing, or convince Hindenburg to appoint Hitler as chancellor with unrestricted powers. Opinions polarized, as they inevitably did among Hitler's lieutenants, with the "objectivists"—Strasser, Frank, Frick—advocating a course of action that was both pragmatic and legal, while the "radicals"—Göring, Goebbels, Röhm—wanted to "liberate" the German people from democratic structures and processes and the shackles of the Treaty of Versailles, whether by backroom political bargaining or by violent revolution. Röhm's storm troopers were ready to march. That evening, Hitler sat with Goebbels on the Haus Wachenfeld veranda. "Wonderful evening," Goebbels wrote in his diary. "Shooting stars. We make wishes for good fortune and freedom."

During those same late-night hours, in a remote village in the industrial region of Upper Silesia, in the easternmost reaches of the country, an event was taking place that would further complicate Hitler's plans and compel him to choose—in the most public way possible—between the pragmatic exigencies of electoral politics and his personal commitment to the principles of his political movement.

CHAPTER 2

VICTIMS OF DEMOCRACY

The list of political acts of terror was lengthened yesterday
by countless new shootings.

—*Vossische Zeitung*, MORNING EDITION, AUGUST 10, 1932

Except for a wedding reception at the tavern owned by Paul
Lachmann, the evening of August 9, 1932, was relatively
quiet in Potempa, an isolated village situated in a forest on
the edge of the industrial wasteland of Upper Silesia, a wil-
derness of smokestacks and mine shafts where even on clear
nights the stars did not shine. In this backwater community,
connected to the rest of the world by three country roads and
a single telephone line, Potempa had been spared much of
the political violence that had plagued towns and cities across
the country as the paramilitaries of rival political movements
clashed that summer in pitched street battles. Papen's lifting
of the ban on demonstrations, on June 16, coupled with the
scheduling of Reichstag elections for July 31, was a politically
toxic combination that Papen himself belatedly recognized as
"an act of state suicide."

As tens of thousands of storm troopers staged pre-
election marches and rallies in Social Democrat and Com-

munist strongholds, violence surged. On the third weekend
of July, Communist snipers fired on a procession of eighteen
hundred National Socialists from a wayside tavern along the
Aurich-Norden high road on the North Sea coast, leaving
five men seriously wounded. A skirmish with handguns in
the coastal town of Greifswald left two dead and twenty-five
wounded. Four National Socialists were stabbed in Frankfurt
an der Oder. A shootout in the city of Rheydt, fifteen miles
west of Düsseldorf, left six wounded, most of them women
and children.

The worst violence that weekend occurred on Sunday,
July 17, outside Hamburg, when 20,000 storm troopers,
wearing brown uniforms and swastika armbands, converged
on Altona, a bastion of Communist support. Assembling in
columns six men across, the storm troopers marched into the
narrow, cobbled streets, provoking sniper fire from windows
and rooftops that killed two storm troopers instantly. When
the police intervened, a full-blown street battle erupted. By
day's end, there were five dead, with another seven fatally
wounded, and dozens more with serious injuries. The violence produced the sort of headlines Hitler had hoped for—
"Reds Shoot at Nazis from Roofs in Altona," in *The New York
Times*, for example—and created opportunities for framing
the National Socialists as victims.

Wilhelm Frick exploited the moment to incite further
violence. "For Germany, it would be a blessing if 10,000,
or even better 15,000, Marxist boys were to vanish from the
face of the earth," Frick declared at a pre-election rally in
Königsberg. As legal protection against accusations of public
incitement, Frick added wryly, "With that I do not mean to
say in the least that I want to unleash a murder spree." Two
days later, Hans Frank stoked National Socialists' outrage:
"If, within twenty-four hours, the government is not able to

guarantee order for the law-abiding citizens of Germany, we will take care of this murderous rabble ourselves." Embold-ened by public rhetoric and the prospect of Hitler's appoint-ment as chancellor, storm troopers adapted the lyrics to a popular song: "When the hour for revenge finally arrives, we will be ready to commit mass murder."

In another era, in another country, it might have seemed incomprehensible that a government would tolerate politi-cally aligned paramilitaries, most of them larger than the standing army, but the federated republic of the German Reich—that was the official name of the Weimar Republic—was a country ruled as much by the Treaty of Versailles as by its own constitution. With the Reichswehr restricted to 100,000 soldiers, the government allowed right-wing private political armies to proliferate, sometimes channeling weap-ons from military stockpiles, as defense against a potential Communist insurgency. Confronting Hitler's 400,000 storm troopers was the Red Front Fighters' League, the under-ground paramilitary of the Communist Party, supported with financing and weapons from Moscow, smuggled mostly over the borders from Belgium and Czechoslovakia. The milita-rized wing of the Social Democratic Party, known as the Iron Front, saw itself as defenders of the constitutional republic in a two-front war battling fascists and Communists alike. The Steel Helmets, or Stahlhelm, were the defense force of the conservative center, mainly veterans of the Great War, with many looking to the restoration of the monarchy. As these armies clashed, casualties accumulated, with nearly a thou-sand dead in pre-election violence, and an additional dozen deaths on the July 31 election day. The killings continued unabated into August, with newspapers publishing "casualty lists" from the country's ongoing *Bürgerkrieg*, or civil war.

Until that summer, the most common criminal activity

in Potempa appeared to have been the smuggling of illegal immigrants across the Polish border, less than a mile to the east. Fifteen zlotys, or 7.50 reichsmarks (about $39 today*), could buy safe passage through the forested porous "green border" into Germany, or for 50 zlotys (25 RM; about $132 today), you could arrange for facilitation through an official border crossing, where Polish border guards aimed both rifle barrels and gazes to the heavens. "The smuggling of people across the German border in the east is a thriving business," the *Vossische Zeitung* reported. "Only in the rarest of cases does this involve criminals who cross the border with the help of professional human traffickers." Mostly, the illegal immigrants were in search of work in mines or factories, or as day laborers and farmhands, or were young men escaping military service in the Polish army. Some came hoping to enroll in a university.

There had been rumors of potential political violence in Potempa in advance of the July 31 Reichstag election. A left-wing activist was told that he would be hanged from the large linden tree in the village square. A teacher avoided sleeping at home for fear of attacks by right-wing extremists. Potempa was too small to have its own police force, so gendarmes were brought in from surrounding towns. Except for a few stones thrown through windows, election day passed without incident. The officers departed. But in the days that followed, local Communists, who had done exceptionally well at the polls, allegedly grew belligerent.

As head of the village council and Potempa's only card-carrying National Socialist, Lachmann had done his part in

---

* The conversion is 4.2 RM to $1 in 1932. For calculating the value today, see MeasuringWorth's Purchasing Power calculator: https://www.measuringworth.com /calculators/uscompare/relativevalue.php.

Hitler's recent electoral victories, helping to nearly triple the number of National Socialist votes in Upper Silesia over the past two years. Every fifty votes, Lachmann told his friends, had cost him a keg of beer. *Time* magazine also highlighted the role of beer in buoying National Socialist recruitment. "Adolf Hitler gave thousands of young Germans a chance to escape from reality," *Time* wrote in December 1931. "Hitlerites had uniforms, brass bands, roaring mass meetings, plenty of free beer. In 1930 when Germany had over 3,000,000 unemployed, Hitler had 6,000,000 followers and with 107 delegates controlled the Reichstag's second-largest party."

Lachmann had officially registered with the party on March 1, 1931, number 479,709, which placed him within the movement's first 500,000 members and thus qualified him to be designated an *Alter Kämpfer*, or old warrior, a distinction he shared with the movement's founding members. Included in this incoming class of March 1 inductees was Albert Speer, a twenty-five-year-old postgraduate student in architecture, who had attended a Hitler rally the previous December. "Hitler made his appearance to a thunderous welcome by his countless followers as well as the students," Speer recalled. "This enthusiasm alone made a deep impression on me." Until then, Speer had known Hitler only from posters and photographs, in his brown shirt with the swastika armband, his hair swept across a sweat-beaded face in the midst of a tirade. "But now Hitler appeared in a nicely tailored blue suit. Obviously demonstrated bourgeois correctness, everything projecting the impression of reasonable modesty," Speer remembered. Hitler had made such an impression on Speer that within the month he had applied to join the party and had become party member 474,481.

For party member 479,709, the allure of National Socialism can be traced to Article 88 of the Treaty of Versailles.

Beyond the humiliation of Article 231, the "war guilt" clause assigning full responsibility of the war to Germans, and the concomitant articles framing reparation payments, calculated at 132 billion gold marks—more than half a trillion dollars today—treaty Article 88 caused Lachmann irreparable personal harm. With enough remorse and time, war guilt could be expunged. Reparations, regardless of how vast the sums, could eventually be repaid. But Article 88 belonged to a set of seven treaty articles, 87 to 93, that seceded irrevocably German territory to its neighbors, including a swath of land known as the Polish Corridor that left East Prussia orphaned in the east.

Lachmann was born in Erdmannshain, a mining town in the easternmost reaches of Upper Silesia, where an ethnically interlaced mix of Germans and Poles had lived variously under Polish, Lithuanian, Austrian, and Prussian domination. On March 20, 1921, thanks to Article 88 of the Treaty of Versailles, they were "called upon to indicate by a vote whether they wish to be attached to Germany or to Poland." The Upper Silesian plebiscite was conducted under the auspices of an Allied control commission and supported by French, British, and Italian troops. Article 88 explicitly bound the German and Polish governments "to conduct no prosecutions on any part of their territory and to take no exceptional proceedings" in the plebiscite region. However, when the votes were tallied, with 60 percent voting to remain with Germany, armed Polish insurgents marched into the plebiscite region, seizing mines and factories. Kattowitz, the "coal capital of Silesia," where 22,800 residents had voted to remain with Germany, compared to about 4,000 for Poland, was encircled and besieged. Poles cut off electricity and water. Coal transports were seized. Atrocities followed.

"It is reported here that at Ruda, eighteen Germans were

murdered by insurgents, who gouged out the eyes and cut off the noses of their victims," a *New York Times* reporter wrote. Houses were looted, women raped. French troops looked on with "secret sympathy" at Polish excesses. Berlin watched the atrocities with practiced patience. "Of course there have been losses from Polish terror but victory is ours," Foreign Minister Walter Simons declared in triumph. "Let everyone hold their head and heart high in the firm belief that no power, no injustice is capable of separating Upper Silesia from the German Reich." It was politics, not power, that ultimately separated Upper Silesia from Germany.

Berlin balked at sending troops for fear of antagonizing the Allies. When former frontline soldiers sought to organize militias, known as *Freikorps*, or free corps, the government closed the borders. Even the left-wing press could not suppress its outrage. "Only Poland is allowed to send troops to Upper Silesia," the *Danziger Volksstimme* reported. "In order to prevent the movement of volunteers to Upper Silesia, measures are being put in place that will block their access to the plebiscite region."

In desperation, local activists formed the Upper Silesian Militia, known as the Selbstschutz Oberschlesien, only to be abandoned by those in Berlin who had agreed to cede the eastern third of Upper Silesia, with 80 percent of the region's industrial capacity, to Poland; this included not only Kattowitz but also Lachmann's town of Erdmannshain, located in the district of Lublinitz, despite its majority vote of 52 percent to remain with Germany. At age twenty-eight, Lachmann found himself betrayed by the democratic process, abandoned by a democratically elected government, and excluded from the constitutional protections that had guaranteed "sanctuary" and the "inviolability" of one's home.

When Hitler railed against the Treaty of Versailles, he

spoke to people like Lachmann and millions of others who felt marginalized by this constitutional democracy. "Take Upper Silesia away from Germany, and you deprive 15 million human beings of their livelihood," Hitler wrote in the *Völkischer Beobachter* a few days before the March 1921 plebiscite. "In this case our people are left with one choice: Either starvation, and most likely a fast rather than slow starvation, or resistance." At the time, Hitler was an insignificant figure on the radical fringe of Bavarian beer-hall politics, with a meager two thousand followers. But by early 1931, he commanded more than six million voters.

Lachmann had sympathized for a time with Communists, greeting friends with "Heil Moscow!" before aligning himself with Brüning's Center Party, then lurching to the radical right. While it is impossible to identify the exact moment of Lachmann's conversion to National Socialism, a dramatic event in the Reichstag in early February 1931 suggests the sort of motivating force, if not the trigger, that transformed Lachmann from conservative centrist to right-wing nationalist.

On the afternoon of February 8, 1931, the Reichstag convened its twentieth session, with Johannes Bell, founder of the Center Party, taking the floor. As a leading jurist, Bell embodied the collective sins of Weimar for National Socialists. Not only had he been one of two German signatories to the Versailles Treaty, in June 1919, but two months later Bell had also affixed his name to the new constitution establishing the German Reich as a federated republic. As Bell began to speak, the National Socialists heckled him, drowning his remarks in catcalls while the Reichstag president clanged the bell calling the delegates to order. Amid the chaos, Franz Stöhr rose to speak. Like Lachmann, Stöhr had come from former German lands to the east, deprived of house and homeland by Bell's signature in Versailles.

"The day will come, and will come very soon, when you will have to pay for your shameless behavior!" Stöhr bellowed into the chaos. As part of a choreographed action, Stöhr added, "We are leaving this chamber in protest." The National Socialist delegates broke into a thundering chorus of the "Horst Wessel Song," their party anthem, chanted *"Heil Hitler,"* then trooped out of the plenary hall, leaving a wide swath of vacant seats.

"Does one recall the scene at the opening session of the Reichstag [in the autumn of 1930] when the National Socialists in their brown shirts trooped into the chamber, in complete silence, and took their 107 seats?" the *Vossische Zeitung* asked, referring to the first session after the September 1930 election. "That was clearly theater, but it did make an impression." Five months later, the National Socialists were flaunting their defiance of democratic norms and decorum. "Such antics would seem laughable if one did not fear that they could potentially become deadly," a reporter for the newspaper wrote. Three weeks later, Lachmann joined the National Socialists and appeared to introduce the same mendacious belligerence to village politics. He was known to many as the *Dorftyrann*, or the village tyrant.

By early August, Lachmann claimed, he feared for his life. Konrad Pietzuch had entered his tavern and verbally accosted patrons, then boasted that the Communists had already killed 450 storm troopers and more killings would follow. Lachmann had scuffled with Pietzuch back in February. Pietzuch had drawn a knife on Lachmann's friend Paul Golombek, the local butcher, and threatened Lachmann with a gun.

On August 9, 1932, an exposé had appeared in the *Nationalsozialistische Parteikorrespondenz*, a biweekly publication published by Gregor Strasser and his brother Otto, under the headline "Street Terror Ordered by the Communist Party." The article detailed a clandestine meeting, allegedly held in Berlin on August 2, of the leadership of the Red Front Fighters' League, the banned paramilitary wing of the German Communist Party. Having gone underground in 1929, after being designated an "extremist organization," the Red Front fighters were believed to number as many as 130,000, larger than the Reichswehr.

Allegedly fearing for his safety, Lachmann called Georg Hoppe, who ran a tavern in the neighboring village of Tworog. On Tuesday evening, August 9, a vehicle arrived in Potempa with nine men, two of whom belonged to the Upper Silesian Militia. The rest were storm troopers, from Sturm 25 in Rokittnitz and Sturm 26 in Broslawitz. It was odd company, to say the least. Ludwig Nowak was a former Broslawitz police officer. August Gräupner and Hypolit Hadamik were miners from Rokittnitz. Georg Hoppe ran a beer distribution business in Tworog, along with his tavern. Reinhold Kottisch, a trained electrician, and Rufin Wolnitza, a miner, were both from Mikultschütz, a mining town. Helmuth Müller, who clocked miners on their shifts, was from Friedrichswille, a nearby hamlet. Their ages ranged from twenty-five to forty-three.

Lachmann led his guests into the kitchen of his tavern, where he plied them with beer, schnapps, and cigarettes for the next two hours. Sometime after one o'clock in the morning, Lachmann offered a final round, then handed the men three pistols, two rubber police truncheons, a broken billiard cue weighted with lead, a flashlight, and a list with the names of four local Communists. "If you're going to do it, do it right," Lachmann instructed the men. He dispatched them in the company of his friend Golombek. Lachmann stayed behind. He was later seen on a stepladder with gardening shears, cutting the village telephone line.

Golombek led the men to the house of Florian Schwinge, whose name was first on the hit list, where he knocked on the door, then stepped aside so as not to be recognized. When Schwinge's wife refused to open the door, Golombek ordered Kottisch to knock down the door and shoot her. Kottisch refused. Schwinge watched from an upstairs window as Golombek then led the men across the square to the Pietzuch residence, where they found the door unlocked. Marie Pietzuch awoke to the sound of shuffling feet and muffled voices in the hallway outside the bedroom she shared with her two grown sons, Konrad and Alfons. As the door opened, a flashlight sliced the blackness. "Who's there?" she said. The sixty-nine-year-old widow bolted upright in bed and found herself staring into the barrel of a pistol. "Shut up or you're dead," a man said. Someone else shouted at her sons: "Get up, you damned Communist dogs! Hands up!" Then someone said, "Beat the shit out of the fat one!" There was scuffling. The flashlight tumbled. The room plunged into blackness. More scuffling, then kicking, then throttling—deep, blunt blows—then scrambling. "Alfons! Alfons!" A door slammed. Then the order "Up against the wall!" Then "Shoot!" The pistol flashed. Marie screamed, "You killed my son!" and ran for help. Alfons rushed to his brother, who lay on the floor gasping for air. By the time his mother returned, Konrad was dead and the intruders had fled.

Golombek then led his men to their next target, a man named Emil whose surname no one could remember. When a dog barked as they approached the property, Golombek stopped. They decided to call it a night.

*

In those same late-night hours, Hans Burgmaier was sitting on a bench in Potempa's village square when he heard a gunshot. As deputy customs officer, Burgmaier was responsible for patrolling the village streets for nighttime traffickers and insurgents smuggled across the "green border" from Poland. Burgmaier saw several men appear in the darkened street. When he ordered them to stop, they broke into a run. Burgmaier gave pursuit, overtaking one of the men, who was clearly inebriated but willing to talk. He said his name was Rufin Wolnitza from Mikultschütz. Burgmaier looked at his watch. It was shortly before two o'clock in the morning. The time would prove to be crucial.

CHAPTER 3

TRANQUILITY

Acts of political murder will be punished
with a death sentence.

—PRESIDENTIAL DECREE AGAINST POLITICAL TERROR, ARTICLE I,
EFFECTIVE MIDNIGHT, AUGUST 10, 1932

The headline-making news on the morning of August 10, 1932, just hours after Konrad Pietzuch had been beaten to death, was a presidential decree imposing the death sentence for acts of political murder. The news was carried in every major newspaper in Germany and rippled across the Atlantic, onto the front page of *The New York Times.* "The German Cabinet, at a special session lasting more than two hours this afternoon, put into final shape the Presidential decree increasing the penalty for political acts of violence," Fred Birchall wired from Berlin on Tuesday evening. "The decree was then telephoned to President von Hindenburg at Neudeck and provisionally approved by him." By the summer of 1932, the eighty-four-year-old Reich president, Paul von Hindenburg, was conducting most matters of state by telegraph or telephone from Neudeck, his ancestral home in East Prussia. Couriers shuttled confidential matters of state between Berlin and Neudeck, as Werner von Alversleben had done that spring on a daily basis so that Schleicher could keep Hindenburg apprised of his efforts during his negotiations with Hitler.

While the journey could be accomplished with a brief airplane ride, Hindenburg preferred to travel by train. According to Otto Meissner, Hindenburg's omnipresent chief of staff, the Reich president found the overnight rail journey deeply disturbing, passing as it did through the Polish Corridor, a trajectory fraught with border controls and occasional peril. More than once a train had caused injury by derailing, either through Polish negligence or sabotage, as happened in May 1925, when several carriages tumbled down a twenty-foot embankment, killing twenty-five persons, including twelve women and two children, and injuring thirty others. It was later discovered the rail spikes had been lifted and the skirting removed. The German press bewailed the fact that Germany was forced to entrust the safety of its citizens to "Polish management." For Hindenburg, who had protected this swath of Prussia from invading Russian armies with his legendary victory at Tannenberg in August 1914, it was particularly galling to watch the territory negotiated away at Versailles, where the French had sought to exact the greatest revenge possible on Germany. Meissner noted that it required "several days" to calm the old field marshal each time he traversed the former German lands between Neudeck and Berlin. In September 1931, when Hindenburg traveled to Berlin to receive Aristide Briand, the French prime minister found the Reich president detached and distracted. Hindenburg talked mostly about the weather. "The journey [from Neudeck] was clearly tiring for the old gentleman," Briand remarked afterward.

Hindenburg was generally a charming and animated host. "He often interrupts the conversation with short, genial

questions, humor frequently breaking through," one observer
noted in those same months. Once when a friend asked what
Hindenburg did when he was nervous, Hindenburg said that
he whistled. "But I have never heard you whistle," the friend
observed. "Well, I have never whistled," Hindenburg replied.
At eighty-four, Hindenburg was as steady and firm as the
stone monument honoring him on the Tannenberg battlefield. He made a strong impression on Daniel Binchy, the
Irish ambassador to Berlin. Binchy recalled presenting his
credentials at the diplomatic salon of the presential palace:
"Hindenburg's gigantic figure, held stiffly to attention with
the broad shoulders squared and the mighty chest glittering
with innumerable orders seemed to dwarf even the stately
proportions of the reception room." He said Hindenburg
looked like a figure from "some remote age," as if he had
stepped "straight out of a Germanic saga."

John Wheeler-Bennett served as an aide to Sir Neill
Malcolm, the chief of the British Military Mission in Berlin.
Wheeler-Bennett was not dazzled by Hindenburg. For him,
Hindenburg was "a man of service, without ambition, and
no love of pomp and ceremony," whose life was determined
by his imposing physical stature, a corpulent six-foot-six,
and equally impressive aristocratic name, Paul Ludwig Hans
Anton von Beneckendorff und von Hindenburg. Hindenburg
"very rarely dominated the events of his long lifetime . . . His
misfortune was the sudden attainment of almost supernatural
adoration on the part of the German people, who elevated
him to the position of a god and expected from him god-like
achievements," Wheeler-Bennett observed. He called Hindenburg a "wooden titan."

Indeed, Hindenburg had been called out of retirement,
in 1914, to serve country and kaiser in the Great War, only
to retire again, in 1918, and only to be called into service

yet again, in 1925, this time as Reich president. Hindenburg
had intended to retire in spring 1932, after completing his
first seven-year presidential term, but Chancellor Brüning
convinced him to extend his service for an additional two
years to allow the German economy and political situation
to stabilize. Had conservatives and centrists banded together,
they could have delivered the two-thirds Reichstag majority required by the constitution to prolong Hindenburg's
presidential term. Hitler wanted none of it. The National
Socialist movement thrived on political chaos and economic
despair. Hitler hoped that Hindenburg, faced with another
seven years in office, which would take him to age ninety-
one, would decline to run for reelection, leaving a field of
candidates that guaranteed Hitler an election triumph. When
the proposal to extend Hindenburg's term was blocked in the
Reichstag, Hindenburg was forced to run for a second term.
In April 1932, he crushed Hitler at the polls by more than six
million votes. His reelection to another seven-year term was
tantamount to a death sentence. If the "wooden titan" was
to die in office, he wanted to die at home and be laid to rest
beside his late wife—"my companion and dearest friend"—in
the Neudeck family plot.

Hindenburg had been coming to Neudeck since the
1850s, when his grandparents were resident on the sprawl-
ing property set in the wooded moorlands of East Prussia.
Hindenburg's youngest brother, Bernhard, who died at age
seventy-three, just two weeks before Hindenburg announced
his reelection campaign, had written fondly of the ancient
house, "with its old-fashioned roof, the poplar trees right and
left, and the thick bushes with wild red and yellow roses,"
beyond which lay the forest paths where the three Hindenburg boys and their sister, Ida, used to play. Evenings were
spent in the sitting room—two long sofas back to back and an

adjacent round dining table with a brass chandelier—listening to family lore. As a young cadet at the military academy in Berlin, Hindenburg had traveled to Neudeck for holidays in "slow, unheated trains" and even slower post coaches over rutted country roads.

Hindenburg recalled his grandfather's stories of Napoleon Bonaparte, who was resident in a nearby palace, in the winter of 1806, when soldiers of the Grande Armée beat back advancing Russian troops at a bridge on the Hindenburg estate. A French officer was shot by a stray bullet through one of Neudeck's attic windows. The aging family gardener recounted his service in the army of Frederick the Great. "In this way, it may be said, this last ray of the glorious Frederician past fell upon my young self," Hindenburg recalled in memoirs.

Otto ran the family estate until his death in March 1908, after which it was managed by his widow, Lina von Benneckendorff. The property gradually fell into disrepair and financial distress. Elard von Oldenburg, a "conservative country squire to the bone," according to *The New York Times*, lived on the nearby estate of Januschau. On one visit he found Hindenburg in a despondent state. When asked what was wrong, Hindenburg lamented that this "last Hindenburg property" could no longer be maintained. "Since the field marshal was not in a position to buy Neudeck himself, I decided to find a way to acquire the property and give it to the Hindenburg family," Oldenburg recalled. He proposed a public fundraising campaign, the *Hindenburgpfennig*, or Penny for Hindenburg, to purchase the property, but Hindenburg would not hear of it. Any money raised in his name, he insisted, was to be given "entirely to the benefit of disabled veterans or the families of war dead." Oldenburg discreetly solicited financing for Neudeck from wealthy friends and industrialists, negotiating with the tax authorities "so that we were able to offer Neudeck as a gift to the field marshal without additional cost." The deed to the property was presented to Hindenburg on his eightieth birthday, in October 1927.

Neudeck was restored, and an additional story was added, along with a handsome mansard roof. The interior rooms were hung with family portraits and antlers from ancient hunts, along with a full-sized painting of Hindenburg as Reich president. Beside his desk, Hindenburg kept an aging piece of paper inscribed with the words *Ora et labora*—"Pray and work"—given to him by his father. On the front porch, where flowerpots would normally have stood, Hindenburg positioned two field guns from the Battle of Tannenberg, still with their frontline splinter shields.

The house was managed by Hindenburg's daughter-in-law, Margarete, who served as an ersatz first lady, while Hindenburg's only son, Oskar, acted as his father's aide-de-camp. "The young Hindenburgs are both most unattractive. They are ungracious and haughty," observed Bella Fromm. Fromm wrote that Margarete had all the charm of a "Prussian petty officer in petticoats." Oskar exuded a "morose gloom." Diarist Harry Kessler considered Oskar "incompetent militarily and in every other way" and plagued by immense feelings of insecurity. Schleicher credited Oskar's career to his blood association with *Haus Hindenburg*. Hitler called Oskar "*ein seltenes Abbild der Doofheit*," or a paragon of stupidity.

But Oskar was his father's son. Hindenburg included him in briefings, sent him to greet dignitaries at the train station, and occasionally dispatched him on errands. "Oskar Hindenburg wants a detailed report on the effective strength and equipment of the *Reichswehr*, for 'papa,'" a *Reichswehr* general reported derisively in his diary that July. During his father's first presidential election bid in 1925, Oskar followed the returns on the radio all night and rushed into his father's bedroom at seven a.m. with news of victory. Hindenburg berated his son for the disturbance. The news, he said, would have been "just as true an hour later." Then he went back to sleep.

*

By August 9, not even Neudeck's comforts and isolation could protect Hindenburg from the troubles of the beleaguered republic. That morning, he received a frantic telegram from political leaders in the state of Silesia, whose political landscape was as fraught as neighboring Upper Silesia. "Last night, there were eleven revolver and hand grenade attacks on supporters of the republic in central Silesia alone," they reported. "The population of Silesia, which supports the republic, pleads for your protection." A copy was also sent to Interior Minister Gayl, with the request for an "energetic defense against the terror to which all citizens supporting the republic are being exposed."

Hindenburg was no stranger to bloodshed. He had devoted his life to killing, first as a frontline soldier and later as a field marshal. As a teenager, Hindenburg had watched his fellow cadets blown to pieces in an artillery barrage during Prussia's war with Austria in 1866 and was himself briefly knocked unconscious when a cluster shot pierced his helmet and grazed his head. (Hindenburg kept the "shattered helmet," which he proudly showed visitors decades later.) He recovered and pressed the assault, capturing a cannon and returning fire on fleeing riders, whose "white cloaks made excellent targets." In 1870, Hindenburg, as troop commander, was ordered to lead his men to battle against the French. He later observed that it was an instance when "advanced weapons" first met "obsolete tactics." His battalion suffered heavy losses.

After his great victory at Tannenberg in August 1914, Hindenburg was elevated to field marshal and was ultimately responsible for three million German war deaths, along with millions more French, British, and American, including the twelve hundred passengers and crew members killed when the *Lusitania* was sunk by the Hindenburg-approved strategy of unrestricted submarine warfare. He was accused of war crimes but never tried. Hindenburg had blood on his hands, but he was a soldier, not a killer. During the war, he sought to intervene with his Turkish allies to prevent the mass killing of the Armenians but was rebuffed. Hindenburg came to realize that the passions unleashed by politics and religion were vastly more dangerous than war. He wore the cloak of the war with solemnity. He avoided politics.

"As an active soldier I had always kept more of a distance from the domestic politics of the day," Hindenburg later explained. "Even after my transition into retirement, I was engaged only in the context of a quiet observer." He intended to pass his waning years, as he wrote in his memoirs, in "the shade of the tree" planted in the "ethical and political soil" tilled by the Hohenzollern monarchy. At heart, he was a monarchist.

Hindenburg initially declined suggestions to run for office following the death of Reich president Friedrich Ebert, in 1925, but coaxing by friends and a petition with three million signatures, collected in two weeks, convinced him to run as a nonaligned candidate. On May 12, 1925, Hindenburg entered the Reichstag to be sworn in as Reich president. In his acceptance speech he said, "Whereas the Reichstag is the place where opposing views and political convictions clash in

partisan conflict, the Reich president's duty should be dedicated to the non-partisan task of uniting and coordinating the
nation's constructive and progressive elements for the common welfare of our people, without regard for party consideration." He went on to swear his oath before "the Almighty,
All-Knowing God" to devote all his energies to the welfare
of the German people, to increase their prosperity, to protect
them from injury, to preserve the constitution and laws of the
republic, and to perform his duties "conscientiously and to
deal justly with all."

The preamble to the Reich constitution, which Hindenburg had vowed to protect as Reich president, promised to
unite Germans "in all their racial elements," to promote "liberty and justice," to preserve "peace at home and abroad."
The aspirational sentiments imbedded in this foundational
federal document—its 181 articles were meticulously crafted
by the finest legal minds of the day—appeared to be failing
on every count, thanks at least in part to the fearmongering
and fomenting of a single man.

Hindenburg had first met Hitler in October 1931. The
man had ranted, in his distinctly Austrian accent, for nearly
an hour, not letting the Reich president say a word. Hindenburg had sought to appeal to Hitler's love of the fatherland
and of the German people, to his sense of honor as a decorated war veteran, all to no visible effect, which left Hindenburg convinced that he wanted nothing further to do with
"that Bohemian corporal," as he told Otto Meissner afterward. Less than six months later, Hindenburg found himself
confronting Hitler again, this time in a presidential election.

In announcing his candidacy in February 1932, Hin-
denburg spoke to the public for the first time on the radio:
"When I was asked the first time, seven years ago, to run for
Germany's highest office, I deliberately avoided speaking at

partisan meetings, and have therefore spoken only once to the entire nation."

Hindenburg was concerned over the fracturing of the polity, and especially the dangers to the German Reich posed by the prospective candidates. He did not mention them by name, but he was clearly worried about both Ernst Thäl-mann, the Communist leader on the extreme left, and Adolf Hitler on the extreme right. Hindenburg said he was not going to present a political platform. He was not going to hold rallies. He would not seek to justify himself to the public. He preferred to let his life and his life's work "speak to his single driving motivation, to fulfill his sense of duty to the Fatherland." He asked no more of every voter than what he had done: to set aside personal interests and agendas and do what was best for the country. He raised his voice only twice during the address, once in towering indignation over a right-wing smear campaign against his character, and again in the final words when he appealed to the nation's people to set contention and differences aside for the sake of the country. The radio address lasted four minutes and ten seconds but delivered him a second term of "this sadly distraught republic," to borrow Birchall's phrase.

Less than six months later, Hitler was back at the polls. Having failed in his bid for the Reich presidency, he was now determined to win a majority in the Reichstag and, with it, a claim to the Reich chancellorship. If he couldn't be head of state, he would become head of government. His 37 percent of the vote did not achieve that. Then came the August 4 call from Schleicher.

But just as Schleicher was placing his call to Hitler on the Obersalzberg to test the waters for his potential inter-est in the chancellorship, Hindenburg received his own tele-phone call at Neudeck from Papen, who briefed him on his

continuing efforts to forge the nationalist parties into a conservative Reichstag majority. Papen told Hindenburg that it
was his sense that Hitler had reached his political high-water
mark in the July 31 elections, and that for all the jubilation
of his supporters, Hitler was disappointed that he had failed
to secure an outright majority. Papen knew that the radical
elements in the National Socialist movement were escalating
post-election violence in an attempt to force the president to
place Hitler in power. "The recent acts of terror are part of
this plan," Papen told Hindenburg. Papen said there was talk
of a "March on Berlin," like Mussolini's demonstration in
Rome a decade earlier, which brought Papen to the issue of
additional measures to restore public security.

Papen said that in the cabinet meeting he had just convened, the reestablishment of public security had been high
on the agenda. Interior Minister Gayl suggested introducing
special courts for dealing with political violence and stressed
the need to sharpen the existing gun-control legislation. "For
those who injure or kill political opponents with a weapon,"
Gayl said, "a death sentence has to be introduced." A heated
discussion ensued. One cabinet member felt that the "boule-
vard press" had created an artificial sense of crisis, suggesting that reports of public violence were exaggerated. Might
it not be better to promote responsible reporting in the press
instead of death sentences for street brawlers? He was concerned that state authorities, already politically polarized,
would flout any federal dictates on gun control. A second
cabinet member cautioned against introducing the death
sentence for practical reasons. Given the current epidemic
of political murder, the courts would be turned into killing
machines.

The discussion turned to an earlier potential solution,
that of a general disarmament in which gun owners would

willingly deposit their weapons at neutral points. In Breslau, local authorities had introduced a municipal "disarmament action" that permitted anyone in possession of an unregistered weapon, in violation of the 1928 law, to hand it over to local authorities with impunity. It was pointed out that it was wholly unreasonable to think one could disarm the entire country when the nation was awash with weapons, when one could buy a revolver on any street corner for five or six reichsmarks (about $32 today). That very week, a police raid on an SA arsenal hidden in a storage facility for farm equipment had seized a motorcycle loaded with ammunition, twenty-three potato-masher hand grenades, a heavy machine gun—mounted on skids—with sixteen belts of ammunition, an army knife, a revolver, and a rubber truncheon weighted with lead. Konstantin von Neurath, the foreign minister and one of the oldest and most sober-minded cabinet members, warned, "The current situation is so tense that only the more peaceable elements would follow such an order, thus leaving the troublemakers as the only ones in the possession of weapons."

A death-sentence decree appeared to be the best—possibly the only remaining—solution for quelling the epidemic of murder sweeping the country. On August 9, a draft of the "Presidential Decree Against Political Terror" was telegraphed to Neudeck for approval. Paragraph 1 imposed a mandatory death sentence on "anyone who commits murder as the aggressor based on political motivations." A companion decree established special courts for dealing with political murder in an expeditious manner. Both decrees went into effect as of midnight, August 10, 1932.

The next morning, the press greeted the new "anti-terrorism" decree with boldfaced headlines, skepticism, even derision. "Do people really believe that the grenade throwers and sharpshooters from the Hitler army would let themselves be deterred from their thuggish activities by the threat of a death penalty when they are celebrated as heroes and martyrs in their party organs at the same time?" a writer for *Vorwärts* asked in its morning edition. The National Socialists applauded the murder decree. The *Völkischer Beobachter* saw it as a "beginning to the annihilation of the red murder banditry." Hitler himself weighed in with a personal commentary. "One would expect that these new decrees are not just words on paper," he wrote, "but will be used with all severity against the Marxist commandos and snipers." In the past, the president had exercised emergency powers, accorded him by Article 48 of the constitution, in order to suppress National Socialist violence, especially attacks on synagogues and Jews. Hitler now welcomed a decree aimed at his political opponents, though, he noted, a "National Socialist emergency decree," while equally draconian, would provide for the "immediate arrest and conviction of all Communist and Social Democratic party functionaries."

Hitler's endorsement was based, in good part, on the fact that the majority of the alleged political murders were perpetrated by Red Front fighters, with a noticeable decline in SA-related killings, as Hitler sought to position his movement for political power. Following a pre-election rally in Königsberg, on July 17, Hitler dispatched a telegram to Gayl, with copies to Hindenburg and Papen. "The SA conducted themselves in exemplary fashion during a propaganda march through the city," Hitler wrote. "As the columns marched past me, I was witness to such outrageous provocations by the Königsberg police that only the unbounded discipline of my followers prevented a catastrophe." The telegram was prompted by an altercation between the local police chief and Gauleiter Erich Koch, who threatened to unleash his storm troopers on police officers seeking to control the crowds. If not for the "discipline" and "restraint" of the National Socialists, Hitler said, the incident would have escalated into a "bloody catastrophe." The incident, like the telegram, belied ongoing SA attempts to incite and provoke public violence, along with almost daily incidents of stabbings, shootings, and bombings. A storm trooper in Reichenbach was blown apart when a grenade he was preparing to throw exploded in his hand. Another survived an exchange of gunfire with a Communist in Ortelsburg. Beatings and other abuses were beyond counting.

Two years earlier, Hitler had talked publicly about how difficult it was to restrain, let alone disarm, men with weapons. He spoke of *"eine innere Liebe zur Waffe,"* or a man's "inner love for a weapon." "Even if I could order that the SA could no longer own a weapon, don't you think they would secretly disobey me?" Hitler asked, noting that this was especially true when Social Democrats and Communists were armed to the teeth. "It would be completely impossible, aside from being insane," Hitler added. As self-serving and cynical as Hitler's public confession of his limited control over his storm troopers may have been, his observation about a man's inborn love of weapons did ring with nonpartisan truth.

When Hitler welcomed Hindenburg's draconian measures against political violence, he assumed the decree would be used to target Communists and Social Democrats. Hitler knew that the application of laws and decrees was ultimately left to prosecutors and judges, who were generally conservative and often exercised judicial leniency in cases involving National Socialists. In a 1922 statistical study, *Four Years of Political Violence*, Emil Gumbel criticized the judicial system for the disturbingly frequent number of acquittals in cases involving right-wing defendants. "Subtly [the judge's] soul sways along with the murderer, covered by a mask of proper procedure," Gumbel wrote. "The murderer goes free."

Hitler himself could have faced extradition, extended imprisonment, or even execution for high treason following his attempted 1923 putsch. Instead, he was given a scandalously light prison sentence. The presiding judge allowed Hitler to use the courtroom for extended tirades and spoke of the defendant's "noble" and "unselfish" motivations. The prosecutor, in his closing statement, praised Hitler for his "honest efforts to inspire belief in the German cause."*

Hitler understood that any law or decree, no matter how draconian, was only as effective as the individuals entrusted with its implementation. Hindenburg had issued a series of presidential decrees seeking to quell public violence, to protect Jewish places of worship, to bridle the rising National Socialist movement, all to little effect. The 1932 presidential decree prohibiting storm troopers from wearing uniforms in public, displaying swastika banners, and conducting mass rallies had been whispered away in a backroom deal with the promise of National Socialist tolerance of a Papen chancellorship and agreement to participate in a coalition government. There was no reason to assume that the latest presidential decree could not be subverted, manipulated, or eventually rescinded, and even if implemented, would target, as Hitler wrote in the *Völkischer Beobachter*, Communist or Social Democratic perpetrators rather than National Socialists.

---

* Hitler served less than eight months of a five-year sentence in a minimum-security facility with a private suite of rooms.

CHAPTER 4

THE HITLER GAMBIT

Crazy things are going on. With guns and things like that.

—JOSEPH GOEBBELS, DIARY ENTRY, AUGUST 12, 1932

For all the precautions taken to keep the August 5 meeting between Hitler and Schleicher out of the public eye, details of their deliberations quickly found their way into the press, albeit in wildly corrupted and fanciful form. "Schleicher advocates that Adolf Hitler become Reich president," *Die Schwarze Front* reported the next morning. That right-wing—though decidedly anti–National Socialist—newspaper, published by Gregor Strasser's brother Otto, who had broken with the National Socialist movement, announced that Hitler was to replace Hindenburg as the ultimate constitutional power in the country. Schleicher would be appointed Reich chancellor, with Hitler agreeing to retain the Schleicher cabinet for a minimum of two years—enough time, the newspaper said, to eradicate the Communist threat and increase military spending as top priorities. By Monday, the *Frankfurter Zeitung* was offering a more plausible though equally unnerving prospect: that Hitler was to be appointed chancellor.

By the morning of Tuesday, August 9, the *Vossische Zeitung* had reported on the "secret" that all of Berlin was talking about. The next day, *Vorwärts* splashed the news in a banner headline, "Hitler wants to rule!" The editors were frantic at the thought. "The appointment of Hitler is out of the question because he lacks even the most basic qualifications," they wrote. "You cannot entrust a government to the leader of a party that in recent days has been responsible for perpetrating countless horrific acts of violence without discrediting the authority of the German state before the eyes of the entire world, not to mention the majority of its own people." There was also the fact that Hitler had served prison time for treason against the very state he was now seeking to rule.

Unlike Hitler's anti-Semitism, a toxic brew of pseudo-scientific readings and malignant mentoring, Hitler's hatred of the Weimar Republic was the result of personal observation of political processes. He hated the haggling and compromise of coalition politics inherent in multiparty political systems. "Is it really a nation when there are thirty political parties?" he wondered. "Do you think it's thanks to them that Germany even continues to exist today?" Hitler was particularly troubled by the absence of personal accountability and individual responsibility, as well as the immunities accorded elected representatives to legislative bodies. "Parliament can take any kind of decision, regardless of how devastating the circumstances, and no one carries any responsibility for that, no one can be held to account," he wrote in *Mein Kampf*.

At his 1924 trial for treason, Hitler used the courtroom to grandstand against weak-kneed democracies and lectured the court on the relationship between violent force and rule of law. He quoted Frederick the Great: "Law is worthless unless it is defended with the tip of a sword." He cited Otto von Bismarck, the "blood and iron" chancellor, who had forged the German Reich against the will of the Reichstag, which had opposed him in a vote of 160 to 11. "How was Bismarck described by everyone in the opposition press?" Hitler asked. "As a violator of the constitution, as a traitor!" Had Bismarck failed, Hitler said, he would have been tried for treason. Instead, he was a hero. Ditto Mussolini. "How do you legalize a coup d'état?" Hitler continued. You eliminate the political opposition, he answered. You restructure government. You rewrite laws. "The legalization of the 'March on Rome' was not completed until after Mussolini had undertaken an enormous cleansing process," Hitler said. "That's how you legalize high treason." According to Hitler, his only crime was failure.

He had expressed this same anti-democratic conviction before the Reich Supreme Court in Leipzig in September 1930, when he was called to testify in defense of three young Reichswehr officers charged with treason. The men had allegedly committed the crime as part of a National Socialist plot to overthrow the government. Rather than answer questions related directly to the case at hand, Hitler took the opportunity to rage against the republic. He insisted that he was not a putschist. He was not a tyrant. He was simply fighting for the honor of the German people. Invoking Article 1 of the Reich constitution, Hitler reminded the judges that the power of the state emanated from the will of the people. "The constitution only prescribes the field of battle, but not the ultimate goal," he said. "When we are finally in possession of the constitutionally guaranteed rights and powers, we will pour the state into the form that we think is best."

It seemed an astonishingly brazen admission, but no less astonishing was the judge's follow-on question: "So, only by constitutional means?" Hitler's reply was crisp and pointed: "*Jawohl!*" Hitler repeated his intentions almost verbatim in an interview the following December. "The National Social-ist movement will achieve power in Germany by methods permitted by the present Constitution—in a purely legal way," he told *The New York Times*. "It will then give the Ger-man people the form of organization and government that suits our purposes."

After his August 5, 1932, meeting with Schleicher, Hitler had every reason to assume he would be chancellor by week's end, as reflected in the increasingly fevered newspaper head-lines that week. "In the course of the day the press has been filling with reports that Hitler will be chancellor," Kessler wrote in his diary that Thursday evening. When he returned to his apartment sometime after ten o'clock, Kessler noticed that the basement room of his servant, a fervent National Socialist, was open to the street. The lights were on. Music blared. "Jubilation and victory in the air," Kessler wrote. "The people are already living in the Third Reich!"

*

As the left-wing press panicked and the right-wing press cheered, Hitler prepared for his meeting with Hindenburg. By midweek, most of his lieutenants had departed. Röhm was preparing his private army for the long-awaited "March on Berlin." Goebbels noted in his diary that calling the SA to Berlin "makes the gentlemen very nervous. That is the pur-pose of the maneuver." Meanwhile, Strasser was conducting further reconnaissance in Berlin.

Goebbels and his wife remained on the Obersalzberg, planning to travel with Hitler to Munich, then Berlin by car. But on the evening of August 10, Hitler received an unexpected call from Munich, possibly from his friend and personal photographer Heinrich Hoffmann or from his Munich housekeeper, Anni Winter. Eva Braun, a young woman Hitler had been seeing discreetly, was in the hospital in Munich. The twenty-year-old blonde had shot herself in the neck in a failed suicide attempt.*

Goebbels's diary entries tend to be a reliable barometer for measuring emotions and concerns within Hitler's inner circle. Following a disagreement with Strasser in January 1930, Goebbels reported, "Hitler is as furious as a hand grenade." Goebbels writes of "jubilation beyond all measure" after a local electoral victory in Saxony in June 1930. A performance of Wagner's *Meistersinger* in the spring of 1931 left Hitler calm and reflective, musing on "style, culture, and civilization." "He is so clear-headed, a truly brilliant thinker," Goebbels wrote in April 1931. On August 11, there is no mention by Goebbels of Eva's suicide attempt. Goebbels writes, "Departure from Obersalzberg. Hitler comes along. Scorching heat."

With Hitler in the passenger seat and his chauffeur at the wheel, they proceeded down the series of switchbacks to Berchtesgaden, and from there up the valley to Bad Reichenhall, arriving at Prien-am-Chiemsee, a lakeside town midway to Munich, where Strasser was waiting with news. It wasn't good. Papen and Schleicher had tested the idea of a Hitler chancellorship on Hindenburg. Strasser reported, "The old man is resisting." In fact, Hindenburg had been more direct

---

* There is some dispute over the actual date of Eva Braun's suicide attempt. Heinrich Hoffmann mentioned early November 1932 in his memoirs, a date used by eminent Hitler biographers such as Ian Kershaw and Volker Ullrich. Heike Görtemaker, a leading Braun biographer, places the suicide attempt in mid-August, a date supported by Harald Sandner in *Hitler: Das Itinerar,* a day-by-day accounting of Hitler's life by location.

in his response: conditio sine qua non. Under no conditions was he going to appoint Hitler as chancellor.

It was difficult to determine from a lakeside terrace in rural Bavaria what the former Prussian field marshal was thinking. Perhaps the conditio sine qua non was in response to being presented with a fait accompli. Perhaps the leaks to the press of a potential Hitler chancellorship had irritated him. *Vorwärts* ran an admonishing banner headline: "Warning! Those Who Play with Fascism Play with Germany's Ruin." Or perhaps the Hero of Tannenberg bristled at the suggestion that he could be intimidated by an army of storm troopers descending on Berlin. How could one know? The man was impenetrable and, in Goebbels's words, *"unberechenbar,"* or unpredictable. Papen reacted differently.

Harry Kessler read that Papen, "terrified by the idea" of an imminent march on Berlin, had declared his willingness to step down and leave the chancellor position to Hitler. Another rumor tangled the chancellorship and a storm trooper coup yet further: "Goebbels and Strasser were said to have wanted to launch the 'March on Berlin' but Hitler realized the right moment had passed and, both furious and disappointed, had returned to Munich without even waiting for his appointment with Hindenburg," Kessler wrote.

Sitting on the lakeside terrace, Hitler now huddled with his closest lieutenants. Goebbels panicked, as he so often did, leaving Strasser to master the moment. Why not turn Hitler's problem into Papen's problem, Strasser proposed. With 37 percent of the electorate and 230 seats in the Reichstag, Hitler had the capacity to paralyze the legislative process. If Papen and Schleicher could not deliver the chancellorship to Hitler, the National Socialists would simply go into obstructionist mode. Papen would be forced to rule by executive decree. The Communists would mobilize, the Papen government would collapse, and Hindenburg would be left with the starkest of choices: Hitler or chaos. The Strasser strategy seemed clear, simple, and sensible. Goebbels calmed down. "In any event, we need to keep our nerves and stay strong," said Goebbels, reprising the collective lakeside sentiment. "We are all of one mind. Strasser is already readying himself for the interior minister position."

Hitler arrived in Munich in time for lunch. Goebbels and his wife, Magda, proceeded north to their country house in Caputh near Potsdam, with Hitler remaining behind and visiting the hospitalized Braun. He had been seeing the blue-eyed photo-shop assistant discreetly on and off for the past two years. Braun had first come to his attention in October 1930, when he stopped by Hoffmann's photo studio. She recalled this "man with a funny moustache, a light-colored English-style overcoat and a big felt hat in his hand." Braun, who had shortened her dress earlier that day, noticed Hitler looking at her legs. Hitler began inviting the young woman to the theater, to dinner. She kept the relationship from her parents for as long as she could, knowing they would not approve. Hitler also kept the increasingly intimate relationship discreet. Hoffmann knew, as did Anni Winter, but almost no one else in his inner circle.

Hitler's mentor, Dietrich Eckart, allegedly told Hitler that he needed to stay single so all the women of Germany could imagine him as their own. Germany was his bride. Hitler's personal pilot, Hans Baur, suggested a more practical reason. "I saw Hitler surrounded by a group of attractive girls," Baur recalled. "None of the girls had eyes for anyone but him." But Hitler kept a noticeably practiced distance. When Baur mentioned this, Hitler replied, "As a matter of fact you are right. And I have to keep it that way. I'm in the spotlight of publicity and anything of that sort could be very damaging." Were Baur to have an affair, Hitler continued, no one would notice or care. "But if I did, there'd be hell to pay," he said. "And women can never keep their mouths shut."

The press was unrelenting in exposing and exploiting irregularities in Hitler's private life. Hitler's father had been born out of wedlock, was originally named Schicklgruber, and had married a cousin who was barely half his age. His sister in Vienna was said to be mentally impaired. His brother in Hamburg was a convicted felon and bigamist. There were rumors of Jewish blood in the Hitler family lineage. Indeed, the National Socialist leader could not provide the incontrovertible evidence of a pure Aryan lineage that he was demanding from his own followers.

On September 18, 1931, Hitler was in his car with Hoffmann on his way to a weekend rally in Erlangen when Julius Schreck, their driver, was flagged down thirty minutes outside Nuremberg by a speeding car dispatched from the Grand Hotel in Nuremberg, where Hitler had spent Thursday night. Anni Winter had called the hotel saying that she urgently needed to speak with Hitler. When Hitler called, she told him that something terrible had happened to his twenty-three-year-old niece, Geli Raubal, who kept a room in Hitler's Prinzregentenplatz apartment. Schreck raced back to Munich "with the accelerator jammed to the floor." "In the driving mirror I could see the reflection of Hitler's face," Hoffmann said. "He sat with compressed lips, staring with unseeing eyes through the windscreen."

By the time they arrived at the apartment, Strasser was already there, interrogating Winter, managing the police, speaking to the reporters who swarmed the entrance. Hitler's youth leader, Baldur von Schirach, who was Hoffmann's son-in-law, had called Adolf Dresler, head of the party's press section in the Brown House, and instructed him to issue a statement explaining that Hitler was "in deep grief" over his niece's suicide. "Dr. Dresler had just fulfilled the instructions when Schirach called back on the telephone," Hitler's close associate and foreign press adviser Ernst "Putzi" Hanfstaengl remembered. "In fact, the press release should make no mention of suicide as the cause of death, rather it should simply refer to an unfortunate accident." By then it was too late.

On September 21, the *Münchner Merkur* reported on an alleged altercation between Hitler and his niece that had preceded the suicide. "Neighbors heard screaming and shouting in the apartment," the newspaper reported. The *Münchner Post*, a decidedly anti-Hitler newspaper, ran the headline "A Puzzling Affair—Suicide of Hitler's Niece" and supplied graphic details, suggesting physical abuse. A letter was allegedly found, written by Geli, saying she was moving to Vienna. By Monday afternoon, the puzzling affair had become lurid. "A mysterious darkness envelops the niece's suicide in the house of Hitler," *Vorwärts* reported in its evening edition. "Officially she has lived for the past two years as subletter with a married couple who live on the same floor as Hitler and keep house for him." But she was often seen in her uncle's company "when going to the movies or other places of entertainment."

The report was followed by that of a case of incest between a niece and her uncle, a prominent Social Democrat in the Mecklenburg region who had hanged himself after unrelenting coverage in the National Socialist press. *Vorwärts* framed the story as a cautionary tale. "In the luxuriously decorated Munich apartment of her uncle, a young woman commits suicide," *Vorwärts* concluded. "The uncle's name is Adolf Hitler. But how are the Nazis planning to respond after establishing their concepts of morality in the Mecklenburg [incest] case?"

Beyond stories of abuse and incest, rumors proliferated. Geli was desperate to move to Vienna to study singing. She was in love with Hitler's driver. She was pregnant by a Jewish music instructor. Anni Winter later claimed that Geli found a letter from Eva Braun in Hitler's coat pocket, tore it to pieces, then shot herself. Winter recalled piecing the scraps together: "Dear Herr Hitler, thank you for the wonderful invitation to the theater. It was a memorable evening." Braun looked forward to seeing Hitler in the future.

Hitler sought refuge in the country house of his printer, Adolf Müller, on the Tegernsee, where he paced his room, day and night, refusing to eat or sleep; he told Frank he was abandoning politics. He could not bear to read the press, to appear in public ever again. Schreck hid Hitler's pistol to prevent another suicide. Hoffmann eventually convinced Hitler to eat. Göring provided a comforting lie: Geli had mishandled the pistol and accidentally shot herself. Hanfstaengl recalled Hitler's eyes filling with tears as he embraced Göring. "Yes, yes, that is exactly what happened, my dear Göring," Hitler said. "Now I know who my true friend is!"

Now, less than a year later, Eva Braun, four years younger than Geli, had shot herself, and just before he expected to be named chancellor. That afternoon, Hoffmann accompanied Hitler to the hospital to see Braun. Hitler asked the surgeon, "Do you think that Fräulein Braun shot herself simply to become an interesting patient and to draw my attention to herself?" The doctor told Hitler it had been a serious suicide attempt, that the young woman felt desperately neglected. Hitler turned to Hoffmann. "You see, the girl did it out of love for me. But I have given her no cause that could justify such a deed." He murmured, "Obviously, I must now look after the girl." Hoffmann objected. He said that Hitler had not obligated himself in any way. "And who, do you think, would believe that?" Hitler replied. Within a day, Hitler was on his way to Berlin.

Meanwhile, the opposition press was processing a more public Hitler scandal. That same day, *Vorwärts* ran a front-page headline, "Bestial Murder in Upper Silesia," over an article on a savage killing in the village of Potempa "perpetrated by soldiers of the prospective chancellor candidate Hitler." In reaffirming his commitment to a legal path to power, Hitler had sought to balance the expectations of the violent extremists in his movement with his sworn oath before the country's highest court. A cartoon that week showed Hitler, in an SA uniform with a swastika armband, leading a storm trooper on a leash while the storm trooper gleefully tosses bombs over his shoulder. The caption read, "I have the SA in hand, but what the SA have in their hands is none of my business." For all its intended irony, the caricature raised a serious question: How much control did Hitler have over his most fanatic followers—or, for that matter, over Ernst Röhm?

The former Reichswehr captain possessed a fierce and occasionally unhinged independence. In 1925, he broke with Hitler and bolted for Bolivia, not returning until 1931, when Hitler handed him the SA leadership. "I had an honest friendship with Hitler," Röhm once said. "Precisely because he was so beset with flatterers who worshipped him unconditionally and never dared contradict him, I felt duty-bound to speak freely, as his true friend." Röhm addressed Hitler as "Adolf" or "Adi," and always with the second-person familiar *du*.

Röhm shared Hitler's tenacity. He was the last holdout during the 1923 putsch. His men had barricaded themselves in the Bavarian War Ministry, where "machine guns poked out from every window." The rear of the building, facing the English Garden, was protected by barbed wire. Röhm remained defiant as the Reichswehr prepared to lay siege. "The artillery brought up a field gun to Schönfeld Strasse and aimed it at us," Röhm wrote. "Machine guns were installed in a building across from us in the Ludwig Strasse, and the mortar company set up on the side of the road." Even after learning that the putsch had collapsed amid a hail of gunfire on the Odeon Square, with Hitler wounded and whisked away in a waiting vehicle, Röhm refused to surrender. Only when orders came from General Erich Ludendorff, who had joined Hitler in the march through the city, did Röhm relent.

Associated Press reporter Louis Lochner remembers meeting Röhm in January or February 1930 when Röhm came to the AP office in Berlin to arrange an interview with Hitler. Lochner found him to be "a rather stout, squatty, heavy-set man" who wore a hat pulled over his eyes. "When he took off his hat I saw a badly cut-up face," Lochner recalled, "that had been horribly mangled in the first world war and had been further scarred by attempts at facial surgery."

As a decorated veteran of the Great War, Röhm wore his scar and Iron Cross, first class, with belligerent pride. For him, as for Kurt von Schleicher, politics was war by other means, which was why he preferred General Ludendorff to Field Marshal Hindenburg, the twin heroes of Tannenberg. "Hindenburg was a figurehead," Röhm said, "but the leadership of the Army and the heavy work of organization was borne mainly on Ludendorff's shoulders." While Hindenburg withdrew after the war to write his memoirs, Ludendorff joined Hitler in the putsch, standing erect amid the hail of bullets as others fell or fled. Unlike Hitler, who emerged from prison committed to following "the legal path" to power, Röhm remained committed to the violent overthrow of the constitutional republic. "It was the old story: as soon as a power bloc formed outside parliament and became significant, its own bosses made war on it and destroyed it." Strasser had indeed advocated the dissolution of the SA. "Parliamentarians cannot tolerate any other gods around them," Röhm said.

Röhm was outraged by the government's abandonment of the paramilitary victories in Upper Silesia, in 1921, and their subsequent efforts in the Ruhr, in 1923, when the German political leadership acquiesced to Allied demands. Röhm liked to quote Field Marshal Gebhard von Blücher after Waterloo. "I most respectfully request that the diplomats," the victorious Prussian commander said, "be instructed not to lose what the soldier has won for us with his blood." When Röhm entered the Reichstag as a delegate, he reminded his fellow National Socialists that they had not been elected "to wear a top hat and tails, but a trench helmet."

Brüning had moved against the SA in the spring of 1932, closing their offices and confiscating their arsenals, only to have the ban lifted in advance of the July 31 elections, in exchange for a promise from Hitler of orderly behavior. The storm troopers had shown restraint, but they marched into Communist and Social Democrat strongholds as provocations, subjecting themselves to jeers and stones and sniper attacks, on the expectation that the election would see Hitler elevated to chancellor. But ten days after the 37 percent triumph, Hitler was still not in power. The storm troopers grew impatient and increasingly violent as they awaited Hitler's ascendence to the chancellorship. "Every adjournment, every postponement of the seizure of power, results in increasing unrest among these National Socialists who have been most primed to take action," wrote *Die Weltbühne*. "It is this very pressure that keeps forcing Hitler again and again into negotiating." *Vorwärts* distilled Hitler's dilemma to a simple existential question: "To revolt or negotiate, that is the question." By week's end, with rumors confirmed that Hitler would be meeting with Hindenburg, tens of thousands of storm troopers "marched" on Berlin in anticipation of the appointment of their Führer as chancellor. They were instructed to pack razors, along with their weapons, so they could be clean-shaven after what promised to be a long night.

*

Goebbels spent August 12 at his country house in Caputh awaiting Hitler's arrival from Munich. In the evening hours he fretted and stewed about the heat, about Magda's health, about the machinations of Himmler and Röhm, whom he suspected would begin vying for power once Hitler was appointed chancellor—"They all smell the prey"—and about the growing restlessness among the storm troopers. "It is hardest for them," Goebbels wrote. "Who knows whether the units can be held together. Nothing is harder than telling triumphant troops that their victory has slipped out of their hands." Goebbels feared that Röhm would lose control of his men. He feared that "crazy things" might happen, especially with the men armed to the teeth with "weapons and such things."

Mostly, though, Goebbels worried that evening about the upcoming meeting with Hindenburg. Schleicher and Papen were willing, Goebbels knew. Now, only the Reich president had to be managed. Hitler would be received. Then the die would be cast. It was a make-or-break moment for the National Socialist movement. "The Führer stands before serious decisions. Without complete power he will not be able to master the situation," Goebbels calculated. "If he is not given full power, then he will have to decline [the chancellor position]. If he declines, the result will be an immense depression in our movement and in the electorate." Or worse.

Hitler arrived at Goebbels's country house around ten o'clock that evening, in a state of nervous distraction and still uncertain whether Hindenburg would actually receive him the next day. Goebbels remembers him pacing the house until late in the night.

CHAPTER 5

SATURDAY THE THIRTEENTH

There are few days in the history of the NSDAP that were of such fateful consequence for the new Germany than August 13, 1932.

—OTTO DIETRICH, PRESS SPOKESMAN,
NATIONAL SOCIALIST GERMAN WORKERS PARTY

Berlin on the second weekend in August 1932 saw the continuation of clear skies and spiking temperatures—34 degrees Celsius, or 93 degrees Fahrenheit, in the shade—that had helped make that year's Constitution Day, August 11, both solemn and sweltering. The Americans had celebrated that year's Fourth of July with parades and fireworks, despite the Dow Jones Industrial Average plunging that week to 41.22, the bottom of the Great Depression. The French had danced in the streets on Bastille Day. Germans had passed their Constitution Day in dour reflection.

"Looking back on the thirteen-year existence of our constitution," Wilhelm von Gayl said in his ceremonial address before the Reichstag, "we must recognize that it is in need of reform." As interior minister, Gayl was not only protector of national security but also guardian of the constitution. But on this afternoon, August 11, the bespectacled jurist enumerated his charge's myriad failings. This foundational document, designed to unite all Germans in "equality and justice," had left the country divided and embittered. Proportional representation had fractured and polarized the political landscape and left it increasingly violent.

"It is not the guilt of any one person but rather the construction of our constitution, when practically every attempt at reform is crushed in the gears of party politics," Gayl observed. Faced with legislative gridlock, Hindenburg was increasingly relying on his Article 48 powers, essentially functioning as a constitutionally empowered dictator.

Amid the fraught political processes, Gayl also saw the fracturing of a collective moral vision for the nation, as voters cleaved right and left and the center fell away. "The stronger these moral stirrings become in one section of our nation, the stronger becomes the resistance of those feeling their world outlook threatened," Gayl continued. "And now our nation is divided in two factions between which rages an embittered fight for political power." Which is exactly what Hitler and company hoped would happen. Goebbels wrote in his diary, "Last Constitution Day ever. Hope you enjoy yourselves."

Hindenburg had arrived in Berlin from Neudeck by train the previous morning and was accommodated in Papen's private quarters in the Reich Chancellery, since the presidential palace was undergoing a long-overdue refurbishment: new roof, updated heating, an en suite bathroom for the decrepit presidential apartment. He was furious to learn that Schleicher had been in negotiations with Hitler. A notation in the official record reads: "He said that he found it a bit much"—"*ein starkes Stück*," literally "a strong piece"—"that he was supposed to appoint the Bohemian corporal as Reich chancellor. He wanted to avoid that if at all possible and perhaps it would be good to meet again with Hitler to convince him to finally abandon that hope."

On Thursday, August 11, precisely at noon, Hindenburg, in his role as president of Germany's first federated, constitutional republic, ascended the steps of the Reichstag, constructed with reparations exacted from France after the Franco-Prussian War of 1870–71, over whose entrance was carved the words "For the German People." Standing a full head taller than everyone else, the stately Reich president proceeded to his place of honor on the high dais overlooking the wreckage of his country's democratic structures. Every seat in the vast glass-domed plenary hall was filled, but not a single delegate of the three major political parties, representing nearly three-quarters of the country's electorate, was present. Instead, dutiful civil servants had brought their wives and friends to guarantee a full house. Camill Hoffmann was the Czechoslovak cultural attaché in Berlin. Sitting in the diplomatic loge, he felt as though he was observing a state funeral rather than an anniversary celebration of a constitution. From the packed press gallery, Fred Birchall of the *Times* noted the absence of Reichstag delegates and that "behind the chairman's vacant desk were banked mournful purple hydrangeas."

By August 1932, Hindenburg represented the final bastion in the defense of democracy in his country. He made the point that afternoon when he entered the Reichstag in the company of Minister of Defense Kurt von Schleicher, who appeared in uniform and full military regalia, his chest spangled with war decorations. Chancellor Papen—ever dapper in his suit and top hat—sported two war medals. Hindenburg could have filled his expansive chest with ribboned and medallioned glory, but he had dispensed with uniform and military decorations. He appeared on this Constitution Day dressed in a three-piece civilian suit and top hat, as duly elected president of the constitutional republic he had vowed to protect and defend.

The ceremony in the Reichstag opened with selections of nonpartisan music from Beethoven (Egmont Overture) and Brahms (Fourth Symphony) and concluded with the national anthem, whose lyrics promised *"Einigkeit und Recht und Freiheit"*—unity, justice, freedom—for "the German Fatherland." As the final notes drifted through the thickening heat, the "Father of the Fatherland," as Fred Birchall called Hindenburg, rose in all his statuesque grandeur and strode from the plenary hall into the blazing heat on the front steps of the Reichstag, where he was greeted with cheers of adulation and invocation of the final word from the national anthem's refrain: "Freedom!"

Normally, Hindenburg would have returned that same day to Neudeck and its cooler temperatures. Instead, he was compelled to remain in the capital to deal with the crisis of a deadlocked Reichstag and the need to form a new government and, worst of all, to weigh the possibility of receiving "the Bohemian corporal." Bella Fromm met with the wife of Hindenburg's aide Otto Meissner on the morning of August 13, noting in her diary, "I saw Frau Meissner today, who told me confidentially, Otto and the major"—meaning Meissner and Papen—"have persuaded Hindenburg to receive Hitler this afternoon. Papen is rehearsing Hitler for the audience this minute." The "rehearsal" was not going well.

That morning, when Hitler visited Schleicher in his Bendlerstrasse office to finalize details for his meeting with Hindenburg, the *"maître de l'intrigue politique"* informed Hitler of a hitch in his appointment as chancellor: Hindenburg refused. Hitler had trusted Schleicher's proven capacities to deliver on his promises. Schleicher had engineered the dismissal of Brüning, the loyal chancellor who had run Hindenburg's successful reelection campaign. Schleicher had arranged the appointment of a virtually unknown state delegate, Papen, as the next chancellor. Schleicher had convinced Hindenburg to suspend the Brüning ban on SA uniforms and public demonstrations, to dissolve the Reichstag and schedule new elections, and, most important, to arrange a personal meeting between Hitler and Hindenburg to confirm these arrangements. There had been no reason to assume Schleicher could not make good on his promise to have Hitler appointed chancellor.

There was, however, an elegant solution, as Papen explained to Hitler later that morning in his Wilhelmstrasse apartment. Hitler could serve for a time as Papen's vice chancellor until he had gained Hindenburg's confidence. Papen would willingly step aside and allow Hitler to assume the chancellorship. With the National Socialists now holding 230 seats in the Reichstag, Hitler headed the largest political party in the country. He had every right to the chancellorship and to be accorded the same presidial powers as Brüning and Papen. "Hitler was staggered," Wheeler-Bennett recalled. "The Nazis were being fobbed off with offers of secondary positions." If he were denied the chancellorship, Hitler threatened, he would unleash Röhm's storm troopers and take the government by force. He would eradicate, if necessary, the republic's multiparty system with "fire and sword." The real challenge, as Hitler explained afterward in Goebbels's apartment, in a fashionable Charlottenburg neighborhood on the west side of town, was balancing storm trooper frustration with voter expectation, while trying to discern Schleicher's and Papen's real intentions. "They try to convince him [Hitler] to be satisfied with the vice chancellorship," Goebbels observed, expressing fear that the real goal was to lure Hitler away from the party and splinter the movement. Goebbels's assessment was stark: "If the Führer agrees to this, he is ruined." Hitler also feared that he had been taken into false confidences by Schleicher, lured to Berlin on sham expectations, with the goal of discrediting him with the public and his followers, when in fact Hindenburg never had any intention of appointing him as chancellor, or so Hitler thought, until three o'clock that afternoon, when the telephone rang in Goebbels's apartment. State Secretary Planck was on the line: the Reich president wanted to meet with Hitler. "If the decision has already been made, then there is no reason for the Führer to come," Goebbels told Planck. Planck replied, "The Reich president wants to speak with him personally." Expectations lifted. An hour later, Hitler arrived at the Reich Chancellery.

For his August 5 meeting with Schleicher, Hitler had brought Strasser. Now, for his meeting with Hindenburg, he arrived flanked by the Janus-headed entourage of Frick and Röhm. As Bella Fromm suggested, Hitler knew his game. Frick was the first National Socialist to hold a state ministerial position and signaled Hitler's implied willingness to embrace responsible, albeit conservative governance. Frick was most likely unknown to Hindenburg. Röhm needed no introduction. Beyond his high-profile role as head of Hitler's 400,000 storm troopers, Röhm had made headlines that spring when personal correspondence had been published revealing his "same-sex inclinations," which he admitted to first "discovering" in 1924, at age thirty-seven, but had long sensed through "a series of feelings and acts back into my childhood." Munich's public prosecutor had placed further awkward revelations in the public record when an unemployed accountant named Peter Granninger was convicted under Paragraph 175 of the penal code, which criminalized "unnatural fornication." In court, Granninger detailed his encounters with Röhm in graphic and often lurid descriptions, which went verbatim into the opposition press. Hitler stood by Röhm, denouncing this "dirtiest and most disgusting witch hunt" in public but seething in private. Hanfstaengl kept an office in the Brown House. "Hitler yelled for hours so loudly that the window rattled," Hanfstaengl recalled. Rumors held that Hitler and Röhm were lovers.

Hindenburg expressed to Meissner his discomfort at the idea of shaking hands with that *"Hinterlader,"* or breech loader, a double entendre alluding to military hardware as well as a sexual act.

Hitler and his entourage were shown into the Reich Chancellery library, where, Otto Meissner recalled, an awkward formality prevailed. There were chasms between the former Prussian field marshal and the Bohemian corporal in terms of military rank, social status, and political convictions, made all the greater by Hitler's breach of his gentleman's agreement, at the May meeting, to support the Papen regime and contain storm trooper violence.

Hindenburg greeted Hitler, Röhm, and Frick at precisely 4:15 p.m. in the Reich Chancellery library without a handshake. He did not offer his guests seats. Otto Meissner was present, and recalled that Hindenburg stood leaning on his walking stick, "a veritable monument of a man, towering over them by a full head and a half."

Hindenburg did not mince words: "Herr Hitler, I called for you in order to pose a simple question very officially: Are you personally willing to place yourself at my disposal for participating in the government?" Hitler replied, "I have already gone over in detail with the Reich chancellor the reasons why it is impossible to participate in a government in which we do not have the leadership." Hindenburg asked, "So this means that you are demanding the entire government?" According to the meeting protocol, Hitler replied that, given the "significance of the National Socialist movement," meaning 37 percent of the electorate, he had to demand for the party and himself complete leadership of the government and the state. "To this," the protocol states, "the Herr Reich President declared with decisiveness that to this demand he had to answer with a clear and definitive '*Nein*.'"

Hindenburg recalled the pre-election promise that Hitler had made that spring to enter into a coalition government if Hindenburg would dissolve the Reichstag under Article 25 to permit new elections, to lift the ban on the SA, and to permit the wearing of the brown-shirt uniform in public. "I kept my promises," Hindenburg said. He had expected the same of Hitler. Hindenburg was also troubled by the hatred and violence that was being fomented by Hitler's followers.

By Saturday morning, nine suspects had been taken into custody for the "bestial murder" of Konrad Pietzuch, perpetrated, in the words of *Vorwärts*, "by soldiers of Reich chancellor candidate Hitler!" Hindenburg told Hitler in no uncertain terms that he could never entrust a government to a political party whose members were so "intolerant, undisciplined, and, in addition, so violent in their behavior." Hitler asked the "Herr Reich President" to "have a bit of understanding that his people sometimes get a little excited," adding that the storm troopers felt threatened by Communists and were "not adequately protected by the police." Hindenburg did not mince words. He told Hitler that he could not justify before "God, his conscience, or the Fatherland" placing the entire powers of government into the hands of a single political party, especially one that was so intolerant of others. Hitler held his ground. He insisted that single-party rule was the only possible solution for the country's myriad problems.

"So, you will then go into opposition?" Hindenburg asked.

"I have no other choice," Hitler said.

"Then let me warn you to conduct yourself in opposition in an honorable manner and remember your responsibility and duty to the Fatherland," Hindenburg said. "I have no doubt as to your love of the Fatherland."

Hindenburg also let Hitler know that he would prosecute "with the severest means possible any acts of terror or violence perpetrated by members of the SA detachments." The former field marshal extended his hand to the former corporal. "We are both old comrades and want to remain so, since perhaps our paths will cross in the future," Hindenburg said. "Thus, I want us now to shake hands as comrades." Hitler nodded, bowed politely, and extended his hand. The meeting lasted less than twenty minutes.

Afterward Hitler spoke with Papen and Meissner in the corridor outside the library. He was furious. He had barely gotten a word in edgewise. The field marshal had given him no room to maneuver, Hitler told Meissner: "It was not possible since Herr Reich President said from the outset that his position was fixed." Hitler felt he had been led into a trap. He told Papen, "Clearly, I will have to go into opposition against your government, since the way you have run the country, as I have already said, has won back two to three million votes for the Communists." Hitler vowed to make life difficult not only for Papen but for Hindenburg as well, as Papen later reported to his cabinet. "Herr Hitler stated that the further developments would inevitably lead to his proposed solution, or to the fall of the Reich president," Papen told his ministers, noting that Hitler had said that "things will become very sharp and he would take no responsibility for the results." But the field marshal was not through with the Bohemian corporal. Before departing for Neudeck, Hindenburg gave instructions that the protocol of his confidential meeting with Hitler be released to the press. Hindenburg also issued a polite but stern directive to the chancellor's office: "Herr Reich President wishes that no new negotiations are to be undertaken with the National Socialists without him first being made aware of them and being able to take a position." Wheeler-Bennett observed that Hindenburg had come to appreciate Papen and had "no thought of exchanging this delightful companion for the wild eccentricities of Adolf Hitler." Helene Nostitz, Hindenburg's niece, recalled that "Uncle Hindenburg" was possessed of such a dislike of Hitler that the name could not even be mentioned in his presence.

That evening, as Hindenburg's train rolled eastward toward the East Prussian moorlands, Hitler huddled in Goebbels's apartment with his key lieutenants, briefing them on the debacle. Goebbels called the notion that Hitler ever serve as Papen's vice chancellor "grotesque nonsense." They also discussed damage control. First and foremost, there was the SA. Röhm worried that expectations had heightened dangerously. Tens of thousands of storm troopers awaited news of the meeting, poised for their "March on Berlin" either to celebrate Hitler's appointment as chancellor with a torchlight parade through the Brandenburg Gate or to launch a violent revolution; 90 percent of the SA leaders were said to be ready "for immediate attack." Equally unsettling was the potential discontent among the voters who had supported Hitler on the promise and expectation that the National Socialists would enter a coalition government. They, too, would need to be appeased. Konrad Heiden was a journalist who wrote for the *Frankfurter Zeitung* and *Vossische Zeitung* and was one of the most astute commentators of the political scene. "The entire German nation watched as Hitler ascended the stairs to power," Heiden later wrote. "The entire German nation then watched as Hitler went flying back down those same stairs."

Dietrich, the NSDAP press spokesperson, who was there that evening, recalled that Hitler remained unmoved. He ordered the entire SA placed on a two-week furlough to let tempers cool. He refused to entertain any discussion of a coalition government. Hitler said, "I would rather besiege a fortress than be a prisoner in one."

It was left to Dietrich to reframe expectations for the press and salvage what he could from what had clearly been a debacle, but before a strategy could be framed, he was overtaken by events. "Hardly had the Führer returned to Dr. Goebbels's apartment when the government press office began, as if on command, to release the deliberations of the 'confidential' meeting with its own spin," Dietrich recalled. Headlines followed: "Hitler Demands Full Power!" "Hitler Dressed Down by the Reich President." Word on the street had it that when the idea of appointing Hitler chancellor was initially broached, Hindenburg had said that if he were to give Hitler any position in the government it would be as postmaster general, "so he can lick me from behind on my stamps."

The French newspaper *Le Matin* reported that Hitler had suffered a nervous breakdown and was now in a sanatorium, with Strasser having assumed responsibility for leadership of the movement; these rumors made quick headlines in the German press. *Vorwärts* considered the rumors, regardless of their inherent efficacy, as affirming Hitler's long-evident "mental instability" and Strasser's obvious leadership capacities, but such news stories were quickly and vehemently denounced by the Brown House press office. *The New York*

Times also dismissed the rumors with a curt statement—"It is untrue"—and a confirming though fancifully inaccurate detail—"Hitler went fishing yesterday."

Hindenburg's unequivocal rejection of Hitler was received with relief by Hammerstein. At a meeting that spring, Hammerstein had told Hitler bluntly, "Herr Hitler, if you achieve power legally, that would be fine with me. If the circumstances are different, I will use arms." As the Reichswehr chief of staff, Hammerstein was well aware of the military's frustration with the liberties and excesses taken by Hitler's storm troopers and its own bridled inaction against them. After Hindenburg's rebuke, Hammerstein wrote in his diary that same day, "I can sleep easily again now since I know that, if need be, I can order the troops to fire on the Nazis."

Kessler first heard the news of the Hitler debacle on arrival in Marseille on Sunday morning. He wondered how his porter in Berlin was absorbing the news—or, for that matter, Ernst Röhm and his "two million" storm troopers. "The decisive meeting between Hindenburg and Hitler lasted only thirteen [*sic*] minutes," Kessler wrote. "What now? Civil war or the inglorious disintegration of the Nazi movement?"

CHAPTER 6

MAJORITY RULES

My plan is now to get 51 percent of the votes,
or an even larger percentage.

—ADOLF HITLER, AUGUST 18, 1932

"I must flatly deny the implication that I asked the president for 'everything or nothing,'" Hitler said. "Holding only
37 percent of the nation's votes, how could I demand all the
portfolios?" It was August 17, and Hitler sat on the Haus
Wachenfeld veranda in the midsummer heat with Karl von
Wiegand, a reporter for the William Randolph Hearst media
empire, while two other American correspondents, Louis
Lochner of the Associated Press and Hans van Kaltenborn of
CBS radio, the "Dean of American Commentators," listened
to daily by millions, awaited their turn.

Hitler generally conducted interviews with reporters
in impersonal settings, as he did with *The New York Times*
and the Japanese daily *Tokyo Asahi Shimbun* at his office at
the Brown House in Munich. Unlike Mussolini, who welcomed banter and repartee, especially with attractive female
journalists, Hitler was awkward in one-on-one settings. For
all his beer-hall belligerence, he generally avoided personal

confrontation. He was, according to Kaltenborn, essentially a shy, awkward man who "compensated for his timidity by raucous self-assertion," protecting himself behind a wall of bluster even in private settings. When Harold Callender conducted an interview for *The New York Times* in the Brown House office, he found Hitler posturing and ranting almost exactly as he had at a public rally the night before. "He rose from his chair, walked about the room, sat upon a table, but was never at rest," Callender reported, remarking, in particular, on Hitler's "nervous gestures" and habit of "checking his rapid flow of speech to make sure his words were carefully noted."

But on this mid-August Wednesday morning, four days after the Hindenburg debacle, Hitler had agreed to sit down in his most private and protected space with Wiegand, Lochner, and Kaltenborn. Hitler had held a press conference for foreign reporters at the Hotel Kaiserhof the previous December, much to the surprise and consternation of the political establishment. The government was blindsided by the event. August Weber, head of the Reichstag's German Democratic Party, a left-leaning centrist faction, told his fellow Reichstag delegates that it was "simply intolerable" that Hitler could appear to be running a "separate government" from the Hotel Kaiserhof, as if he were "about to come to power." Hitler defiantly scheduled a second press conference the following week, this time exclusively for British and American journalists, but canceled it at the last moment amid rumors of a police raid. Instead, Hitler arranged a live radio broadcast to address the American public directly over the CBS radio network, but this too was prevented when the German postmaster general, Georg Schätzel, banned Hitler's access to state-owned radio cables. Hitler eventually found accommodation with William Randolph Hearst, who published the text of the scuttled speech in the *New York American*. That December, *Time* magazine featured Hitler on its cover, confirming Reichstag delegate Weber's worst fears. *Time* observed, "Adolf Hitler sat in Berlin giving press interviews as though he were already Chief of State." *Paris-Midi* marveled at *"les tribulations héroï-comiques"* of Hitler as he sought an audience outside his right-wing echo chamber. Now Hitler was having another go, this time on the Obersalzberg, but on this August morning neither as gesture nor as provocation but as political triage, the last recourse to repair political damage.

Hitler had found himself blindsided by the Hindenburg protocol detailing the president's dressing-down of the National Socialist leader. Within hours, he had dispatched a pointed letter to Meissner and Planck: "The official communication published this evening diverges on important points so significantly from the actual course of events that I cannot allow the public to be informed in such a one-sided and distorted manner." Hitler included his own version of the meeting, correcting what he saw as distortions of his words and intent. When Hindenburg said, "So, you are demanding control of the entire government?," Hitler insisted, he had, in fact, provided a more nuanced response: "I said that is not definitive. There would still need to be further negotiations over the configuration of the cabinet, which cannot be resolved from today to tomorrow." When Hindenburg allegedly faulted Hitler for reneging on agreeing to tolerate the Papen government in exchange for Hindenburg lifting the ban on the SA and dissolving the Reichstag to allow for new elections, Hitler said that Hindenburg had added, "I will not hold this against you since I understand that you feel forced by circumstances beyond your control." Hitler went on to detail his post-meeting discussion with Papen in the corridor and Papen's apparent diffidence, indeed arrogance, toward parliamentary process. "Oh, the Reichstag!" Papen allegedly said with a brisk wave of his hand. "I am surprised that you even care about the Reichstag."

If the official protocol was not retracted, Hitler threatened, he would issue his own protocol to the press the next day. Meissner replied immediately: The government stood by every word. As promised, Hitler released his account of the Hindenburg meeting on Monday morning, to deafening silence in the mainstream press. Not a single news service picked up the story. The following day, Tuesday, August 16, the *Völkischer Beobachter* featured the Hitler protocol verbatim in a full front-page story, while the *Rheinisch-Westfälische Zeitung*, a local newspaper, owned by press secretary Dietrich's father-in-law, published an extensive Hitler interview with softball questions that allowed Hitler to reaffirm his account of the meeting and to suggest that Hindenburg had violated the provisions of the Weimar constitution.

"I consider the involvement of the Reich president in the process of building a government as a transfer of responsibility from the shoulders of the Reich chancellor to the shoulders of the Reich president," Hitler said in his interview, noting that this represented a brazen violation of Article 53 of the constitution that empowered the Reich president to appoint and dismiss the Reich chancellor, but not necessarily to negotiate the positions in the cabinet. Hitler further pointed out that *that* responsibility, according to Article 58, was left to the Reich chancellor. One cannot help but hear echoes of Hans Frank's legal counsel here. Hitler also wondered why the National Socialists, as the country's largest political party, were not allowed to run the government. With a nod to a classic Bismarck adage, Hitler quipped, "Politics is no longer the art of the possible, but rather the art of the impossible."

"If you tell a lie big enough and keep repeating it, people

will eventually come to believe it," Goebbels allegedly said; this was in fact the distillation of a cynical truth Hitler had commented on in a chapter on reasons for Germany's surrender at the end of the First World War in the first volume of *Mein Kampf*. But big lies require big audiences. The Hitler correctives to the Hindenburg meeting were extensive, pointed, and useless. "Our press could not make it through the noise," Dietrich recalled. "The [Hindenburg] maneuver succeeded." Goebbels's comment was more to the point— "Hitler fell into Hindenburg's trap"—which appeared to have been designed by Schleicher. Hitler was left scrambling for an audience of last resort—the foreign press.

As foreign press adviser, Hanfstaengl belonged to a tight circle of well-heeled individuals, including Carl and Helene Bechstein in Berlin and Hugo and Elsa Bruckmann in Munich, who had supported Hitler since his earliest years in politics. Hanfstaengl, a graduate of Harvard University, was the son of a wealthy Munich publisher, a giant of a man with a "strangely distorted head" in the words of Bella Fromm, and hands of "frightening dimensions," who played piano to calm Hitler in private and stage-managed his foreign press relations, not always with success. In November 1931, Hanfstaengl arranged an interview with Dorothy Thompson, an American reporter married to the Nobel Prize–winning author Sinclair Lewis. Thompson arrived for the interview reeking of alcohol, Hanfstaengl recalled, and ultimately wrote a disparaging profile of Hitler as "the very prototype of the Little Man." Hitler said afterward, "Don't ever bring me anyone like that again, Hanfstaengl."

For the Obersalzberg interview, Hanfstaengl reached out to Kaltenborn, one of his best friends from his Harvard days. Kaltenborn happened to be in Berlin, staying at the Hotel Kaiserhof. Hanfstaengl sent him a telegram offering an inter-

view with Hitler. Hanfstaengl sent an identical telegram to
Lochner. Lochner had interviewed Hitler in 1925, shortly
after the publication of *Mein Kampf*, and again in December
1931, two days after the Kaiserhof foreign press conference.
When Lochner had asked how Hitler thought the press conference had gone, Hitler replied, "Judging by the way the
German opposition press is jumping on me, they now at least
have something to write about." At the time, Hitler was feeling ebullient over his public relations coup. He wasn't smiling
on this mid-August Wednesday. Kaltenborn recalled that "the
Führer had been chary about receiving American correspondents" ever since his encounter with Dorothy Thompson.

Lochner and Kaltenborn took an overnight train to
Munich, where Hanfstaengl was waiting with Hitler's private
car and driver. They drove to Berchtesgaden, then up the
series of switchbacks to the Hotel Türken, an Obersalzberg
guesthouse with a beer garden, a favorite gathering place for
"Hitler pilgrims" because of its unobstructed view of Haus
Wachenfeld. The two men were surprised to encounter Wiegand, who had been invited separately by Dietrich.

Wiegand had known Hitler since 1921 and took lasting
pride in having first introduced him to the American public.
Wiegand called Hitler "one of the most interesting charac-
ters" he had encountered, noting his "toothbrush moustache"
and "eyes that spurt fire when in action." He christened Hitler the Mussolini of Germany. By the summer of 1932, Wiegand had been in contact with Hitler for over a decade and
never had any problem arranging interviews. "On a number
of occasions, he has called on me to have a chat," Wiegand
observed. The two men would meet in Hitler's office or for
lunch or dinner. On this August morning Wiegand asserted
proprietary rights, insisting that he be allowed to conduct a
one-on-one interview with Hitler. Lochner and Kaltenborn

waited beneath a tree in the beer garden. Wiegand returned a short while later in a state of high irritation. "That man is hopeless," he said. "I got nothing out of him. Ask him a question and he makes a speech. This whole trip has been a waste of time."

Now it was time for Lochner and Kaltenborn. As the two men approached Haus Wachenfeld, in the company of Hanfstaengl, Lochner noticed the laundry that Hitler's sister had hung out to dry. Hitler was waiting at the front door, dressed in a black suit and black tie, with a swastika lapel pin as the only dash of color. Hanfstaengl whispered the two journalists' names into Hitler's ear. Hitler greeted his guests without a smile—indeed, with "latent hostility," as Kaltenborn later recalled.

"In your antagonism towards the Jews, do you differentiate between German Jews and the Jews who have come to Germany from other countries?" Kaltenborn asked Hitler in German. Hitler paused. His eyes bored into his guest. Kaltenborn remembered them as being fiercely blue. "We believe in a Monroe Doctrine for Germany," Hitler said. "You exclude any would-be immigrants you do not care to admit. You regulate their number. You demand that they come with a certain physical standard." Hitler added that he couldn't care less about Jews in other countries; he was concerned only with those in Germany, and their attitude toward Germany, especially those with indications of disloyalty or anti-German attitudes. "And," he added, "we demand the right to deal with them as we see fit."

The men took seats in chairs beneath the open windows, listening to the chirping of canaries from inside and watching Hitler's three dogs bound about the yard. Hitler's sister brought coffee and cake. Now Lochner struck. "Did you promise Hindenburg to tolerate the von Papen government?" he asked. This was exactly the question Hitler had wanted. "No, I only promised to tolerate them so long as they were bearable," he lied. "A general promise of toleration would have been sheer madness." Hitler launched into the barrage of rhetoric behind which he liked to hide in close quarters. He talked domestic and international politics. He denounced the war reparations that devastated the German economy. He denounced every treaty that came to mind—Lausanne, Rapallo, the Young Plan (scheduling the reparations payments), and, most of all, the Treaty of Versailles. He went on to enumerate the failings of the French, the British, the Soviets, at which point Lochner sought to bring Hitler back to the point of the discussion.

"Herr Hitler," Lochner said. "It is reported in the German press that in your interview with the Reich president you asked for the creation of a Nazi government in which you would exercise a power equivalent to that of Mussolini in Italy."

"I never made such a demand in the form quoted," Hitler said with annoyance. "How could I have demanded any such power when I was willing to leave the Reichswehr outside of my control? That would have provided an ample safeguard against any absolutism." Nevertheless, Hitler added, he had the right to complete control of the government. Kaltenborn jumped in. "But you don't have a majority vote," he said.

"Under the rules of democracy a majority of 51 percent governs," Hitler said. "I have 37 percent of the total vote which means I have 75 percent of the power that is necessary to govern." By his calculations, Hitler possessed the majority of the majority. "That means I am entitled to three-quarters of the power and my opponents to one-fourth." With 13.7 million voters, Hitler went on to say, he was in a "safe position" with the electorate. "Next time I will have fourteen to fifteen million and so it will go," he predicted. "That is my hard-earned capital which no one can take from me. I slaved for it and risked my life for it." He laid out the Strasser game plan, pointing out that since he had the largest party in the Reichstag, it was impossible to create a functioning majority without him. He could cripple the Reichstag and, with it, the democratic process. Hitler's mood brightened at the thought. "Without my party no one can rule Germany today," he said. He could make or break any government.

At this point, one of his dogs, who'd been coursing about the yard, bounded onto the terrace, interrupting Hitler, who pointed with his hand and ordered irritably, *"Platz!"* The dog slunk dutifully down the stairs and back to the lawn. Hitler then expanded on his stranglehold on the democratic process. "Europe cannot maintain itself in the uncertain currents of democracy," he said. "Europe needs some form of authoritarian government." He cited kings, the Catholic Church, and the Holy Roman Empire as examples of the continent's long and enduring undemocratic legacies. "The authority can assume different forms," Hitler continued. "But parliamentarism is not native to us and does not belong to our tradition. The parliamentarian system has never functioned in Europe." He said that dictatorship represented the only viable future for Germany, but not one imposed on the country—rather, one embraced by the people, in which "the people declare their confidence in one man and ask him to lead."

Sitting on the terrace, where he and Goebbels had cast their hopes upon the stars, Hitler repeated his vow to destroy democracy through democratic process. He called his storm troopers the "best disciplined body imaginable" and brushed away the notion of a rumored March on Berlin. "I don't have to march on Berlin as they say I propose to do," Hitler said, then added with a wisp of whimsy, "I am already there. The question is who will march out of Berlin?" Lochner noticed Hitler growing restless, his glance drifting beyond the terrace. Lochner tossed out a final question: "Do you expect to follow the paths of legality in your future steps?" "Oh, yes," Hitler said dismissively with a brief smile. Then his glance fixed beyond them. They turned and saw Röhm, in his brown SA uniform, striding across the green lawn against the fierce blue sky.

As they rose, Hanfstaengl suggested he take a group photo with Lochner's camera. Hitler looked annoyed but conceded, standing between Lochner and Kaltenborn, with Wiegand to the side. In the photograph, Lochner and Kaltenborn are beaming, Kaltenborn with the smug, knowing smile of an American who looks forward to telling America about "this man on the hill," and Lochner with the self-satisfied look of having landed a scoop. Hitler stands with his arms locked across his chest, scowling.

Hitler's ad hoc Obersalzberg press conference generated exactly the sort of press he had hoped for. The interview found its way into hundreds of local American newspapers across the Hearst empire, and into the pages of *The New York Times*, which picked up Lochner's story from the Associated Press wire. "High up in the Bavarian mountains 107 miles from Munich," *The New York Times* wrote, "Herr Hitler is calmly awaiting further political developments, declaring he is certain that no matter what Cabinet is established after the Reichstag meets on August 30 his Nazis will have at least 75 percent representation in the government." But by the time the stories made it into American newspapers, the German news cycle had turned its focus to a local news story with implications not only for the nation but for millions of voters who needed to decide whether to cast their ballot for Hitler and his National Socialist movement.

CHAPTER 7

BOYS OF BEUTHEN

I had been hit in the head and was completely dazed.

—ALFONS PIETZUCH, AUGUST 19, 1932, BEUTHEN DISTRICT
COURTHOUSE, UPPER SILESIA

For men facing possible death sentences, the nine defendants who appeared in the dock for the murder of Konrad
Pietzuch were a notably spirited lot. They greeted fellow
National Socialists arriving in the Beuthen district courtroom with stiff-armed salutes and cries of *"Heil Hitler!"* The
local gauleiter for Upper Silesia shook hands with each of
them. "This is how the leaders under Hitler demonstrate
clear solidarity with bestial criminal murderers," a reporter
for *Die Rote Fahne*, a leading Communist newspaper, wrote.
"They laugh, make jokes and act as though they were already
acquitted."

The Potempa defendants were the first to be tried under
the new law seeking to curb political violence. With the
authorities promising expeditious implementation of the
decree, evidence had been collected, indictments issued,
and suspects arrested and charged and now placed on trial
in barely a week and a half. The only missing defendant was

Paul Golombek, who had served as the killers' late-night
Potempa guide. Golombek had been placed under house
arrest but had convinced his guard that he would just go
outside to "pick mushrooms in the woods," and then vanished. He was thought to have fled across the green border
to Poland. The rest of the suspects had willingly surren-
dered themselves, knowing that the courts tended to treat
right-wing violence with leniency. Kottisch, the electrician
who had put the bullet into Pietzuch, later said, "I thought
I would get a dressing-down or a slap on the wrist." He had
not expected a potential death sentence.

As with so many things that year, the Potempa murder
trial left the country bitterly divided. Local authorities had
attempted to avoid the exploitation of the killing by removing
Pietzuch's corpse from Potempa immediately and forgoing
forensic photographs that could be leaked to the public. Nevertheless, gruesome details found their way into the press.
Under the headline "Bestial Killing," *Vorwärts* detailed the
late-night savagery. *Die Rote Fahne* ran the headline "How
Hitler's Stormtroopers Butcher Workers." François-Poncet
recalled the rumor that Pietzuch had been stabbed with a
dagger twenty-eight times. The *Völkischer Beobachter* said it
was a "scandal that, considering the numerous horrible Communist murders, most of which have remained unpunished to
this day, the National Socialists of all people are the first to be
dragged before the bars of a special court."

Alfred Rosenberg was the party's chief ideologue and editor of the *Völkischer Beobachter*. Rosenberg defended the Pietzuch murder by drawing a parallel with the killing of Blacks in
the American South. Rosenberg observed that while the U.S.
Constitution guaranteed "formal equality between the white
man and the Negro," southern whites had developed extra-
judicial remedies such as lynching "to keep America's Black

population in place." Rosenberg argued that ethnic Germans should follow America's example and apply a similar "lethal rebalancing" against Slavs and Jews, citing the Pietzuch murder as a prime example.

Röhm invoked legal principles and his own sense of honor. "I see it as my sworn duty to stand by these men who acted in self-defense, and who have been subjected to prosecution and punishment." Support for the Potempa defendants resonated in the right-wing press. "The defendants aren't guilty of murder," *Ostfront*, a National Socialist–aligned Silesian newspaper, wrote, "it's Prussia's state minister of interior who belongs in the dock," along with the former minister of justice, whose liberal policies had forced "patriotic" Germans to take matters into their own hands.

From the third-floor legal department in the Brown House, Hans Frank assumed immediate responsibility for the case and brought the files to Hitler on the Obersalzberg. Frank claimed to have overseen 2,400 cases for the party and represented Hitler in 140 personal lawsuits, mostly for libel and defamation, which Frank frequently turned to his client's advantage. When Hitler was rumored to have spit out a communion host in his youth, Frank used the lawsuit to highlight Hitler's religious upbringing, a fact that allegedly resonated particularly with Roman Catholic voters.

"His opponents always ended up causing more harm to themselves," Frank once boasted, "even though they thought they were damaging this ascending figure with their slander."

But with Potempa, Frank counseled caution against prevailing defensive sentiments within the Brown House corridors. Frank warned against attempts to justify the Pietzuch murder, arguing that it was not legally tenable in court. Homicide was homicide. Frank feared that belligerent defense of the appalling murder could alienate segments of the law-abiding electorate who had cast their vote for the National Socialists in July.

As it was, Walter Luetgebrune, the head of Röhm's own legal department within the SA, not Hans Frank, was assigned to designing the defense for the men of Beuthen. Luetgebrune had successfully defended Erich Ludendorff, Hitler's co-defendant in the beer-hall putsch trial, in 1924. Ludendorff was acquitted of charges of treason. Luetgebrune also defended Röhm for violations detailed in Section 175 of Germany's criminal code for homosexual activities, getting him acquitted of charges on six occasions, despite Röhm's well-known predation of young men and his membership in the League for Human Rights, one of the country's leading organizations advocating for same-sex relations.

The Potempa murder trial commenced on Friday morning, August 19, punctually at nine o'clock, with opening remarks by the judge. Statements by the five primary defendants—those facing death sentences—followed. The first to take the stand was Reinhold Kottisch. Kottisch informed the court that he was neither a National Socialist nor a storm trooper but a member of the Upper Silesian Militia. Kottisch said he had been asked to accompany a group of storm troopers to Potempa, where he was given excessive amounts of beer and hard liquor, handed a pistol, then dispatched by Lachmann to "get the job done." Kottisch was so inebriated that he dropped the pistol. Someone picked it up for him. He was then led by a man whose name he did not know [Paul Golombek] to the residence of Florian Schwinge, where he was instructed to shoot Schwinge's wife through the window. Kottisch had refused. He was then led into the Pietzuch house, where he was ordered to shoot Konrad Pietzuch.

"You went heavily armed to people who were asleep, and

who had no idea what was happening?" the judge asked. "And then you actually shot a man who was frightened out of his sleep?" Kottisch replied, "I was drunk, and besides, I was just following orders." After shooting Pietzuch, Kottisch fled the house with the others. Only when he lit a cigarette, he said, did he notice that he had blood on his hands.

The next defendant was Rufin Wolnitza. Like Kottisch, he belonged to the Upper Silesian Militia. Like Kottisch, he had been plied with schnapps and beer. He was given a rubber truncheon and asked to wait outside the Pietzuch house. "We could see right through the window that Emil [*sic*]* was being beaten," Wolnitza said. He had been so inebriated that night that he had not even gotten the victim's name right. The third defendant was August Gräupner, who was indeed a storm trooper—with Sturm 25, in Broselwitz—and had accompanied Kottisch into the house. He said the visit had been intended as a warning. Had they been intent on homicide, Gräupner said, they would have killed Konrad's brother Alfons Pietzuch, too. Lachmann, the main defendant, took the stand to detail the repeated intrusions and harassment by Konrad Pietzuch, how he felt himself threatened, especially after Pietzuch burst into his tavern and shouted, "The National Socialists here will be shot just the way 450 other National Socialists have already been killed."

That afternoon, Alfons Pietzuch appeared as the first witness for the prosecution. Unfortunately, he was a poor eyewitness. He said that he had seen very little, literally, in the darkness, compelling the judge to press him for specifics about his brother's actions. "Did he jump up and throw a blanket over the defendant's head?" the judge asked. "I didn't see that," Alfons replied. "They pulled Konrad by his feet out

---

* Wolnitza misspoke; he meant "Konrad."

of the bed and began beating him up." Beyond that, Alfons
had seen nothing. "The intruders kept turning the flashlight
on and off," he said. "I was sharing the bed with my brother
and when the intruders hit me I turned over and saw nothing
further." It was only after the pistol had been fired and the
men had fled that Alfons risked leaving the bed. He found his
brother on the floor, gasping for air.

Marie Pietzuch saw even less than her son. In court, the
widow appeared weary and shaken. She gave her testimony
in Polish through an interpreter. She had heard the scuffling
and shouting. She had screamed into the chaos, "Children,
what will happen to you?" but had little to add in the way of
material evidence. That was left to the forensic pathologist, a
Dr. Weimann, whose autopsy report registered twenty-nine
wounds. "The corpse was extremely bruised around the neck,"
Weimann told the court. "The outer carotid artery was completely shredded. There was a large hole in the larynx." The
most serious injuries appeared to have been inflicted not by
the truncheons or the billiard cue, or even the gunshot, but,
rather, by repeated kicking while Konrad was on the floor.
His carotid artery had ruptured, causing blood to enter the
respiratory tract. Pietzuch had suffocated on his own blood.

In framing his defense strategy, Luetgebrune had one
overriding consideration: to prevent the prosecution from
developing a chain-of-command argument that could impli-
cate Röhm and possibly Hitler. At the end of the day, Luetgebrune knew, Hitler was the one on trial. Thus, Luetgebrune
first moved to have the case dismissed on technical grounds.
The defendants had intended only to deliver a "warning,"
not to kill Pietzuch, he argued, meaning the trial fell out of
the jurisdiction of the special court for premeditated political murder. When this failed, Luetgebrune argued that the
murder had occurred on Tuesday evening, August 9, before

the presidential decree went into effect, an assertion that was refuted by multiple witnesses. Florian Schwinge testified that the defendants had knocked on his door sometime around one-thirty a.m. Both Alfons and Marie Pietzuch confirmed the time of Konrad's killing as two a.m. Luetgebrune countered, arguing that the initial gathering in Lachmann's tavern, around eleven p.m. Tuesday evening, should be seen as the commencement of the crime.

Luetgebrune then invoked the principle of latent self-defense, a legal precedent that justified proactive physical aggression against a perceived threat. He spoke of ethnic tensions along the Polish-German border. He cited statistics indicating that Communist attacks on National Socialists outweighed National Socialist attacks on Communists by a margin of three to one. He recalled a recent precedent-setting court decision, in Gleiwitz, in which a National Socialist defendant was acquitted on the grounds of "latent self-defense."

Finally, Luetgebrune argued that if anyone was responsible for the Pietzuch murder, it was Golombek, who had led the defendants from the Lachmann tavern, had given them instructions, and had ultimately ordered Kottisch to shoot the victim. Golombek, of course, was still at large. The defendants, Luetgebrune argued, were in fact victims of "an accumulation of unfortunate circumstances."

*

Hitler followed the trial from the Obersalzberg with irritation but, like miner Wolnitza, assumed that the court would acquit the defendants. It was thus an unpleasant surprise when, on the afternoon of August 22, the judge issued the verdict: five death sentences, with Lachmann identified as the mastermind of the killing. Two others were sentenced to five years of imprisonment as accessories to murder. Two others were acquitted. "This verdict is so outrageous, it's hard to believe," Goebbels raged. Röhm rushed to Beuthen to comfort his men, as did Alfred Rosenberg. Göring dispatched a telegram. "Inconsolably embittered, I am outraged at the horrific verdict that has befallen you," he wrote. "I give you, comrades, my assurance that from now on our entire fight is devoted to your freedom." Göring initiated a fundraising campaign among friends to collect a thousand reichsmarks (about $5,300 today) as a sign of solidarity with, and concrete assistance to, those found guilty. "Stay strong!" he urged. "Fourteen million of the best Germans have rallied to your cause."

Like Frank, Strasser took a dim view of the Potempa Five. He now saw strategic benefit in their conviction. As he had told Schleicher in their secret meeting, he would disband the SA if appointed interior minister. The death sentences served a double purpose for Strasser. They signaled to the party radicals, especially Röhm and his army of storm troopers, that there would henceforth be accountability for excessive violence. They also provided a sobering message to a party leadership hoping to secure a majority of votes in the upcoming Reichstag elections. As *Vorwärts* wrote, "Doesn't Herr Göring understand the disgrace he is putting on the fourteen million Hitler voters when he expresses solidarity with the murderers of Potempa?"

Hermann Rauschning, a Hitler associate from Danzig, was on the Obersalzberg with Hitler when news of the Potempa verdict arrived. Hitler "lambasted the court's death sentence, calling it a mockery of justice," Rauschning later wrote. "The vehemence of his tone showed how angry he was. Such 'blood judgments,' he said, 'people will never forget.'" If it came to street fighting and twenty to thirty thousand

Germans lost their lives, the nation would be able to recover from that, Hitler said. There would be suffering, mourning, but people would endure. The wounds to the nation would heal, as they did after a war. "But a miscarriage of justice, a death sentence pronounced after cool deliberation, and pronounced and carried out against the people's unerring sense of justice, an execution of men who had acted in national passion, like those who had been sentenced at Potempa as common murderers," Hitler raged, "that would never be forgotten." Hitler was furious with the verdict, with the court, and, in particular, with Papen, whom he held responsible for permitting the special court to go ahead with the trial. "Papen will have to answer for this," Hitler told Rauschning.

That afternoon, Hitler dispatched a telegram to the Potempa Five. He wrote: "My comrades! In the face of this monstrous blood sentence, I feel bound to you in eternal loyalty." Hitler wrote that their freedom was "from that moment on, a matter of our honour and duty to fight a government that made this [verdict] possible." Hitler followed the telegram with a front-page article, filled with fury, in the *Völkischer Beobachter* and reprinted in Goebbels's *Der Angriff*. "More than 300 [National Socialists] massacred, some of them literally butchered alive, this is the tally of our martyrs," Hitler wrote. "Tens of thousands more have been injured and many crippled for life." Hitler railed against the government and border policies that permitted "insurgents" like Konrad Pietzuch to enter the country with impunity. Turning the debacle of his August 13 meeting with Hindenburg into political capital, Hitler wrote that he hoped that anyone with a sense of national pride and honor would now understand why he refused to be part of a government that could place the life of a foreigner above that of an ethnic German. Hitler feared for the future of Germany under the current government. "Justice under von Papen may end up condemning thousands of Nazis to death," he continued. "But I am not suited to be the hangman of the German people's freedom fighters." Hitler vowed that if he were ever appointed chancellor, his government would never place a foreigner's life above that of a German.

Fred Birchall of the *Times* was in the Beuthen courtroom when the verdict was read. There was "complete silence" as the defendants, their legal counsel, and assembled reporters absorbed the sentence. "Then Edmund Heines, commander of the Nazi 'storm detachments' in Silesia, who had attended the trial in full uniform, rose and shouted, 'The German people will pass a different sentence. This Beuthen verdict will become a beacon for German liberty,'" Birchall reported. "Thereupon most of the spectators, including many reporters, shouted, '*Heil Hitler!*'" That afternoon, 10,000 storm troopers took to the streets of Beuthen in open battles with police and military units that raged for the next three days.

*

Harry Kessler was at a friend's seaside estate outside Cannes attending a wedding and enjoying the sunshine and the surroundings when news of the Potempa verdict arrived. "The death sentence passed by the Beuthen court on five Nazi murderers appears, according to the local newspapers, to have caused tremendous excitement throughout the Nazi Party, which until now appears to have considered itself above the law, even if they committed the most serious crimes," Kessler wrote in his diary. "Hitler personally telegraphed the murderers, expressing his sympathy with them and that it would be a 'matter of honor!' to declare them pardoned. These people are supposed to be running the country!"

CHAPTER 8

DETERRENT EFFECT

Personally, I am inclined to commute the death sentences.

—PAUL VON HINDENBURG, AUGUST 30, 1932

If there was any indication as to where the epicenter of German political power rested by the summer of 1932, it can be seen in a photograph taken on the garden terrace of Neudeck on the afternoon of August 30, 1932. Hindenburg sits between his bespectacled interior minister, Gayl, and his bald-headed defense minister, Schleicher, a full head taller than both, with Hindenburg's aide Meissner as notetaker just to the left. The Reich chancellor sits opposite Hindenburg, when, in fact, he should have been in Berlin attending the opening session of the Reichstag, a traditional courtesy shown by the head of government. Papen sits in jovial company on a balustraded terrace at a table covered with a lace cloth and set with porcelain for afternoon cake and coffee. Papen and Schleicher laugh. Gayl smiles. Hindenburg looks bemused. It is a deceptively relaxed tableau for a group of men who have gathered to decide the fate of democracy in their country.

For the past half century, since the days of Bismarck,

decisions of such import had taken place in the rarefied confines of the former Radziwill Palace, on the Wilhelmstrasse, which now served as the Reich chancellor's residence, or in the adjacent presidential palace, once owned by the emperor before his abdication, also on the Wilhelmstrasse. The street also accommodated the foreign and interior ministries, with several power embassies—French, British, American—clustered around the Brandenburg Gate, at one end of the Wilhelmstrasse, and the Hotel Kaiserhof, Hitler's unofficial Berlin residence—a second-floor salon—at the other end. The façades of the Wilhelmstrasse ministries and residences presented a stern stone face to the public but were connected from behind by an enclosed park that permitted intercourse among the ministers, beyond public scrutiny and the press. In the early days of his Reich presidency, when he was resident full-time in Berlin, Hindenburg strolled the park's gravel paths in the morning hours, greeting the gardeners and giving suggestions on horticulture, before returning to the presidential palace to take breakfast on the glassed veranda. The rest of the day was filled, often until eleven o'clock at night, with ministerial meetings, private consultations, representational appearances, diplomatic receptions, and state visits by leaders from around the world. According to the Lutheran pastor Martin Niemöller, there was only one place of higher calling—"höhere Instanz"—than the Wilhelmstrasse, and that was the realm of divine powers. Except perhaps for the Hindenburg estate in East Prussia.

By the summer of 1932, Neudeck had increasingly become a place of consultation, deliberation, critical decision-making (as with Brüning's demission), and, on occasion, pilgrimage. On the last weekend in August, Hindenburg had received a "regiment" of university students who were traveling to Berlin to join a Steel Helmet rally scheduled to coincide with the opening of the new Reichstag. Sporting gray uniforms and trench helmets, the students had made a pilgrimage to a "fortress of the dead"—five stone towers arranged in a circular pattern in imitation of Stonehenge—on the moorlands of the Tannenberg battlefield, then continued to the estate of Elard von Oldenburg, where the former Reichstag delegate and avowed enemy of the republic made a pitch for the return of the kaiser. "The royal crown of Prussia lies at the bottom of the Vistula [the Polish border river] and it has to be recovered," Oldenburg told them that Saturday morning. "Without a German emperor there is no German Reich and there is no Prussia without a King of Prussia." Oldenburg said he hoped that his neighbor, the current president, would find "the strength" to continue to run the country with or without the Reichstag, then added, "probably without." The students then trooped off to Neudeck, where Hindenburg was waiting with a very different message.

"Dear young men, it is a great pleasure for me to greet you here at my home, in the narrower sense—you come from Tannenberg, that hallowed ground that I defended as I have defended and shall continue to defend our entire country," Hindenburg said to the uniformed students who had assembled in orderly ranks on his front lawn. "At that time, the German people were yet united and powerful, and in consequence capable of great deeds." Unfortunately, this was no longer the case, Hindenburg said. He did not reference any political figure in particular but called on the assembled youths to place the fatherland above any personal or political interests. He appealed to their sense of patriotism and their responsibility as citizens of the country, then gave a rousing, full-throated call: "Long live our beloved Fatherland!" The students cheered. Hindenburg then walked along their ranks in review, stopping here and there to pose a question, before sending them on their way. "Once more I thank you for coming to see me and for giving so much pleasure to this old man. Good luck to you all!" As the students marched off, the Reich president stood in the doorway to Neudeck, flanked by his two artillery pieces, waving a handkerchief.

Hindenburg was an unlikely standard-bearer of European democracy by any measure, a former field marshal and closet monarchist who was said to have adhered to the articles of the constitution the way a junior officer followed instructions in a field manual. As Reich president, he had exercised a light-handed executive rule in his first years, with the country running as any representative constitutional democracy was supposed to run: citizens who were elected as delegates to the Reichstag legislated; the chancellor and a cabinet of ministers administrated; the president presided. "For the most part, he supported the respective Reich chancellor, believing that by doing so he was fulfilling his constitutional duties," Oldenburg recalled. Of course, there were fascists on the far right and Communists on the far left, though the center mostly held. But with the financial crash of 1929, the radical right and the radical left surged at the polls. With the legislative branch blocked by factionalism and obstructionist politics, Hindenburg found himself resorting increasingly often to his constitutionally mandated emergency powers. During his first five years in office, Hindenburg had not issued a single Article 48 decree. Between December 1930 and April 1931, there were nineteen pieces of legislation compared with two Article 48 decrees. From April 1931 to December 1931, the Reichstag was unable to pass a single law, while Hindenburg issued forty emergency decrees. In 1932, there were fifty-nine presidential decrees, compared with only five pieces of legislation. *Time* magazine dryly observed that the government appeared to be trying to "out-Hitler Hitler" in its tilt toward authoritarian rule.

Hindenburg found himself running the country with a combination of three constitutional articles, known as the "25-48-53" formula. Article 25 empowered the Reich president to dissolve the Reichstag at will and exercise his Article 48 powers to issue emergency decrees, while Article 53 permitted him to appoint and dismiss chancellors at will. When Oldenburg pointed out the myriad failings of democratic structures and processes and urged Hindenburg to suspend the Reichstag and restore the monarchy or establish himself as authoritarian ruler, Hindenburg replied, "Be still, I know all that. But don't forget that I swore an oath to the constitution." It was in this spirit that, on the last Tuesday in August, Hindenburg convened his chancellor and key cabinet members on the garden terrace at Neudeck, to listen to arguments for suspending one of Europe's last surviving constitutional democracies.

"Even if there were a parliamentary majority, the constitution specifies that the Reich president cannot appoint a specific person to be chancellor and transfer the political leadership to him," Papen said to Hindenburg. "Furthermore, the Reich president must address certain questions to those holding a majority, namely whether they recognize the presidential emergency decrees as vital, and whether they are in compliance with the constitution and the laws." It was shortly after noon on August 30, and Papen sat comfortably on the Neudeck terrace, taking in its view of the gardens and the surrounding moorland forests, with their loam-softened air, which provided a welcome respite from the relentless heat of Berlin. Papen had traveled in the company of Schleicher and Meissner, to report to the Reich president on the government's efforts to fashion a Reichstag majority from the conservative Center Party and the National Socialists, in accordance with Hindenburg's explicit request to return the country to parliamentary rule.

Papen and Schleicher reported on their lunch with Hitler the previous day. Hitler had waffled between caustic belligerence and fawning desperation. He had begun the meeting declaring that he no longer had any interest in being appointed chancellor. Indeed, he would reject an offer of the chancellorship, be it from the centrists or the Reich president. He did not want favors. He intended to fight until the National Socialists could come to power on their own and claim the government on their own terms with a 51 percent Reichstag majority. But Hitler moderated his tone as the meeting proceeded, presenting "somewhat calmer opinions," according to Papen, with few substantive arguments against Papen's proposed program for social and economic reform.

That did not mean, Papen told Hindenburg, that he was necessarily endorsing a Hitler chancellorship. Both Papen and Schleicher warned Hindenburg that the National Socialists and the centrists both had a double agenda. The centrists wanted to avoid dissolution of the Reichstag and to "saddle" the National Socialists with running the government, in an effort to "wear them down." Hitler, for his part, was interested in entering a coalition in order to deliver the Reichstag majority that Hindenburg was allegedly demanding, knowing full well that Hindenburg would reject a Hitler cabinet; this would, in turn, discredit Hindenburg in the eyes of the country. It was proposed that Hindenburg exercise his Article 25 powers and simply dissolve the Reichstag. Hindenburg concurred that there was little hope for establishing "a serious working majority" with the current parliament.

Schleicher observed that the Reichstag would, in any

event, have a delay of ten days after its opening session to attempt to build a majority coalition, but he predicted that it would not end well. Given the Reich president's popularity, Hindenburg could form his own party with an instant majority in the Reichstag and thus turn the country's government into one-party rule with a handpicked chancellor and cabinet. Papen was taken by the idea, especially since he was already serving as Hindenburg's chosen chancellor. Papen knew he was in power only through the machinations of Schleicher, who had convinced Hindenburg to dismiss Heinrich Brüning, the head of the Center Party, that spring, thereby allowing Papen to head a "cabinet of barons," which was widely despised and derided by virtually the entire country.

Interior Minister Gayl cautioned that the constitution required the president to set new elections within sixty days of dissolving the Reichstag. Papen saw a way around this for Hindenburg. "If the Field Marshal and Reich President von Hindenburg, who has always been so faithful to every word of the constitution, decides to deviate from it due to a political crisis," Papen said, "I am certain the German people will have understanding for that." Gayl expressed concern that the Reichstag could put forward a "no confidence" vote in the Papen government under Article 54. "Since we have to be prepared for this possibility from one day to the next, we need to have a full authority from the Reich president to dissolve the Reichstag," Gayl said. "This could be conveyed over the telephone at the same moment that the order would be officially made. The dissolution of the Reichstag would certainly meet with public approval, as would the postponement of new elections." Gayl said that both the press and the electorate were, in any event, not anticipating new elections. "For us the only real question is whether we are doing what is necessary for Germany and whether we are hindering ourselves by adhering too closely to a strict reading of the constitution. If one determines that there is a state of emergency, then we can in good conscience disregard the article that stipulates that one must hold an election for a new Reichstag within sixty days."

Hindenburg pointed out that in the case of a serious crisis, he could indeed justify "to his conscience" the postponement of elections. "As far as the present government is concerned, I personally see no reason to dissolve it simply because some parties have asked for this," Hindenburg continued. "I am in complete agreement with the current ministers and I also approve of their actions, which are based on patriotic motives. If the Reichstag takes a different view, it can make use of its constitutional right, to which they have every recourse—I do not wish to deny them that—and decide on a vote of no confidence. But even in this case I will not abandon the current government." The discussion returned to the issue of new elections, the impact on the economy, and the justification for extended postponement. Hindenburg agreed to draft a decree dissolving the Reichstag but leave the date blank to keep his options open.

A similar decision was taken on the Potempa murder convictions. Hindenburg said that he was personally inclined to commute the death sentences, not based on political considerations but "solely on legal grounds because the commission of the crime had taken place only an hour and a half after the law had come into force, and it could therefore not be assumed that the perpetrators had been aware of the heightened penalties." Papen noted that any deliberations on possibly commuting the sentence should await the appeals process, which he was certain would follow. He also thought that a lingering death sentence could have a "deterring effect."

*

In those same hours, Reichstag delegates were gathering in the overheated plenary hall of the Reichstag for the first time with the National Socialists as the largest political faction, for what was expected to be one of the most chaotic parliamentary sessions of any modern democracy. *The New York Times* anticipated disruptions, not least because Reichstag protocol required that the session open with remarks by the eldest delegate, who happened to be Clara Zetkin.

The seventy-five-year-old Communist militant and friend of Lenin's—"The principal feature of Lenin's nature was his simplicity and sincerity," she said in a eulogy—had been continuously reelected to the Reichstag since 1919. Zetkin was in failing health and now spent most of her time in Moscow. She had returned to Berlin for the express purpose of opening the new Reichstag session. Her presence in the Reichstag was expected to cause outrage and possibly physical violence. The impending drama was heightened by the 200,000 Steel Helmets, including the "regiment" of students from East Prussia, who were assembling for the opening of the Reichstag in a show of force under the motto of unifying patriotism: "No party, no class, no interest groups, only Germany."

Papen heightened tensions further with a radio address to the nation, denouncing the rise in political violence. "Both sides demand that their political opponent be put beyond the pale of the protections of the law, that in political strife manslaughter and revenge be permissible and that their opponents be outlawed," he said, condemning left- as well as right-wing violence. Papen noted that he intended to halt "this brutalization of political morals," citing the Potempa killers. He then turned his attention explicitly to Hitler. In December 1931, Brüning had rebuked Hitler on national radio, chastising him for his vow to eliminate due process. "When one declares that on assuming power legally one will destroy legal protections, that is not legality," Brüning said. This professorial Reich chancellor with "searching eyes behind spectacles," animated by what one observer called a "subdued inner fire," subsequently banned brown shirts, swastikas, and public demonstrations, then launched a nationwide police raid on SA headquarters. Papen was even more strident in his rhetoric but more flexible in his response.

"I do not concede to him [Hitler] the right to regard that minority which troops behind his banner as 'the German nation' or the right to treat the rest as outlaws," Papen said in his radio address. "If, in opposition to Hitler, I stand up for a constitutional commonwealth of the people and for an authoritarian conduct of the government, it is I and not he who stand for what millions of his adherents have for years ardently desired." It was a "fighting speech," delivered in a "forceful, vigorous voice, far different from his usual mild tones," according to Fred Birchall. Metaphorically, Papen had removed his top hat and donned fighting gloves. Papen denounced Hitler on Sunday. He lunched with him on Monday. But Birchall said that Papen's speech "contained enough dynamite to change completely the political situation in the Reich."

CHAPTER 9

ARSENAL OF DEMOCRACY

We do not come as friends, and not as neutrals.
We come as enemies!

—JOSEPH GOEBBELS, "IN PARLIAMENT,"
Der Angriff, OCTOBER 17, 1927

"It is a rule in this house that its oldest member shall preside over the opening of the new session," Clara Zetkin said at the inaugural session of the sixth Reichstag, shortly after lunch on the afternoon of August 30, 1932. "I was born on July 5, 1857. Is there anyone older here?" Hunched over the microphone on the tribune, Zetkin paused to survey the plenary hall, then continued, her voice "hoarse and weak," according to Fred Birchall, who watched from the press gallery.

Zetkin, unlike some of her fellow Communist leaders, was a survivor. Karl Liebknecht had been gunned down in a forest outside Berlin in January 1919, his corpse delivered as an "unknown body" opposite the Eden Hotel. Rosa Luxemburg had her skull bludgeoned with the butt of a gun before a bullet was put through her temple that same day, her body dumped in the Landwehr Canal. Zetkin had survived elections and assassinations to become the grand dame of communism of the German parliamentary assembly. She now leveraged

the privilege of age and protocol to take the podium, supported by two assistants, before the assembled Reichstag
delegates. Zetkin railed against the capitalist system that had
created the "murder and annihilation machinery of the last
world war." She denounced a capitalist "beggars society" that
left millions of workers unemployed and impoverished. She
condemned "the terror of the fascists, the cowardice of the
bourgeois liberals, and the passivity of a large portion of
the working class." She demanded the removal of Papen and
his "cabinet of barons" and called for the impeachment of
the Reich president for myriad violations of the constitution.

Zetkin spoke for nearly an hour, in a dry, fragile voice,
struggling at points to complete single words, pausing to take
a drink of water, wiping her lips repeatedly. The plenary hall
of the Reichstag, for all the quiet dignity accorded by the plush
carpets, leather seats, and wood-paneled walls, was generally
a place of impatient politics and frequent heckling, resounding with choruses of partisan protest and orchestrated outrage. Elard von Oldenburg, Hindenburg's friend, had served
as an East Prussian delegate to the Reichstag from 1902 until
1912, as a staunch defender of the kaiser. He returned to the
Reichstag in 1930 as a delegate with the anti-democratic German National People's Party. "Back in the years before the
war, the men in parliament, regardless of their politics, were
personalities far superior in their comportment to the average man, especially compared to the mediocrity that dominated the field in 1930," Oldenburg observed. He considered
Social Democrats a *"Schweinebande,"* or "mob of pigs."

With a hard-line Communist presiding over the opening Reichstag session, and with half the plenary seats filled
with brown shirts and right-wing nationalists, one could have
anticipated a scene of utter chaos. *Volksblatt* expressed outrage
that a "traitor to the country" who spent most of her time in

Moscow should be presiding over the Reichstag's opening session. But on this Tuesday morning, respectful silence reigned as the feeble but fierce grande dame of left-wing politics carried on with a tedious polemic before concluding with a final provocation: "I open the Reichstag in fulfillment of my duty as the eldest delegate and in the hope that despite my current infirmities I will have the good fortune to live long enough to see Germany ruled as a Soviet republic." Here there followed cheers from the ninety Communists. The National Socialist faction listened quietly, seemingly respectfully, as the strident opposition delegate had her say.

When Hitler wrote of his disdain for democracy in *Mein Kampf*, he reserved particular ire for parliaments—"an assembly of idiots"—which he saw as the linchpin for destroying the system, but on this Tuesday afternoon he had instructed his 230 delegates to provide a respectful reception to the aging Communist delegate. There was to be no heckling, no sneering, no catcalling, and certainly no fisticuffs. The world was watching, along with the packed press gallery. The National Socialists needed to demonstrate restraint and discipline, since protocol required that after the eldest delegate had opened the Reichstag, the assembled delegates, in keeping with democratic practice, would vote for a new Reichstag president, and although there were four candidates on the ballot, everyone in the hall knew it was a done deal.

The left-wing parties could not manage a majority since the Social Democrats would never vote for a Communist and the centrists would never vote for a socialist. The right-wing and centrist delegates, including the National Socialist, German Nationalist, Center, and Bavarian Peoples parties, coalesced to deliver a comfortable majority of 367 votes to the handsome, thirty-nine-year-old decorated war hero Hermann Göring, with his Blue Max, brown uniform, and swastika armband, making him, after the Reich chancellor and, of course, the Reich president, the most powerful man in the country.

"The big joke on democracy is that it gives its mortal enemies the tools to its own destruction," Goebbels had written in May 1928. That year, he had just been elected to the Reichstag along with eleven other National Socialists. Thanks to the constitutional principle of "proportional representation" guaranteed by Article 22 of the constitution, the thirty-year-old Reichstag delegate representing the voting district of Berlin now enjoyed the same parliamentary privileges as the old men with the centrist parties, most of whom were twice his age. He traveled in first-class coaches, at taxpayer expense, enjoyed parliamentary immunities that allowed him to say things in public that would land the average citizen behind bars, and dined in the elegantly appointed Reichstag dining room—oak-paneled walls and club chairs— where conservatives and Communists enjoyed their "Wiener schnitzel and pork chops" in equal measure.

Goebbels was neither charmed nor distracted by parliamentary privilege. "We enter the Reichstag to use the arsenal of democracy in order to assault it with its own weapons," he said. "We will become Reichstag delegates in order to paralyze the Weimar process with its own mechanism." With just 12 delegates, the National Socialists were among the Reichstag's smallest political factions, more than ten times smaller than the Social Democrats, with 153 seats; smaller than the German National People's Party with 73 delegates; and smaller even than the Communists, with 54. With a mere 2.6 percent of the electorate, the "Hitler movement" shared the bottom of the ballot with other splinter groups, like the parties of "Rural Christians" and "Victims of Inflation" and "Justice for Renters." All that changed after the Crash of 1929.

As the economy plummeted, the National Socialist percentage soared from 12 to 107 Reichstag seats. "Overnight the little heap of despised and reviled delegates became leaders of a mass political movement of the grandest style," Goebbels wrote in his diary on September 21, 1930, as the election returns came in, making the National Socialists the second-largest political faction in the Reichstag, behind only the Social Democrats. "A dark day for Germany," Harry Kessler observed. "The Nazis have increased their mandate tenfold." The National Socialists more than doubled that two years later in the July 1932 elections. Hitler, as we have seen, commanded the largest political party in the Reichstag, which afforded the National Socialists claim to the Reichstag presidency. Göring was handpicked for the role by Hitler himself.

Hitler's delegates now dominated the plenary floor, filling nearly half of the vast hall, all of them in brown storm trooper uniforms, all with blazing red swastika armbands. Since the days of Bismarck, Reichstag presidents had worn tails on the opening day of the Reichstag session, but Göring sported a street suit with a brown shirt and tie, a fashionably tasteless reminder of his political affiliation. He strode to the podium, tall, handsome, supremely confident, perhaps not as slender as he once was, but still an imposing and impressive figure. He was greeted by the National Socialist delegates rising as one to offer a stiff-armed Hitler salute. Göring, exercising his presidential authority, ended the session before it began.

That evening, Hitler received his Reichstag contingent for a presentation at the Hotel Kaiserhof. All were present except for delegate Paul Moder, from the northern German town of Pinneberg, who had been arrested and imprisoned for his role in hand grenade attacks by SS men in ten villages in the state of Schleswig-Holstein. Bella Fromm was in the Kaiserhof lobby when the flood of delegates swept into the room, a vast brown tide, and "strutted around like peacocks, happily unaware of their absurdity," their wide-cut trousers flapping like wings. "Intoxicated by their own masquerade," they passed through the room "with a certain grimly juvenile belligerence" and proceeded into the ballroom, where they dutifully awaited the arrival of their Führer. Fromm observed Hitler's arrival. "He crossed the lobby, his face bearing a seriously warlike expression," she recalled. As Hitler entered the ballroom, a collective *"Heil"* thundered through the room and into the lobby. Hitler did not respond. He did not linger. "He is careful not to spoil his people with an overdose of his divine presence," Fromm continued. "He looked at no one, then vanished through a side door."

For all the public pomp, the real power play was taking place behind closed doors. Just two weeks after the Hindenburg fiasco, Hitler was positioning himself for his next move. Unlike the moderate conservatives, he did not have wealthy businessmen and landowners to back him. Unlike the Social Democrats, he did not have three generations of engagement with the public. And unlike the Communists, he did not have the backing of Moscow. All Hitler had was thirteen years of fierce and unrelenting determination, as he had repeatedly said that week in rallies in Hamburg, Dortmund, and Munich. Hitler's only asset was momentum. If he could not be the chancellor, he would play the obstructionist. He would gridlock the Reichstag. He would bring the government down. He would sow political and social chaos. He would drive the country into civil war. Hitler was ready for battle. "The Kaiserhof has once again become political headquarters," Goebbels wrote. Meanwhile, Gregor Strasser was hoping to give coalition politics a last try.

On the day after Hitler's meeting with Hindenburg, former chancellor Brüning and a leading figure in the Center Party were traveling on the night train from Berlin to Munich when a Strasser emissary boarded in Halle with a message for him. "Shortly before Munich as I stepped into the corridor from my sleeping compartment, I ran into Strasser's adjutant, Lieutenant Schulz, who had been looking for me the entire night," Brüning recalled. "He requested that I visit him in his apartment that same day and inform him whether I was prepared to meet with Strasser." Brüning called on Schulz. Strasser was hoping to discuss a potential coalition with the Center Party. Had it been another National Socialist, Brüning would have declined. A meeting with Hitler that past January had convinced him of the impossibility of dealing with the National Socialist leader, but Brüning knew that as a fellow Reichstag delegate, Strasser was less strident, more amenable to compromise.

That night, Brüning reflected on his terms for exploratory discussions. Being the largest political party, the National Socialists certainly had claim to the Reichstag presidency, but they needed to abide by protocol and proper election procedures. Brüning would also demand a month-long moratorium on debate over the new government's program to allow for reflection and revision.

At their meeting, Strasser presented a tempered version of National Socialism, purged of the more radical elements, with the prospect of potential alignments with Brüning's Center Party. Most important, Strasser believed "that in the end Hitler would forgo the chancellorship" if a few cabinet posts were assigned to National Socialists and there was a long-term prospect of Hitler becoming chancellor. Brüning dismissed any notion of Hitler serving as chancellor, but said he was willing to meet with him. Plans were made for a secret meeting in Berlin on August 29, though Brüning knew full well that Papen and Schleicher would learn of the rendezvous through the military intelligence service agents who had infiltrated the National Socialist movement.

The morning of the meeting, Brüning arrived at a private residence to find heavily armed SS guards in the foyer and front rooms. "I could not help but smile," he recalled. He watched as Röhm, Göring, Goebbels, Strasser, and Frank trooped out of a room, and then he was ushered in for his tête-a-tête with Hitler. Hitler launched into an extended exegesis, after which Brüning stated, in no uncertain terms, his conditions for a possible coalition, emphasizing that he would never agree to National Socialist control over the Ministry of the Interior or the security services, at the state or federal level, let alone permit Hitler to assume the chancellorship. "Hitler appeared to agree to all these conditions," Brüning recalled. The meeting ended with polite ambivalence, as did a subsequent lunch meeting with Papen and Schleicher. "It's all talk and negotiation. Nothing really comes out of it," Goebbels complained in his diary. Brüning did come away with one terrifying realization: if Hindenburg was impeached, as Clara Zetkin was proposing, Hitler would be elected Reich president.

At precisely three o'clock in the afternoon on September 12, the Reichstag reconvened as the newly elected Reichstag president strode to the podium. Papen sat with Foreign Minister Neurath and Interior Minister Gayl on the government tribune, anxiously awaiting his debut Reichstag speech as chancellor, a carefully crafted twenty-page rescue plan for the country. Ambassadors from France, Britain, Spain, and Italy were seated in the dignitary gallery. Reporters packed the press section. Birchall of the *Times* called it the most "crucial moment in any modern democracy."

Before Göring could open the session, something unexpected happened. Delegate Ernst Torgler rose from the Communist Party ranks. He had two motions to add to the day's agenda. The first motion was a vote to overturn the presidential emergency decree. The second was aimed at the new chancellor. Torgler requested "a vote of no confidence against Papen's starvation regime," then shouted, "Down with the Papen regime! Down with his starvation decrees!" The Communist faction applauded. Suddenly a Social Democrat was on his feet, demanding that a Social Democrat motion on workers' rights, postponed from the previous Reichstag session, take precedence. This was followed by cheers from the Social Democrats. Göring was nonplussed. He asked if there were any objections to the motion. There were none. Göring continued, "I now declare that—" but delegate Frick from the National Socialist faction was on his feet. He called for a half-hour recess. There was applause, then laughter. Göring adjourned the session. The delegates rose to their feet in confusion. Papen rushed from the hall. Someone shouted, "Look, he's running away." More laughter. Göring approached Frick. "The Reichstag president is taking lessons," a Communist delegate sniped. Göring and Frick left the hall to call Hitler. A half hour later, they were back. The bell rang. The delegates reassembled. Papen took his seat, a red leather folio with Hindenburg's dissolution order in hand. Göring assumed his place at the podium. Then things *really* got strange.

"We will now take a vote," Göring began, confident and composed. "Since there have been no objections raised against the new agenda, we will now vote on the Torgler motion."

"A roll-call vote," Torgler shouted.

"It will be a roll-call vote," Göring confirmed. Now

Papen had his hand in the air, waving to Göring. The Reichstag president ignored him. Papen waved frantically. Göring proceeded with the vote. Papen got to his feet, all eyes on him, and headed to the podium. The Reichstag president ignored him. Papen held out the red folio. Göring took it and set it aside. "We are taking the vote," Göring said to the delegates. "We were already voting and I must complete the count before I can address other matters." Shouts rose from the delegates. The German Nationalists protested. The chancellor has the right to speak whenever he wants, they pointed out. The Communists and National Socialists protested the protest. Göring sought to calm the delegates as Papen pointed his thumb over his shoulder, indicating to his ministers that it was time to leave. Papen walked to the door and with a wave of his hand signaled that the Reichstag was dissolved.

Göring proceeded with the vote. The National Socialists found themselves suddenly, and awkwardly, voting with the Communists. Shortly after four o'clock, the final votes were in. "Of the 550 votes cast, there are 5 abstentions, 32 nays, and 513 yeas," Göring announced. The Papen government was dissolved. Triumphal applause rose from the Communist and National Socialist factions. "Ladies and gentlemen!" Göring said as the applause subsided. "After the roll call had already begun, the Reich chancellor requested to take the floor. When the vote was completed I gave him [Papen] the floor in keeping with protocol." Shouts of protests arose from the centrists, with countering shouts from the Communists and the National Socialists. "During the roll call the Reich chancellor handed me a countersigned document, which, coming from a cabinet that has been dissolved by a no-confidence vote by the people's assembly, can no longer be considered valid," Göring explained. A storm of applause followed. Göring then opened the red folio and read its contents. It was a written presidential decree suspending the Reichstag as of September 12, 1932. The hall exploded in shouts and protests. It was the sound of constitutional crisis.

"It is my position that this document provisionally has no validity, that it is countersigned by a ministry whose authority has been suspended by a no-confidence vote by the people's assembly," Göring shouted into the chaos. He went on to underscore, for the sake of the journalists and diplomats present, the fact that the Papen government was the most unpopular government in the history of a democracy. Göring adjourned the Reichstag until the following day. Göring claimed afterward that Papen, "in his agitation," had placed the dissolution order with the reverse side up, "so that I was unable to see what it even was," Göring said. "It is not my job to turn over papers like that."

In the press gallery, Birchall had been counting the minutes and the cost to the taxpayer. The entire Reichstag session had lasted exactly forty minutes. "Each election costs the government approximately $840,000," Birchall wrote. "The last produced the shortest-lived Reichstag on record." By Birchall's calculation, there had been six hours in total, with five hours devoted to "preparation" and only fifty minutes to actual parliamentary business. "Thus, it cost about $16,800 per minute. Under the same reckoning Clara Zetkin's tirade on the opening day cost the government more than $12,000." One reporter dubbed the Papen cabinet a "government without people." The French assessment was brief: *"Les allemandes sont fous"*—the Germans are crazy.

The Reichstag did not convene the following day. Hindenburg informed Göring in no uncertain terms that his decree stood as written. The Reichstag was dissolved. Papen remained chancellor. There would be new elections in November. Birchall's wire story that evening produced a morning headline, "Papen Is Victorious as Reichstag Yields," with the subheadline "Deputies Abandon Attempt to Continue as Nazi Chairman Is Reproved by Hindenburg." Birchall marveled at the resilience of the Weimar political system. Despite the chaos and uncertainty, "the government goes on as smoothly, efficiently and peacefully as in any of the world's well-established democracies, a marvelous tribute to the inherent law-abidingness and solid characteristics of the German people." They now awaited a date to be set for the next election.

The next day, Hitler assembled his delegates in the now-suspended Reichstag to announce his new election campaign. He was not going to compromise his principles. He was not going to sell his movement for a title or a position. He would be no part of a government that could condemn to death five Germans for the sake of a Polish insurgent. That evening, Hitler took the same message to a fanatical crowd of ten thousand at the Zirkus Krone. He repeated the vow the following evening in Munich before five thousand storm troopers and SS men. He condemned the Papen regime, which was held in place, he said, only through "violations of the constitution." He said he would not "sell" the party for a title or a position. He reminded them of Article 1 of the constitution. The power of the state emanated from the people. With the Reichstag dissolved, there would now be new elections. He vowed that this time he would secure 51 percent of the vote and, with it, the chancellorship and full power of the state. He told them to wait and see what happened in a few weeks' time, saying, *"Das Volk wird in drei Wochen 'wild werden'"*—in three weeks the people were going to go wild.

*

Hitler rose early on the morning of Sunday, September 18, 1932, sometime after five o'clock, which was highly unusual for him; he was normally a creature of late-night hours. He got up at the break of dawn to drive with Goebbels and his chauffeur Julius Schreck on a family matter to Vienna, where his half sister, Angela, was waiting. When CBS correspondent Kaltenborn remarked on Hitler's shyness, his need to hide his true self behind a wall of rhetoric and tirade, even in small groups, he was touching on an essential part of Hitler's character. Hitler was an exceedingly private person. He kept a tight circle of trusted intimates and an even tighter family circle. In *Mein Kampf,* Hitler devoted fifty pages to his childhood without ever mentioning Angela or his older half brother, Alois, let alone his full-blood kid sister, Paula, except in an inadvertent observation, when he writes of the collective family grief over the death of "our father." Paula Hitler once remarked that her entire existence had been reduced to a possessive pronoun.

Hitler had not attended his niece Geli's funeral on September 24, 1931, fearing that his presence would expose him to unwanted media attention, but the following Saturday, September 26, 1931, he arrived in Vienna in the company of Heinrich Hoffman and an adjutant, Julius Schaub. He saw Angela and her daughter, Elfriede, at a hotel, then continued to the cemetery. Hoffmann remained in the car while Hitler stood at the grave in the pouring rain for half an hour. They returned to Munich that same day. Hitler did not mention his niece's suicide once during the entire drive—or the visit with his sister—except for saying that he intended to have Geli's remains brought back to Munich as soon as possible, where he would provide for "a beautiful grave." The visit passed without a mention in the press, though the border police recorded the exact time of the morning entry, as well as his arrival in Vienna, his visit to the cemetery, and his exit from Austria.

Now, on the first anniversary of Geli's death, Hitler returned to Vienna, once again noted in the police records, as well as in Goebbels's diary. "The Führer has driven to Vienna for a private visit," Goebbels wrote on September 19, 1932. "No one knows about it in order to prevent any crowds. Schaub has arranged a hotel room for him under the name of 'Huber.' He intends to visit Geli's grave." Goebbels noted that they also saw his sister. "Frau Raubal, the good soul, visited me in the hotel and had a good cry," Goebbels wrote. "I comforted her as much as I could. Poor, dear Geli."

In those same Sunday hours as Hitler gathered with family at his niece's grave in Vienna, Strasser was in the grand salon of the Hotel Kaiserhof, meeting with Hubert Knickerbocker. The Pulitzer Prize–winning journalist had interviewed Chancellor von Papen across the street: "We sat at a wide window of the Reichs Chancellery opening on the Wilhelmstrasse." Now he sat in imperial opulence—chandeliers, palms, portraits of king and kaiser—with the man credited with helping transform a regional political party into a nationwide movement, and who remained an enigmatic and threatening figure for some. "When businessmen grow frightened of the Nazis, they are frightened of Gregor Strasser," Knickerbocker wrote. "They think they know the views of Adolf Hitler. They think he is safe. They are not sure of Herr Strasser."

Knickerbocker was referring to Strasser's distinctively socialist rhetoric. In a speech before the Reichstag that spring, Strasser had talked about the desperation of the common man for "bread and work," of the need for agricultural reform for farmers, of industrial restructuring for workers, of an economic system that benefits all. Strasser put the "socialist" into National Socialism. It was what lured voters from the Social Democratic and even the Communist camps into the National Socialist fold. It is also what scared businessmen.

But now, sitting in the elegance of the Hotel Kaiserhof, the blue-eyed Strasser was at once charming, compelling, and, most of all, moderate. "We recognize private property. We recognize private initiative," Strasser told Knickerbocker. "We are against the nationalization of industry. We are against the nationalization of trade. We are against a planned national economy in the Soviet sense. We are against inflation. We are for the gold standard." Strasser spoke with a natural ease and warmth that was foreign to Hitler, ready to explicate rather than agitate, better suited to an interview with an award-winning journalist than a sweat-sodden room of beer-hall fanatics. Strasser cited inflation rates, trade imbalances, and statistics with confidence. He explained the need to regulate the domestic budget and to realign trade deficits, leaving Knickerbocker with an impression that was becoming increasingly apparent to many. "When Hitler comes to power and fails to establish socialism, or when Hitler fails to come to power and the masses of the people leave him," Knickerbocker wrote, "Gregor Strasser will be their leader."

CHAPTER 10

EMPIRE OF LIES

I don't need your golden rain.

—ADOLF HITLER, OCTOBER 19, 1932

By the autumn of 1932, the foreign press appeared to be the last resort for National Socialist leaders seeking a "fair hearing" with an audience outside the echo chamber of their own press, whether it be the diligent but hardly credible reporting of the *Völkischer Beobachter*, managed by Alfred Rosenberg, in Munich, the shrill and occasionally hysterical editorializing in Goebbels's *Der Angriff*, in Berlin, or the prurient political pornography of Julius Streicher's rabidly anti-Semitic *Der Stürmer*, in Nuremberg. The biweekly *Nationalsozialistische Briefe*, claiming to represent the movement's intellectual weltanschauung, was a vehicle for the less strident Strasser wing of the party.

The centrist liberal press, which was openly hostile to Hitler and National Socialism, was dominated by newspapers like the *Frankfurter Zeitung* and the *Vossische Zeitung* owned by the Ullstein Publishers, a family-run company that was unapologetically pacifist, internationalist, and Jewish. "They were five, like the erstwhile Rothschilds, and also Jews," wrote Ullstein editor Arthur Koestler, author of the dystopian classic *Darkness at Noon.* "Their motto was political liberalism and modern culture." The Social Democrat daily *Vorwärts* also splashed unfriendly ink over National Socialism and its leadership, as did the strident Communist newspaper *Rote Fahne,* which featured the names of the murdered co-founders, Rosa Luxemburg and Karl Liebknecht, beneath its daily headlines.

If there was any potential accommodation for sympathetic coverage for National Socialism in the mainstream press, it should have been the sixteen hundred newspapers affiliated largely with the Telegraph Union news agency. Controlled by Alfred Hugenberg, the Telegraph Union was belligerently nationalistic, fiercely anti-democratic, and decidedly anti-Semitic, with a devoted readership in the country's conservative heartland. Having amassed a fortune from inheritance and as director of the Krupp armament concern during the war, when he was known as the *Kanonenkönig,* or king of cannons, Hugenberg built his media empire as a counterforce to what he perceived as the Jewish-controlled liberal press.

Hitler and Hugenberg should have made the perfect political couple. Both men were anti-Communist, anti-democratic, anti-immigrant, and anti-Semitic, but their attempts to forge a partnership failed repeatedly. Hitler tended to emerge red-faced and furious after his meetings with Hugenberg. Goebbels described Hitler's mood with evocative words like *Sauwut,* angry as a pig, and *Scheisswut,* mad as shit. *Vorwärts* attributed the men's differences to their nationalities—"Hugenberg the Prussian" and "Hitler the Austrian."

The problem lay not so much in the two men's differences as in their similarities. Like Hitler, Hugenberg was known for his inflexibility, stubbornness, and self-righteousness. Like Hitler, he was the subject of incessant scrutiny and critique. "No politician in post-war Germany had to endure the personal spitefulness, misrepresentation, and lies to which Hugenberg was subjected," his authorized biographer wrote. Hugenberg fancied himself as the future leader of a "Third Reich," as he called it, with himself as *Reichsverweser*, or regent of the Reich. Hugenberg adherents responded to cries of *"Heil Hitler"* with counter-choruses of *"Heil Hugenberg!"*

As the vehicle for his political ambitions, in the 1920s Hugenberg began to use his business interests to bankroll the German National People's Party, the leading right-wing, anti-democratic political party, with seventy-three Reichstag seats compared to twelve National Socialist delegates. "Today there is a man in the German National People's Party for whom I cannot fail to express my admiration and respect," Hitler wrote in the *Völkischer Beobachter*. "Hugenberg, he said, is a good German patriot with a decent and honorable disposition." Hugenberg took a more measured view of Hitler and the National Socialist movement. He applauded Hitler's belligerent nationalism and desire to destroy democracy, but he feared that Hitler's intransigence in entering a coalition would prevent a conservative majority in the Reichstag. Hitler needed to help unify, not divide, Hugenberg felt. Hitler could not, in Hugenberg's words, command election outcomes through *Führerbefehl*, or through "the Führer's orders."

Vorwärts compared the Hitler-Hugenberg rivalry to the race between the tortoise and the hare, in which a frenetic and frantic rabbit ultimately loses to his plodding but steady hard-shelled opponent. Hitler scurried about incessantly, in planes, trains, and cars, making speeches, stirring outrage, keeping all eyes fixed on his every word and move, while

Hugenberg trundled along, generally unnoticed and under-estimated, but invariably appeared at the finish line well ahead of his rival. "Two hours before the Führer appeared for his meeting on Saturday evening with the Reich president, two representatives from the German National People's Party had already been there," the *Pommerische Zeitung* reported in its article about Hitler's August 13 debacle with Hindenburg. Hugenberg was one of them. *Vorwärts* minted a moniker: *"Hase Hitler,"* or Hitler the Hare.

For all their competing similarities in politics and personality, the two men could not have been more different in appearance. Hugenberg was short and squat, with enormous jowls and flared whiskers, "as funny a sight as ever, with his military haircut, full-spread moustache, small eyes hidden in rolls of fat, and a perpetual leer on his face," wrote Bella Fromm. She called him "Sturdy Alfred." *Vorwärts* caricatured him as a puffed-up frog with his signature spectacles, spiked hair, and flared moustache on a tiny head. Hugenberg's most common appellation, even among friends and associates, was *"Der Hamster,"* which infuriated him. Hitler called him a "woof woof"—*"Wauwau"*—to be trotted out before the public to perform political tricks.

Hugenberg possessed neither Hindenburg's stature nor his pedigree. The imperial whiskers that imbued the Reich president with majestic dignity sat comically on Hugenberg's jowled face. Embittered by all the things that money could not buy, Hugenberg grew arrogant, irascible, intransigent, vengeful. André François-Poncet had encountered Hugenberg on numerous occasions. The French ambassador said the man with the "gold-rimmed spectacles," prominent paunch, and flared white moustache projected the confidence of a "diligent country doctor" but in reality was stubborn, narrow-minded, violently sectarian, ferociously partisan. He called him *"un des mauvais génies de l'Allemagne,"* one of the most evil geniuses in Germany.

Hugenberg and Hitler first attempted to cooperate in early 1929 when the National Socialists were seeking to expand their Reichstag representation. Hugenberg thought Hitler's efforts to dismantle democratic processes were as misplaced and naïve as his failed beer-hall putsch six years earlier. Hugenberg believed that the best way to bring down the existing political structure was through a strategy he called *Katastrophenpolitik*, or the politics of catastrophe. Rather than targeting the Reichstag, Hugenberg aimed to fragment and polarize the electorate, as a means of hollowing out, then destroying the political center and, with it, the collective understanding that sustained the democratic polity. With the center fragmented, he thought, the political system would collapse of its own accord. Hugenberg's idea was to move inflammatory public policy issues, which were generally debated within the space and protocol of the Reichstag, onto the national agenda and into neighborhoods, taverns, and living rooms across the country. Such actions would place the government in an awkward position, and force neighbors, friends, and family members to confront one another with uncomfortable opinions. Civil discourse would fracture, opinions would polarize, public consensus would collapse. It was madness, of course, but there was constitutional method to the Hugenberg madness.

Article 73 of the Reich constitution stipulated that the Reichstag could be forced to debate proposed legislation through a public petition signed by more than 10 percent of the electorate. If the Reichstag did not pass the law in a majority vote, the proposed legislation could be placed on a public referendum; if more than a two-thirds majority was gained, it would then pass into law regardless of the Reichstag vote. Hugenberg intended to put his media empire to work elevating exceptionally divisive issues, then, thanks to constitutionally guaranteed press freedoms, flood the public space with inflammatory news stories, half-truths, rumors, and outright lies.

There were, however, laws against defamation and incitement. "The press must refrain from any kind of inflaming of public passions, even through inadvertent errors in reporting," Franz Bracht, the Prussian state interior minister, warned. "Otherwise they will have to face the gravest restrictions on their freedom of expression." But these restrictions were most often reserved for the left-wing press, while the radical right generally got a free pass, as was the case with Goebbels's *Der Angriff* in reporting the death of an SS man who was killed in Breslau. "Blown to Bits," *Der Angriff* reported in a banner headline. "Horrible Murder of an SS Man." The victim had been walking home when "Marxists" hiding in nearby bushes allegedly hurled a hand grenade "that literally blew his body to shreds by an explosion that was heard far and wide." In fact, the SS man had died, it was later revealed, when a hand grenade he had been preparing to throw exploded in his hand. When *Der Angriff* was called out for fomenting public violence with fake news, the newspaper doubled down on the false reporting. "We opened the pages of *Der Angriff*, curious to see if we could find a mention of this [retraction] on the editorial pages, and found nothing," the *Vossische Zeitung* wrote. Instead there was a further threat to an opposition leader, cautioning him, lest he discover a bomb on his feather bed. "So the tone *Der Angriff* uses in writing is not one to incite passion," the *Vossische Zeitung* wrote ironically.

Hugenberg chose a hot-button issue for his *Katastrophenpolitik* campaign: wartime reparations. The Hugenberg referendum, proposing the draft "law against the enslavement of the German people"—also known as the *Freiheitsgesetz,* or Liberty Law—called for the abrogation of the Treaty of Versailles and, with it, the withdrawal of foreign forces from the country, the return of the Alsace region, and the suspension of reparation payments. Section IV of the Liberty Law contained the most inflammatory demand: any German official who was a signatory to the Young Plan or involved in its reparation implementation was to be arrested and tried for high treason.

Hugenberg lobbed the explosive draft law into contentious Reichstag debates over the Young Plan, a proposal for reducing and rescheduling German reparation payments.* While centrist political leaders recognized the legal obligations of reparations and the implications of German war guilt, right-wing nationalists bristled at any suggestion of postwar responsibility or reparation outlined in the Treaty of Versailles or subsequent agreements.

"We do not see these treaties as law, rather as something forced on us," Hitler had told the Leipzig court in September 1930. "We do not accept the guilt for this war." Hitler vowed to abrogate the Versailles Treaty through either legal or illegal means and to exact revenge. "If our movement succeeds in winning our justified battle, then a German state court will be established and November 1918 will be avenged, and heads will roll." *The New York Times* ran the headline "Hitler

---

* The Young Plan, advanced in 1929 by Owen D. Young, an American industrialist who had been involved in a previous rescheduling agreement known as the Dawes Plan (1924), reduced German reparation obligations by 20 percent and extended the payment period until 1988. Payment was calculated in gold marks, backed by gold reserves, rather than the volatile reichsmarks, which were subject to inflation. The final debt obligation was met in October 2010, ninety-two years after the end of World War I.

Would Scrap Versailles Treaty and Use Guillotine." When Hitler threatened consequences, he did so as a private person. He had no official or legal status at the time. He was not a Reichstag delegate. He had not yet gained German citizenship. With the Liberty Law, Hugenberg wanted these threats codified as law.

There had been only two previous Article 73 referenda, both put forward by the Communists and both limited in scope; both failed. The proposed Liberty Law secured 10.2 percent of the electorate, thanks to an aggressive Hugenberg press campaign, allowing the petition to move to the Reichstag for debate and a vote. The Reichstag debate, as Hugenberg intended, was fierce and included objections within his own party, which split over the Article IV criminal clause. The draft law was voted down by a landslide, 430 to 16, but not before the issue was showcased. Gottfried Feder, a founding member of the National Socialist Party and among its first twelve delegates to the Reichstag, incited outrage and a formal censure from the Reichstag president Paul Löbe over a proposed amendment to Article IV. Observing that prison time was "too limited" a punishment for any German signing or implementing the Young Plan, Feder proposed "that they be hanged." The proposed law, rejected by the Reichstag, moved from the plenary hall into the public space for a national referendum.

Hugenberg mobilized his Telegraph Union network of sixteen hundred newspapers. Front-page stories appeared on the Liberty Law referendum, along with editorials on the onerous burdens of war reparations and the added vexations of the Young Plan that extended the payment obligations across the next three generations. The *Lippische Tages-Zeitung*, a regional newspaper for Detmold-Lippe, one of the smallest federated states in the country, welcomed the referendum in a banner headline, "The Defensive Battle Has Commenced." The paper reprised the "horrific" impact of the Treaty of Versailles on the German people, ranging from consumer goods, "automobiles, margarine, paper, shoes, firewood, nylon, etc., etc.," to the vast outflows of capital from the country, to the despair of the common working man. According to the newspaper, a single advertisement for six positions in Brazil drew 2,370 applications in two weeks. And this was before the November 1929 market crash.

The Berlin *Lokalanzeiger*, a Hugenberg newspaper, published a story claiming that the Young Plan contained a provision for "human export and slave sales"—"*Menschenausfuhr und Sklavenverkauf*"—of German citizens to British and French colonies. There was to be an "annual governmental review of German boys and girls to determine their exportability"—"*Exportfähigkeit*"—as part of the reparations package. The political establishment decried the Hugenberg rumormongering as irresponsible and dangerous. In a joint statement, the Center Party and Bavarian Peoples Party denounced the Liberty Law language as "provocative and inflammatory" and called the referendum a "fateful step in further polarizing the German people." Which was, in fact, exactly what Hugenberg intended.

"Ladies and gentlemen, on behalf of the National Socialist movement, I must declare that we are joining the effort to abolish the Paris dictate in a direct appeal to the German people," Hitler said in an address on July 9, 1929, in Berlin endorsing the proposed Liberty Law. By his side on the podium were Hugenberg and industrialist Fritz Thyssen. "Over the last ten years we have repeatedly witnessed attempts to suppress the desires of the German people; witnessed how the will of the people is forced into the will of the government." His tone grew accusatory: "We witnessed again and again that there could be no resistance to any decree." The political leadership needed to be held to account. They needed to take personal responsibility for enslaving the German nation to a legacy of unfounded guilt and crushing reparations that threatened to burden the future of their children and their children's children. How many more years, Hitler wanted to know—ten, twenty, thirty—were to be lost to an imposed and fake war guilt?

"There must come a time when the honor and future of the nation will no longer be sacrificed for the rights of living in the present," Hitler continued. "Because in the end the German people will not shake off their chains by giving in to them, but by throwing off their inner vices of cowardice and disunity." Hitler issued a "call to arms" in the "fight against the Paris tribute plan built on the extortion of war guilt." The call to arms echoed across the Hugenberg media empire, giving the National Socialist leader unprecedented exposure. However, Hitler was presented as playing second fiddle. "The main player is Hugenberg," Goebbels seethed in his diary. "In the middle stands Adolf Hitler. That is a knife through the heart." On the other hand, the campaign also brought Hitler financing: "Hugenberg has had to cough up money so that we can work," Goebbels noted. Even more important, they gained votes at the expense of Hugenberg. In a local election in the state of Baden in October of that year, the National Socialist ticket surged from 8,000 to 65,000 votes, adding six more Reichstag delegates, while Hugenberg's delegates fell from nine to three. The party financing also helped Hitler to move from his small three-room apartment in Munich's Thierschstrasse to an elegant second-floor apartment on the Prinzregentenplatz.

On December 21, a day before the referendum, Hitler held a final rally, at the Zirkus Krone in Munich, and issued an urgent call to action, imploring his audience, "with all means possible, to encourage people to participate. You have to shake people up and bring them in. You have to educate them to be rebels, and to resist the demands that would bring down the German nation."

The Liberty Law referendum was a disaster. Of 42 million registered voters, only about 6.2 million went to the polls, not even 15 percent of the electorate. *Vorwärts* ran a headline trumpeting Hugenberg's "pathetic political bankruptcy," and went on to calculate that the Article 73 folly had cost taxpayers 3.5 million reichsmarks (about $18.5 million today) in logistical costs, not to mention the millions more spent in countering Hugenberg's deluge of half-truths and outright lies. Hugenberg's own newspapers spun the debacle as best they could, declaring the referendum a triumph. Of those who participated in the referendum, one newspaper noted, "only a tiny minority voted against the law." Of those who voted, 98 percent cast their ballot in favor of the Liberty Law. A cartoon in *Vorwärts* depicted Hugenberg as a snowman, with drooping jowls and mustache, melting in the sunshine of democracy.

Hitler was furious at the public humiliation but rewarded at the ballot box. Legitimized by association with Hugenberg's German National People's Party, and fueled by the stock market crash of 1929, the National Socialists surged in the September 1930 Reichstag elections, with nearly a ninefold increase to 107, while Hugenberg candidates took a shellacking. Hugenberg never forgot, nor forgave, Hitler for the favor he had done him. The two men continued to clash in public and collude in private. The *Berliner Tageblatt* reported a telephone conversation between the two on April 9, 1931, during which Hugenberg allegedly discussed the prevailing political climate and Hitler allegedly solicited financial support. "The claim is untrue from start to finish," Hitler responded in the *Völkischer Beobachter*. "I never had a telephone conversation with Hugenberg. . . . Neither the NSDAP nor I have ever sought any form of financial support from Hugenberg, either directly or through an intermediary." That was, in fact, not true.

"Putzi" Hanfstaengl recalled a failed Hitler attempt to extract money from Hugenberg. "Hitler was in the library with Hugenberg at the time and tried to get financial support out of him for hours, but without success," Hanfstaengl said. "Finally, exhausted, Hitler came down the stairs, saw me, and asked, as he usually did in moments of depression: Hanfstaengl, play me something." They retired to a piano. Hanfstaengl improvised on passages from *Tosca* and *Madama Butterfly*.

Hitler and Hugenberg had another go during the summer of 1931. In an attempt to unify the right—using *Sammlungspolitik*, politics of aggregation—Hugenberg announced a two-day meeting scheduled for October in the town of Bad Harzburg. Known as the Harzburg Front, the right-wing leaders would gather in common cause and parade their respective paramilitaries—the storm troopers for the National Socialists, and the Steel Helmets for the right-wing nationalists. Hitler threatened to pull out when Hugenberg did not intervene after two National Socialists—one was Wilhelm Frick—lost their positions in state governments over local politics. In a stern letter to Hugenberg, Hitler spoke of "deception" and "betrayal." He feared that Hugenberg might lure him into an insidious strangulation of the National Socialist movement. "I now solemnly declare that I refuse to continue to uphold any association from which I have received such poor proof of the concept of loyalty," he wrote. How could Hitler ever trust Hugenberg in a coalition

cabinet? He could not imagine what it would be like to share
seats in a Reich cabinet with him. Hitler said he would not
allow himself to be "knifed in the back." "If German libera-
tion is supposed to come from such treachery and from such
insidiousness," Hitler said, "then I no longer have any faith
in it."

Hugenberg punched back. He was surprised that Hitler
could threaten to separate from a political partnership so easily.
He wondered whether Hitler was forced to terminate their
strategic partnership because "in your own party opposition
to a national united front from elsewhere is growing strong."
Perhaps, Hugenberg suggested, Hitler needed to exercise
more control over his followers. The men sparred, then compromised. Hugenberg accommodated. Hitler acquiesced. But
the two men continued to posture and scuffle. Hitler arrived
late in Bad Harzburg, insulted other right-wing leaders from
the podium, and departed early. In a staged bit of political
theater, he watched from his Mercedes as his storm troopers paraded past, then drove off before the Steel Helmet bat-
talions began to march. For his part, Hugenberg positioned
Hitler as a Harzburg Front tagalong. Photographs show Hitler in the rarest of poses: seated in the audience, along with
Frick, Göring, and Strasser, while Hugenberg commands
center stage. Another shot shows Hugenberg greeting a
crowd in his three-piece suit while Hitler looks on, two steps
behind, in a rumpled storm trooper uniform, his arms bolted
across his chest, a scowl on his face.

Hitler and Hugenberg tangled yet again a few months
later, in January 1932. The *Danziger Volksstimme*, a non–
Hugenberg affiliated newspaper, reported on a particularly
fraught Hitler-Hugenberg negotiation over the upcoming
presidential election. "They have been deliberating among
themselves since Thursday and keep postponing their deci-

sion from one day to the next," the newspaper wrote, observing that the two men rescheduled a joint statement for Saturday afternoon, January 9, then, suddenly, for Saturday evening. That evening, they delayed until Sunday, then to Monday morning, and a few hours later to Monday evening.

Meanwhile, Hugenberg sought to secure Crown Prince Wilhelm of Prussia as his candidate; Wilhelm, in turn, secretly sought to secure Hitler as his chancellor. The heir to the upended imperial and royal throne, who passed his days attending motorcycle races and tennis matches and being photographed with pretty young women, discreetly summoned Hitler to his family palace in Potsdam with the proposal that he himself run for president, with Hitler as his chancellor. Hitler liked the idea. Prince Wilhelm's father, the kaiser, did not.

"If you accept this position, then you have to swear an oath to the republic. If you do that and hold to it, then I am finished with you. I will disinherit you and ban you from my house," the abdicated kaiser wrote to his son from exile in the Netherlands. If, on the other hand, the crown prince broke his presidential oath to uphold the republic, "then you would commit perjury, and you are no longer a gentleman. And for me, you are done for." Hohenzollerns always kept their word. The plan was dropped.

Hugenberg was furious over Hitler's back-channel machinations and selected Theodor Duesterberg, a leader of the Steel Helmets, as the German National party candidate. Hitler decided to enter the race himself, his first attempt to run for political office. By 1932, Hitler had been engaged in German politics for thirteen years, given hundreds of speeches, appeared before millions of people, and yet had never entered an election—because he was a stateless immigrant. Having renounced his Austrian citizenship in 1925, Hitler had assumed "that I earned my citizenship on the battlefield," as a corporal in the 16th Bavarian Reserve Infantry Regiment. In fact, his failed Munich putsch had scuttled any prospect of securing citizenship in Bavaria.

In 1930, Frick used his authority as state interior minister for Thuringia—citizenship was issued by state rather than federal authorities—to hire Hitler as a village gendarme, which automatically accorded him German citizenship. In a closed ceremony, Hitler swore an oath and co-signed his appointment certificate, as well as an official attestation. "I immediately realized that I could not take [the appointment] on," Hitler later recalled, having understood that the position would open him to ridicule and mockery. On returning to Munich, he burned the signed certificate, then told Frick to destroy the signed attestation. But by then it was too late.

Under the headline "The Gendarme of Hildburghausen," the *Vossische Zeitung* wrote: "We do not wish to disparage the honorable post of a gendarmerie commissioner, but the absurdity lies in the outspoken peacock vanity of the ruler of the Brown House, who suddenly wants to settle down in a small post in the remote town of Hildburghausen, as if he really wanted to command seven gendarmes and three police officers." The Ullstein newspaper *Tempo* reported, "As of yesterday, all of Europe is laughing about Adolf Hitler." *Das Volk* went for a broader reaction: "The whole world is laughing about Gendarme Hitler." Hitler's appointment was also reported in *The New York Times*, which detected "more merriment than indignation in political circles." Goebbels regretted this "bottomless slop pail" that had been delivered to the opposition press.

Hitler's attempt to gain citizenship in Thuringia ended in fiasco and produced a fiercely worded legal opinion about his ever serving in public office: "There is no justification for the nomination of a foreigner, such as Hitler, or a stateless person, to a civil servant post solely for the purpose of allowing him to run for the office of Reich president. Such a nomination would be null and untenable." Nevertheless, Hitler tried again in January 1932, when Dietrich Klagges, a National Socialist in the state of Braunschweig, was appointed state interior minister. Klagges first sought to have Hitler appointed as professor for "Organic Sociology and Politics" at the Braunschweig Technical University, only to have the proposal rejected by both the rector and the dean. They noted that Hitler had never completed high school, let alone attended university. A week later, Klagges proposed Hitler for a post as a mid-level civil servant in the state's department of land surveying, with an assignment to the Braunschweig legation in Berlin. This time, Klagges prevailed.

At two p.m. on February 26, Hitler appeared before Braunschweig state officials to swear an oath of loyalty to the constitution, to obey the laws, and to "diligently perform my duties as a civil servant." A photograph shows Hitler emerging from the Braunschweig legation in a double-breasted winter coat, fedora in hand, as a freshly minted German citizen and civil servant, with an annual salary of 5,238RM (about $27,350 today) and a generous retirement plan "effective immediately."

In an article headlined "Hitler Appointed Civil Servant," *Vorwärts* wrote, "We can already see Mr. Adolf Hitler with his briefcase under his arm." If Hitler failed in his presidential bid, *Vorwärts* continued, one should assume he would move to Braunschweig as a "diligent" civil servant to fulfill his duties until mandatory retirement at age sixty-five, in 1954.

It was reported that Hitler tripped on the carpet as he entered the room to take his oath of office at the Braunschweig legation, leaving his entourage caught in awkward stiff-armed salutes to their stumbling Führer. One observer compared it to Napoleon "appearing on the world stage in his underwear." The newspaper *Germania* described the ceremony as a "constitutional comedy" ready-made for the stage. The next day Hitler entered the presidential race, having secured a leave of absence from his superior in the surveyance department. That evening, he announced his candidacy before a roaring crowd in the Berlin Sportpalast, taking direct aim at Hindenburg: "We once served the General Field Marshal loyally and obediently. Today we say to him: you are too venerable to allow those who want to destroy [the Reich] to hide behind you. You must step aside."

Had Brüning's efforts in the Reichstag to secure a two-year extension of the Hindenburg presidency succeeded, the eighty-four-year-old head of state could have served out his extended first term then withdrawn into a well-deserved retirement, but now the aging field marshal could not let the Bohemian corporal's challenge go unanswered. "Were President von Hindenburg really to withdraw from the political arena when his present term ends it would mean a fundamental change in Germany, for the prestige of his name, the confidence felt in him by great masses of the people . . . these attributes he can transfer to no successor," *The New York Times* reported, highlighting Hindenburg's "quite special relation to the Reichswehr, the sole organized armed force in the German Reich and the only bulwark against revolution from the Left to Right." Hitler knew that he was a long-shot candidate for the presidency, but his odds would increase dramatically with Hindenburg out of the race. The prospect of Hitler invested with the ability to appoint a chancellor and invested, also, with the near-dictatorial powers provided by Article 48 was nothing short of terrifying for many. As it was, Hindenburg entered the race.

The March 13 election saw Hindenburg, who ran as an independent, as he had in his first election campaign, pitted against Hitler representing the National Socialists, Duesterberg as the German Nationalists candidate financed by Hugenberg, and Ernst Thälmann, supported by the German Communist Party, with financial backing from Moscow. Hindenburg won 49.54 percent of the popular vote, just short of an absolute majority, forcing a runoff.

Brown House researchers revealed that Duesterberg had a Jewish grandfather who had converted in 1818. The National Socialists piled on insults, especially Walther Darré, the Hitler expert on blood and soil. In the old-school tradition, Duesterberg challenged Darré to a duel. Darré declined. He said it would be beneath him to fight a Jew. Damaged by the National Socialist propaganda, Duesterberg withdrew his candidacy, having received a meager 6.8 percent of the vote in the election's first round. In addition to losing his presidential candidate, Hugenberg suffered the indignity of watching Crown Prince Wilhelm place his lot with Hitler, as did Hugenberg's industrialist friend Fritz Thyssen, who issued a statement blaming Hugenberg for the failure of the Harzburg Front and transferring his endorsement to Hitler, along with financing. This latest kerfuffle cost Hitler access to the Telegraph Union's affiliated newspapers just before a crucial election, but Hitler remained defiant. He said he would manage just fine without the "golden rain"—*Goldregen*—of the Hugenberg media empire. Hitler had other plans for reaching the voting public.

CHAPTER 11

"GOLDEN RAIN"

Let the battle begin.
In four weeks we will emerge victorious.

—ADOLF HITLER, OCTOBER 6, 1932

"Tomorrow morning at six o'clock I shall be in Herr Hitler's airplane, the only newspaper representative to accompany the Fascist leader on the whirlwind with which he is winding up his campaign in the presidential election," Sefton "Tom" Delmer reported in London's *Daily Express*. Delmer had attended Hindenburg's eightieth birthday celebration in 1927. He had witnessed a zeppelin departure. "But both of these great days faded into nothingness compared with the spontaneous and unprepared demonstration that greeted the smiling, bare-headed Herr Hitler," Delmer wrote of a mass gathering in Berlin's Lustgarten, "where 120,000 fanatical Berliners were waiting to hear him speak." On April 3, campaigning in the runoff, Delmer joined Goebbels, Hanfstaengl, Hoffmann, Hitler, and Rudolf Hess, Hitler's personal secretary, at Munich's Oberwiesenfeld Airport. The leased trimotor Lufthansa passenger aircraft, piloted by Hans Baur, departed Munich for Dresden under clear skies. Half an hour after Hitler spoke in Dresden, they flew on to Leipzig, and three-quarters of an hour after that, on to Chemnitz, then Plauen, with the National Socialist press keeping tally of fanatic crowds that greeted him—"70,000 in Leipzig," "90,000 in Chemnitz."

"The next morning at nine o'clock we flew to Berlin," Baur recalled, where they were met by a large crowd of admirers at Tempelhof Airport. That evening there was a fanatic throng in the Sportpalast. The next morning, however, they were greeted by a hostile press. "The speech disappointed even those who listened attentively," the *Vossische Zeitung* reported, saying that Hitler appeared defensive, had nothing of sub-stance to say, and, perhaps worst of all, sounded rehearsed, repeating parts of previous speeches word for word. *Vorwärts* challenged Hitler's disparagement of the democratic repub-lic and his embrace of the "orderliness" of society under the kaiser. The paper denounced Hitler's endorsement of Hohenzollern rule with the banner headline *"Hitlers dümmste Lüge!,"* or "Hitler's Dumbest Lie." The next day, Hitler flew to Würzburg, where he was greeted by Crown Prince Wil-helm. A photograph shows the prince clasping Hitler's hand with the Lufthansa airplane as backdrop.

For the July Reichstag elections, Hitler leased a Luft-hansa plane yet again, again with Baur as pilot, and repeated the same breakneck air tour.

"Hitler usually sat in the front on the left or right side of the plane and stared ahead or checked the map with the terrain below," Hanfstaengl recalled. Hitler tended to keep to himself on the flights, usually reading, studying notes, or staring out the window. On one occasion, near the coastal city of Wismar, when the plane was running low on fuel, Hit-ler glanced out the window. "That's the North Sea," he said nervously. "Then we'll soon be in England," Hanfstaengl replied, "and finally have ourselves a cup of decent tea." Hitler ignored the comment. "In my opinion we should be keeping our course to the south; then we will be close to land," Hitler said. He then sat silently, opening and closing his fist. "Hitler had an aversion to water," Hanfstaengl wrote. "He couldn't swim."

Hitler took a film crew with him during the July election campaign and afterward produced a fifty-minute newsreel-style documentary, *Hitler über Deutschland*. In the black-and-white footage, Hitler sits in the cabin staring out the window, with cutaways to the German countryside in some scenes and aerial views of cityscapes in others. Hitler is seen stepping from the airplane and welcomed by young women, who hand him flowers. He signs an autograph. He chats with children. He visits a farmer and addresses vast crowds in stadiums and open fields. One subtitle reads, "100,000 in Hamburg," and another, "30,000 farmers in Lüneberg." In Cologne, the crowd broke into a chorus of *"Deutschland, Deutschland über alles."* In Hannover, where the camera pans across a crowd estimated at 120,000, the subtitle reads, "The mainstream press wrote: The audience was small, there was no mass demonstration, the Hitler movement is in decline everywhere." Along with the northern cities of Hamburg, Bremen, and Königsberg, the film chronicles Hitler's visits to Berlin, Leipzig, Dresden, Munich, and the Ruhr industrial region. According to Otto Dietrich, Hitler logged more than 40,000 air miles during his 1932 election campaigns, the equivalent of circumnavigating the globe. Dietrich claimed that Hitler held more than two hundred rallies in cities, towns, and villages, reaching a total audience of fifteen million, nearly one in every four Germans. Even allowing for the requisite hyperbole and spin of a press strategist, Hitler's five 1932 air campaigns were momentous, the first in German history, possibly one of the first in political history.

For the first two tours Hitler had leased from Lufthansa a ten-seater Rohrbach Roland II. The plane had a heated, sound-insulated cabin—though he was still forced to stuff cotton in his ears to dampen the noise—and an onboard toilet, a first in the German airline industry. For the July tour, Hitler leased a trimotor Junkers 52 passenger plane. In August, a state-of-the-art Junker made its world premiere at the Zürich Air Show. The upgraded Junkers had more headroom than the Rohrbach, could seat as many as seventeen passengers, and, most important, flew twenty miles an hour faster. Hitler informed Baur that he wanted to lease the new plane for a month in advance of the November 6 election.

Lufthansa management declined. The company needed the aircraft for its transalpine route. Hitler turned to Göring. As president of the Reichstag and former leader of Baron von Richthofen's legendary "Flying Circus," Göring used his political clout and hero status to convince the Lufthansa board to release the new plane for one month, once again with Baur as pilot.

*

A hard wind buffeted the Junkers passenger plane as it bumped and lurched through the nighttime storm to deliver Hitler to the October 17 rally in the town of Insterburg. There, emergency crews had stacked sandbags in a last-ditch attempt to keep the swollen banks of the Sieg River from flooding the factory hall where Hitler was to appear, while storm troopers stood watch against sabotage. Loudspeaker cables had been slashed at rallies in Halle and Essen. "Autumn flying conditions were poor as usual, and I had a good many difficulties to contend with," Baur later recounted. Outside Hamburg, the plane was tethered to the tarmac against a fierce North Sea wind that threatened to topple the aircraft. In Ulm, preparing for a late-night departure, Baur purchased ten hurricane lamps to stake out a makeshift runway in a field. In Königsberg, airfield mechanics refused to attend to "Adolf Hitler's plane" out of political protest. Baur argued that the aircraft belonged to Lufthansa, not Hitler, but when he arrived the next morning at eleven, the aircraft had still not been serviced. "I was informed that unless the SA guards were withdrawn no mechanic would touch the plane," Baur said. He secured the departure of the SA men, and the plane was fueled and prepared for flight. Despite the difficulties Baur had to deal with, he wrote, "I overcame them all, and not a single one of the many meetings had to be canceled on account of any failure in our flight program."

At rally after rally, Hitler beat the same drum. "I know that those of you who have come here today have one question: Why did I, on August 13, refuse to join the government?" he said in Breslau. He would not take part in a government he did not believe in, in a government that would achieve nothing. In towns and villages he stoked nationalist anger, claiming the government was not protecting Germany's borders. They let in foreigners from the east who brought chaos and crime and havoc into the country, he said, to undermine the political system and society, to despoil and violate the purity of the German race. Hitler once again evoked the specter of Potempa: "Here one Polish insurgent was killed, and for killing a Polish mass murderer, five Germans are being hanged." Could one ever imagine the French or British or Polish doing this to their own people? he asked. "This most despicable political class considers a Polish insurgent more worthy than five Germans who fought and bled for their people and their Fatherland. That says it all!" Hitler railed against Papen, faulting him for this outrage against the German people. He said he would never be a member of a government that would place a Polish life over a German one. He vowed that this would never happen if he were chancellor, which brought him to the issue of titles. He did not need the title of the chancellor, he declared. He did not need any title. He was mandated by Article 1 of the constitution, which invested the power of the state in the people. He had the common man behind him and not the aging president and not the cabinet of barons, not von Papen. "Many say that the constitution is outdated, and I say the constitution only now has found its purpose, because only now is the will of the people coming into force."

Hitler repeated what he had told Kaltenborn in August. A government required a majority of the electorate to be legitimate: "Of the 51 percent, we have 37 percent," Hitler said. "This means we have three-quarters [*sic*] of the votes needed to be legal." He said he had more votes than anyone else in the country, in particular Chancellor von Papen. Hitler mocked Hindenburg. "My great opponent, the Reich president, is eighty-five years old and I am forty-three and am completely healthy," he smugly observed. Then added that he would still be alive and healthy when Herr Reich president was "long gone." And, of course, there was "the Hamster."

"When Mr. Hugenberg says to me, 'Be smart, give in!' then I say: 'No, no, I'm happy to be the stupid one, but I will not give in! . . . The words 'give in' are not in our National Socialist dictionary. And if Mr. Hugenberg says that the smarter ones give in, then I would rather be the stupid one." That August, during the sensitive negotiations leading up to Hitler's meeting with Hindenburg, Hugenberg had received a late-night call from a newspaper editor informing him that Papen was willing to step down as chancellor to allow Hitler to ascend to the chancellorship. The next morning, Hugenberg met with Papen, in the company of close associates, and convinced Papen to reverse his position. After Hitler's failed audience with the Reich president, Hugenberg publicly questioned Hitler's intelligence and political judgment for refusing to enter into a coalition. "You should have taken it," Hugenberg chastised Hitler in an editorial. He said that if Hitler had been smart, he would have been flexible and joined in a coalition government and come to power instead of betting on all or nothing.

"Don't worry, Mr. Hugenberg, worry about your own!" Hitler responded. "At least I held my own for thirteen years and didn't surrender. Rest assured, I will be doing the same in the fourteenth year!" Hitler waved the Hugenberg admonishment like a red flag at his bullish opponent, asking, "Do you really think I would sell out the movement for a few ministerial seats?" Hitler said that he needed neither Hugenberg's advice, nor his financing, nor his sixteen hundred newspapers. Hitler had managed just fine on his own for thirteen years. He would continue to do so in the coming election.

*

By the evening of November 1, Hitler had flown from Bonn to Mannheim, with rallies in both cities; he then traveled by car to Pirmasens, addressed a crowd of sixty thousand, then drove to Karlsruhe, spoke to another seventy thousand, then boarded the Junkers for Berlin.

The plane landed sometime after midnight, and a waiting car drove Hitler to the Hotel Kaiserhof, where he was to prepare for one of his final speeches of the election campaign.

The next evening, November 2, shortly after nine o'clock, following an opening speech by Goebbels, Hitler entered the Sportpalast to "storms of applause" from the thronging crowd that packed the main floor and three tiers of viewing stands in the city's largest public venue. When constructed back in 1910, the vast concrete hall with a steel-and-glass ceiling had housed the largest ice-skating rink in the world; it subsequently hosted twenty-four-hour bike-a-thons, jitter-bug dance-a-thons, and boxing matches, and in recent years it had been the site of political rallies of all stripes. Two days before Hitler appeared, the leader of the Communist Party in Germany, Ernst Thälmann, had entered the Sportpalast to speak before forty thousand cheering followers. The Social Democrats would rent the facility the following evening.

While Hitler was greeted by a hurricane roar of jubilant National Socialists, hundreds more tried to battle their way in. The police sealed the doors, and pitched battles between National Socialists and Communists were fought in the sur-rounding streets. At a nearby park, twelve Communists and National Socialists were shot or stabbed, three of them fatally. As in Karlsruhe, Hitler modulated between piercing irony, which evoked waves of laughter and applause, and fierce determination that he would never be bribed or coerced into a coalition government. He said he carried too much "bag-gage" to enter a political office and then leave, like the last three chancellors and their bevy of ministers, who entered and exited government posts on regular rotation. "For thir-teen years they believed they could besiege us through the Weimar constitution, but this movement grew despite that," Hitler said. He added that he had been "dragged into court-rooms" more times than he could remember. "They believed that in the end the constitution would destroy our move-ment. And when that did not happen, they tried to bribe me with titles and power." Here he paused to let the thunderous applause subside. Hitler knew where the real power lay.

"When Papen says: 'I have the power,' then I must answer, 'No, you don't,'" Hitler said emphatically. "The police and the army are not power, they are violence. The power lies with the people, in the faith and in the strength of the people. . . ." Hitler spoke of the power of the common man and the will of the people and the coming of a Third Reich, which would bring a rebirth of the German nation, and would be a Reich of prosperity and unity for all Germans. Then he paused to conjure the presence of the chancellor into the hall and addressed him: "That, Mr. von Papen, is not your Reich, that is ours!"

Leni Riefenstahl was present that evening. The film star and aspiring director had met Hitler earlier that year after he had seen her star turn in the film *Das Blaue Licht* (The Blue Light). She had seen him speak at one previous rally. But that evening she was mesmerized. "He spoke without a script and with such force that his words seemed to lash the spectators," she later recalled. "He appeared demonic as he swore to them that he would create a new Germany and put an end to unemployment and poverty. When he said, 'Collective good takes precedence over individual good,' his words struck at my heart."

Hitler departed Berlin the next day, speaking at rallies in Hannover and Göttingen on Thursday and Kassel and Ulm on Friday. He arrived at Munich's Oberwiesenfeld Airport just before midnight, then proceeded to his residence on the Prinzregentenplatz in the center of town. The next day, he and Eva Braun visited an exhibition. Hitler gave two more speeches that afternoon, one at three forty-five and another at four-thirty, then dined with Hoffmann and his wife. The polls would open the next morning. Otto Dietrich, the

NSDAP press spokesperson, told journalists that Hitler was confident in the election outcome. "The storm of enthusiasm from five or ten rallies in bastions of National Socialist support could be deceptive as to the general mood," Dietrich said to the press Saturday evening, "but everything that we have seen and heard on our travels across the entire country absolutely excludes any possibility of deception." Dietrich predicted a landslide. He added, "We will crush them, these enemies of the people."

*

Election Sunday in Berlin was partially cloudy, with gradually clearing skies and a northerly wind that brought falling temperatures to an eerily still city. A transit strike, endorsed by the Communists and National Socialists in a politically awkward alliance as an appeal to the working-class vote, had brought the subways, buses, and tramlines to a standstill. There had been hope of continued service on Saturday when 219 trams were reported to be running along thirty-one lines—out of the usual 1,000 trams on seventy-two lines—but by eight o'clock that evening even these had stopped. Sunday dawned with the tramlines silenced and the grates to subway entrances closed. On this election day, Berliners literally voted with their feet.

"Everything is calm, but a heavy, oppressive atmosphere lies over Berlin," Goebbels noted in his diary that day. He had secured an additional ten thousand reichsmarks for an eleventh-hour propaganda effort on Saturday but was unable to have the posters printed and placed. The printing company, the Berliner Plakatgesellschaft, refused the order. Instead, Goebbels stationed storm troopers in front of opposition placards to explain the National Socialist position, to little effect. "This counter-maneuver can't be completely successful in such a short time," he wrote. Despite the strike, voters appeared at the polling places in unexpectedly high numbers. Unlike the July Reichstag elections, the day passed without serious altercations.

Meanwhile, election officials prepared for the polling results on the second floor of the city hall, just off the Alexanderplatz, where a state-of-the-art, American-made Smith Premier tabulator had been installed to verify the election returns and avert allegations of voter fraud and the sort of courtroom antics that had plagued previous elections. When Hitler had challenged the election results following his failed presidential bid, Hans Frank had appeared before the Election Review Court, arguing that Hitler's ban from national radio had infringed on his constitutional right to free speech. National Socialist election posters and flyers had been prohibited, election rallies canceled. Frank also cited irregularities and harassment at polling stations. When an opposition attorney began listing acts of "terrorism" by National Socialists, Frank leaped to his feet in loud protest, refusing to sit down until the presiding judge, Johannes Bell, the Center Party jurist who had signed the Versailles Treaty and been heckled in the Reichstag, instructed Frank, in no uncertain terms, "how one was to behave in a court of law." Only then did Frank fall silent. The court dismissed the Hitler suit. Following his 37 percent triumph in the July 31 Reichstag election, Hitler had lodged no objections, but the Social Democrats, who had taken a beating at the polls, had their own litany of claims about "irregularities and fraud." Three hundred thousand mail-in ballots were said to have been in circulation in Berlin alone.

For the November 6 Reichstag elections, the Berlin government was taking no chances. But with fourteen parties holding seats in the Reichstag, and three dozen on the ballot, the November 1932 election strained even the capacities of the Smith Premier "miracle of technology," along with the political system of the thirteen-year-old constitutional republic.

The polls closed at six p.m. Goebbels followed the state-by-state returns on the radio late into the night. "Every update is another defeat," he noted. "It's a disaster." Hitler had vowed to destroy democracy with democracy, but that Sunday evening, as the Smith Premier tabulated the polling results, it appeared that democracy had outdone him. President Hindenburg followed the initial election counts, and when assured of Hitler's defeat, he went to bed.

In mid-October, the *Vossische Zeitung* had predicted a National Socialist defeat following a local election in the town of Selb, where the National Socialists had lost 25 percent of the vote just two days after Hitler had held an election rally there. "If 12,000 farmers and workers truly 'experienced' the Führer, as the *Völkischer Beobachter* had claimed, why was it that despite this experience barely a fifth of them voted National Socialist on Sunday?" the *Vossische Zeitung* asked its readership. The trend seemed to have played out across Germany. Fred Birchall had also expected a National Socialist defeat. "The country is getting tired of the Nazis," he wrote. "They had their chance last August when President von Hindenburg offered a share of the government to Herr Hitler and he refused." Birchall called the results in July Hitler's "high-water mark." Word circulated even among Hitler's closest associates: *"Der Führer hat verspielt."* Hitler had misplayed his cards.

CHAPTER 12

TRIUMPH OF THE SHRILL

Hitler is a man with a great future behind him.

—KURT ERICH SUCKERT, A.K.A. CURZIO MALAPARTE

On Monday morning, November 7, 1932, just hours after the Smith Premier tapped out the final election results at forty-five minutes after midnight and the lights went dark in the city hall, the first newspapers hit the stands with headlines trumpeting Hitler's election debacle. Most galling of all, Hugenberg had picked up eight hundred thousand votes, and an additional fourteen seats in the Reichstag, mostly at Hitler's expense. *Vorwärts* declared, "CRUSHING DEFEAT FOR HITLER!" in a banner headline, highlighting the National Socialist loss of two million votes. "The most important result of November 6: decline of the National Socialists. They cannot move forward, they can't hold on, they're sliding backward," the article noted. Two-thirds of the German people had rejected Hitler, it continued. Observing that Hitler's demand for one-party rule had seemed an "outrage" after the July election, the article suggested that it now looked more like a *"Donquichoterie,"* a bit of Don Quixotism. The electorate had made one thing clear: Germans did not want a Hitler dictatorship. A front-page political cartoon later that day showed Hitler slouched against a table holding a broken swastika in his hand, like a kid moping over a broken toy. The *Vossische Zeitung* offered the sobering headline "NSDAP Decline Begins—Hugenberg in Key Position."

The mood in party offices and SA headquarters across the country was dark. Goebbels wrote the following evening, "Miserable mood in the district. And a lot of anger, worry and drudgery. Evening at the district office, studied press reports. Everywhere [reports of] our defeat." A party-wide depression set in.

Following his poor showing in the first round of the presidential election in March, Hitler had reacted as one might expect. He had assumed that with the party's meteoric rise in recent Reichstag elections he would easily clear the 50 percent hurdle and succeed Hindenburg as the next Reich president. "Our expectations had been set far too high based on our own desires during the heat of battle," Otto Dietrich recalled. As we know, Hitler barely cleared 30 percent, compared to 49.54 percent for Hindenburg. In a meeting with his advisers, Hitler sat in stunned silence. It was obvious to all that he would never prevail in the runoff against Hindenburg. Goebbels was in total despair. Göring observed coolly that Hindenburg was over eighty and could hardly be expected to serve out the full seven-year term. Perhaps it was wiser to abandon the next election round. Dietrich advised that instead of "bleeding to death" financially in a runoff they would lose, perhaps they should concentrate their resources on local elections—or mobilize the storm troopers in an armed insurrection, overthrow the government, and install Hitler as dictator, putting an end to the republic once and for all. Like Hans Frank, Hanfstaengl felt that Hitler should continue to follow the legal route and use the democratic form of government to install himself as dictator.

According to Dietrich, Hitler listened in silence, then dictated a statement for a supplement to the *Völkischer Beobachter* that was just going to press. "We must renew our attack immediately and ruthlessly," Hitler said. "The National Socialist, recognizing his enemy, never relents until his vision is fulfilled." Hitler then declared his candidacy for the runoff election scheduled for Sunday, April 10. Hanf-staengl had a different account. "Well, we'll see," he recalled Hitler saying. Then, without another word, Hitler stood up, put on his coat, and walked out the door. After the election, Hanfstaengl called on him at his Prinzregentenstrasse apartment. He found Hitler sitting in a darkened room brooding: "a classic example of a disappointed and deflated gambler who had overplayed his hand and had bet well beyond his means."

Now, eight months later, in the face of an electoral set-back that had cost him two million votes and a swath of seats in the Reichstag, Hitler proclaimed victory. "The most difficult battle in the history of our party lies behind us," he declared in a message to party leaders. "A massive attack against the movement and the rights of the German people has been repelled. Von Papen and his government—despite using all the political means at their disposal, and despite the use of the greatest propaganda tool, the radio, and despite the backing of almost the entire media and special newspaper reports—have suffered a crushing defeat."

Two days after the election, Hitler gathered his lieutenants for a post-election debrief in a back room of the Stern-eckerbräu beer hall in downtown Munich. Adolf Wagner, the gauleiter of Munich, was there, as were Hanfstaengl and Hans Frank. Goebbels had come down from Berlin on an overnight train, where he'd encountered Leni Riefenstahl. He'd invited her to come along to the meeting.

Hitler's choice of the Sterneckerbräu had a signal effect that everyone present understood. Hitler had first come to the Sterneckerbräu in September 1919 as a thirty-year-old military intelligence officer, less than a year from the front, to look into a right-wing political movement. He had found seven men sitting around a table. Thirteen years later, as he reminded everyone repeatedly in those months, he was the head of a movement that now had more than thirteen million followers across the country. Hitler's message was clear that Tuesday morning. It was time to return to the roots and reassess. His mood surprised Riefenstahl. "Hitler spoke as if he had won the election," she thought.

It is hard to know how much of Hitler's response was bravado, how much wishful thinking, or even mere delusion. While Goebbels's diary entries and occasional recordings allow one to track Hitler's fluctuating, often hysterical responses to crises—Hanfstaengl, Rauschning, and others also make such notes in their memoirs, including Hitler's alleged threats of suicide—Hitler appears to have been possessed of a nature resilient to adversity. Whether that was as a result of some form of emotional or psychological imbalance that inclined him toward the delusional or of a fierce, even ruthless determination that steeled him against acquiescence in the face of impending defeat is not clear. But his resilience inured him against public humiliations large and small, blinded him to seemingly insurmountable obstacles, allowed him to countenance defeats and setbacks and cling to even the flimsiest sliver of hope for rescue or salvation in the most dire situations, and permitted him to double down without flinching, without compromise in the face of threatening ruin. On occasions when Hitler threatened suicide, he was almost certainly envisioning a scenario in which every last option and resource had been exhausted. There would be no surrender. One of Hitler's most cherished quotes by Frederick the Great, which he repeated throughout his life, literally until his dying day, was "The commander who throws his last battalion into the battle will be the victor."

Goebbels arrived at the Sterneckerbräu loaded with bad news. The electoral results in Berlin had been catastrophic: in the Kreuzberg voting precinct, the Communist vote defeated the National Socialists, 79,000 to 54,000. Even in conservative strongholds like Charlottenburg and Schöneberg, the National Socialists barely held their own. He reported a miserable mood in the NSDAP district offices. Goebbels feared a hemorrhaging of membership and finances. *Vorwärts* described Hitler's followers not as an "army of loyal and disciplined soldiers" but, rather, as a band of "mercenaries" looking to plunder the country for their own gain. Hitler may have been inclined to agree. "I know exactly why the gauleiters ask me to come and give speeches," he complained. "They rent the largest halls in the city but cannot fill them. [When I am there,] I fill them to the ceiling and they stick the proceeds into their pockets. I have to race around Germany like a crazy person in order for [the party] not to have to declare bankruptcy."

The Social Democrats had launched a last-minute poster campaign equating the National Socialists with the Communists for backing the transit strike. Goebbels's attempted counterpunch was too little, too late. Worse still, Papen had given a radio address after the election denouncing Hitler's ambitions for dictatorial powers, as well as Hitler's endorsement of acts of public violence committed by his followers across the country, mostly against Jews. It was a stern public reprimand and repudiation of National Socialist extremism heard by millions.

Frank had an even more unsettling explanation. The 37 percent surge in July had been driven primarily by independent voters who had initially seen Hitler as a bulwark against the radical left and assumed that he would enter into a coalition with centrist conservative parties, bringing stability to years of political chaos. When Hitler refused to join a coalition in August, demanding full power for himself, independent voters abandoned him, having tired of his radicalizing and polarizing rhetoric. Hitler's Potempa telegram had not helped matters. As someone in the party who was critical of Hitler's position on the Potempa Five, Frank later recalled that the Papen radio address had delivered perhaps the most devastating blow: "[The address] was the last upstanding voice against Hitler and was an oratorical demonstration of the best thinking of the [German] people."

Hitler wrote in *Mein Kampf* that even the severest canings by his father had been unable to shake his resolve. A tongue-lashing by Franz von Papen left Hitler unmoved, as did the election results. Sitting in the back room of the Sterneckerbräu, Hitler summoned the same determination that had transformed a clutch of seven men sitting around a wooden table in the back room of a beer hall into the most powerful political movement in the country. Riefenstahl recalled Hitler saying, "Only the weak have deserted us and that is good." Hitler also noted, "In the next local elections in Lippe"—scheduled for mid-January 1933—"we need to go to every house to fight for every vote—we will win the next election and finally achieve our breakthrough." Assuming there was enough money.

*

Walther Karsch, editor of *Die Weltbühne*, one of the political left's leading cultural publications, made his own written contributions under the pseudonym Quietus. In March 1932, Karsch published an investigation into National Socialist finances. "Until the first election, everything went well. The money from industry flowed plentifully, and one was able to take on loans with the promise that Hitler as Reich president would take care of the open bills," Karsch wrote. Beyond the leasing of the Lufthansa aircraft and the fees for a pilot and the expense of the speaking venues, there was the film crew hired for the documentary *Hitler über Deutschland*, along with the cost of a ten-minute film of Hitler speaking to be played on public squares. Fifty thousand gramophone records of Hitler's speeches had also been produced, the disks small enough to be mailed in an envelope. There were also costs for printing flyers and posters, for renting cars and trucks, hotel bills, tent rentals, and rentals of sound systems. Karsch discovered deficits at every turn. In Freiburg, a local National Socialist newspaper, *Der Alemanne*, was carrying a debt of 30,000 RM (about 158,000 in current U.S. dollars). Franz Eher Verlag, the publisher of Hitler's *Mein Kampf* and Alfred Rosenberg's *The Myth of the Twentieth Century*, was down 220,000 RM (about $1.16 million). The party office for the state of Hessen was running a 325,000 RM ($1.7 million) deficit. The biggest financial drain, according to Karsch, was Röhm's army of storm troopers. "It's no longer a secret that many jobless found their way to [Hitler] only because being a member of the SA meant getting a small salary," Karsch wrote.

Hitler was fully aware of the precarious financial situation within his movement, not only with the operational costs for the Brown House, in Munich, and other offices across the country, but the enormous additional costs of election campaigns. Adolf Müller, a Munich printer whose major sources of revenue were publications for the Catholic Church and the daily print run of the *Völkischer Beobachter*, complained personally to Hitler and threatened to cancel the contract over delinquent payments. "My most tragic moment was in 1932 when I had to sign all sorts of contracts in order to finance our election campaign," Hitler said later. "I signed these contracts in the name of the party, but all the time with the feeling that, if we did not win, all would be lost forever." Former British diplomat John Wheeler-Bennett heard that Hitler did not even have enough money to pay the salaries of his bodyguards.

In October, Hitler appealed to his supporters for financial contributions, ostensibly to help cover the medical costs of injured storm troopers and provide assistance to their families. "Even the smallest amount will help," Hitler wrote. Any contributions were to be sent "as soon as possible" to Account 120 at the Barerstrasse branch of the Bavarian Loan and Exchange Bank in Munich. Whatever the real purpose, the appeal smacked of financial desperation. Hitler's personal finances were hardly better. He had been battling the Munich state tax authorities over annual deductions since 1925, when questions arose about his purchase, in February 1925, of a Mercedes-Benz for 20,000 RM. His tax filings for his time in prison had indicated that he had had no reported income. Hitler explained that he had taken out a loan to purchase the vehicle. He continued to scuffle with tax authorities for the rest of the decade, frequently filing late, one time receiving a "penal order"—*Strafverfügung*—of 10 RM or a day in prison, and submitting deductions for well over half his income. Deductions included 300 RM per month to Rudolf Hess for secretarial services and 200 RM for his driver, as well as 2,000 RM annually for automobile tax and insurance.

"Accordingly in my case as a political writer, the expenses

of my political activity, which is the necessary condition of my professional writing as well as its assurance of financial success, cannot be regarded as subject to taxation," Hitler wrote in one letter. His declared income fluctuated between 11,000 and 15,000 RM (roughly $58,000 to $79,000 today), but when his political fortunes soared, so did royalties from *Mein Kampf*: from 7,664 copies sold in 1929 to 54,086 in 1930, and massive sales thereafter. By 1933, the Bavarian state authorities had assessed Hitler 405,494 RM (about $2.9 million today) in back taxes.

Meanwhile, the federal government had been conducting its own internal investigation into the tangled financing of Hitler's political movement. "It's a fact that all the financial transactions at the Bayerische Vereinsbank in Munich were not linked to an official account but rather to a large number of single accounts with inconsequential names," Hermann Pünder, former state secretary in Chancellor Brüning's cabinet, reported on April 16. It would require investigators to interview each of the "technical people" involved with each of the individual accounts. Over the past twelve months, Pünder noted, substantial sums in foreign cash had been channeled into these accounts through the Schweizerische Kreditanstalt in Zürich.

There had also been an additional 15 million RM (more than $79 million today) generated from domestic sources—membership dues, entrance fees to Hitler rallies, the sale of political pamphlets—plus an additional 5 million RM ($26.4 million today) from "so-called anti-terror protection premiums," extracted from large business owners, such as Hermann Tietz, the Jewish founder of the Hertie department store chain, and Jacob Schapiro, also Jewish, who owned the Sportpalast, Hitler's preferred Berlin venue for indoor rallies. The 5 million RM also included contributions from German industrialists. "The primary donor in Germany was Fritz Thyssen, loyal member," Pünder noted.

Steel magnate Thyssen was widely known to have helped finance the National Socialist movement for nearly a decade. "My contributions have been very much overestimated, because I have long been rated the richest man in Germany," Thyssen once said, noting that his first subsidy, 100,000 gold marks, had been made in the fall of 1923, in advance of the beer-hall putsch. By Thyssen's estimate, he contributed an estimated million reichsmarks ($5.3 million) over the years. He also facilitated a foreign loan for acquiring and refurbishing the Brown House in Munich. Hitler had repaid only a fraction of the sum.

According to Thyssen, the Berlin piano manufacturer Edwin Bechstein and his wife, Helene, were Hitler's most significant benefactors, along with the Munich publisher Hugo Bruckmann and his wife, Elsa. "Aside from this," Thyssen said, "Hitler did not receive many subsidies from German industrialists." For a time, Hugenberg channeled to the National Socialists about 20 percent of the contributions he collected from industrialists, which Thyssen thought amounted to two million reichsmarks per year.

Most significant, Thyssen made Hitler palatable to fellow industrialists. He had arranged for Hitler to address the Club of Industrialists in Düsseldorf in January 1932, permitting businessmen to judge the National Socialist leader themselves. "The speech made a deep impression on the assembled industrialists, and in consequence of this a number of large contributions flowed from the resources of heavy industry into the treasuries of the National Socialist Party," Thyssen recalled. What interested them in particular was promoting cooperation between Hitler and Hugenberg in forming a conservative bloc against the Communists and Social Democrats. "They gave the money to Dr. Alfred Hugenberg, who placed about one-fifth of donated amounts at the disposal of the National Socialist Party," Thyssen said.

After the run-up to two rounds of presidential elections, two Reichstag campaigns, and various local contests, the party had burned through an estimated 60 million RM ($318.4 million today). By mid-November 1932, Hitler's movement was essentially bankrupt, not only financially but also politically. In addition to Hitler's radicalism and his embrace of the Potempa Five, industrialists were unsettled by the National Socialists finding common cause with Communists—in obstructing the legislative process and public transportation—and frustrated by Hitler's intransigence toward Hindenburg and, of course, their friend and fellow businessman Hugenberg. Even Thyssen cooled. He informed Hitler that he was having financial troubles of his own. His final contribution would be to finance a carload of political pamphlets for the *Völkischer Beobachter*.

"Scarcity of money has become chronic in this campaign," Goebbels wrote on November 2, four days before the election. "We lack the amount necessary for carrying it out effectively." By mid-month, "chronic" had turned to desperate. "Just waves of debt and responsibilities," Goebbels despaired, "and on top of that, with this defeat, the complete impossibility to find large sums of money anywhere." One estimate put the party's debt level at 90 million reichsmarks. Hitler once said, "The ancient Romans were right when they created Mercury, a common god for bankers, thieves, and prostitutes."

By mid-November, the lease had expired on Hitler's Lufthansa plane, which was returned to servicing the airline's transalpine route. Before Hans Baur went back to work for Lufthansa, Hitler asked him to inquire into the cost of a

Junkers 52. Baur reported back that the purchase price was 275,000 reichsmarks (about $1.5 million). "It's too expensive. I will have to wait," Hitler said. "Before long I will be chancellor and then I'll establish an official air service and put you in charge of it."

CHAPTER 13

"HARE HITLER"

Herr Hitler, I wish to hear in your own words
a summary of your ideas.

—PAUL VON HINDENBURG, NOVEMBER 19, 1932

On Monday, November 14, Hitler received a letter from
the Reich chancellor. Papen was extending an olive branch.
"When the Reich president appointed me to head the government on June 1, he instructed the presidial cabinet to
support me in trying to build the widest possible coalition
of nationalist parties," Papen explained. He pointed out that
Hitler had "welcomed the idea in the warmest terms" and
agreed to do whatever was "best for the country." Given that
Hindenburg had made it explicitly clear on August 13 that he
would not appoint Hitler as chancellor, Papen thought it was
perhaps now a good time to explore other options. "With the
November 6 election, a new situation has arisen, and with
it, a new opportunity to try once again to bring together the
different nationalist forces," Papen wrote.

Papen said that he was aware of the National Socialist
press claim that it was impossible to negotiate with the current Reich chancellor, but he wanted to show that he was

indeed willing to enter into good-faith discussions with Hitler. "We must try and forget the bitterness of the election campaign," he wrote, "and put the welfare of the country we serve together above all else." Papen informed Hitler that he was traveling during the first half of the week but would be available for a face-to-face meeting either on Wednesday or Thursday. Hitler smelled blood.

He knew that Papen had met with other party leaders over the past few days in an attempt to fulfill the Hindenburg mandate of forming a coalition government supported by a Reichstag majority. His talks with the Center Party leaders had failed, as had his approaches to the Social Democrats. Even Papen's relationship with Hugenberg had soured. Hugenberg's press had turned on him. Papen found himself increasingly isolated.

On Wednesday, Hitler sent Papen an extended letter saying that he saw no point in a meeting if his demands for absolute power were not met. He assured Papen that he harbored no "bitterness" over the elections, nor over Papen's role in the disastrous meeting with Hindenburg, nor the subsequent public humiliations he had suffered. "I have endured so much persecution and personal attacks during the thirteen years of my struggle for Germany that I have learned to put the great cause I serve above myself," Hitler wrote. There was, in fact, only one thing that filled him with bitterness, he said: watching Papen squander the vast amounts of "hope, belief, and trust" that the German people had placed in him as chancellor, watching that goodwill turn to "pain and grief" amid political chaos and economic misery. It was this betrayal of public trust that had convinced Hitler all the more that he alone could overcome the crisis in the country.

How could Hitler trust Papen? "The discussions that have taken place up to now, which have also been witnessed by others, indicate that the meaning and content of those negotiations are not remembered the same way by the two parties," Hitler continued. How could Hitler ever negotiate in good faith, knowing that his positions and intentions could be misinterpreted or intentionally distorted, then leaked to the public? Hitler dispatched his letter to Papen, then released it to the press.

Without National Socialist support in the Reichstag, Papen knew, his position as chancellor was untenable. Within a day, he had submitted his resignation, which the Reich president duly accepted, though with evident regret. Unlike Brüning, who had been dismissed curtly, without even a handshake, Papen received a letter of warm thanks for his service to the nation. Hindenburg asked him to continue as chancellor in a caretaker role until a replacement could be found. Papen was allowed to retain his Wilhelmstrasse apartment. The Reich president had come to appreciate Papen's pragmatic conservativism, despite his unpopularity in the Reichstag and with the general public. Papen was ridiculed for his "cabinet of monocles" and tainted by his wartime expulsion from the United States on espionage charges while serving in the German embassy in Washington DC, where he left behind pay stubs with the names of his spies.

Papen's sudden demission unleashed a flood of rumors. *Vorwärts* sensed an imminent military coup led by Schleicher. *Vossische Zeitung* saw Gregor Strasser as Papen's most likely successor. The Swiss newspaper *Journal de Genève* reported that Hitler had already been appointed chancellor, and "Göring will probably become vice chancellor and foreign minister." Harry Kessler heard, with sheer horror, that there might be a Papen reprise. Kessler was right. "The Reich president saw Papen as a man he could trust politically and personally, and hoped to entrust him yet again with building a cabinet," Otto Meissner recalled, but first other options needed to be explored.

On Friday morning, November 18, a day after the Papen demission, Hugenberg sat in Hindenburg's office. There was little for Hindenburg to like about Hugenberg. The man was arrogant, presumptuous, and rich. As a director at Krupp, Hugenberg had made a fortune in a war that cost millions of Germans their lives. As the owner of a media empire, he incessantly disparaged the Reich president and the republic. But as the leader of a party that had just culled almost a million votes from Hitler's ranks, and now commanded fifty-one Reichstag delegates, Hugenberg was indispensable to building a conservative Reichstag majority.

Hugenberg lectured the former field marshal on the economy and the high unemployment that he saw driving political radicalism, but he cautioned him against state intervention. The market would right itself, he said. He argued for a presidial cabinet—one that answered to the president rather than the Reichstag and made use of Hindenburg's Article 48 emergency powers—at least until the spring, to give the economy time to stabilize, to counter the Communist opposition. The economy had already turned a corner, he said, and employment would follow. "I am not taking the current crisis so seriously, because it's really only a party crisis, and only a crisis of the centrists and the National Socialists, who don't quite know how to position themselves in the current situation," Hugenberg explained. He also cautioned against dissolving the Reichstag and calling for elections. With his newly won seats, Hugenberg had little interest in another round of voting.

But Hindenburg had wearied of presidial cabinets. He did not want to wait until spring to restore constitutional order. He wanted a centrist conservative cabinet supported by a Reichstag majority. With a coalition of delegates from the nationalist parties—196 National Socialists, 70 Center Party members, and 51 German Nationalists—one could establish a parliamentary consensus. Hindenburg got to the point: Could Hugenberg envision joining a cabinet under Hitler? Hugenberg did not mince words.

"In principle, I negotiated with Hitler before Harzburg on the basis that he, Hitler, wanted neither to become Reich president nor Reich chancellor, but only to remain the leader of his movement. Then Hitler turned around and demanded first the presidency, then the chancellorship," Hugenberg said. "I don't believe Hitler honors the agreements he makes. The way he deals with political matters makes it extremely difficult for Hitler to be given any political leadership." Hugenberg made it clear that he would have "serious concerns" about joining a coalition headed by Hitler.

*

Hitler received word that the Reich president wanted to meet with him almost at the same time as the news hit the press. The announcement was met with cautious expectation and wild speculation. The National Socialist newspapers suspended attacks on the aging Reich president. Saber rattling ceased in the ranks of the SA. The *Vossische Zeitung* observed that Hitler's belligerent rhetoric, his demand for "absolute control," for a "dictatorship without constraints," beyond the authority of the Reich president and the Reichstag, appeared to have evaporated into thin air. *The New York Times* reported, "In place of the arrogant Adolf Hitler of last August a much chastened National Socialist chieftain was received by President von Hindenburg today." *Vorwärts* featured a front-page cartoon with Hitler cowering beneath a bird of prey in whose talons dangle words of warning. "August 13, 1932," the caption reads. "There he is again."

Hitler departed the Hotel Kaiserhof on Saturday morning in the company of Strasser, Göring, and Frick to the cheers of waiting storm troopers, and arrived by car a few minutes later at the gates of the presidential palace, where another clutch of storm troopers waited with stiff-armed salutes and cries of *"Heil Hitler!"* Röhm was nowhere to be seen. Hitler and his entourage arrived punctually at 11:30, exactly twenty-four hours after Hugenberg. Hindenburg wanted a meeting *"unter vier Augen"*—literally, among four eyes—so Hitler entered Hindenburg's office alone. He emerged at 12:45. There were no press statements, no leaked exchanges. The official communiqué was restricted to a single fact: Hindenburg had requested a follow-up meeting in a few days' time.

"I tried to establish contact with the old field marshal by having recourse to comparisons of a military nature," Hitler said afterward. "Connection was made fairly rapidly with the soldier." The two veterans, field marshal and corporal, exchanged recollections and reflections on the war, one of Hindenburg's favorite pastimes, before the conversation moved to matters at hand. Hindenburg explained that Papen's inability to bridge party divides and secure a Reichstag majority had cost him the chancellorship. "I will now earnestly try to bring together both the Center Party and the National Socialist Party under a new government," Hindenburg told Hitler. He had spoken not only with Hugenberg of the German Nationalists but also with Ludwig Kaas of the Center Party and Eduard Dingeldey of the conservative German People's Party. "You, Herr Hitler, are the leader of a large movement, whose national importance I fully recognize," Hindenburg continued. "You have accomplished this significant feat despite all the material hardships of the time, to revitalize large parts of the German people nationally and to fill them with new idealism." Hindenburg respected this achievement. He was now appealing to Hitler's "love for the Fatherland," to his "soldierly sense of duty," to set aside past animosities and personal ambitions for the good of the country. "These times are too serious for individuals to pursue their own personal interests and make their own way," Hindenburg said. "We have to put aside our differences and come together in this time of urgency."

He wanted to hear from Hitler in strict confidence what it would require for him to join a coalition government. As the leader of the largest social movement in the country, Hitler said, he felt that he had a claim to the chancellorship. He wanted a presidial cabinet, to rule by decree, just as the two previous chancellors had done. Hindenburg repeated his desire to return the country to a constitutional basis with majority rule. He said that Hitler could achieve his objectives by participating in a coalition. Indeed, Hindenburg was willing to open several minister posts to Hitler's key lieutenants. "I ask you, Herr Hitler, to reconsider this question and also to discuss it with your fellow party members and also with the other party leaders," Hindenburg continued. "I don't want to give you a definitive answer today, nor do I want a definitive answer from you just yet. We both need to think it over and discuss it again in the next few days."

Hitler said that Hindenburg needed to understand that he could not enter into a government unless he had absolute authority. "I am not only putting forward my name, but my entire movement," Hitler said. He reminded Hindenburg that there were eighteen million Marxists and among them perhaps fourteen or fifteen million Communists who were preparing for violent revolution. Hitler was not going to dilute or fragment his movement by entering into a coalition.

The only bulwark against the Communist threat was a unified government under dictatorial rule, he said. Hitler maintained he was not interested in "power," in and of itself, but rather in *"Führung,"* in leadership that could provide guidance and direction. Of course, he would let other parties speak at the table and participate in the building of the government, he said, but a strong, centralized leadership with popular support was the only way out of the current crisis. Hitler warned Hindenburg against another cabinet, like Papen's, that did not have broad public support.

"Certainly one can govern in an authoritarian manner with a coalition cabinet for some time, supported by the power of the state, but that would not last long. There would be revolution by February," Hitler went on. The government urgently had to address the needs and concerns of the average citizen, Hitler said, the desire for financial stability and for an end to public street violence. "I know that it is no simple task to take over the leadership of the government," Hitler concluded. "The country is desperate. Nevertheless, I would be willing to take on the task in the hope that I could lead Germany out of the current crisis."

When Meissner was summoned into the office, he found Hitler seated before the Reich president "like a schoolboy" on a straight-backed wooden chair, nervously fidgeting with his hands. Meissner watched as Hindenburg feigned sympathy. Hindenburg said he appreciated Hitler's concerns and had no doubt as to the honesty of his intentions, but he doubted that he could entrust Hitler with a *"Parteikabinett,"* a single-party cabinet. Hindenburg again said that he wanted a coalition government with majority support in the Reichstag. Had Hitler even tried to engage with other party leaders? Hindenburg wondered. Hitler replied, "I do not intend to contact other parties, nor do I wish to get involved in party

negotiations." If Hindenburg would entrust him with building a government, Hitler was willing to enter into discussions,
not only about policies but also about proposed ministers.
"I believe that I would find a basis on which the Reichstag
would grant me and the new government the power to make
and enforce laws," Hitler said. "No one but me could get
the Reichstag to grant such an enabling act. That would be
the easiest solution." Hitler knew that proposing an enabling
act, an *Ermächtigungsgesetz*, was a provocation, but Hindenburg had accorded his two previous chancellors, Brüning
and Papen, the same sort of capacity for dictatorial rule. To
Hitler's surprise, Hindenburg did not dismiss the idea out of
hand. He paused. "I will take time to think about the whole
question and I think that we should discuss this matter again,"
Hindenburg said. "I would also ask that you reflect on all this
as well." Hindenburg once again appealed to Hitler's sense of
"duty to the Fatherland" and to the "old camaraderie" that
bound them as soldiers.

Hitler reminded Hindenburg that he, Hitler, had single-
handedly created a *"Millionenbewegung"*—a movement with
millions of followers—in a brief thirteen years. If the "Herr
Field Marshal" wanted a Reichstag majority, Hitler would
deliver a Reichstag majority. But there was one thing on
which Hitler had to insist. He wanted legislation enacted that
would accord him presidial power to run the country as he saw
fit. It went without saying, Hitler added, that "this law would
need to be passed by the Reichstag and then presented to the
Herr Field Marshal for signature." Hitler finally appeared to
be acknowledging not only his accountability to the Reichstag but ultimately to Hindenburg. As Hindenburg nodded
with solemn but seemingly beneficent approval, Meissner
could not help but notice a slightly bemused smile cross the
old man's face. Hindenburg rose to his feet. The meeting

had ended. Meissner escorted Hitler out the door. After the meeting, Hindenburg wondered with Meissner whether "the man was gradually coming to his senses." The encounter left Hitler perplexed. He told his lieutenants, "It is impossible to draw any definitive conclusion with all the contradictory messages coming from the Wilhelmstrasse."

On Monday morning, Hitler returned to Hindenburg's office for a follow-up meeting, this time with a three-page typewritten letter—single-spaced, signed, and dated—detailing his conditions for assuming the chancellorship. Hitler did not want a repeat of August 13 with competing versions of the exchange. Hitler lambasted Papen, lamented the crisis in the country, again presented himself as the only political figure with broad public support, and warned the aging field marshal that a government could not be sustained on the "tips of bayonets." The meeting lasted just fifteen minutes.

There followed an exchange of letters, shuttled on foot across the Wilhelmplatz between the Kaiserhof and the Reich Chancellery. *Vorwärts* wrote of top secret "love letters between the Kaiserhof and Wilhelmstrasse." Hugenberg's Telegraph Union, always in the know, reported that Göring hand-delivered a letter at eight o'clock on Monday evening. By Thursday, Hindenburg had lost patience and confidence. Meissner dispatched a brief note to Hitler: "The Reich president fears that a presidial cabinet led by you would inevitably lead to a party dictatorship with all the attendant consequences of a dangerous exacerbation of the polarization among the German people, which he cannot justify before his oath or his conscience." Meissner then released the entire exchange of letters to the press.

"Hitler had been knocking on the door to power since 1923," the *Vossische Zeitung* wrote. "First he tried to open it by force with his November Putsch in Munich." Then he tried through legal means. Now, when the door was opened wide to him, he turned away. Apparently Hitler was "born" to spend his career knocking on doors, the journalist wrote. *The New York Times* reported the "prevalent view" that Hitler had irrevocably "put himself out of the running by holding out, in substance, if not in so many words, for full power." Louis Lochner watched with glee as the field marshal outmaneuvered the frontline corporal. "It was most amusing to see old Hindy take Adolf out for a ride during the last week [*sic*] of November, and put him in a beautiful hole," Lochner wrote.

Hindenburg had decided to appoint Schleicher chancellor. Goebbels suspected subterfuge. "One cannot shake the feeling that General Schleicher used the negotiations to get rid of us once and for all," he wrote. Hitler agreed. "In calling me to Berlin to cooperate in settling the government crisis, nothing was really intended but to save the Papen cabinet and give me a repetition of August 13," Hitler informed his party leaders. He added ominously, "This system must be smashed if the German nation is not to be destroyed. The fight goes on."

CHAPTER 14

CLUELESS

His lieutenants are clueless only because he is clueless.

—*Vorwärts*, NOVEMBER 30, 1932

"You cannot rule a country against the will of 90 percent of the people," Hitler told Tom Delmer in a vast exaggeration. "It would be impossible in Britain; it is just as impossible here." Perhaps a government in Russia could be "sustained on the tips of bayonets," Hitler continued, but never in Germany. It was November 27, a week after his second Hindenburg debacle, and Hitler was meeting with the head of the *Daily Express*'s Berlin bureau, in Weimar. Hitler knew he could rely on Delmer for good press. Delmer's boss, Lord Rothermere, had traveled to Munich in September 1930 to meet Hitler. "These young Germans have discovered, as I am glad to note, what the young men and women of England are discovering, that it is no good trusting the old politicians," Rothermere said after the meeting. Delmer delivered the sort of copy Rothermere wanted and Hitler craved. He conveyed the fanatic loyalty of Hitler's followers and provided verbatim accounts of the "campaign of terrorism repressions, restriction, lies and calumnies" directed against Hitler by men who were clinging to power "for the sake of personal profit." In return, Hitler sent Delmer notes on personal letterhead with his direct telephone number: 50 1 05 07. He hosted him at Haus Wachenfeld. He took him on airplane rides.

On this last Sunday in November, the party's top brass—Goebbels, Göring, and Frick foremost among them—gathered in the storied Hotel Elephant in Weimar. Hitler was holding a series of rallies in advance of a state election scheduled for the following Sunday. In an age before national polling, local elections were used as a "barometer" of public sentiment. In the elections in the state of Thuringia, one of the bastions of National Socialist support, the state capital of Weimar had delivered 28,072 votes in July, nearly 40 percent of the electorate, but only 20,570 in November. Hitler was there to buck up the vote. It seemed to be working. "In the evening, the Führer and I spoke in the jam-packed Weimar-Halle. This time, the mood, compared to August 13, was indescribably enthusiastic," Goebbels wrote in his diary. "As long as the party doesn't split, we will definitely win the game."

But Delmer sensed that Hitler was not his usual animated self. He spoke in a slow, extended monologue, with frequent asides and diversions. When Delmer asked Hitler if he thought there had been any chance of forming a new cabinet during his recent negotiations with Hindenburg, Hitler said, "Never once. I knew from the outset that thing was a great farce rigged up to deceive the German people into believing that it was having fair play. Well, their plan failed. I was not deceived, nor were the German people." As they talked, Hitler suddenly posed his own question to Delmer, off the record. "Look, I have been told that the English government would like to see the monarchy restored here in Germany and would appreciate my support with such a restoration," Hitler said. "Do you know anything about it? Is that really the view of your government?" Delmer was nonplussed. He told Hitler he had never heard such a thing and could not imagine it being true. "True, true, Germany would go up in flames if someone would try to bring back the Hohenzollerns," Hitler said. Hitler continued, still off the record, that he had absolutely no intention of restoring the monarchy, even though Crown Prince Wilhelm had publicly declared his allegiance to him. "And I certainly have no intention," he added, "to act as a racehorse for an imperial jockey who wants to jump on my back the minute I cross the finish line." Hitler returned to the matters at hand. He predicted dire winter months ahead. "Unemployment will increase this winter," he told Delmer. "There will be grave social unrest, giant strikes and the like. Most important, the government is faced with a catastrophic breakdown of its financial and economic plans; it cannot survive this and it is coming soon."

Delmer found Hitler defensive, depressed, distracted, besieged. "Hitler's reputation was on the wane. He had broken with the leaders of the German [nationalists], who now supported Papen and Schleicher. Hugenberg had withdrawn the support of his journalistic apparatus," Delmer later recalled. But even as Hitler sat with Delmer, offering his wearied belligerence and tattered defiance, predicting an imminent electoral triumph that would turn the tide, he had dispatched Strasser to Berlin to meet with Schleicher in a rearguard action to see what still might be salvaged from the ruins of his political movement.

While we don't have the specifics of Hitler's conversation with Strasser, we can assume that Strasser had explained to Hitler the double-edged threat of voter attrition and the mounting debts. Like Strasser, Hitler knew that each election had cost them two million reichsmarks (more than 10 million dollars today). More consequentially, the elections were costing votes. Perhaps Fred Birchall was right when he'd suggested that 37 percent was their high-water mark. Strasser wanted to leverage the electoral gains and secure a National Socialist foothold in government before there was any further voter attrition. Hitler understood Strasser's utility. He was easy, charming, confidence inspiring. If Hitler's defining gesture was the stiff-armed fascist salute, Strasser's was the firm, deal-closing handshake.

Hindenburg had charged his defense minister, Schleicher, with conducting exploratory discussions with potential coalition partners. Hindenburg knew no one would meet with Papen, who was now serving as caretaker chancellor until the Reich president identified a successor. By Monday, November 28, Schleicher had already consulted with several party leaders, and he was now scheduled to see Strasser the next morning for what promised to be a potential game-changing meeting. A front-page cartoon in *Vorwärts* shows Strasser, bare-chested with muscles flexed, preparing to hoist a "he-man"-sized weight with the words "Reich Government," while Hitler, stooped and clutching a cane, hobbles into oblivion.

Strasser knew that Hindenburg was willing to offer as many as three cabinet seats to National Socialists, possibly Frick or Göring as minister of labor, and Strasser as vice chancellor. Strasser could offer a face-saving solution to Hitler's maximalist demands, as political commentator Konrad Heiden observed. In a commentary titled "*Schach oder matt?*," a play on the German word for "checkmate," Heiden suggested that Hitler had exhausted his political options through intransigence and brinkmanship, having rejected both the chancellorship as well as the continuing possibility of partial power in the state of Prussia." But Strasser knew there were constraints, as did everyone else. The *Vossische Zeitung* wrote that Tuesday morning, "There were already reports yesterday that Hitler has sent Delegate Strasser to Berlin, with explicit instructions not to agree to anything, be it tolerance of the Schleicher cabinet or the agreement to a political armistice for the winter months." Within hours, Strasser had canceled the meeting. He informed Schleicher that "he did not have the mandate to negotiate." If Schleicher wanted to strike a deal, he needed to meet with Hitler. Then came word that Hitler would be on the Tuesday overnight train from Munich to Berlin to negotiate personally with Schleicher.

Strasser was accustomed to being upstaged and publicly humiliated by Hitler. In 1926, at a party conference in Bamberg, he had presented a socialist-leaning political agenda that Strasser and his young assistant, Josef Goebbels, had framed. Hitler denounced the plan as "treason" and demanded adherence to the party's original twenty-five principles. Strasser acquiesced. Goebbels bolted, abandoning Strasser for Hitler, who made him gauleiter for Berlin. "The result of this brilliant stroke was that Gregor's former private secretary assumed a degree of authority over us," recalled Strasser's brother Otto.

When Strasser was invited by Thyssen to speak in Düsseldorf in January 1932, Thyssen happened to mention the event to Hitler. "I think it would be better if I came myself," Hitler had said. Strasser obediently stepped aside. But loyalty was not to be mistaken for fealty. Goebbels, however, practiced blind reverence. "Adolf Hitler, I love you because you are both great and simple at the same time, what one calls a genius," he once wrote. Göring was the doting courtier—suave, well-connected—serving as liaison to Lufthansa, Swedish banks, and the court of the exiled kaiser. Röhm was Hitler's attack dog. Gregor Strasser was different. As a clear-eyed *Realpolitiker*, he exercised pragmatic loyalty to Hitler for the broader sake of their political movement, willingly suppressing emotions and ego to advance the National Socialist cause. Less than a year later, Strasser once again quietly acquiesced to Hitler, only this time it made front-page news.

"In response to Gregor Strasser's announcement that he is not authorized to engage in negotiations with the government, that Hitler and only Hitler is available to meet with the defense minister," the *Vossische Zeitung* reported, "General Schleicher has invited the National Socialist leader to a meeting." The Wednesday morning headline announced, "Hitler Meets with Schleicher Today."

*

On Tuesday night, Hitler had boarded a sleeper car on the overnight train from Munich to Berlin in the company of Röhm and Werner von Zengen. Zengen was a trusted Schleicher associate who had been dispatched by the Reichswehr to accompany Hitler to Berlin. Hitler gave instructions that he wanted to be awakened shortly before the train's 8:01 a.m. arrival at Berlin's Anhalter train station, where Strasser and Frick were scheduled to be waiting, along with Walther von Etzdorf, another trusted Schleicher associate. From "reliable sources," Hugenberg's Telegraph Union already knew that "Hitler should arrive around 9 [*sic*] o'clock in Berlin with the meeting following immediately afterward so that the Reich president can be informed of the results of the discussions toward midday." Otto Meissner was on confidential terms with Reinhold Quaatz, a German Nationalist delegate to the Reichstag. Quaatz, in turn, was on confidential terms with Hugenberg, which may explain the Telegraph Union's capacity for breaking news.

In fact, Hitler never arrived. It was reported that as the train made a brief stop in Jena, at 5:22 a.m., there was shuffling in the corridors, followed by thick-fisted pounding on Hitler's compartment door. Given that Hitler's travel plans had appeared in the press, it was reported that he had possibly feared saboteurs or assassins. "After several tense seconds Hitler appeared half dressed in the doorway and recognized that the intruder was none other than Reichstag president Göring," the *Vossische Zeitung* later wrote. Göring informed Hitler that Goebbels was waiting for him in Weimar, that the trip to Berlin should be canceled. Hitler closed his compartment door and reappeared a few minutes later fully dressed. Awakened by the tumult in the corridor, Röhm scrambled to join them.

Strasser, Frick, and Etzdorf were waiting on the platform at the station when the train arrived without Hitler. Strasser rushed back to his hotel and began making phone calls, only to learn that Göring had intercepted Hitler in Jena and spirited him to Weimar, where Göring and Goebbels convinced him to cancel the meeting with Schleicher. "Furious, Strasser and Frick threw themselves into a car and raced at 100 kilometers an hour to Weimar," according to one account. By late afternoon, Göring's Jena interception had made headlines.

"It is not exactly earth-shattering but then again not completely unimportant that among the National Socialists there is a struggle over the soul of their Führer," the *Vossische Zeitung* reported. "The willingness of Strasser and Frick to enter into a coalition government stands in opposition to the intransigence of Goebbels and Göring." The article was headlined "*Unterhosenszene,*" referring to Hitler's "underwear scene." Parodying the title of a published collection of Hitler photographs by Heinrich Hoffmann, intended to portray the Nazi leader in informal settings, *Vorwärts* ran the headline "Hitler as you've never seen him."

Instead of leaving the story to be buried in the next day's newsprint, the Brown House drew further attention to Hitler's Jena abduction with public denial. "It is not true that Adolf Hitler boarded the Berlin D-Train with SA Chief Röhm and gave instructions to be awakened shortly before Berlin," the disclaimer read. "What is true is SA Chief Röhm was not even in the company of Adolf Hitler"—and so it went with denials about the scheduled Schleicher meeting, the Jena interception, the detour to Weimar. The incident inspired a rhyme that could be translated as: "Hitler's chancellorship is now sunk / Frick and Strasser are in a funk."

For all its farcical absurdity, Hitler's "underwear" moment exposed, both literally and metaphorically, the deep divisions within the National Socialist leadership. In August, *Der Funke*, a left-leaning legal journal, identified two factions within Hitler's inner circle: the "radicals," who insisted that Hitler demand absolute power, and the moderates, "with whom we also rank Hitler, those who are inclined to take the more comfortable and profitable path of compromise and coalition." *Vorwärts* noted a revealing comment from the *Völkischer Beobachter*—"There was one single anxious question to be read on all the faces: Will he remain hard and not concede?"—as evidence of a "power struggle within the NSDAP." Hitler denounced vehemently and repeatedly any suggestion of dissent within his ranks.

Perhaps most consequentially, as the *Vossische Zeitung* pointed out, the incident in the Jena train station suggested how easily Hitler's plans could be derailed. Hitler fashioned himself as a man of single-minded vision and purpose. It was a public construct that belied, in fact, Hitler's incessant shut-

tling between the competing camps within his political movement. Hitler had initially refused to enter into "horse trading"
over cabinet positions, then dispatched Strasser to do it for
him, only to decide to take over the negotiations himself,
only to postpone the meeting from Tuesday to Wednesday,
then cancel it altogether. It was indecisiveness masquerading
as political acumen, not a sovereign field marshal framing a
grand strategic plan for battle but the frontline corporal scur-
rying through a maze of interconnecting entrenched interests, delivering whatever message he happened to be handed.
As *Vorwärts* pointed out, Hitler's lieutenants were "clueless
only because their supreme leader is clueless." In his "underwear moment," Hitler revealed himself to be more waffler
than Führer. Or did Hitler know exactly what he was doing, as
Harry Kessler might have suggested, sowing chaos and confusion all the while with a clear-eyed vision of his endgame?

A cartoon that Friday captured the interpersonal strife
within Hitler's closest circle in all its apparent revelatory
awkwardness and absurdity. Hitler is being dragged from the
train half asleep by Göring in jackboots and a storm trooper
uniform. Hitler's hair and mustache are disheveled. His
spindly legs, covered with spiky hair, protrude from a thin
nightshirt on which he has pinned his Iron Cross. "Move it,
Hitler, you're out of here!" Göring orders. A befuddled Hitler asks, "What's happening? Where are we going?" Göring
barks, "None of your business! Your job as Führer is to do
what I say."

Der Angriff denounced press reports of the Jena intervention as "ridiculous" and a "pack of lies." The Führer had
never intended to travel to Berlin, it reported, where "political chaos" reigned. He was "calmly" continuing with his
scheduled pre-election rallies in Thuringia in the company
of other National Socialist leaders.

Whatever the realities, the news underscored the growing rifts among the senior Hitler advisers who assembled in Weimar's Hotel Elephant that morning. Göring, Goebbels, Röhm, and Hjalmar Schacht held to the *"alles oder nichts"* strategy. Schacht, the former head of the national bank, saw Hitler as the only bulwark against Bolshevism. Strasser restated his belief that the November election results and party finances made it imperative that they begin exploring modalities for joining a coalition government. "Strasser is for coalition. Otherwise sees no hope. Hitler strong against him. Remains unmoved," Goebbels noted. Goebbels and Göring "seconded" Hitler's position, as did Schacht. Frick hedged.

In the midst of their deliberations, a telegram arrived from Berlin. Meissner said that Hindenburg was requesting a meeting with Hitler. Hitler stonewalled. "Since I have already presented my position both verbally and in writing to the Reich president and to the public, and having diligently examined my initial position, I have nothing further to add," Hitler wrote in a carefully worded telegram. Besides, Hitler added, a visit to Berlin would be "very difficult" in the run-up to the Sunday elections in Thuringia. Hitler's rebuke was followed by a similar request from Schleicher. Hitler parried again. "Schleicher's move blocked," Goebbels wrote. "Now he's getting very tired." Hitler knew they were desperate. Göring followed Schleicher's query with a phone call to Berlin. He suggested Schleicher send an envoy to Weimar for exploratory discussions.

On Thursday, Schleicher dispatched his adjutant, Eugen Ott, to the Hotel Elephant. Hitler demanded amnesty for imprisoned storm troopers, a postponement of the Reichstag until after the holidays, and the rescinding of emergency decrees. Otherwise, he would unleash his storm troopers. Hitler was playing hardball. "We've got the upper hand,"

Goebbels noted. After a bruising three-hour tirade, Ott returned to Berlin and reported to Schleicher on the security threat.

Back in September, Hammerstein, the Reichswehr chief of staff, had staged war games based on a theoretical attack on Berlin that involved an *Oderübergang*, or a crossing of the Oder River. The Red Army, commanded by General Fedor von Bock, was to attack Berlin from the east. The Blue Army, commanded by General Gerd von Rundstedt, was to hold a defensive line along the Oder River. "In order to approximate as nearly as possible to reality, the Red Army is equipped with the latest motor devices, while the Blue Army acts in accordance with the conditions laid down by the Treaty of Versailles," an observing general noted. Rundstedt's forces were overwhelmed.

Part of the problem may have lain with Hammerstein. The maneuver was scheduled during hunting season, and Hammerstein, a passionate hunter, was absent during portions of the military exercises. As one critic observed, Hammerstein preferred sitting "in a hunting blind on stilts" rather than standing on the "field marshal's hill." Hammerstein's absence did not go unnoticed by Hindenburg, who later chastised the general. "The old field marshal had gotten angry with Hammerstein during that year," Meissner later recalled, "in particular because he knew how talented his chief of staff was and it annoyed him that he [Hammerstein] had an aversion to regulated work." Hammerstein brushed off the criticism. He warned against soldiers who camouflaged "stupidity" with hard work. "Anyone who is both clever and lazy is qualified for the highest leadership duties," Hammerstein said, "because he possesses the mental clarity and strength of nerve necessary for difficult decisions."

At Schleicher's request, Major Ott presented to Papen

and his cabinet a *Kriegsspiel,* or war game, outlining potential security risks that Ott had developed in consultation with
the Reichswehr and representatives from the police, the train
service, and the post office, which controlled telephone and
telegraph lines. If Hitler launched a violent attack on the
state, Ott posited, the Communists would respond in kind;
the trade unions would strike, crippling transport and communication networks; and Poland might exploit the opportunity to invade and occupy still disputed eastern parts of the
country. With the Treaty of Versailles restricting the German
military to 100,000 men, the Reichswehr could be caught in
a three-front war and overwhelmed. The country would collapse into chaos. "The excellent presentation vividly demonstrated the difficulties such an approach would have. It could
not be successfully countered by force of arms. All the participants had the same shocking impression," Finance Minister
Krosigk noted. *Kriegsspiel Ott* panicked Papen.

Meanwhile, Hitler was back on the campaign trail, with
three days to go before Sunday's election, putting his party's
final cash reserves into a bid for as many seats as possible. Hitler waved his defiance of Hindenburg like a banner of pride.
"I am declining the invitation I received as well as those that
I will be receiving to accept a few cabinet seats. They just
want to give me those so that I will keep my mouth shut,"
he said on Thursday evening. He was speaking to a crowd of
six thousand in the town of Greiz. (The newspaper *Nationalsozialist* reported more than double the actual number, citing
fifteen thousand.) Hitler swore that nothing could blunt his
resolve or divert him from his mission. Had he entered into
a coalition government in August, as some of his own party
members had urged him to do, Hitler said, he would have
been complicit in the "failed" Papen government. This confirmed to Hitler that only his vision could save the country.

"For thirteen years, I have followed its [the vision's] bidding, in good and bad times," Hitler said. "Should I betray it in the fourteenth year because someone promises me a position, a few cabinet seats?"

Hitler spoke for forty-five minutes, then drove to the nearby town of Altenburg, where another two thousand people were gathered in a large tent. Once again, Hitler said that he would not be coerced, could not be bought with a generous salary or bribed with an impressive title or position. He called himself a "prophet" for predicting the collapse of the Papen cabinet. He was not going to be lured into another failed government, he said. No one was going to silence him by placing "a golden lock" on his mouth. He would continue to fight. The word "surrender" did not exist in the National Socialist vocabulary.

Hitler repeated himself the following day, Friday, December 2, in Gotha and Jena, and again, in a final push on Saturday, in Eisfeld, Effelder, and Sonneberg. He urged his listeners to go to the polls and vote "not as citizen, laborer, craftsman, or farmer, not as Catholic or Protestant, but rather singularly and solely as a German." Despite Hitler's efforts, the *Ostthüringer Volkszeitung* found that he'd delivered a "dull, listless speech that offered nothing new." In Altenburg, several hundred people walked out of the tent even before Hitler had finished speaking.

"The Führer spoke today in Gotha and Jena," the *Völkischer Beobachter* reported. "Once again tens of thousands cheered, confirming with their enthusiastic applause just how passionate people are about the correctness of his response to the current political situation."

Election day, December 4, brought a surprisingly high voter turnout, as high as 80 percent in some districts, suggesting little sign of election fatigue. As the polls closed and the election results came in, the voters had indeed passed judgment on Hitler's political direction, handing him a loss of 160,000 votes, a nearly 25 percent drop since July, as voters returned their votes to moderate political parties. In the city of Weimar, where Hitler had told Delmer just days earlier that he enjoyed 90 percent approval ratings, the National Socialist votes plummeted from 28,072 in July to 15,778 in December. Another local election, in the northern city of Bremen, appeared to confirm receding voter support, with even more precipitous declines, from 1,843 votes to 894 in one local contest, a loss of more than 50 percent. Even student elections saw significant declines. The National Socialists lost six hundred votes and two seats on the student council at Munich's Technical University. At the University of Würzburg, National Socialist representation dropped from fourteen seats to ten on the student council as "the majority of the student body distanced itself from National Socialist brawling and terror tactics." "The situation in the Reich is catastrophic," Goebbels wrote in his diary. "In Thuringia we have suffered a forty percent loss since July." *Vorwärts* reported a "horrific bloodletting." By then, Hitler was back in Berlin, in the Hotel Kaiserhof, strategizing with his lieutenants on the opening session of the new Reichstag that Tuesday. In those same hours, Strasser was across the street quietly conferring with Schleicher, who was discussing the position of vice chancellor with him.

"The nimbus of the inexorable rise has vanished, the effects of sensationalist propaganda has worn off, the superlative promises now fall on deaf ears," the *Vossische Zeitung* wrote. "The healing can now begin." Sunday also brought the heartening news that Hindenburg had approved Schleicher as chancellor. On Monday, the stock market ticked upward.

CHAPTER 15

BETRAYAL

If the party collapses,
I will put a bullet in my head in three minutes.

—ADOLF HITLER, DECEMBER 7, 1932

"Tell your boss that Mr. Streeter has gone to see Mr. Creeper."
It was in the first days of December, perhaps Saturday but
most likely Sunday. The *Daily Mail*'s correspondent and Hitler sympathizer Tom Delmer was on the phone to his friend
"Putzi" Hanfstaengl. At Harvard, Hanfstaengl was known
as "Hanfy." To friends in Munich, he was "Putzi." Delmer
called him "Hempstalk," a literal translation of Hanfstaengl.
Delmer liked morphemic transpositions and espionage.
Hanfstaengl knew, of course, that "Mr. Streeter" was Strasser, just as "Mr. Creeper" was Schleicher. The German verb
schleichen means to creep or crawl. As the polls had been closing Sunday evening in Thuringia on yet another National
Socialist electoral debacle, Strasser was in Berlin in discussions with Schleicher about a joint political future.

For Hitler, the difficulty with Strasser had long been
discerning political pragmatism from potential duplicity.
Strasser never exhibited Goebbels's blind devotion, nor the

call-and-command obedience of Göring, a man of impressive stature and wartime achievement, but without vision, a paladin waiting to fulfill Hitler's every beck or command. Strasser practiced a noticeably calculated deference. He addressed Hitler as *"Herr Hitler,"* never *"Mein Führer,"* and frequently stated contrarian views or opinions, though he never challenged Hitler's ultimate authority.

Even as Hitler sat in Landsberg Prison, a time when Strasser had engineered his own release and reentry into politics, Strasser stated unequivocally that there was "one man who tirelessly works to reveal the truth to the German people and shows the way to a new, strong, and free Germany: Adolf Hitler." Strasser bowed to Hitler's authority two years later, in Bamberg, when Hitler rejected publicly and vehemently Strasser's vision for a more socialist form of National Socialism, as he did again when his brother, Otto, came into direct conflict with Hitler. On one occasion, when Gregor was away, Hitler called on Otto unannounced, seating himself at Gregor's desk, opposite Otto in their Berlin office. Hitler threatened to send ten storm troopers to pull him into line. Otto drew a large revolver from his desk drawer. "I have eight shots, Herr Hitler," he said. "That means eight fewer storm troopers."

In 1930, when Otto finally broke with Hitler, resigning from the party, Gregor was forced to choose his loyalty: his brother or Hitler. Gregor chose Hitler. That autumn, Strasser inscribed a book to Hitler "in eternal loyalty." "Thank God, we didn't lose Gregor Strasser, a blessing for all of us!" Hitler said at the time. When Geli committed suicide, Strasser was said to have comforted him "like a brother." Alfred Rosenberg, the NSDAP's ideologue, recalled that Strasser often closed his speeches with the words, "I fought as a Hitler man, and I will go to my grave as a Hitler man."

But by late summer 1932, Hitler began to have doubts. "For the first time, he [Hitler] spoke openly about the activities of the Strasser clique in the party. Here, too, he sees what's going on even if he is not saying anything," Goebbels observed. By September, Hitler was airing his concerns about a Strasser subterfuge. "I had a long talk with the Führer," Goebbels wrote on September 3. "He strongly mistrusts Strasser and wants to strip him of any power." But by September, there was nothing to be done. With the November 6 elections just two months away, Hitler needed every vote. On Sunday evening, amid the devastating electoral results in Thuringia, came the call from Tom Delmer about the Strasser meeting with Schleicher. Goebbels summarized, "That is nothing less than the worst betrayal of the Führer and the party."

On Monday morning, Hitler convened the senior party leadership, including Strasser, in advance of a general meeting with the election-thinned ranks of the Reichstag delegates. There is no verbatim transcript of the discussions that followed, but meeting participants reported sharp exchanges and clashing opinions as to the best way forward for the movement. Strasser and Frick argued for a moderated course, especially in light of the November 6 election and the Sunday results in Thuringia. Everyone, including Hitler, Strasser, Goebbels, Göring, and Frick, had done everything to drive the vote but to no avail. As Birchall had suggested, the German people appeared to be tiring of the Nazis. Worse still, the election campaigns had exhausted financial resources. Strasser feared that if Schleicher were to call for new elections, it would not only precipitate further losses at the polls but drive the party into bankruptcy. Strasser said it was time for compromise. Hitler would hear nothing of it. "Strasser argued that Schleicher had to be tolerated," Goebbels observed.

"The Führer clashed as fiercely with him as I have ever seen. As is becoming increasingly more frequent, Strasser painted the situation in the party blacker than black." No mention was made of the Delmer phone call to Hanfstaengl, not a word about the reported meeting with Schleicher. But fissures in party leadership were obvious to all, as Heiden made evident in his *"Schach oder matt?"* commentary: "Gregor Strasser considers it a potentially fatal mistake at this increasingly obvious turning point in the development of the party that the party leader [Hitler] would accept neither the authority over the Reich offered him by Hindenburg nor partial authority, which he can still have, over Prussia."

That evening, the newly elected National Socialist Reichstag delegates assembled in the palace of the Reichstag president, Göring's official residence at Sonnenstrasse 30, just opposite the Reichstag building, to prepare for the opening of the new Reichstag the next day. "No great movement has ever succeeded when it took the path of compromise," Hitler told the 196 assembled delegates. "The more circumstances press for a decision, the more one has to be willing to sacrifice to the fight." Hitler let it be known the party was at war. He spoke of battle. He invoked his favored Frederick the Great adage: "Whoever throws the last reserves and the last battalion into the battle," Hitler said, "wins at the polling booth." Hitler proclaimed the Sunday election in Thuringia a victory. "It is not true that the NSDAP suffered defeat," he said, in defiance of press reports and election returns. He told the delegates that the Communists were the ones who had actually lost. Compared to the Communist losses, Hitler said, the National Socialists had actually gained in percentage points. "In many communities the voting numbers had actually exceeded the last Reichstag election," Hitler said, which was, in fact, the case compared with the December 2, 1928, results.

"The National Socialist movement will not waver for even an hour in its determination and fighting spirit," Hitler continued. "It has the greater endurance and therefore will lay claim to the final victory." He said that "the power and strength of the NSDAP came first and foremost, in its collective will, in life as in death, against which all attacks will shatter." Hitler went on for a full hour like this, impassioned, unrelenting, unwilling to broach any opposition or compromise, condemning defeatists in the party ranks. There would be no talk of acquiescing. This had nothing to do with his person, Hitler said, but rather with "the honor and prestige of the party."

Hitler had written in the second volume of *Mein Kampf* that the highest priority—"*höchste Aufgabe*"—of the National Socialist Party was to guarantee that "no internal disagreements among members of the movement lead to a split [within the party ranks] and with it the weakening of the work of the movement." On this November evening, Hitler now sought to avert such a scenario. When Hitler had finished, Frick rose. Speaking on behalf of the assembled Reichstag delegates, Frick assured Hitler of their "unshakable and inviolable loyalty." Goebbels noted that Strasser sat silent, his face "turned to stone." Hitler told Goebbels afterward, "If the party collapses, I will put a bullet in my head in three minutes."

Riefenstahl saw Hitler in his hotel suite following the meeting. He was drenched in sweat from his tirade. He was still fuming. "Those traitors, those cowards—and this shortly before the final victory—those fools—we've struggled and labored and given our all for the last thirteen years, we've survived the worst crises, and now this betrayal just before the goal," Hitler raged. He paced the room, holding his head, not once looking at Riefenstahl. He threatened suicide then hesitated. He spoke of all those who depended on him. He mentioned Göring and Goebbels by name. He could not let them down. "We're going to keep fighting, even if we have to start again from the very beginning," Hitler said. But if the movement failed, if it disintegrated, he added, he would put a bullet in his head.

*

Tuesday's inaugural session of the Reichstag on December 6 began peaceably enough. The opening address was delivered by Karl Litzmann, an eighty-two-year-old former general who had displaced Zetkin as the assembly's eldest delegate. During the November 6 election, Litzmann had been pressed into service by the National Socialists and placed on the ballot in a safely conservative precinct in order to guarantee his rank as the eldest Reichstag delegate, with the goal of averting a repeat performance by Zetkin.

Reading from prepared remarks, Litzmann expressed wonder that the Reich president had accorded previous chancellors dictatorial powers. Just last year, Hindenburg had appointed Brüning. Then he'd appointed Papen. And now, just two days before, Schleicher—to rule the country with a presidial cabinet. And yet he had refused to grant Hitler the same courtesy and capacity, despite the fact that Hitler was the single most popular political figure in the country. Litzmann went on to fault Hindenburg for not eradicating Marxism and for not addressing the country's social and economic despair. He noted that there had been 193 suicides in Berlin in October alone. Litzmann then got personal. He reminded the Reichstag that it was he, not Hindenburg, who was the real victor in the last war, for having countered a Russian invasion. *Vorwärts* noted afterward: "The old Herr

Litzmann completely forgot that Germany lost the war."
Litzmann fumbled with his papers, appearing to have misplaced his last page, then ended abruptly. There was no
applause.

The Reichstag reelected Göring as Reichstag president
with the thinnest of majorities, then, in rare bipartisan agreement between National Socialists and Communists, voted
on legislation amnestying perpetrators of political violence.
The National Socialists' proposal that Hugenberg become
Reichstag "notetaker" was then met with gales of laughter
and applause "that lasted several minutes." An enthusiastic
majority voted for the proposal. Red-faced and seething,
Hugenberg declined the "honor." The house again erupted
in laughter.

Wednesday morning matters took a serious turn. When
the National Socialists proposed legislation to amend presidential succession in case Hindenburg was incapacitated or
died in office—shifting responsibility from the chancellor to
the chief justice to prevent an aggregation of power in the
hands of Schleicher—a Communist delegate rose to his feet
and denounced Hindenburg as the "president of a dictatorship," "oppressor of the people," "implementer of the shame-
ful Treaty of Versailles." The vice president of the chamber
called the delegate to order three times, then censored him.
The Communist delegates roared, "Down with von Hindenburg!" A protester catcalled from the guest tribune. Back in
September, the National Socialist Reichstag delegates had
been ordered to be on their best behavior. With the ranks
thinned by thirty delegates after the November 6 shellacking
and having taken a beating in the state elections in Thuringia,
the delegates dropped any pretense to decorum. As a Reichstag security officer attempted to remove the protester, several
National Socialists rushed to the officer's aid. Communists

bolted from their seats. A tussle ensued. Reichstag delegates joined the fray, which gradually moved from the plenary hall to the corridor, where a pitched battle developed. Spittoons and ashtrays flew. Wooden tables were hoisted and hurled. Brass carpet rods became pikes and spears. One journalist reported that "a wild fracas was going on outside between National Socialists and Communists." The Communist delegate Heinz Hörnke returned to the plenary hall after a few minutes "with a bleeding head." Delegate Hinrich Lohse, the gauleiter for Schleswig-Holstein, took a telephone to the head.

Reichstag security forces came under bipartisan assault as they sought to intervene. "Heavy injuries were suffered especially by the police officers, who tried to break up the fights," *Vorwärts* reported. After an hour, the Reichstag delegates returned to the plenary hall, bloodied and bruised, to continue their legislative deliberations. They took the decision to postpone their next session at least until after the Christmas holidays, possibly indefinitely. The raucous parliament made headlines. "WILD NAZI-RED FIGHT HALTS REICHSTAG," *The New York Times* bannered, reporting that "combatants hurled inkwells, phones and other missiles."

*

Hitler was in his suite at the Hotel Kaiserhof on Thursday morning when he received a letter, hand-delivered from a Strasser emissary, informing him that Strasser no longer wished to be part of a plan that involved plunging the country into chaos and peril just so that the National Socialists could secure absolute control, with Hitler as chancellor, and then work to rebuild what had been destroyed. Strasser was therefore resigning his party positions. He would, however,

retain his party membership, *Mitgliedsnummer 9*, and return
to the movement's rank and file. Strasser further informed
Hitler that he was taking a two-week leave of absence. He
concluded his missive by reiterating his commitment and
loyalty to the National Socialist movement and its goals. Hitler had seen this coming.

Bernhard Rust, the gauleiter for Hannover and Braunschweig, had already alerted Hitler to the Strasser letter and
briefed him on a meeting that Strasser had convened with the
party's ten *Landesinspektoren*, or state inspectors. Strasser had
created these positions as a way to oversee the other thirty-
four gauleiter spread across the country. Goebbels, the state
inspector for Berlin, had not attended, but seven others who
were in Berlin had been there, including Hinrich Lohse, who
had been hit with a telephone during the Wednesday Reichstag brawl, as well as Robert Ley, one of the two *Reichsinspe-
ktoren* charged with monitoring their fellow state inspectors.
It was a pyramid of accountability built on trust that was
based on loyalty. These were mostly Strasser men, especially
Robert Ley, whom Strasser had brought to the Brown House
to serve as his deputy.

Just as Hitler knew how to whip ten thousand party stalwarts into a frenzy in the Berlin Sportpalast, or five thousand
villagers in a wind-blown tent in a rural village, he knew how
to read a room. Hitler had browbeat the 196 Reichstag delegates on Monday, but now he modulated his tone to match
the disquiet among the seven men assembled in his hotel
suite. "If one individual turns disloyal and abandons me in
the most difficult hour of the party, I can survive that," Hitler
told them. "If you all decide to abandon me, my life's work
and my struggle for it no longer make any sense, and the
movement will collapse."

Hitler spoke in a subdued, serious tone. But there was

noticeable disquiet among those assembled, a general sense of discouragement over the Strasser resignation and perhaps even more so over the reasons for his resignation. Hitler possessed, as Kessler once observed, a "lightning-fast ability to assess a situation, and to react with astonishing speed and effectiveness." Hitler grew solemn. He spoke of his own demise. He envisioned a casket draped with a swastika banner as a symbol of the movement that would be buried with him.

When Hitler asked the assembled leaders exactly what Strasser had said to them, Ley took the floor as Strasser's former deputy. Ley had suffered permanent brain damage while serving as an artillery reconnaissance officer during the war, which left him with a stutter and lisp made worse by excessive drinking. Recordings of Ley speeches reveal a man sometimes struggling to navigate his thoughts through an alcohol-muddled mind. He frequently talked nonsense. He proposed introducing an "eight-day week" and claimed that after conquering Germany and the world, Hitler would invade the planets. Goebbels disliked and distrusted Ley. "Dr. Ley is an idiot and perhaps a schemer," Goebbels had observed. Goebbels mused with poisoned intent, "Is Ley perhaps a Levy with a missing consonant?" But what the addled lieutenant lacked in intelligence and eloquence, he now compensated in loyalty to Hitler.

Standing now in Hitler's hotel suite, the former Strasser deputy was focused, lucid, candid. Ley told Hitler that Strasser had told the seven *Landesinspektoren* that Hitler's *"alles oder nichts"* strategy was misplaced. Strasser did not particularly disagree with Hitler on the National Socialist political agenda but complained about the apparent absence of a discernible and coherent strategy for attaining power since Hitler's disastrous August encounter with Hindenburg. Strasser did not care whether they pursued the legal path to power, as developed by Frank, or unleashed Röhm's storm troopers in a violent coup. What Strasser could not countenance was watching the political movement that he had helped build over the past decade fracture and fray for the sake of Hitler's single-minded drive for the chancellorship. Had Hitler only accepted Hindenburg's offer of the vice chancellor position in August, Strasser argued, the National Socialists would have had the necessary foothold for the progressive seizure of power. Strasser was also vexed, Ley reported, by his exclusion from meetings with Goebbels, Göring, and Röhm. Strasser said he was resigning his official duties and taking a two-week vacation in northern Italy. He planned to return just before the Christmas holidays, as a rank-and-file member of the party.

Hitler listened to Ley in silence. He sensed the disquiet and doubt that Strasser had sowed among his seven *Landes-inspektoren*, who in turn were responsible for their respective gauleiter, who were in turn responsible for the eight hundred thousand registered party members, as well as the millions of voters. He knew this was a time not for ranting and raving. Hitler began with a point-by-point response. Had he accepted the position of vice chancellor in August, Hitler explained, he would have eventually found himself at odds with Papen and been forced to resign. This would have played into the hands of those, Hitler said, who claimed that the National Socialists were not fit to serve in government. Had Hitler entered into compromise with Papen, the millions of National Socialists who had placed their faith in Hitler and the movement would have felt abandoned and betrayed. It would have meant the end of the movement. "I refuse to go down this road and will wait until I am offered the chancellorship," Hitler said. "That day will come probably sooner than you think."

Hitler also dismissed Strasser's proposal of attempting

another coup d'état, as he had attempted in 1923. Hitler had no doubt that Schleicher and Hindenburg would not hesitate to crush any attempt by brute force. "Gentlemen, I am not so irresponsible as to hound Germany's youth or the war generation, the best of our nation's manhood"—"*das beste Mannestum der Nation*"—"in front of police and Reichswehr machine guns," Hitler said. "Gregor Strasser will never see the day when that happens." Hitler then turned to Strasser himself. He said that he had noticed how Strasser had become "reserved, somber, reticent" as of late. Was Hitler to be blamed for that? "How can I help it if Göring and Goebbels show up for uninvited visits more than Strasser?" Hitler asked. "Are these sufficient reasons for one of my most intimate and oldest colleagues to turn his back on the movement?" It went on like this for two hours.

Lohse found Hitler "quieter and more human, more friendly and appealing" than he had ever experienced him. He sensed that Hitler was seeking to untangle the confusion Strasser had wrought and to make a warm appeal, to talk to the men as "their friend, their comrade, their leader," helping to free "each one again out of the completely muddled situation that Strasser had presented, convincing them emotionally and intellectually." When Hitler approached each of the seven men individually, "The old bond with him was again sealed by those present with a handshake."

Fractiousness, divisiveness, and competition within National Socialism's senior-most ranks had long been evident to outside observers. "First it was Strasser against Hitler, Goebbels against Hitler, then suddenly Goebbels for Hitler and against Strasser," Konrad Heiden once wrote, noting that other Hitler lieutenants, like Göring and Röhm, were also entangled in intraparty power struggles, but all with the understanding that Hitler remained the unchallenged leader of the movement, with Strasser, as Heiden added, "the unquestioned leader of the party after Hitler." But what happened when the power dynamic threatened to tilt?

Oswald Spengler knew both men. The author of the two-volume landmark treatise *Decline of the West* was considered one of the leading conservative thinkers of the day. Spengler found Hitler to be "clueless, indecisive, in a word, 'dumb.'" He placed his bets with Strasser, as did Hermann Rauschning, the Hitler associate in the port city of Danzig. "Hitler's nature was incomprehensible to the North German," Rauschning recalled. Instead, he praised "the big, broad-shouldered Strasser" who was "practical, clear-headed, quick to act, without bombast and bathos, with a sound peasant judgment." Strasser drank beer. He smoked cigars. Strasser was a man, Rauschning said, "we could all understand."

The weekly journal *Die Weltbühne* had taken measure of the two men in spring 1932. "It doesn't require much prophetic skill to be of the opinion that in the not-too-distant future Strasser will press his lord and master Hitler into a corner and take the reins of the party," *Die Weltbühne* predicted. "Today he is already known by his most intimate associates as 'Gregor the Great.'" Strasser may, in fact, have been "greater" than contemporary pundits realized.

On Thursday morning, December 8, the Brown House press department issued a curt two-line statement responding to the Strasser letter that belied the internal turmoil in the party: "Party comrade Gregor Strasser has taken a three-week sick leave with the Führer's approval. Any other observations related to this issue have no basis in reality." The opposition press had a field day with the two-line explanation. A feeding frenzy followed. *Vorwärts* observed that Strasser had appeared in the Reichstag on Tuesday in "best Bavarian health" and wondered how "Hitler's approved illness" had suddenly befallen Strasser, and what "inventions" in the press were being denounced before a single article had even appeared. The *Frankfurter Zeitung* published leaked excerpts from the Strasser resignation letter. According to the newspaper, Strasser was fed up with the "radicals" in the party who were seeking to create "chaos" in the country and were willing to avail themselves of "brute force" to achieve their ends. They refused to cooperate with other parties on either side of the political aisle in pursuit of their "all or nothing" politics. Strasser had had enough of the likes of Göring, Goebbels, and Röhm. He had wearied of Hitler's "politics of lost opportunities." The article was titled "Strasser's Declaration of War Against Hitler."

Hitler spent a restless night in his suite at the Hotel Kaiserhof. An advance Friday morning copy of the *Tägliche Rundschau* left him sleepless and surly. The conservative daily had once championed him as chancellor, but its editor, Hans Zehrer, had turned on Hitler after his August 13 meeting with Hindenburg. Hitler called Goebbels at two a.m. and summoned him to the Kaiserhof. Röhm and Himmler were there with the offending article, which proclaimed "Strasser as the great man." Hugenberg's Telegraph Union added fuel to the fire, with details from leaks it always seemed to be tapping. "As we hear," the news service reported in its Friday morning edition, Gottfried Feder had also resigned out of "general dissatisfaction over Hitler's dictatorial demeanor and the lack of visible success in the NSDAP." The news of the Feder resignation was equal to, if not more consequential than, Strasser's.

Feder was "a man of the first hour," one of the seven people Hitler had found sitting at the table when he'd first entered the back room at the Sterneckerbräu in September 1919. "After I heard the first lecture by Gottfried Feder, I had my first inkling for one of the most important founding principles of the party," Hitler wrote in *Mein Kampf*. Feder railed against "Jewish finance capitalism" and "the shackles of interest rates." Feder helped author the National Socialists' Twenty-Five-Point Program, the "catechism of the movement." When Hitler promised "bread and work," as he did in his shellac-disc address that July, he was quoting a slogan coined by Feder. Now Feder too was reportedly taking his leave. *Vorwärts* reported on the fracturing in a headline: "Feder Is Also Rebelling!"

Hitler generally tolerated Darwinian logic divisiveness among his senior staff. Competition allowed Hitler to select the lieutenant or idea he deemed best suited to his purpose. It also kept political opponents, along with the press, guessing at his next move. With the Strasser rupture, constructive chaos became potential political calamity. The *Deutsche Allgemeine Zeitung*, a leading conservative newspaper, warned of "disaster for the nation if the largest right-wing movement were to tear itself to pieces." *The New York Times* reported that "the smoldering conflict within the Nazi Party has broken into flame." Seeking to quash rumors of a fracture in the party ranks, Goebbels ran a banner headline in *Der Angriff*: "They Lie! They Lie!"

*

When Schleicher offered Strasser the position of vice chancellor, he was acting on covert intelligence from a leak within the Brown House that had gone undetected by the fourth-floor Sicherheitsdienst, the Security Service, run by Himmler's young assistant, Reinhard Heydrich. Along with maintaining a "card system" that profiled "every publicist, captain of industry, savant, scientist, and other person of importance as to his political opinions, racial origin, ability, private life," according to Louis Lochner, "down to the smallest village constable," the twenty-eight-year-old Heydrich oversaw a network of operatives intended to ferret out spies and traitors, but had missed Schleicher's well-placed mole. Schleicher knew his game.

Schleicher deployed information the way other generals used sharpshooters, machine guns, or heavy artillery, taking aim at the enemy and employing whatever weapon was most effective. Heinrich Brüning, whose chancellorship had been upended by Schleicher, spoke of the general's masterful use of "*divide et impera*" strategy, to divide and conquer. Treviranus, who lost his cabinet post when Schleicher toppled Brüning, called the general a "master of counterintelligence and surveillance." Schleicher was adept with the anonymous leak, knowing how much or how little information to release, whether in poisonous drips or flooding the public space with distractions and disinformation. He would target military rivals within the defense ministry with the same calculating ruthlessness as political enemies.

Werner von Blomberg had been the Reichswehr chief of staff, a former frontline officer who, like Göring, had earned the Pour le Mérite medal during the Great War. Blomberg was a general's general who focused his attentions on military matters and avoided politics. He had worked with Schleicher to develop *Grenzschutz*, or border protection, a covert policy to equip and train paramilitaries along the Polish border. In 1929, Blomberg sought to extend the *Grenzschutz* actions, which violated the Treaty of Versailles, to the border with France, against Schleicher's advice. Schleicher feared complicating diplomatic negotiations. When Blomberg attended training exercises with paramilitaries in the Rhineland in August 1929, Schleicher leaked the information to the press. Called to task by Defense Minister Wilhelm Groener, Blomberg assumed Schleicher would abide by the Reichswehr unwritten code of honor and deny the rumors. Instead, Schleicher denounced Blomberg, who was demoted as chief of staff and replaced by Kurt von Hammerstein, one of Schleicher's closest friends. "I was never part of Schleicher's inner circle of friends," Blomberg said afterward. "I never joined his fraternity of cultivated, self-satisfied old boys."

Along with the discreet, well-timed leak, Schleicher could flood the political landscape with information and disinformation, as he did repeatedly with the National Socialists. "You can no longer see your way through the whole mess," Goebbels wrote in August 1932. "Who is betraying, who is being betrayed?" Goebbels was certain of only one thing: "Schleicher is the pike in the carp pond," the wolf in the sheep pen.

As the crisis between Hitler and Strasser unfolded that December, Schleicher was apace with firsthand insider knowledge and actionable intelligence. "H. [Schleicher's shorthand for Hitler] has once again completely misread, as far as my knowledge reaches, the situation within his party," Schleicher's Brown House mole reported on Wednesday, December 21. "He considers Strasser a closed case, seeing in fact Strasser's departure as 'strengthening the party,' since it has helped consolidate matters, and has, as he says, 'liberated him from a nightmare.' In truth, the whole matter has caused him considerable damage and is by no means over." The two-page memorandum, written as a briefing paper and referencing Schleicher in the third person, had been passed along to Crown Prince Wilhelm of Prussia with the salutation "Your Imperial Highness! Most Serene Prince and Lord!," who, despite his public support of Hitler, was also serving as a secret courier for his long-standing friend Schleicher. "Kurt and Willi" had known each other since their days together as cadets. A brief cover note included with one briefing note concludes, "With heartfelt greetings, yours, Wilhelm." A royal mule for a Brown House mole.

"Schleicher's plans were simple," Otto Strasser later recalled. "He wanted to get rid of Hitler while preserving the good and useful elements of National Socialism. He wanted a government resting on a broad basis, on the Reichswehr, the trade unions, and the intellectuals. Whom could he choose to second him if not Gregor Strasser, excellent organizer, true socialist?" Hanfstaengl agreed. "The idea was by no means so ill-conceived and amid the momentary demoralization and monetary confusion in the Nazi ranks," the Hitler adviser later conceded.

Schleicher's most effective intelligence was also to become his most public. On Saturday evening, December 10, sometime between eleven and eleven-thirty, Schleicher received a phone call in his apartment. Bernhard Wilhelm von Bülow, the state secretary in the foreign office, was on the line. Bülow had just heard from Foreign Minister Konstantin von Neurath, who was in Geneva seeking to lift restrictions on the German military. Neurath had detected a "shift in sentiment" on the part of the British, who recognized that the Treaty of Versailles had left the Germans, in Neurath's German translation, *"gehandicapt."* Following nine hours of intense negotiations, the French had now been moved to "accord" Germany "equality of rights in a system that would provide security for all nations." Neurath had upended one of the most onerous provisions of Versailles. Germany would now sit as an equal at the negotiating table.

This was followed four days later with news from the German ambassador in Washington, Friedrich von Prittwitz, of the "willingness of the American government to begin negotiations for a rescheduling of the debt payments."

Debt relief compounded the interest on the political capital earned on the earlier suspension of reparation payments. "The reparations were now dead, 'dead as a doornail,' as Dickens would have said," Minister of Finance Krosigk recalled. Krosigk had also framed a radical economic plan to create as many as two million new jobs, reducing unemployment by as much as 40 percent. According to journalist Hubert Knickerbocker, the plan allowed the government "to have [its] cake and eat it too." "The Government remits $500,000,000 of taxes to industry, yet the Government keeps the taxes," Knickerbocker explained. "This paradoxical process will be accompanied by the banks lending money to industry today with which to pay taxes a year from now." Schleicher just needed to bide time for the return of political and economic stability.

Schleicher secured this political breathing room when he convinced the Reichstag to recess through the holidays before reviewing his political and economic agenda. It was the first time since 1920 that a new government had been spared the ordeal of partisan debate or a humiliating confrontation, as with Papen. With the dismantling of the two most contentious dictates of Versailles, and postponement of divisive parliamentary debate, Schleicher had deprived Hitler of the tinder and hearth for igniting further political conflagrations.

On Thursday, December 15, Schleicher went public with the good news. In a national radio broadcast, Schleicher assured his listeners, with characteristic wit and charm, that even though he was a general, no one should worry about a military dictatorship. He informed his listeners that he was wearing a suit, not a uniform. Indeed, Schleicher said that he saw himself as an interim chancellor, in part out of respect for his predecessor and "good friend," whom he had been forced to replace out of political necessity. Schleicher had not even wanted the job, he told his listeners. As chancellor, Schleicher set himself a single, simple objective: to improve the life of the common man by reducing unemployment and stabilizing the economy. He spoke for an hour "in a quiet and even voice," according to Fred Birchall, that contrasted with the overheated rhetoric of Papen and the political tirades of Hitler.

Schleicher met with the Associated Press's Louis Lochner for an off-the-record discussion during those same days. "My policy is one of steadying the jarred nerves of the German people, and especially our politicians," Schleicher told Lochner. "That policy is succeeding. Take today: everything is quiet. Why?" Because, Schleicher told Lochner, he had succeeded in convincing the political leadership of the major parties, including Hitler, that they should make a "Christmas truce" and suspend the political infighting. "After the Christmas season is over I shall find other occasions for calling a political truce," Schleicher continued, "and before we know it, the whole excitement that has characterized recent weeks and months will have subsided and we can go back to our constructive tasks again." The Schleicher strategy was simple. "Ruhe, Ruhe, Ruhe," he told Lochner. "Calm, calm, calm."

CHAPTER 16

GHOST OF CHRISTMAS PRESENT

Strasser's Ghost Is Making the Rounds!

—*Volksblatt* HEADLINE, DECEMBER 19, 1932

Hitler was furious. "*Vorwärts, Frankfurter Zeitung,* and other newspapers are reporting that I allegedly said in Halle that Gregor Strasser had been 'punished' by me. I allegedly said that because I had shown great restraint in my first clash with the Strasser brothers, and I was now going to show no mercy," Hitler raged. "In fact, I had not even mentioned the situation with Strasser, not even the name Gregor Strasser." It was a week before Christmas, and Hitler was denouncing what he called a "witch hunt of lies," or *Lügenhetze,* to which he responded with a deluge of denials, obfuscations, and his own countertide of lies. He condemned reports in the *Frankfurter Zeitung* and *Vorwärts* about a supposed brawl between opposing factions—Hitler versus Strasser, SS men versus storm troopers—that had broken out while Hitler was addressing a meeting of local party officials in Halle. Hitler insisted that no Strasser supporters had forced their way into the hall. There was no scuffling. There were no fistfights.

"The streets did have to be cleared of rampaging Communists by the police," Hitler said. As *Vorwärts* observed, the steady stream of denials coming from Hitler and his Brown House press office on virtually any matter, regardless of how vital or insignificant, not only helped draw public attention to the incident but also had the effect "that many people have begun viewing these denials as necessary confirmation that the supposedly false news reports were in fact true."

The alleged non-incident in Halle took place on December 18, as Hitler was making a final round of speeches to extract pre-holiday vows of subservience and obedience from his followers. He had addressed four thousand party stalwarts in Magdeburg at eleven o'clock that morning, where he spoke for an hour. The event ended with a collective "Oath of Loyalty to the Führer." Hitler then proceeded south to the industrial city of Halle, a Communist stronghold, to speak to an additional two thousand local functionaries. On arrival, Hitler's Mercedes was swarmed by 400 storm troopers, who attempted to divert their Führer to a separate meeting of disgruntled followers. Julius Schreck navigated the Mercedes through the crowd to the scheduled location, the Stadtschützenhaus, where Hitler was to speak at two-thirty p.m. There, Hitler talked about Strasser's temporary sick leave, then demanded the requisite vows. At that point Strasser supporters forced their way into the hall and began battling Hitler loyalists. Chaos followed.

Amid the scuffling, Hitler collected his loyalty pledges, then escaped south to Nuremberg, arriving toward midnight at a Christmas party for the SA Motor-Sturm M 2/4, where he delivered a brief speech, consecrated a swastika banner, then went to bed. He awoke to news reports about National Socialist functionaries "throttling" one another in open battles. "It shows how deep the differences are in the NSDAP," *Vorwärts* reported.

The fissures created by the opposing factions of Hitler and Strasser loyalists were widened by financial strains. "Strasser's exit was just the beginning. Who is supposed to raise the money?" the Brown House mole wrote to Schleicher. That same day, two storm troop detachments mutinied in Kassel when they were told to pay for SA supplies with their own money. Six hundred of them were expelled from the party. The detachments ended up selling three hundred tons of potatoes to cover their costs. In Berlin, eight storm troop detachments, 10,000 out of the city's 16,000 storm troopers, mutinied over shortages of funds. "The hatred is directed in the first instance at Goebbels," Hugenberg's adviser Reinhold Quaatz observed. "Unbelievable circumstances. The people are starving and still have to pay."

The Bendlerstrasse was fully apprised of the crisis. "The financial collapse of the Nazis is slowly assuming grotesque forms," one general noted. "Whole companies of storm troopers are mutinying because they are no longer being paid enough for their political 'convictions.'" Fights between SS and SA personnel, and fractures in Kiel, Flensburg, Neumünster, Schleswig, and Simtshausen were reported. Three Hitler Youth leaders in Halle had their houses vandalized, not by Social Democrats or Communists but by their own members.

A dispute over loyalty oaths in a Munich café led to a melee with broken table legs that ended with three men being carried out with severe head injuries. A fight between National Socialists in a Munich beer hall resulted in an SA man being pummeled to death with a glass beer mug. *"Es kracht und bricht"* ("It cracks and breaks"), as one newspaper reported. Local detachments fought and splintered. Chaos reigned.

The cause célèbre of this "foment and fracture" was the killing of Herbert Hentsch, a twenty-six-year-old SA man, who was beaten, shot, stuffed into a bag with his feet bound, weighted with rocks, and thrown from a bridge into a reservoir outside Dresden. Hans Frank brought the news to the Obersalzberg. Goebbels dismissed the killing as yet another "*Dummheit*," or "stupidity" by "our people." Hitler refused to believe it. "Those can't be SA men," Hitler said, to which Frank replied, "Yes, they belong to the party." Frank recalled Hitler leaping to his feet. "Get them out of the party now! Get rid of them altogether!" Hitler raged. He then fell silent. After a moment's reflection, Hitler added, "Sure, the Communists have killed more than three hundred of our men. It's all so horrifying." According to Frank, Hitler continued. "Will this torrent of blood around me ever cease? There has to be an end to this now!"

When Hentsch's mother sent a letter to the Brown House asking Hitler and Röhm for an explanation and a bit of sympathy "for a mother," she received a curt reply indicating that there was no record of Hentsch's SA membership. The press dubbed the killing "Potempa II" for its callous, unbridled brutality. "In Potempa the National Socialists murdered a son before the eyes of his mother, then threw his mangled corpse at her feet," *Vorwärts* observed. "In Dresden, a mother waits day and night for three long weeks," only to receive a letter from Röhm that states, "I am sorry, I do not know your son." The SA man suspected of the killing hinted that it had been a hit job ordered from above, then escaped to Italy. His disappearance was followed by the disappearance of his superior. The police scrambled to investigate. No one knew

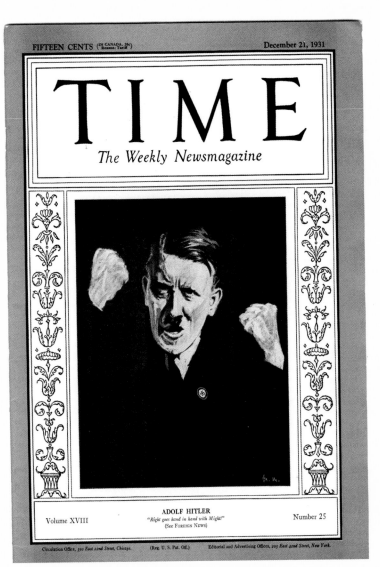

FIFTEEN CENTS (IN CANADA, 20c) ("Reason: Tariff")   December 21, 1931

TIME

The Weekly Newsmagazine

ADOLF HITLER
"Right goes hand in hand with Might!"
(See FOREIGN NEWS)

Volume XVIII   Number 25

Circulation Office, 350 East 22nd Street, Chicago.   (Reg. U. S. Pat. Off.)   Editorial and Advertising Offices, 205 East 42nd Street, New York.

Adolf Hitler vowed to destroy democracy through the democratic process. In December 1931, *Time* magazine wrote that Hitler was acting "as though he were already Chief of State."

Hitler ran for president in spring 1932. He lost by nearly six million votes but went to court to have the results overturned. Here, Hitler speaks at an April 4 pre-election rally in Berlin. Joseph Goebbels is in the background.

President Paul von Hindenburg ran for reelection to prevent a Hitler presidency. For the eighty-four-year-old incumbent, the April 10 victory was tantamount to a death sentence in office.

Campaigners for the July 31 Reichstag elections. Absent an outright majority, Hitler argued that 37 percent represented 75 percent of 51 percent and demanded the chancellorship.

Poftonfel Hitler.

clockwise from top: Hitler, wearing a hat in the front passenger seat of his Mercedes, departs following a disastrous meeting with Hindenburg on August 13.

Harry Kessler was a well-traveled count and dedicated diarist. He was on the Côte d'Azur when he learned of Hindenburg's refusal to appoint Hitler chancellor. "What now? Civil war or the inglorious disintegration of the Nazi movement?" Kessler wrote.

Eva Braun's attempted suicide on the evening of August 11 threatened to complicate Hitler's political ambitions.

Rejecting Hitler as chancellor, Hindenburg was rumored to have quipped that, at most, he would appoint Hitler as postmaster general "so he can lick me from behind on my stamps." This cartoon from *Vorwärts* is titled "Postman Hitler."

top left: Franz von Papen was seen as a puppet of Defense Minister Kurt von Schleicher. With the support of only thirty-two out of more than six hundred Reichstag delegates, Papen remains the most unpopular chancellor in German history.

top center: Schleicher viewed politics as war by other means. The French ambassador to Berlin called the Prussian general a *"maître de l'intrigue politique."*

top right: Otto Meissner was Hindenburg's chief of staff and a close Schleicher associate. Meissner played a central role in the intrigues and power politics of the day.

By summer 1932, Hindenburg was conducting government business from Neudeck, his family estate in East Prussia. From left to right are Oskar von Hindenburg, Franz von Papen, Wilhelm von Gayl, Paul von Hindenburg, and Kurt von Schleicher in late August.

top: Gregor Strasser was second only to Hitler in the National Socialist movement and was considered superior to him by some. *Die Weltbühne* called Strasser "Gregor the Great" and predicted that he would eventually replace Hitler as party leader.

left: Hitler invariably emerged from meetings with Alfred Hugenberg (left) in a "*Sauwut,*" or angry as a pig. The media mogul had the capacity to make or break Hitler's bid for the chancellorship.

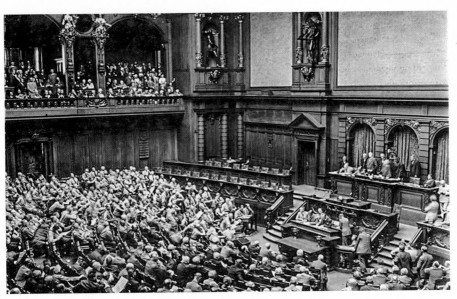

Hitler was able to gridlock the legislative process with 37 percent of the Reichstag vote. As an incoming delegate, Goebbels once wrote, "We do not come as friends, and not as neutrals. We come as enemies!"

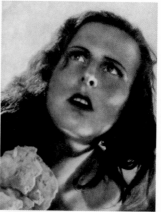

clockwise from top left: Hitler leased Lufthansa planes for the 1932 elections, a first in German politics. A film chronicling the July Reichstag campaign was titled *Hitler über Deutschland*, or *Hitler over Germany*.

Hitler met Leni Riefenstahl after seeing the twenty-nine-year-old actor/director star in her 1932 film, *The Blue Light*. Riefenstahl became a Hitler confidante.

Hitler casting his vote in Munich. The National Socialists shed two million votes in the November 6 Reichstag elections, throwing the party into turmoil.

SS guards in the Brown House, the national headquarters for the Nazi movement, protected the corridors but were useless against a Schleicher "mole" in the senior party ranks.

top: On learning that Strasser (front left) had been offered the vice chancellorship, Hitler convened a crisis meeting on December 7. Hitler told Riefenstahl afterward that he would shoot himself if his movement collapsed.

right: "The year 1932 has been one long streak of bad luck," Goebbels wrote in his diary over the Christmas holiday on the Obersalzberg. Hitler with Goebbels (center) and press spokesman Otto Dietrich (right) keeping warm near a porcelain stove in Haus Wachenfeld in early 1933.

Hitler staked his political fortunes on local elections in the mini-state of Lippe on January 15, 1933. The banner reads, "Lippers who love their homeland."

Der neue Hamlet

„Für Schleicher sein oder nicht sein, das ist hier die Frage!"

Hitler as "the new Hamlet" stands in the graveyard of his political movement as Schleicher digs his own grave and Strasser patiently waits his turn to assume party leadership. This cartoon appeared in *Vorwärts* on January 24, 1933. Within a week, Hitler was chancellor.

This still, taken from film footage, shows Hitler with his cabinet on January 30, 1933, his first day as chancellor. Seated left to right: Hermann Göring, Adolf Hitler, Franz von Papen. Standing left to right: Franz Seldte, Günther Gereke, Lutz Graf Schwerin von Krosigk, Wilhelm Frick, Werner von Blomberg, Alfred Hugenberg.

how far up the Brown House hierarchy the culpability would reach.

Der Funke ran an exposé implicating Hitler in the Hentsch killing. The newspaper reported, based on "material" supplied by "disaffected former Nazis," that Hentsch had served for a time as an operative in the Nazi Security Service—Sicherheitsdienst—run by Reinhard Heydrich from the third floor of the Brown House. As a Heydrich operative, the newspaper surmised, "Hentsch probably had such deep knowledge that after leaving the 'secret service' a radical form of muzzling—*Mundtotmachung*—was desired." *Der Funke* also found "threads" linking the Hentsch killing outside Dresden directly to the Brown House in Munich. "It is simply impossible that Hitler and his senior staff knew nothing of this murderous organization," *Der Funke* wrote. "Didn't Hitler for his part stand behind the murderers of Potempa?" The front-page article asked in a boldface headline, "Where Is the Indictment Against Hitler?"

Amid the rising chaos in the ranks, word had it that Hitler was backtracking. He realized that his movement might not survive without Strasser. Along with Strasser and Feder's resignations, General Litzmann had left the party, complaining that he had been exploited by the Nazis. The *Bayerische Staatszeitung* reported that Hitler and Strasser knew that they needed to reconcile for their mutual political survival. There were rumors that once tempers cooled, Strasser would return in a new position as "secretary-general of the NSDAP," with the mandate to negotiate with other political parties as well as the government, resolving the state of crisis in the Schleicher government. The *Vossische Zeitung* ran a front-page story suggesting the shifting power dynamic within the party: "If Strasser were to return, he would not come as a subject, docilely submitting to his master's bidding, but rather as the dominant force." The boldfaced front-page headline crystalized the crisis: "Strasser's Demands: Will Hitler Have to Concede?"

*

For Hitler, December had long been the cruelest month, a time of agitation, turmoil, and deep-seated grief. His mother had died in the night hours of December 21, 1907, following a merciless months-long battle with breast cancer. He had spent Christmas 1924, fresh from Landsberg Prison, listlessly listening to Hanfstaengl on the piano, slumped against his friend's wife. Christmas 1930 was fraught with family discord. "I am surrounded by idiots, yes, you are all idiots!" Hitler raged after a nephew gave an interview to the English press. "You are destroying everything that I have built with my own hands." A few months after Geli's suicide, Hitler spent Christmas 1931 alone with Schreck at the Hotel Bube in the Bavarian village of Bad Berneck. They were the only guests. Christmas 1932 was racked by political turmoil and headlines predicting doom.

That Christmas Eve, Hitler and Eva Braun arrived in Munich, where they attended a party at Hoffmann's photo studio. The next day, Hitler departed for Haus Wachenfeld, apparently without Braun. Angela did not approve of her forty-three-year-old brother associating with a twenty-year-old shop assistant who did not possess the appropriate age or stature. Hitler spent Monday and Tuesday on the Obersalzberg, alone with Angela and her younger daughter Elfriede, along with their three dogs and a cage of canaries, and a book he had been given as a Christmas present by Elsa Bruckmann, who regularly gave him books she thought useful or entertaining. While Hitler was in Landsberg, in May 1924, Bruckmann had written an inscription in an eight-hundred-page "introduction" to Kantian philosophy: "In loyalty that is so deeply rooted it can endure anything."

For Christmas 1932, Bruckmann gave Hitler a slender, 120-page treatise on the biological origins of leadership personalities by Hans Prinzhorn, who had already written on Hitler's rhetoric capacities. Cobbling together scraps of philosophy from Schopenhauer and Nietzsche, and laced with pseudoscientific jargon cribbed from Darwin, Prinzhorn parsed mankind into those with the inherent capacity to lead and those who welcomed subservience and subjugation. Bruckmann certainly knew that the Prinzhorn book was just the sort of Christmas reading that would provide Hitler with solace and reassurance in this most recent winter of despair.

On December 28, Hitler's archrival sent him a three-page letter and an olive branch. Hugenberg wrote of his "deep concern" about the long-term future of the conservative nationalist movement as a whole. He worried that the centrists were planning to siphon votes from the radical right into a coalition with the Social Democrats, tipping the political scales dangerously to the left, possibly into the hands of the Communists. Hugenberg's "deep concern" were based on rumors he had gathered over the Christmas holidays. On December 16, Hugenberg had met with Quaatz, who had met with Meissner. It seemed that Schleicher had not, as promised, advanced a proposal of a potential Hugenberg cabinet with Hindenburg. Hindenburg was cooling toward Schleicher and drawing closer to Papen again.

When Quaatz told Meissner on December 24 that Hugenberg was also cooling toward Schleicher, Meissner reversed himself. "This time, he did not mention any criticism [of Schleicher] and emphasized that Schleicher's star was rising [with Hindenburg]," Quaatz reported to Hugenberg that evening. Quaatz also informed Hugenberg that Schleicher was in discussion with the Center Party and the Social Democrats about a possible coalition, as a means of "distancing himself" from the right-wing nationalists. Worst of all for Hugenberg, Thyssen was threatening to pull out of UFA, divesting his financial stake of 500,000 RM, which had permitted Hugenberg to acquire the film studio. Hugenberg now feared that Thyssen would use the liquidated investment to bulk up Hitler's struggling political enterprise. But Hugenberg also knew from Meissner, via Quaatz, that Hitler himself was 14 million RM in debt. It was time to strike a deal and revive the Harzburg Front.

"History will find it astonishing that [the Harzburg Front] was missing at this most serious moment. Our internal and external situation is perhaps more critical now than it has ever been," Hugenberg concluded. "Therefore I feel myself obligated to suggest that we at least try negotiating one more time to see if we might not reestablish some form of unity." When Hugenberg had written to Hitler in the spring of 1932, Hitler had responded with his own typewritten broadside. This time, the Hugenberg letter was met with silence. Hitler had other plans, at least for the moment.

*

Goebbels arrived on the Obersalzberg a day after the Hugenberg letter, on Thursday, December 29, along with other Hitler lieutenants. Frank and Hoffman were there, as was Robert Ley, who had assumed Strasser's duties as chief of staff in the Brown House.

Hitler had spent the pre-Christmas weeks railing against Strasser in speeches in Breslau, Dresden, Chemnitz, and

Leipzig. He continued to unpack his fury on the Obersalzberg, not only against Strasser but also against Gregor's
brother Otto, who had developed his own brand of right-
wing nationalism that further frayed the party fringes. "The
Strassers have inflicted immense damage on us," Goebbels
noted. With his venom spent, Hitler turned his attentions
to his New Year's message. He tended to outline his talking
points on paper, then dictate the text while Hess took notes,
as they had done with *Mein Kampf* in Landsberg Prison, and
most of Hitler's speeches since then. It didn't seem to matter
whether the text was intended for print or pulpit. The mesmerizing rhythms and cadences that Prinzhorn had identified
were there. "Hitler has been dictating the entire morning on
his [New Year's] message," Goebbels wrote that Friday. "We
can hear him all the way over here. Will be good." That evening, Hitler assembled his guests for a reading of the first
complete draft.

"One day, the year 1932 will go down in history as one
of the great and successful chapters in our struggle," Hitler began. "After twelve years of fateful and uncertain battle our movement succeeded in its thirteenth year to strike
such a powerful blow against Marxist rule that the old parties of November [1918] were forced to surrender and abandon their positions in Prussia and the Reich and withdraw."
Never in history, he said, had a political party achieved such
unprecedented and unimaginable heights. As with most end-
of-year messages, the Hitler address was Janus-headed, with
a glimpse into the future and an extended retrospective gaze
into the past year. On this occasion, Hitler mused back to the
start of the movement with the fateful meeting in 1919 in
the Sterneckerbräu, and then the grim years that followed
the failed beer-hall putsch—"A sad time. I sat in prison"—
and the hundreds of "martyrs" who had sacrificed their lives

to the movement in the subsequent years, not to mention the "30,000 injured and wounded." Hitler recounted the myriad injustices and persecutions the National Socialists had endured, by the individual states, by the federal government, by the courts. There was a nod to the Potempa Five—"so mercilessly persecuted by the courts"—who had been excluded from a year-end pardon. Hitler tallied, then rallied. In the first six months of 1932, there had been bans on speeches, rallies, and uniforms, indeed a ban on the SA itself, and yet by July, the National Socialists had established themselves as the largest political party in the country. "If the last Reichstag election had been held just four weeks later, we would have had an even greater success," Hitler said. "Then this time as well my prophesies would have been fulfilled more than 100 percent!" In his campaign speeches before the July elections, Hitler had mostly refrained from anti-Semitic diatribes, as he had on his two-disk "Appeal to the Nation" recording, focusing instead on Communists, Social Democrats, and "November criminals," those who accepted the Treaty of Versailles. For the November 6 election, Hitler showed no such restraint. He railed against "Jewish-internationalist Bolshevism." He spoke of a "plague" upon the continent of Europe. "Either the German people will escape from the hands of the Jews or it will degenerate into nothing," Hitler told a crowd in Essen on October 30. Now Hitler ended the year with a broadside against the "Jewish press" and "Jewish Bolshevism." He then turned to Gregor Strasser.

Hitler dismissed reports of "revolts and insurrections" within the party, of "altercations and mutinies" among the storm troopers, not to mention "leadership conflicts" within the party's most senior ranks. He denounced the "flood of lies" as an attempt to "undermine and splinter" his political movement. When all had failed, his enemies had attempted to lure Strasser into a coalition. "We know our opponents and we know their thinking," Hitler said. "They involve the party in the government so that it will be burdened with the responsibility but without being able to determine anything." The party would become a "prisoner" to the system: either strangled by government structures and exigencies and forced to abandon its vision and values or, if it tried to escape, losing its followers, who would become disillusioned by their party's inability to deliver on its promises. It was an existential issue.

"When I resisted these temptations on August 13 and November 25, I made the hardest and most consequential decisions of my life," Hitler continued. He had never wanted to be considered a "statesman," he said, because statesmen were the "gravediggers of the people." Hitler was the leader of a movement, not a party, of a weltanschauung. He would not become beholden to a system. He would never lead his movement into a political trap and would never allow others to do it, either. "Anyone who betrayed the movement, who broke with its discipline and obedience, was from that moment on a dead man," he said.

"No reconciliation! Fight to the death. Down with Strasser," Goebbels wrote afterward in his diary.

The year 1933 would be the year of triumph, Hitler predicted, time to crush the opposition, to unite all Germans in a single nation, in a single race. "This has been the greatest task of our people for the past thousand years," Hitler concluded. "The movement that achieves this will engrave its name forever in the immortal book of the history of our nation."

The National Socialist press splashed the Hitler triumphalism across the front pages of its New Year's Day editions, while much of the mainstream press took a different measure of the moment. The *Vossische Zeitung* recalled

Hitler's disastrous midsummer meeting with Hindenburg. "Hitler's decline began with August 13, slowly at first, then with increasing speed," the newspaper observed, describing the "historical audience" with Hindenburg as "the turning point for the year 1932, possibly the turning point in post-war German history." *Vorwärts* announced a political implosion of unprecedented dimension: "A decline on such a scale, especially in its outward manifestations, which no political movement has ever experienced before." The *Frankfurter Zeitung* was convinced that the "violent National Socialist assault on the democratic state" had been crushed once and for all. *Volksstimme* ran the headline *"Hitler auf sinkendem Schiff,"* or "Hitler on a Sinking Ship." The popular weekly *Simplissimus* put it most succinctly: *"Dieses 'Führers' Zeit ist um"*—that is, the time is up for this particular Führer. A leading Italian political commentator called Hitler "a man with a great future behind him." Goebbels relegated Hitler's annus horribilis to the dustbin of history. "The year 1932 has been one long streak of bad luck," he wrote. "One has to smash it to pieces."

CHAPTER 17

HITLER IN LIPPERLAND

No, not till a hot January.

—WILLIAM SHAKESPEARE, *As You Like It*, ACT I, SCENE I

January 1933 was as cold as August 1932 had been hot, with temperatures as low as minus 30 degrees Celsius, or 22 degrees below zero Fahrenheit, some of the most mercilessly frigid temperatures on record. The Rhine was choked with ice, trapping barges and idling five thousand dockworkers. The nearly two-mile expanse of sea between Stralsund and the island of Rügen froze so solid that a "road" was opened for automobile traffic. Lufthansa made emergency landings on ice to deliver supplies to stranded ships. Berlin was "encased in ice." A corpse was seen frozen in a canal in the district of Spandau, but was churned into oblivion by an icebreaker before the police arrived. One national headline announced the return of the Ice Age to Germany. Goebbels reported "bone-chilling cold."

Hitler and Goebbels had parted company on New Year's Day, Goebbels traveling to Berlin and Hitler spending the afternoon alone with Eva Braun in Munich. They visited the city museum on Sankt-Jakobs-Platz and attended a performance of *Die Meistersinger*. Afterward, Hitler and Braun had coffee with the Hanfstaengls. Hanfstaengl had met Braun in the Hoffmann photo studio, but this was the first time he had seen Hitler and Braun as a couple. "She was an attractive blond girl, nicely shaped, with blue eyes, charming in her modesty and hesitancy," Hanfstaengl recalled. That evening, Hitler was as relaxed as Hanfstaengl had seen him since the early 1920s. Hitler hummed and whistled passages from *Die Meistersinger*. As they were departing, Hitler and Braun each signed the guestbook. Hitler added, "On the first day of the New Year." He said to Hanfstaengl, "This year belongs to us. I give that to you in writing." Whether plagued by delusional triumphalism or driven by fierce blind determination, Hitler entered the new year apparently undeterred and seemingly free of Strasser.

A year earlier, Hitler anticipated his potential election as Reich president and Strasser as his chancellor. The question of the party leadership arose: "Someone has to manage the party, either Hitler or I," Strasser had told one of the party's economic advisers Otto Wagener at the time. "If the party ever comes to power, the gauleiter and *Landesinspektoren* will become megalomaniacal." With Strasser gone, and with no personal interest or inclination for administration, Hitler engaged Ley to clear the Brown House of Strasser loyalists. "Department fumigated," Goebbels wrote. "A third have been let go." But Ley missed the Schleicher mole.

On Tuesday, January 3, Hitler held his first speech of the year, delivering a thinly veiled attack on Strasser and those whose faith in ultimate victory had wavered.

He addressed party stalwarts at the Brown House, lecturing on *Blut und Boden*, the concept framed by party ally Walther Darré, whom Hitler had tipped as minister of agriculture back in August. Darré defended *"Notzucht"*—literally forced breeding—or rape as a guarantor of *"Blutschutz,"* or protection of racial purity. Hitler said that "blood" represented the true "constitution of a people," defining it as a racial group, dictating its laws and structures, just as "soil" circumscribed its national borders. It was the constitutional duty of the government to protect both against foreign influences—purity of the blood, integrity of the soil. Extending the *Blut und Boden* metaphor, Hitler compared himself as Führer to a tiller of this national soil. "Just like the farmer who every year has to plant his crop and believe he will harvest it, without knowing whether the wind or weather will destroy it," Hitler told the assembled party stalwarts, "so we must have the courage to do what must be done"—and now came a jab at the weak-hearted and wavering—"even if success is visible or not."

He then departed the Brown House and was driven to the train station, where he caught an overnight train to the Rhineland, allegedly to begin his tour in the Free State of Lippe to drum up support for upcoming local elections.

The following morning, Hitler and his entourage deboarded the train in Bonn. Hitler had a quick breakfast at the Hotel Dreesen, then departed in an automobile with curtained windows, accompanied only by a chauffeur. "The destination was unknown to us," press spokesman Dietrich recalled. "The Führer had given us directions earlier to stay in his car without him and to stop outside of Cologne, on the road to Düsseldorf." Dietrich and Schreck waited in the penetrating winter cold for the next two hours. Hitler eventually returned in the curtained vehicle, then joined them in his own car. "We sat freezing inside the car," Dietrich recalled. "No one dared ask a question. The Führer sat silent again. We never learned where he was or with whom."

The secrecy was understandable because that day, the

first Wednesday in the new year, Hitler had met with Papen, the man he had belittled in the run-up to the November elections and whose chancellorship he had scuttled shortly thereafter. Hitler had a defamation suit in appellate court pending against the Stuttgart paper *Schwäbische Tagwacht* over an article suggesting that the two men were colluding. For Papen, the need for secrecy was essential because he was serving as a personal adviser to the new chancellor, Schleicher. Kurt Baron von Schröder, a financier and SS brigade leader, had facilitated the meeting in Cologne following a discussion with Papen at a gathering of the Herrenclub. What had appeared to be political disaster to most now looked to a banker like a promising investment. Schröder was of the opinion that business wanted a strong leader to come to power in Germany and build a regime that would remain for a long time. With this in mind, he had called on Hitler on the Obersalzberg the Thursday after Christmas. They had agreed to meet the following Tuesday.

Shortly after nine o'clock on Tuesday morning, Hitler ascended the steps to the Schröder villa with private secretary Hess, SS chief Himmler, and financial adviser Wilhelm Keppler. No one noticed the elderly gentleman with the camera lingering nearby. "Hitler, Papen and I went into my study, where a two-hour discussion took place," Schröder recalled. "Hess, Himmler, and Keppler did not take part but were in the adjoining room." The confidential meeting was intended to explore the potential for offering Hindenburg, yet again, a cabinet that could unite the conservative parties with a Reichstag majority, with the financial backing of big business as a means to stabilize the country and create a bulwark against the rising left-wing radicalism of the Communists and Social Democrats. But first Hitler needed to off-load his grievances. "Hitler raked me over the coals about the Potempa case and about the verdict I approved," Papen recalled. Hitler faulted Papen for endorsing the Hindenburg decree against political murder and upholding the convictions of the five Potempa felons, even though Papen had commuted their death sentences to life in prison. Once Hitler had finished his rant, the two men turned to the business at hand.

"Papen went on to say that he thought it best to form a government in which the conservative and nationalist elements that had supported him were represented together with the Nazis," Schröder recalled. "He suggested that this new government should, if possible, be led by Hitler and himself together." Hitler launched into an extended monologue. If he became chancellor, Papen's followers could participate in his government as ministers as long as they were willing to support his policies, which included the weeding out of all Social Democrats, Communists, and Jews from leading positions in the country. Knowing of Hindenburg's resistance to a Hitler chancellorship, Papen suggested that Hitler serve as vice chancellor, as Papen had proposed in August, or that senior National Socialists be given cabinet positions to pave the way to an eventual Hitler chancellorship. At this point in the conversation, Schröder came into the room and invited the two men to breakfast. While no definitive conclusions had been reached, it was agreed that there could be a chance for cooperation and that exploratory discussions should continue, once again in absolute secrecy, either in Berlin or another suitable place. Hitler and Papen each departed around eleven o'clock that morning.

The supposed secret meeting made headlines within hours. On Wednesday morning, January 5, the *Tägliche Rundschau*, a centrist conservative newspaper closely associated with Schleicher, ran a headline story of a meeting between the two sworn enemies, with photographic evidence of Hitler and Papen entering and exiting the Schröder villa. Papen looked dapper, with his signature walking stick and top hat. Hitler was flanked by his entourage. The press went wild. One newspaper called the images of the two archenemies together a "hair-raising improbability." The front-page headline of the January 7–8, 1933, *Rheinische Zeitung* read, "Adolf and Little Franz: Earth-Shattering News That Left the World Shaking with Laughter," beneath a photograph of the Schröder villa.

For Papen, the revelation could not have been more embarrassing. He said it was the "most awkward moment" and admitted that Schleicher's astonishment was to a certain degree justifiable. John Wheeler-Bennett surmised that Papen had been tripped up by "the itch of ambition" coupled with a "lust to revenge himself on Schleicher." Papen was convinced that Schleicher had been tapping his telephone line. Dietrich assumed they had been tailed. "Schleicher's intelligence services and his accomplices who followed us everywhere did a good job," Dietrich surmised.

For Hitler, the revelation was not only inopportune but politically perilous. "If he is sitting with Papen at a table, he can't swear that he has nothing to do with Papen," *Vorwärts* wrote, referring to Hitler's lawsuit against the *Schwäbische Tagwacht*. Beyond the mundane hypocrisy of domestic politics, the Schröder breakfast focused press attention on the precarious financial situation in the Hitler political movement and his questionable attempts to remedy matters via members of the Herrenclub. Hitler had long denounced and ridiculed these "fine people" who exploited the common man. One political cartoon showed Hitler on his knees, kissing the oversized stomach of steel magnate Thyssen. Highlighting Hitler's rabid anti-Semitism, *Vorwärts* dryly observed that Baron von Schröder was involved with "Aryan firms" like Stein, Levy, Salomon, and Oppenheim. One rumor held that

Schröder himself was "a Jewish banker and stock exchange king."

In an article titled "Swedish Money Pump," *Vorwärts* reported on Göring's meetings with the Swedish banker Carl Wallenberg, whose name, another newspaper noted, sounded "suspiciously Jewish." The most sensational rumor that year held that Hitler had received $10 million from "Sidney Warburg," allegedly a son of American banker Paul M. Warburg, followed by another 200 million RM (more than one billion dollars today), with the understanding that he would seize power only through legal means. An additional $15 million was said to have come from a consortium of foreign banks—a third coming from the Mendelssohn Company in Amsterdam, a third through the Rotterdamsche Bankvereeniging, and the final tranche from Banca Commerciale Italiana in Rome.

"I don't know what contributions he received for the Lippe elections," Papen said later. "Schröder, Thyssen, and others may have paid contributions, although it seems hard to believe that two hundred million reichsmarks were raised."

Hitler and Papen responded with a joint statement denouncing the "incorrect inventions in the press," insisting that the alleged meeting had simply been a casual conversation over breakfast. Papen awkwardly told the press that he was simply on his way to visit his mother in Düsseldorf and happened to encounter Hitler.

Hitler issued a fierce denial of everything. "In recent days, the government-aligned press has been systematically flooding the public with untrue assertions about the NSDAP and my own person," Hitler wrote in a press statement. He denied that his movement could no longer cover its expenses, that an industrialist had served as a middleman between him and Papen, that he was seeking financial support in exchange for political favors, that he had approached "a Swedish banker with the Jewish name Marcus Wallenberg" about a loan for four million reichsmarks. Hitler insisted, "All these assertions are inventions and lies from start to finish." In puzzling over Hitler's broadside denial, *Vossische Zeitung* archly wondered, "Everything isn't true, but what is true?" Marcus Wallenberg, for his part, patently denied having any dealing with the National Socialists, which was in fact the case.

For Hitler, the real measure of the potential political damage from the Schröder fiasco would be measured at the ballot boxes in Lipperland. Regardless of the embarrassment, for Hitler it was worth the price. Gottfried Treviranus recalled that "Hitler could breathe a sigh of relief because he thought he could count on Schröder's help to remedy the party's financial troubles in the long term. Schröder had raised Hitler's debt ceiling from thirteen to thirty million reichsmarks." Goebbels recorded the event in his diary: "Finances have suddenly improved."

Hitler had enough money at least to attempt to score an electoral victory in Lipperland, pouring his party's final cash reserves into a bid for as many seats as possible in the state's twenty-one-member "mini-parliament."

*

With 160,000 inhabitants, the federal state of Lippe, an obscure patch of villages and farmland tucked between the Weser and Lippe Rivers just east of the Ruhr industrial heartland, represented one of the smallest electorates in the country. Once ruled by the Lords of Lippe, the mini-state represented a rural bastion of centrist conservativism whose election outcomes were of no interest to a "single person" except for Adolf Hitler, according to the *Vossische Zeitung*. But for Hitler the stakes could not have been higher. Despite its size and obscurity, the Lipperland electorate was crucial for the National Socialists, especially in light of recent polling setbacks and losses.

In the last election in Thuringia, a province farther east, the National Socialists had lost 40 percent of the support they had held there in the July 31 elections. The *Vossische Zeitung* saw the results as a barometric reading of the country's overall political climate. "The election results show that the radical excitement that at times threatens to disrupt the very fabric of our state is on the wane," the paper wrote. It predicted that the "nimbus of unceasing success" had burst. "Mass propaganda has lost its sensational power; the most superlative promises reach deadened ears." A month later, Hitler turned his attention to Lipperland.

It promised to be a daunting fight. In November, Lippe had registered some of Hitler's worst polling results in the country, with the Center Party claiming 32 percent of the vote, the Social Democrats 23 percent, and the National Socialists trailing third, with 20 percent. Now Hitler mobilized his "brown legions" and "oral artillery"—*Rede-Kanonen*—to conquer the voters of this isolated farming community, without asking, according to the *Vossische Zeitung*, whether the locals needed or even wanted the "salvation" Hitler was promising. He more than quadrupled the number of planned campaign stops, intending to hold sixteen speeches in ten days.

For campaign quarters, Hitler and his entourage settled into Gut Grevenburg, the country residence of a local baron, Adolf von Oeynhausen, who was a National Socialist sympathizer. Hitler, Hess, Himmler, Goebbels, and Dietrich passed their days huddled in front of a roaring fire in the ancient and drafty country house, framing their battle plan. Dietrich remembered, "Each evening around six p.m. we would leave the castle and head out across the country for two or three meetings. At midnight or even later we would return to our idyllic castle. We managed to keep this beautiful respite top secret. No hounding reporters spotted us, none found our scent. We arrived and disappeared at will; no one knew whence and whereto."

Hitler's first speech, in the late-night hours of Wednesday, January 4, was in Bösingfeld, a small town with a population of four thousand, and almost four thousand more in the surrounding countryside. "When Hitler arrived at the lectern, the SA men fell to their knees, as if they were worshipping an idol, and stayed in that degrading position for a while," *Volksblatt* reported, observing that the scene felt like an adulation of Hitler and his party. Hitler spoke of the common man that evening, of the need to bridge class differences for a common cause, and how "the wall of prejudice and contempt must come down." He railed against the aging politicians, who had not delivered to the people, and spoke of his own struggle for the common man: "I have worked hard for thirteen years. What have they done? How have they made things better? Why haven't they done their work?" Hitler said that he could have entered the government on August 13. He could be sitting in Berlin at that very moment. Instead, he was here with them in a tent on a cold, wet winter night, along with them, in Bösingfeld. He could be chancellor if he wanted to. Instead, he was here in Lipperland. "[They can] keep the government, I am reaching for the people!" His speech was followed by thunderous applause.

Hitler then set off, with Schreck at the wheel, along a two-lane country road, through the chill and drizzle of a brief January thaw, past the town of Lemgo, through the village of Dörentrup, and arrived in Detmold, the capital city of the Free State of Lippe, just before midnight, where another five thousand followers awaited him in a tent. "If given the choice to become Reich chancellor or to recruit new people, then I choose the latter," Hitler told the crowd in Detmold.

Hitler vowed to fight in every street, every village, every town, every city across the country. He was interested not in titles or positions but only in people. Without the people behind you, you have no real power, he said. "And even if we lose a few percentages, it is important that we are the ones in Germany making history." He spoke of miracles. "Our hour will come!" he said. "And if our opponents say that our movement is losing ground, then I say, the wave will come! And it will begin in the villages. And then state elections will count as nothing more than markers in the resurrection of the nation." Hitler went on like this until one o'clock in the morning, then drove to his castle retreat, with its roaring fire.

And so it went for ten days, through the towns and villages of Oerlinghausen, Augustdorf, Kalldorf, and Lipperode, with only the briefest interruption for meetings in Berlin—a six-hour train ride away—with speeches in towns, villages, and hamlets in the run-up to election day. In the village of Leopoldshöhe, the site of an ancient Teutonic victory over the Romans, Hitler addressed another crowd of five thousand. "From this historic ground, we see again and again that over-coming inner conflict radiates power," he said. "Germany collapsed into need and misery because it collapsed politically. I want to eliminate this need, and I have to start here."

"Hitler Hits the Villages!" one headline read. Another reported "A Triumphant Victory March Through Lipperland." The *Vossische Zeitung* proclaimed Hitler the "Oracle of Lippe." The election was scheduled for January 15. Time would tell whether Hitler's efforts would bring results. Meanwhile, Gregor Strasser was back in Berlin for a meeting with Schleicher and Hindenburg to continue talks about his possible appointment as vice chancellor.

CHAPTER 18

THE STRASSER CALIBRATION

There have been discussions for weeks about the possibility of Gregor Strasser joining [Schleicher's] cabinet.

—*Vossische Zeitung*, JANUARY 14, 1933

Strasser appeared to have been stunned by Hitler's bare-knuckle attack in early December. "I ran into Strasser that morning when I arrived in Hitler's anteroom at the Hotel Kaiserhof," Alfred Rosenberg recalled. "I started to greet him, but he merely made a hopeless gesture with his hand and left the room. I heard that he had just resigned all his posts." Brüning heard that Strasser had stumbled out of the hotel and wandered aimlessly across the Wilhelmplatz. Of the nearly two hundred National Socialist Reichstag delegates assembled in the hotel, not a single one rose in Strasser's defense. Erich Koch, the gauleiter from Königsberg, offered a flicker of belated support. "However things may be in reality, one thing is certain: Gregor Strasser will never take a step which could be detrimental to the movement," the *Preussische Zeitung*, a Königsberg newspaper, quoted him as saying. "Gregor Strasser is also not a man who could easily withdraw from the movement overnight, he helped build it, and a large part of what happened within the National Socialist German workers' movement is forever associated with his name."

Wilhelm Kube was head of the National Socialist faction in the Prussian state assembly. Deeply religious and virulently anti-Semitic, Kube rallied Christian voters to the National Socialist movement. Kube called Strasser a "man of honor" who would never break his word: "He, in particular, one of the oldest warriors of the NSDAP, knows that the idea and movement are inseparable from the Führer." Kube said that Strasser frequently ended his speeches with the assurance, "I am a Hitlerman and remain a Hitlerman."

Krosigk had heard that Strasser was "deeply wounded" by Hitler's accusations of "deception and betrayal." Hans Frank visited Strasser at the Hotel Excelsior, where Strasser stayed when he was in Berlin. Frank knew Strasser to be one of "the most confident and pragmatic men" he had ever met, but on this occasion the altercation with Hitler had left him undone. "Hitler seems to me to be completely in the hands of Himmler and his sycophants," Strasser told Frank. "Hindenburg and honorable men offer cooperation, and here stands the 'Wagner-Lohengrin Hitler from the Wahnfried' with his shady guys from the Gralsberg," he added, making a disparaging allusion to Hitler's reverence for Wagnerian opera. Frank said that Strasser was dismayed by the increasing influence of the party radicals, especially Goebbels, Göring, and Röhm, over the movement's clear-sighted pragmatists like Frick, Frank, and himself. "Frank, this is horrific," Strasser said. "Göring is a brutal egotist who couldn't care less about Germany, Goebbels is a clubfooted devil, Röhm is a pig. These are the Führer's guards."

In fact, Frick was working to undo the damage. Feder had recanted. He denounced "inaccurate interpretations of my relationship to the NSDAP" and professed his "loyalty and unshakeable devotion" to "my Führer." For Christmas, Feder inscribed an advance copy of his latest book, *Battle Against High Finance*, to Hitler in "deepest devotion." Frick now sought to have Hitler reconcile with Strasser.

It was impossible to know, Frick told Hitler, what portion of the National Socialist movement consisted of Strasser loyalists. A complete break with Strasser, especially at such a politically and financially perilous moment, risked fracturing the movement irreparably. Frick urged Hitler to meet with Strasser and repair the breach, to reconsider the prospect of coalition government, the possibility of a Strasser vice chancellorship within a Schleicher cabinet as a foothold to power. Hitler acquiesced, and Frick set out to locate Strasser in what Konrad Heiden has described as "a series of tragic-comic concatenations." Frick discovered that Strasser had settled his bill and checked out of the hotel that morning, depositing his suitcases at the luggage depot at the Anhalter Bahnhof, then vanished. While Hitler waited in his suite at the Hotel Kaiserhof, and Frick vainly scoured the city, Strasser sat with a close friend, Ewald Moritz, a right-wing author who wrote under the pseudonym Gottfried Zarnow, before catching an evening train to Munich, and from there, departed for Italy with his wife and two sons for a two-week respite. "If Strasser knew how the entire party was waiting for him, how everyone was fretting and pacing their hotel room waiting for a miracle," Heiden recalled, "perhaps he would have stayed in Berlin."

Gauleiter Hinrich Lohse saw Strasser's return to Munich and subsequent travel to Italy as Strasser's final defeat. "[Hitler had] triumphed and proved to his wavering, but upright and indispensable fighters in this toughest test of the movement, that he was the master and Strasser the apprentice,"

Lohse recalled. "So he remained the ultimate victor also in this last and most serious attack." Hanfstaengl thought Schleicher had miscalculated: "He underestimated Hitler and overestimated Strasser."

On the evening of January 3, as Hitler boarded the train to Lipperland, Strasser was on his way back to Berlin. The *Vossische Zeitung* had reported, "The first round of the party's wrestling match for power is over, and if there's no mistake, the winner is Goebbels, Strasser's chief opponent." The article added that "Strasser has now lost his important post in the party; it remains to be seen what his countermove will be." Bella Fromm was delighted. "For a whole month, Gregor Strasser and Hitler have been at each other's throats," she wrote. "It is good to know that they are weakening the party by their constant frictions."

Strasser, of course, already knew what his next move would be, since Schleicher had offered to make him vice chancellor. One of the first people Strasser saw in Berlin was former chancellor Brüning. Strasser told Brüning that Schleicher had approached him about the vice chancellorship, the same position they had discussed in December and, before that, in August, before Hitler blew their chance with his meeting with Hindenburg. But now Schleicher was raising the prospect of a vice chancellorship yet again, only this time Schleicher was chancellor and not just minister of defense. Brüning told Strasser to be careful. Schleicher "is clever but not loyal," he said. "Therefore you have to nail this down in the presence of the Reich president. Otherwise I see a catastrophe coming not only for Germany but for you."

On the second Friday in January, Schleicher sat with the latest secret dispatch: a detailed briefing on the discussion between Hitler and Papen at the Schröder villa the previous week. "The aim of the discussion on the H. side was to persuade the Reich president, through Papen's mediation, to withdraw his confidence in the chancellor before the new elections and to replace him with some type of alternative scenario," the memo read. It questioned Papen's potential motivations for the meeting with Hitler. "If Papen is Schleicher's friend and an honest player, then his objective must be to humiliate H., and to make him do whatever the chancellor wants." That was obviously not the case. Papen had not informed Schleicher of the meeting. "If Papen is not a friend of the chancellor, then it can be assumed that the objective was the same on both sides"—i.e., the dissolution of the Schleicher government. The mole said that no credence should be given to press reports that Hitler might consider the positions of minister of defense, minister of the interior, or the head of the state government of Prussia. As long as the Reich president holds firm, the memo concluded, Schleicher's position would be fine. "If the Reich president doesn't yield, then the situation for the chancellor's government is not at all bad."

In fact, assuming Schleicher could bring Strasser into his government, and assuming Strasser could bring a significant number of voters with him, Schleicher could cobble together a functioning government with Reichstag support—also assuming, of course, that Hindenburg would approve Strasser as a member of the cabinet. Unlike Hitler, whose belligerent nationalism, hard-line conservatism, and vicious anti-Semitism allowed him to be easily pigeonholed within right-wing politics, Strasser was more complex. He railed against the Treaty of Versailles, the Weimar constitution, and alleged Jewish conspiracies with all the vigor of a right-wing extremist. He was a fierce nationalist, as he had demonstrated on national radio when he'd sworn allegiance to "Germany, only Germany, and nothing but Germany."

But he was equally passionate in his denunciation of the

"slave market of capitalism" and the "political domination of money" with all the vigor of a Social Democrat. "The German people are protesting against an economic system that thinks only about money, profit, and dividends, and which forgets about labor and performance," Strasser told the Reichstag in a speech in May 1932. It was the sort of rhetoric that unnerved the conservative center. Hindenburg had met Hitler variously in the company of Göring, Frick, and even Röhm, never Strasser. But Schleicher felt that offering Strasser a post was worth the risk. Hindenburg agreed to meet Strasser, albeit under strict, confidential circumstances, with no recorded protocol. But there was, inevitably, a leak. When news of the meeting broke, the presidential office firmly denied the assertion. It was, however, eventually forced to concede that the two men had met.

"The Reich president had the wish to meet the renowned Herr Gregor Strasser, and had invited him for this purpose a few days ago," the official statement read on January 11, 1933. "The Reich president declined to comment on what Mr. Strasser presented to him, and therefore did not attach any importance to making this known in order that personal conclusions would not be drawn from [the meeting]." There are no minutes or references in the official protocol, but the discussion must have gone well, as Otto Meissner, Hindenburg's aide, reported afterward. "Even the Reich president, in his conversation with Strasser, found nothing revolutionary to criticize in regard to his political and social views, and agreed to Schleicher's proposal to appoint Strasser vice chancellor," Meissner wrote. With presidential approval, Schleicher could now bring Strasser into his cabinet and, with him, the prospect of a cross-aisle centrist majority in the Reichstag.

Five days later, on Monday, January 16, Schleicher convened his cabinet. The prospective Strasser appointment topped the agenda. Schleicher underscored the fact that Hindenburg had repeatedly expressed his desire to establish a government with a "broad base" in the Reichstag. Schleicher believed that securing a majority would require a wide coalition, extending from Strasser's National Socialists to Hugenberg's German Nationalists and possibly including the Center Party. One cabinet member wondered whether Strasser was really willing to join the Schleicher cabinet and, equally important, whether he could bring enough delegates to secure a ruling majority. Schleicher confirmed Strasser's willingness to accept a cabinet position. There was no certainty concerning the number of delegates he could bring. One "optimistic" estimate placed the number of potential Strasser defectors at forty. These were thought to be National Socialist Reichstag delegates who feared losing their seats in tightly contested voting districts if the party held to its radical "all or nothing" strategy. There was another caveat: in the event that he joined the cabinet, Strasser did not want to leave the National Socialist Party but would reform it "in a positive direction."

Günther Gereke had helped lead Hindenburg's reelection campaign. He wondered how wise it was to appoint Strasser just now. He feared that Hitler would press for new elections to prevent Strasser from gaining traction within the party. Perhaps it would be more prudent to wait with the Strasser appointment. Perhaps Schleicher could convince the Reichstag to tolerate his government as it stood. Schleicher stuck by his candidate. Of all the National Socialists, he said, Strasser was the only one he could imagine serving in their government. He suggested that if Strasser were paired with Hugenberg, it could anchor the government within conservative circles. The Center Party might not want to cooperate with Strasser and Hugenberg, but Schleicher was certain that they could anchor a solid conservative coalition.

Gereke disagreed, arguing that a majority in the Reichstag would not be achieved even if the cabinet was reorganized according to Schleicher's suggestion. Schleicher conceded that a parliamentary majority could be achieved only with Hitler, but added that if the government was given time to show results, especially on the economic and unemployment fronts, it would effect "a gradual change in the mood of the population that would work in the cabinet's favor." Schleicher was buying time.

With Hitler pressing hard for new Reichstag elections, Schleicher knew he needed to make a case for postponement for as long as possible, ideally until the autumn. The ministers were skeptical that the situation in the autumn would be much different than it was currently. At one point, Meissner intervened to express concern that the Reich president could view the postponement beyond sixty days as a violation of the constitution. Schleicher told Meissner not to worry about Hindenburg; he had the old man well in hand. The cabinet meeting concluded with general agreement that one should wait to engage further with Strasser until after the results of the previous day's Lippe election.

When Schleicher informed his cabinet that Strasser would insist on retaining his party membership, he was speaking not only on the basis of his discussions with Strasser but also with regard to talking points presented by his Brown House mole, who had parsed possible future scenarios following the Hitler-Strasser rupture, with pointedly cautionary observations. Schleicher knew from the intelligence gathered that both Hitler and Strasser recognized their mutual dependency. That was why Hitler did not expel Strasser from the party, and why Strasser resigned from his positions but not from the party. As tempers cooled, Hitler and Strasser would find their way back to each other in a more tempered, less strident National Socialist movement. "I consider it a mistake that [Schleicher] still regards the movement as a single force in his calculation. If the chancellor is to lead a government, he can only do this if Hitler and Strasser reach some kind of agreement, in which Strasser leads the restored collective movement. That healing process has not happened yet," the mole wrote in a confidential letter to Prince Wilhelm.

To court Strasser and split the party or to let the party potentially heal and temper? That was the question, at least from the intelligence gained at the Brown House.

*

Beyond the political awkwardness of the Schröder villa fiasco, and the subsequent feeding frenzy in the press, not to mention anticipation over the ultimate outcome and potential impact of the Lippe election, Hitler had a more protracted concern: Who had leaked the Schröder meeting? Papen thought it was Schleicher. "Apparently he had my phone monitored to keep track of my movements," Papen maintained. Strasser's dentist, Dr. Hellmuth Elbrechter, who circulated in conservative circles and was a suspect, had helped facilitate the initial meeting between Schleicher and Hitler in the spring of 1932. He was now rumored to have learned of the Schröder meeting through either a patient or the editor of a right-wing newspaper, *Die Tat*, for which he occasionally wrote. Elbrechter had indeed called the chancellor with a brief warning: *"Fränzchen hat Sie verraten"*—your little friend Franz has betrayed you.

By then, Schleicher had already been alerted through a circuitous royal route. Hitler's financial adviser, Keppler, had mentioned the upcoming Schröder villa meeting to a Munich banker friend, who, in turn, mentioned it to Crown Prince Wilhelm. The prince subsequently delivered that intelligence to Schleicher on New Year's Day. Schleicher recruited a former member of his entourage, a retired military captain, to stake out the Schröder villa with a camera. The press did the rest.

Confronted by incontrovertible evidence—photographs of Hitler and Papen on the steps of the Schröder villa— Hitler did what he always did in the face of uncomfortable fact: he denied it publicly and vociferously. On January 5, in the joint statement with Papen, he denounced the "false assumptions." He claimed "that the discussions dealt exclusively with the question of the possibility of a large national political front" and insisted that there had not been any talk about an incumbent Reich cabinet within the framework of this general debate. As we've seen, Papen gave Schleicher a similar assurance.

Within a week, Papen and Hitler were meeting in secret yet again, this time at the villa of Joachim and Annelies von Ribbentrop, in the fashionable Berlin neighborhood of Dahlem.

CHAPTER 19

VISITATIONS

Papen visits Hindenburg, Hitler visits Papen, Hitler and
Papen visit Schleicher, Hugenberg visits Hindenburg and
finds he's out.

—CHRISTOPHER ISHERWOOD,
Christopher and His Kind, 1929–1939

"I recall with particular clarity that the meeting took place
on the night of January 10 to 11, 1933, because that was the
evening I met Adolf Hitler for the first time," Annelies von
Ribbentrop recalled. "I greeted him in my husband's study,
where he was conducting a confidential discussion with Herr
von Papen."

The Ribbentrops were among the Berlin social elite,
handsome, monied, and titled. Joachim had his pedigree
thanks to a midlife adoption in 1925 by an aunt, Gertrude
von Ribbentrop, to ensure the continuation of the family's
aristocratic lineage. His wife, née Henkell, was heiress to
a sparkling-wine enterprise, one of the country's premier
brands and a victim of Article 236 of the Versailles Treaty,
which forbade Germans to apply the term "champagne" to its
effervescent wines. Bella Fromm had known Annelies since
the early 1920s. "She was never a very bright girl," Fromm
observed. "The years have not made her any brighter." But

Annelies was stately, wealthy, and ambitious, considered a latter-day Lady Macbeth by some. For the eldest Ribbentrop son, Rudolf, who was eleven at the time, politics was as much a part of family life as his piano lessons. Papen was a regular guest, as was Count von Helldorff, who had fought in the same regiment as Rudolf's father during the war and now headed Berlin's storm troop detachments.

In August 1932, just days after the Hitler-Hindenburg tête-à-tête, Joachim Ribbentrop asked Helldorff to arrange a meeting with the National Socialist leader. "Helldorff did so, as far as I remember, through the mediation of Herr Röhm," Ribbentrop recalled. "I visited Adolf Hitler [on the Obersalzberg] and had a long discussion with him." Ribbentrop thought that Hitler would be best served working with Papen and Hindenburg's son, Oskar. Hitler insisted that General Schleicher was the better man. "A Prussian general does not break his word," Hitler told Ribbentrop." The two men parted company. "When Father came back from Berchtesgaden, [my mother] told me that Hitler had not agreed to his suggestions," Rudolf recalled. The young Ribbentrop was sworn to secrecy.

One day in early January 1933, two gentlemen came for lunch at the Ribbentrop villa and were first taken on a stroll around the garden. Usually there was chatter and banter at the lunch table, but on this occasion, the discussion was serious and sullen. The two men were Himmler and Keppler. Hitler had charged them with exploring the possibility of whether Ribbentrop could facilitate a meeting for him with Papen and possibly Oskar Hindenburg. "A few days after the visit by Himmler and Keppler, we children were seated at supper when Father came into the dining room and gave the butler instructions for the visit of several gentlemen he was expecting," Rudolf remembered.

This was unusual, since his father rarely involved himself in arrangements for visitors. That evening a driver was dispatched to pick up Papen, who then waited in the Ribbentrop study. Hitler was at a performance of *La Traviata*. Instead of returning to the Hotel Kaiserhof, Hitler was driven to Dahlem.

The purpose of the January 10 meeting was to explore the potential for forging a coalition of conservative parties with a Reichstag majority that could be presented to Hindenburg as an alternative to the Schleicher cabinet. As in Cologne, Papen proposed himself as chancellor with Hitler as vice chancellor, a suggestion he had also made in August. And just as in August, Hitler refused to consider any position but that of chancellor, despite the fractiousness and discord within the party ranks. The SA had begun to fragment, as we know, with detachments in Berlin, Essen, and Halle breaking away and creating their own organizations. Worse still, everyone was aware that Strasser was in negotiations with Schleicher and willing to take the vice chancellorship. If Strasser broke with the National Socialists and established his own political party, he could split the movement and deprive Hitler of much of his dwindling base. The meeting ended with testy uncertainty. Hitler did not want to see Papen again before the Lippe election, Annelies recorded in the minutes of the meeting. Afterward, Hitler spoke with Goebbels, who jotted a note in his diary: "Papen strongly opposed to Schleicher. Wants to bring him down or get rid of him entirely. Still has the old man's ear."

Papen conveyed a very different message to Finance Minister Krosigk, namely that Papen, on behalf of the Reich president, had repeatedly tried to reach out to the National Socialists, not in order to overthrow Schleicher but to finally establish the national front that his good friend Schleicher

had been seeking. But now, Papen disingenuously told Krosigk, "all these attempts by the Reich Chancellery were tor-
pedoed by reports in the press, premature announcements
of names, etc." Papen knew he was playing a perilous game,
as did Hitler. Everything depended on the Lipperland vote.
And on Hugenberg.

Vorwärts reported on January 14 that Hugenberg had
met with Schleicher for more than two hours the previous
day. With details undisclosed, the question remained: Would
Hugenberg play along with Hitler and deliver his 51 German Nationalist delegates? Or, would he, as rumors had it,
join a Schleicher cabinet with Strasser as vice chancellor?
It seemed a plausible scenario. With Hugenberg anchor-
ing the conservative business interests in a cabinet post—an
"economic dictator," as Hugenberg imagined—and Strasser drawing in his portion of the National Socialist vote as
well as crossover Social Democrats, Schleicher could create a
viable centrist government with cross-bench Reichstag support. Hindenburg would need to agree. Hitler would become
irrelevant. "Hugenberg was cunningly awaiting the right
moment," Brüning observed. "He watched coolly as his crops
ripened."

As speculation circulated, Hitler was at that moment in
Lipperland in an eleventh-hour attempt to save himself—as
well as the National Socialist movement—from political and
financial ruin. Meanwhile, Hugenberg was in Berlin, where
a meeting with Hindenburg, shrouded in secrecy, had been
arranged. The meeting was seen by some as the penultimate
step in fracturing the National Socialist movement with a
Hugenberg-Strasser coalition. *"Kommt Strasser?"* asked a
Berlin headline. "Is It Finally Strasser's Turn?" "Strasser will
join Schleicher's cabinet and bring a portion of the National
Socialist delegates with him," *Vorwärts* wrote.

The big question—indeed, the biggest question, as everyone knew—was how many voters would support Reichstag candidates from the Strasser faction in a new election. Hitler could browbeat his Reichstag delegates and attempt to coddle and charm his party leaders, but he had no control over the electorate. Industrialist Thyssen said that Strasser was "the most popular among the National Socialists" in the Rhineland. "He was an educated man, a pharmacist by profession, and generally people took him seriously, despite his National Socialist leanings," Thyssen said. When Hanfstaengl toured the Ruhr industrial region with Hitler, he was surprised to see that Strasser posters outnumbered Hitler posters. "Strasser is really quite the man here," he noted, as Hitler just looked away. The north Germans, as Rauschning had observed, preferred Strasser's clearheaded pragmatism to Hitler's "bombast and bathos."

A reshuffle of the Schleicher cabinet with Strasser as vice chancellor, and Hugenberg as a potential economic minister, was entirely possible. Hugenberg had met with Schleicher on Friday and Hindenburg on Saturday. Meanwhile, there was a resounding silence from Hitler on these matters as he prepared, in the words of the *Vossische Zeitung*, his "army" for its "election campaign battle"—"*Wahlfeldzug*"—with 150 events scheduled in the "little land of Lippe." Goebbels had a one-word answer to the news of Strasser's impending vice chancellorship: "Traitor!"

*

On Monday, as the Lippe election results were tabulated, *Vorwärts* proclaimed an electoral triumph for the Social Democrats, gloating over "losses for the Communists" and a stunning setback for the National Socialists. "Hitler falls far behind July election results," the newspaper announced in the headline. The National Socialist leader had once again failed to cross the 50 percent threshold to majority rule, despite committing his last reserves in financing and manpower— Göring, Goebbels, Frick, Frank, and a relentless two weeks of speaking engagements for himself. Statistically, the National Socialists had notched a slight improvement, with 39 percent of the voters, but in fact, with 38,844 votes, had shed nearly four thousand supporters from the high-water mark of 42,280 in July.*

Vorwärts observed smugly, "The elections did not deliver the National Socialists the results they expected." Hugenberg had done even worse. The German Nationalists, who once dwarfed the National Socialists, had lost four thousand votes, nearly half their constituents, reducing them to a single seat in the twenty-one-seat Lippe parliament, compared with nine for Hitler.

Vossische Zeitung hoped that Lippe would provide a final chastening lesson for Hitler and put an end to his dream of an absolute majority, exposing his claim to absolute rule as a "hollow presumption." Hitler saw things differently.

Hitler was in Weimar preparing for a meeting with the gauleiter there when Hans Frank arrived with the election results. Frank recalled watching Hitler in his room at the Hotel Elephant "beaming like a little boy." Hitler told Frank, "That was the final battle to the greatest domestic political struggle in German history." Later that day, Hitler again

---

* In 2018, the *American Political Science Review* published a statistical analysis of Hitler rallies and their impact on voting patterns, based on 455 Hitler speeches in five national elections between 1927 and 1933. The study's authors, Peter Selb and Thomas Munzert, wrote, "Hitler's speeches, while rationally targeted, had a negligible impact on the Nazis' electoral fortunes." In brief, Hitler was preaching to the converted.

invoked a military metaphor and spoke of an electoral triumph of historic proportions.

Hitler looked beyond voter attrition. He ignored the partisan sniping of the opposition press. Instead, he spun his 39 percent at the Lippe polling stations and the nine National Socialist seats in the state mini-parliament into a triumph of historic dimension. "Just like a field marshal, one only learns the quality of a political leader once he has suffered a setback," Hitler told the gathering of three thousand party stalwarts that afternoon in the Weimar Hall. He compared the victory in Lippe to Frederick the Great's greatest battlefield triumphs. He talked about the sacrifices, in effort, money, and blood, that had brought the movement to this point. Hitler railed against those who thought to betray the movement. He promised, "I will never abandon the party!" The brown-shirted crowd rose as one in sustained, thunderous applause, then turned on Strasser, who had been smeared by Goebbels's sustained propaganda attacks of deceptions, deceit, and betrayal, along with the alleged discovery of "Jewish blood" in the Strasser family lineage. "Poor Gregor!" Goebbels wrote. "Slaughtered by his best friends."

Three days later, Hitler was back at the Ribbentrops' for a second meeting with Papen, brandishing his 39.6 percent like a cudgel. "Hitler demands the chancellorship," Annelies Ribbentrop recorded in the meeting minutes. Papen insisted that this was impossible. "Such a demand exceeded his influence with Hindenburg," Papen said. Hitler didn't believe it. Either Papen was protecting his own claim on the chancellorship or he'd overstated his influence on Hindenburg, as he had done last August, with humiliating consequences. Either way, Hitler saw no reason for further discussions.

The next day, Hitler met Hugenberg. The two men had clashed repeatedly since their failed attempt to forge a com-

VISITATIONS   249

mon conservative cause with the Harzburg Front two years
before. Hugenberg's holiday missive went unanswered. Now,
the two men explored a political space vast enough to accommodate their equally oversized egos. As Hugenberg told his
adviser Reinhold Quaatz the night before the meeting, he was
going to propose that the National Socialists and German
Nationalists revive the Harzburg Front and force Schleicher
to bring them into his cabinet, with Hitler as vice chancellor without portfolio—that is, without a specific ministry to
head—and Hugenberg as minister without portfolio, on the
promise of delivering Schleicher the Reichstag majority support he needed. If Schleicher refused, they would threaten
him with a no-confidence vote in the Reichstag and topple
his government.

Hugenberg was aware of Hitler's repeated insistence on
the chancellorship for himself, but he knew that Hitler now
had financial backers who wanted to see a return on their
investment. Indeed, just that week, *Vorwärts* had tallied
the Herrenclub members Hitler had recently solicited: the
banker Schröder and industrialists Otto Wolff and Thyssen.
Thyssen was said to have already invested millions. Kessler
heard that Wolff, who had previously financed Schleicher,
had personally cleared Hitler's private debts to make him
"impervious to poking and probing" from political enemies.
Hitler had obtained the necessary financing. Hitler told
Hugenberg bluntly, "I have to be chancellor." But Hitler now
added an unexpected concession: he would no longer insist
on one-party rule and would appoint Hugenberg as minister
without portfolio and accommodate Schleicher as minister of
defense. Hitler said, "I can tolerate Schleicher, if he gives me
free rein." Hitler also wanted his storm troopers unbridled.
"Marxism must be bludgeoned, but not by state organs," Hitler said. That job would be left to his men.

Hugenberg pushed back at the meeting. He recalled that Hindenburg had repeatedly refused to appoint Hitler as chancellor, for the sake of God, his conscience, and the country. Hugenberg assured Hitler that Hindenburg would never appoint him chancellor. It was not Hindenburg, Hitler snapped back, it was his advisers who were exerting increasing influence over the old man, especially his son, Oskar, and the head of the presidential office, Meissner. This was, in fact, the common wisdom in those months.

Hitler and Hugenberg parted company with a testy but tacit agreement to continue their discussions. Later that day, Hugenberg told Quaatz, "If Hitler sits in the saddle, then I will have the whip." Goebbels wrote, "He [Hitler] was with Hugenberg. But without success." Ribbentrop said Hitler was infuriated by Hugenberg. He insisted on returning to Munich immediately. Göring and Ribbentrop eventually calmed Hitler down and convinced him to remain in Berlin to continue negotiations.

The enclosed park behind the Wilhelmstrasse, with its gravel paths linking the rear entrances to the ministries and residences, permitted Papen, who was still in the apartment he had been given as chancellor, to meet discreetly with Oskar von Hindenburg, who kept an apartment in his father's residence, leaving Schleicher, who had remained in his Defense Ministry apartment near the Bendlerstrasse, without actionable intelligence on their deliberations. It was public knowledge that Hindenburg had granted Papen permission to continue residing in the Wilhelmstrasse, giving rise to the facetious moniker of Papen as Hindenburg's *Vorratskanzler*, or spare chancellor.

On Friday, January 20, Papen informed Ribbentrop that the younger Hindenburg was willing to meet with Hitler at Ribbentrop's home that Sunday. He would be accompanied by Meissner. Hitler agreed to the meeting and said he would be bringing his own entourage. On Sunday evening at ten o'clock, Hitler appeared at the Ribbentrop villa's garden entrance in the company of Frick and Himmler. Göring arrived later that evening. The meeting did not begin well.

"When Hitler asked how the Reich president assessed the situation, I explained to him that nothing had changed in the president's view of Hitler's chancellorship," Papen said later. "But he is of the opinion that the worsening of the situation makes it even more desirable than before to involve his movement in this or in a new government." Hitler flatly rejected participation in the Schleicher government. He emphasized that involvement of his movement would be possible only under his chancellorship. Hitler then launched into a personal attack on Papen. He recalled the August 13 meeting and accused Papen of distorting the protocol that had been released to the public. He, Hitler, had never demanded all the power in the state, he said. He insisted that Papen's account was untrue, adding that he was not demanding that now, either. Hitler said that it would be easy to agree on representation by a good number of ministers from the centrist parties as long as the cabinet was built according to the principle that the ministers were not beholden to their parties. But Hitler did insist on a presidial cabinet, as Brüning and Papen had. He continued to reiterate the same arguments over the course of the evening.

Oskar seemed impressed—at least, that's what Hitler relayed to Goebbels. However, the report Oskar gave his father carried a strong warning: "Once Hitler is in power, neither the first list of ministers nor any of the agreements will be kept. A party dictatorship will result."

*

Bella Fromm dropped by Schleicher's office on Monday morning, January 23, to update him on the political gossip she had been gathering. Schleicher had not attended a soirée the previous week, "a glittering elaborate affair" hosted by Foreign Minister Neurath, "covetous and self-interested, wealthy and mean," whose buxom and bejeweled wife was proud, haughty, and "fully as mean." Fromm saw Schleicher's absence as a bad omen. She had had occasion at the fête to speak with Brigadier General Ferdinand von Bredow, a Schleicher protégé who'd described the "almost inhuman strain" weighing on the chancellor. "He seems to have made up his mind that, at this moment, it would be wise to include the National Socialists in the government," Bredow told Fromm. "Lately he has been having frequent talks with Gregor Strasser. He thinks him a very able man." The party had taken place on Tuesday, January 17, in the same hours that Hitler was delivering the death blow to Strasser's political career before party leaders in Weimar. "Gregor, that shrewd tactician," Goebbels wrote at the week's end. "Come what may, he will never again have any power."

By then word was out that Ribbentrop was facilitating contact between Papen and Hitler, while Papen was also continuing to support Schleicher in public. "It's characteristic of Papen to work both sides of the street," one guest at Neurath's party told Fromm. "At the same time he's waiting to kick the props out from under him [Schleicher]." Fromm noted that there was only one question among the "Herrenclub lunchers" that week: "Should Hitler be given a chance?" Fromm noted, "It's maddening to watch this mass blindness." On Sunday evening, while Hitler was meeting with Oskar Hindenburg, Fromm attended a gala performance for the Berlin charity called Winter Aid, "an exceptionally glamorous affair," albeit one whose atmosphere was chilled by the ominous political gossip.

"People are slowly waking up to the shocking realization of their blunder in having elected Hindenburg," Fromm noted, "and, what is worse, in reelecting him." The Reich president was allegedly losing control of his senses and had fallen into the intrigues of those around him. Fromm heard that Hjalmar Schacht had "definitely hitched his horse to the National Socialist star" and that Papen was in discussion with top Hitler lieutenants as well as the Reich president's son. "Papen has the task of mediating between the various camps," Fromm had learned. "He avails himself fully of Hindenburg's good graces and affection." Meanwhile, Hugenberg was waiting for the right moment to merge the German National People's Party with the National Socialists. Fromm noted, "I am afraid Hitler is just ready to leap, smash the whole lot of them, and grab power for himself."

Fromm wrote that Schleicher knew he had been excluded from "palace intrigues." He no longer had access to Hindenburg. "The slanderous whispers have convinced the childish old man that a revolt in the *Reichswehr* will break out soon if the appointment of a strongman is postponed much longer," she observed. Fromm believed that Hindenburg was deliberately misled by his "devoted" staff. She had also heard that Papen was watching with "growing jealousy the deliberate attempt at a Schleicher–Gregor Strasser coalition."

Papen realized that his only chance of reinserting himself into the government was by aligning himself with Hitler. He had no problem playing "his dirty game" with Oskar Hindenburg, not to mention Göring and Goebbels. Fromm told Schleicher that she had heard that Hitler was just waiting at the Kaiserhof for Papen and the staff of the Hindenburg household to get ready. "Then revolution!" Schleicher was unconcerned. He had had an awkward meeting with Hindenburg on January 6, followed by an "ungracious reception" two days later, but after nearly twenty years, he felt he knew the old man well enough to feel secure in the relationship.

Following Hitler's Lipperland "triumph," Schleicher received an update from his Brown House mole. The man warned Schleicher that a reconciliation between Hitler and Strasser was now unrealistic, eliminating any prospect of Schleicher possibly co-opting the entire National Socialist movement. The only possibility would be for Strasser to "subjugate" himself to Hitler, an unthinkable concession. Schleicher was advised that he might still restructure his cabinet with a coalition of centrist parties to achieve a Reichstag majority, but he should in any event abandon his current efforts with Strasser, since the Lipperland election had demonstrated Hitler's control not only over his gauleiter and Reichstag delegates but also over the electorate. Politically speaking, Strasser was, as Hitler had said, "a dead man." And Hitler found himself emboldened. For Schleicher, engaging with Hitler was out of the question. "Hitler seems to have developed a resolutely entrenched negative attitude toward the chancellor," Schleicher's source observed. "He sees the chancellor as someone who is intent on splintering the NSDAP." But Schleicher needed neither Papen nor Strasser nor Hitler, let alone a Reichstag majority. Hindenburg had already replaced two chancellors in less than seven months. Schleicher calculated that Hindenburg couldn't really afford to make him the third.

CHAPTER 20

HINDENBURG WHISPERERS

He doesn't want me? Rubbish. His advisers don't want me.

—ADOLF HITLER, JANUARY 18, 1933

By late January 1933, Bella Fromm had begun to suspect that Hindenburg was drifting into dementia. She had seen him a few weeks earlier looking frail, disoriented, inattentive, almost childlike in his demeanor, as had an increasing number of presidential observers. "They understand now that Hindenburg has been lulled to sleep by his staff," Fromm wrote. "That he is too weak and senile to resist their influence and their plotting." This clutch of palace policy advisers had been given a name, the *"Kamarilla,"* derived from the Spanish *"camarilla,"* or little chamber of intriguers. Marie von Hindenburg sensed her uncle's failing capacities along with his increasing reliance on his son, Oskar, no longer just a presidential errand boy and geriatric attendant, taking his father's arm as they ascended and descended stairs or entered or exited a vehicle, but now said to be helping shape presidential policy. "Previously, Oskar never had any influence on

him. Quite the opposite. They hardly got along," she told
Harry Kessler over a mid-January afternoon tea.

Former chancellor Brüning found the aging president
more absorbed in recounting war stories and "sentimental memories" than interested in matters of state. Further,
Brüning claimed that Hindenburg was "terrorized" by his
son, whose yelling could be heard outside in the Wilhelmstrasse. Irish ambassador Daniel Binchy also thought Hindenburg was deteriorating. Hindenburg's "jovial manner"
appeared to have given way to "weary listlessness." For his
part, Hitler saw no change. Hindenburg, in his judgment,
had always been a puppet in the hands of palace intriguers,
who scripted his every move and word. Hitler derided Hindenburg's limited and repetitive political vocabulary. "He is a
gramophone record," Hitler said.

In the eyes of his detractors, Hindenburg had long been
in decline. When the Reich president had vanished from public view for ten days in the spring of 1932, rumors of frailty
had abounded. Brüning thought the old man had suffered a
nervous breakdown. Meissner, who dealt with Hindenburg
on a daily basis, knew it was "neither a mental nor a nervous
collapse"; Hindenburg had caught the flu. "Afterward, he
quickly recovered and was until a few days before his death
[in August 1934] in full possession of his mental capabili-
ties," Meissner recalled. Perhaps the most credible witnesses
to Hindenburg's condition in those months are the verbatim
protocols of presidential meetings. They testify to a man in
full command of his mental capacities and his official responsibilities. He listens, probes, commands.

Vorwärts suspected Hindenburg of a grand plan to lead
the republic into political and economic ruin as preparation
for a return of the monarchy, a suspicion for which one could
cite ample evidence. "For the time being a flood of wild pas-

sions and resounding speeches has overwhelmed the ancient traditions of our state and apparently destroyed all our sacred traditions," Hindenburg had written in 1919. "Yet this flood will subside again. Then from the tempestuous seas of our national life will once more emerge that rock—the German Imperial House—to which our fathers clung in days of yore." Was the president of the republic in fact still a closet monarchist? Or, even more unsettling, a scheming, soon-to-be constitutional dictator? On Tuesday, January 17, the Reich president was handed the opportunity to become the latter.

That morning, Hindenburg received a briefing paper outlining the legal basis for suspending the constitution and establishing a presidential dictatorship through his Article 48 powers. The two-page legal brief noted that in every state there were political or social challenges "against which the constitution provided no protections," in particular, the manipulation of legal processes or obstructionist tactics that could lead to legislative gridlock and a constitutional crisis. The paper used the term *"Verfassunglähmung,"* or constitutional paralysis. In the face of legislative gridlock, the president, as the elected representative of the majority of the people, had not only the right but, in fact, the duty—out of "loyalty to the constitution in its totality"—to suspend due process and amend the constitution as he thought appropriate for remedying the governance crisis. In brief, Hindenburg had the legal authority, indeed, the responsibility to shape the state to his will.

By mid-January, a full-blown case of *Verfassungslähmung* appeared to be at hand, with legislation blocked by the National Socialists in the Reichstag and with an electorate so fractured that political consensus seemed impossible. Hindenburg knew he needed a chancellor with the personality and capacity to break that paralysis. His finance minister,

Krosigk, was warming to the idea of Hitler as a chancellor candidate, as were Schacht and General Blomberg. Hindenburg had sent Blomberg to Geneva as head of the German delegation for disarmament talks. The former Schleicher colleague turned bitter rival dispatched a series of cables from Geneva warning Hindenburg that Schleicher was aiming to establish himself as military dictator. Hindenburg's neighbor, Elard von Oldenburg, always a staunch monarchist, was increasingly inclined to Hitler, as was the Hindenburg family friend Viktoria von Dirksen, who had invested much of her late husband's fortune into advancing Hitler's career. Along with Helene Bechstein and Elsa Bruckmann, Dirksen helped make Hitler socially respectable. Kessler called Dirksen "the great benefactor of the Nazis." Goebbels knew that "Frau von Dirksen was working very hard" in trying to convince Hindenburg to appoint Hitler as chancellor. "I don't believe it will work," Goebbels noted in his diary on the evening of Sunday, January 22. Göring exercised his right as Reichstag president to call on Hindenburg and lobbied for a Hitler chancellorship. Hindenburg showed him the door.

As a longtime Hindenburg protégé and canny political strategist, Schleicher depended as much on the weaknesses of his opponents as on his own canny and considerable capacities. In the cases of Blomberg and Brüning, Schleicher helped when needed to set the conditions for their ruin, all the while relying on his friendship with Oskar and his two decades of service as a staff officer in Hindenburg's headquarters during and after the war. After Hindenburg's election as president, in 1925, Schleicher became a regular in *Haus Hindenburg*. The Reich president liked Schleicher's easy style, his self-deprecation, his quick wit, his ease with himself and others. Most of all, Hindenburg appreciated Schleicher's sharp mind and strategic sense, already in evidence during the war, and honed as he became head of political intelligence in the Defense Ministry, then defense minister, then head of government. When appointed chancellor, Schleicher had called himself "the last horse in Hindenburg's stall," a deprecation as witty as it was true that appealed to Hindenburg's appreciation for all things equestrian.

On Monday morning, January 23, Schleicher appeared in Hindenburg's office to outline a plan for overcoming the ongoing political impasse. He told the Reich president that he expected a no-confidence vote when the Reichstag convened on January 31. Schleicher argued that a new Reichstag election "would not change the situation and the country would be in a state of emergency." The best option would be to postpone new elections for a few months. Schleicher proposed a simple solution: "to declare a state of emergency, dissolve the Reichstag, and hold no new elections for the time being." He had met a fellow general the previous evening to review the plan and had been assured of the military's support in the event of public unrest, which was thought to be almost certain to follow. The imposition of martial law for several months, possibly into the autumn, would permit the political and economic situation to stabilize. By then he was certain that negotiations in Switzerland would have reduced and rescheduled reparation payments and established armament parity for Germany, dismantling the two most onerous provisions of the Treaty of Versailles. Deprived of these two points of attack against the republic, the National Socialist Party would either moderate or fracture—one cannot help but hear the words of the Brown House mole in this suggestion— potentially permitting Strasser to establish his own political movement, which could ensure a Reichstag majority and return the country to constitutional order. Without this temporary suspension of the constitution, Schleicher would find himself in an impossible situation. The implication was clear: he was threatening to resign.

The previous spring, Krosigk had watched Brüning's gradual descent from favor with the Reich president. It was always the same: the fading of the warmth, the vanished smile, the polite distancing, a furrowing of the brow. With Hindenburg, Krosigk knew, "the loss of trust was marked by a darkening shadow that clouded his forehead." Krosigk suspected that Schleicher's incessant scheming and his occasional disparaging remarks about Oskar von Hindenburg had found their way back to the senior Hindenburg. On this midwinter day, Meissner was there to take protocol and record the phenomenon as Hindenburg displayed a rare impatience with the man he had once called the "smartest head" on his general staff.

"On the second of December you predicted civil war if Papen's suggestions were to go through. The army and police would be incapable of combating internal unrest and maintaining order and state authority," Hindenburg said, reminding Schleicher of *Kriegsspiel Ott,* the worst-case wargame scenario Schleicher had used to topple the Papen government. "The internal situation has become increasingly aggravated over the past seven weeks; the National Socialists have received new impetus, the left is more radical than ever," Hindenburg said. "If civil war was expected then, how much more likely would it be today?" Hindenburg observed that the army was no more capable of responding to the crisis in January than it had been in December. "Under such circumstances, I cannot accept your recommendation to dissolve the Reichstag and provide you with carte blanche to govern," Hindenburg said. The old field marshal wasn't going to be intimidated. Hoisted by his own petard, Schleicher sat silently for a moment, then said that he would need some time to reflect.

*

Hindenburg's irritation that winter morning was perhaps stoked by weekend developments that had placed the Reich president in awkward circumstances. On Saturday morning, the newspapers' banner headlines had reported a *"Riesen-skandal,"* or "huge scandal," related to federal funds that had been channeled into the coffers of two hundred East Prussian aristocrats. The Reichstag budget committee, at the instigation of the Communist delegate Ernst Torgler, had investigated the government program *"Osthilfe,"* or Eastern Aid, which had allocated hundreds of millions of reichsmarks in state subsidies to farmers in the eastern regions of the country. An effort to keep the budget committee hearings behind closed doors had failed. On Saturday morning the names had been published. There were stories about Hindenburg's East Prussian landowning neighbors, including Hermine von Hohenzollern, a member of the royal family, and Baron von Richthofen, with details about luxury-car purchases and vacations on the Riviera, all paid for from the public purse; Elard von Oldenburg topped the list of beneficiaries. It seems that Hindenburg's friend and neighbor had siphoned public moneys into his private estates, "speculating," in the words of the Social Democrats' Reichstag delegate Kurt Heinig, with 621,000 RM ($3.25 million today), which he had lost, and was now seeking additional financial support to save him from bankruptcy. Worst of all, at least for Hindenburg, was that even though the subsidies had not been used for his estate, the Reich president was implicated in the scandal, either as a dupe or a colluder.

It was suggested that Oldenburg's fundraising campaign to purchase and restore Hindenburg's estate, Neudeck, had been intended to anchor the Reich president in East Prussia in order to keep public moneys pouring into the estates of neighboring landholders. They bought Neudeck, one cynic observed, adding, "But along with Neudeck they bought the old boy." More awkward still, Erich von Ludendorff, the former fellow general turned antagonist, pointed out that the estate had been given "not to the Old Gentleman, but to his son Oskar," to avoid inheritance taxes. Oldenburg came to Hindenburg's defense. As "an old officer" and a gentleman, Oldenburg said, he would normally have responded to Ludendorff "in the usual manner among cavaliers," with a pistol duel, but he would forgo this gentlemanly response because his opponent was socially beneath him.

By the fourth week of January, the newspapers were bannering stories about financial scandal, martial law, and the threat of an imminent coup d'état. Meissner, ever the sober observer, thought that Hindenburg was not so irritated with Schleicher as he was with the republic itself. Hindenburg knew that the constitution was flawed and the possibilities for amendment, under the circumstances, limited. But he understood that it was better to stay with the plan at hand than to take uncertain action in uncertain and changing circumstances. Hindenburg told him, Meissner wrote, that "none of the politicians and statesmen with whom he had been in contact, either in written or by verbal communication, could make a proposition that would be compatible with the constitution other than the one Papen had already made." Except that this plan included Hitler.

That Thursday, January 26, Kurt von Hammerstein called

on Meissner at his office in the presidential palace to express concern about their mutual friend Kurt von Schleicher and Schleicher's growing frustration over trying to manage the government without an extended mandate to rule by decree. Hammerstein worried about social unrest were Schleicher to resign and Papen to return as Reich chancellor, in coalition with Hugenberg, as rumors were suggesting. It was common knowledge that Papen and Hugenberg were disliked by politicians and the public alike. With support from only 7 percent of the Reichstag delegates, Papen was the most unpopular chancellor in the history of the country. A second Papen chancellorship could provoke a violent response. "The army would then have to defend this 7 percent base against 93 percent of the German population," Hammerstein observed. "That would be in the highest degree disquieting. Could it not still be prevented?" Certainly not with Hitler, he added. Didn't Schleicher remain the only viable alternative? Uncertain whether the Hammerstein visit was intended as a warning, a threat, or as reconnaissance for Schleicher, Meissner led Hammerstein into Hindenburg's office. Hammerstein repeated his concerns to the former field marshal. "Hindenburg was extremely sensitive about any kind of political interference, but then said, apparently to placate me, 'You will hardly think me capable of appointing this Austrian corporal as chancellor of the Reich,'" Hammerstein recalled.

That afternoon, the *Vossische Zeitung*, Hindenburg's favorite newspaper, echoed these same sentiments for its readers: "Today Hitler insists, just like he did yesterday, and just as he did a half a year ago, that his party cannot and should not participate in any government that does not bear his name," the newspaper wrote. "And today, the Reich president does not think one iota differently about a Hitler dictatorship than he did before." A cartoon in *Vorwärts* showed Hitler standing in a cemetery filled with swastika-shaped headstones, the grave-yard of his National Socialist movement. While Schleicher digs his own political grave and Strasser looks on with patient bemusement, Hitler appears delusional and disheveled. He stands, contemplating an effigy of his own head that he holds in his hand, muttering the words "To be or not to be." The cartoon is titled "The New Hamlet."

CHAPTER 21

FATEFUL WEEKEND

It has to be Hitler. But how?
The Old Man just won't allow it.

—JOSEPH GOEBBELS, DIARY ENTRY, JANUARY 27, 1933

"States have changed their form, monarchs have gone into exile, but the Press Ball has remained what it has always been, the grand gathering of celebrities, the parade of Berlin's high society," the *Vossische Zeitung* noted, reporting on the city's premier social event of the year, held annually on the last Saturday in January. Everyone who was anyone was in attendance: politicians, businessmen, foreign dignitaries, film directors, actors, playwrights, painters, musicians, writers, as well as the occasional journalist, and five thousand other guests.

On Saturday morning, January 28, Bella Fromm jumped into her car and rushed to see her friend Schleicher about the Friday evening headlines announcing his precarious political situation. *Vorwärts* had bannered its late Friday edition "Crisis in Wilhelmstrasse—Hitler and Papen Chancellor Candidates—Schleicher Toppling." One commentator noted a temperature plunge—*Temperatursturz*—among Schleicher's friends and associates that left the chancellor encased in an "ice sheet of isolation." Fromm's own newspaper, the *Vossische Zeitung*, saw the end of the Schleicher chancellorship as "unavoidable." Less clear was who would be the next chancellor, the paper wrote. Papen? Hugenberg? Hitler?

Schleicher received Fromm with characteristic warmth and candor. He knew that his efforts to fashion a Reichstag majority had failed. The list of enemies plotting his demise had ballooned. There were headlines and rumors of palace intrigues. That was nothing new, Schleicher told Fromm. He understood what it took to stay in power. He would be meeting with Hindenburg at twelve-fifteen that very day to address the ongoing crisis. As in his last meeting with Hindenburg, he intended to propose a state of emergency and dissolution of the Reichstag to allow matters to stabilize for a few months, possibly into the spring, maybe the autumn, however long it took. Of course, the Communists would revolt, and, yes, Hitler's storm troopers would do the same, but Schleicher was confident that the army could crush the dissent. Hammerstein was a close friend, as was General Joachim von Stülpnagel, the head of the garrison in Potsdam. Schleicher felt so secure as defense minister that he once told Meissner, "If Hitler wants to establish a dictatorship in the Reich, then the Reichswehr will be the dictator of the dictator." When a friend had mentioned to Schleicher that Brüning had had sleepless nights during Hindenburg's reelection campaign the previous spring, Schleicher had sniped, "People who cannot sleep at night have no place in politics."

"Don't worry so much, Bella dear," Schleicher told Fromm. "I'll see you tonight at the Press Ball." Fromm returned home to prepare for the evening. She had ordered a rose-colored gown from a Parisian couture house. "When

I left Schleicher this morning," Fromm wrote in her diary, "I thought for a moment that perhaps he was right."

As part of his survival instinct, Schleicher had become a master of deception and apparent self-deception, though he knew exactly what he was doing. Gottfried Treviranus recalled Schleicher saying, "Trevi, you are sooo right!," with his vowels drawn out in velvet-smooth reassurance, even when Schleicher was in complete disagreement.

But by that morning, Schleicher had recognized just how precarious his position had become. He had sensed the shift in mood from the warm confidence he had once enjoyed with the old field marshal and felt the Prussian chill on entering *Haus Hindenburg*, as well as his growing isolation. John Wheeler-Bennett recalled, "His agents deserted him; his marionettes no longer responded to his touch." Behind Schleicher's "façade of assurance," Wheeler-Bennett suspected that Schleicher was "in a panic."

Schleicher brought a controlled, clear-eyed sobriety into the cabinet meeting that morning when he convened his ministers at eleven-thirty. His mood was somber. He told his cabinet that he understood that he could not secure a Reichstag majority to support his government. If anyone had that chance it was Hitler, but he knew the president was, just as before, decidedly against a Hitler chancellorship. He also knew that a cabinet with Papen and Hugenberg would be so unpopular as to precipitate a revolt. Schleicher intended to ask the president for a mandate to dissolve the Reichstag. If the president refused, Schleicher would have to resign. Finance Minister Krosigk challenged Schleicher's grave assessment of a potential Papen-Hugenberg cabinet, suggesting that Hindenburg would first solicit opinions from the other ministers. Foreign Minister Neurath considered the dangers of a Papen-Hugenberg cabinet indeed significant. At ten minutes after twelve, Schleicher excused himself. Five minutes later, he sat across from Hindenburg.

The old man was cloaked in a particularly stern Prussian demeanor. Schleicher knew to keep it formal. He outlined the continuing tense political situation, then the limited range of options for a response. A Hitler cabinet with a Reichstag majority could be a solution, Schleicher told Hindenburg, but he did not believe that it was possible for Hitler to assemble a cabinet whose members could guarantee a Reichstag majority, especially given the kingpin role of Hugenberg and the toxic relationship between the two men. There could, of course, be a Hitler cabinet with a Reichstag minority, essentially handing Hitler his long-desired government with one-party rule, but Schleicher already knew Hindenburg's opinion on that. The third option—a second Papen chancellorship—was not worth mentioning.

The only viable solution, Schleicher explained to Hindenburg, was to retain the current presidial cabinet. This would require the Reich president to exercise his Article 48 powers to dissolve the Reichstag the following Tuesday and suspend the constitution, at least until the spring.

Hindenburg knew that Schleicher was aware of his position on Hitler. Hindenburg also recognized political blackmail when he saw it. Schleicher was, in fact, offering Hindenburg only one option: a Schleicher dictatorship. Hindenburg had finally had enough of Schleicher's maneuvering and machinations. He said that "given the present circumstances," he could not consent to the Schleicher proposal. He appreciated Schleicher's efforts with Strasser, his attempt to forge a functioning Reichstag majority. "Unfortunately, [a majority] was not achieved, and therefore other possibilities need to be tried," Hindenburg said. Schleicher knew he had just been dismissed as chancellor.

Schleicher was the master of the bon mot, of repartee. He had a fitting or cutting comment for every occasion. In the spring of 1932, Schleicher had told the editor of the *Tägliche Rundschau*, "I have something very fine in the works! You will be amazed!" Schleicher delivered on his promise: the shock replacement of Brüning by Papen. Afterward, Schleicher dubbed himself the "head" of the government and Papen its "hat." As Papen began forging his own political course, Schleicher jested, "Look, Little Franz did it all on his own!" But now, sitting across from the stern, unmoving Reich president, Schleicher found himself at a loss for words and wit. He had squandered the trust and, even more, the respect of the old field marshal. Nothing was going to fix that. The curt finality stunned him. Perhaps there were points better conveyed by other cabinet members, Schleicher suggested meekly. Krosigk on the economy, Neurath on foreign responses. Hindenburg responded firmly, "I wish to reserve that option for myself, but it cannot change my decision."

Hindenburg rose to his feet and extended his hand. "I thank you for the loyal service you have rendered the Fatherland in difficult times, and I ask you to convey my thanks to the Reich ministers as well," Hindenburg said, then repeated for good measure, "I am very grateful to all of you." Schleicher had lost the battle but had a final request. "When the Reich government is reconstituted, I would ask that the president not hand the Defense Ministry over to any of Hitler's party members," he said. "That would put the army in great danger." Hindenburg thanked Schleicher for his concern. As commander in chief and former field marshal, Hindenburg knew how to manage the army. Schleicher had entered Hindenburg's office at twelve-fifteen. He departed at twelve forty-five. "I know it sounds strange, but I could not help but feel sorry for Schleicher," Brüning said afterward. "He seemed a broken man."

Hindenburg's irritation with his former protégé had been heightened earlier when he read that day's edition of the *Tägliche Rundschau*. This newspaper was the point of reference for the Wilhelmstrasse. It was not only generally read but also known as an unofficial mouthpiece for Schleicher—though even when that was not the case, it did tend to align with his politics. The writer of the article reviewed the limited options that were left to Hindenburg as Reich president if Schleicher were to be dismissed from office. It concluded that reappointing Papen and investing him with dictatorial powers would inevitably lead to a political cataclysm that could result in a "crisis for the Reich president" himself. That sounded like a threat. Hindenburg asked Meissner to determine whether Schleicher was behind the article. Meissner said he was uncertain how he could determine this, since the editors obviously would not tell him and it was clear that there was no talking to Schleicher about it. But if Schleicher had been behind the article, he would have had to have known how ill-advised it was to seek to intimidate the old field marshal. In any event, it was clear to Meissner that the article ruined any chance that might have existed for Schleicher to serve as chancellor and remain defense minister in a new cabinet, which would, in fact, have been the best option for holding Hitler in check.

Whether out of personal annoyance, political expediency, or perceived constitutional necessity, Hindenburg's decision to dismiss his favored deputy belonged to a pattern of gradual empowerment and sudden abandonment. Erich von Ludendorff had been as much responsible for the victory at Tannenberg as Hindenburg and remained his chief lieutenant, only to be sacrificed at war's end. Heinrich Brüning kept Bolsheviks and fascists in check and championed Hindenburg's tenure as president, running the successful reelection campaign, only to be dismissed six weeks after triumph at the polls. Now it was Schleicher's turn.

Schleicher had barely left Hindenburg's office when Papen arrived to update the Reich president on his ongoing exploratory discussions. Hindenburg shared with Papen his displeasure with Schleicher, then reviewed the remaining options for forming a government, which, according to Papen, led Hindenburg to an unsettling conclusion. "You mean to tell me I have the unpleasant task of appointing this Hitler"—"*diesen Hitler*"—"as the next chancellor?" Hindenburg allegedly asked.

Papen nodded. Hindenburg asked Papen to test the waters to see how other parties would react to a Hitler chancellorship with Papen serving as vice chancellor. "It was quite unusual for the Reich president to ask any person to form a government which would not be headed by the person himself," Papen later recalled. "In the normal course of events Hindenburg should, of course, have entrusted Hitler himself with the formation of a government." But Hindenburg wanted to minimize Hitler's influence in any government as much as possible.

A half hour later, a newswire went out. Schleicher had resigned. Papen had accepted the task of proposing a new government. Papen's first port of call was Hugenberg.

*

Hitler had been meeting with Hugenberg in those same hours, on Ribbentrop's recommendation, to explore the potential for fashioning a Hitler-Hugenberg cabinet supported by a Reichstag majority. Recognizing his own limitations, Hugenberg was willing to serve in the cabinet of a Hitler chancellorship, albeit with conditions. He was adamant that the police and military remain out of the hands of National Socialists, and he vehemently opposed integrating the SA into the military. He also insisted on dictating the majority of cabinet posts. Most important, Hugenberg refused to countenance the thought of another round of Reichstag elections. There had already been four national elections the previous year—two presidential ones and two Reichstag elections, the last one in November, less than three months ago. And besides, Hugenberg had gained an additional eight hundred thousand votes, along with fourteen more seats in the Reichstag. Why would Hugenberg want another election? Hitler departed livid with rage. "I have never seen Hitler in such a state," Joachim Ribbentrop later told Annelies.

That afternoon, Papen called on Hugenberg. Hugenberg was furious with Hitler. The two men had not been able to agree on anything. Hitler wanted presidial power in any Hitler-Hugenberg government. He did not care about a Reichstag majority based on coalitions. Hugenberg himself demanded two seats for his people in the cabinet, even though he had only fifty-two seats in the Reichstag and Hitler had five times that number. Hugenberg understood that without those fifty-two votes, a coalition government was impossible. As always, Hugenberg was pragmatic and blunt. He knew a second Schleicher chancellorship was out of the question, as was Papen's own reappointment. "A Papen dictatorial cabinet would stoke tensions among the people to the boiling point, and would lead to a presidential crisis," Hugenberg said, endangering not only Papen but potentially Hindenburg. Article 43 of the constitution provided for impeachment proceedings against the Reich president.

Hugenberg doubted Hitler's true willingness to join

a conservative coalition that could command the sort of Reichstag majority Hindenburg was seeking. "Hitler will do his utmost not to preside over a coalition government," Hugenberg had told Papen. One would have to reach a compromise with Hitler that would restrict his powers as much as possible. For his part, Hugenberg was game, as long as he could serve as "economic dictator," and with the stipulation that there would be no new elections.

An hour later, Papen met with Hitler. When Papen arrived, Hitler was cool but receptive. Papen had good news. Hindenburg no longer opposed a potential Hitler chancellorship, provided that it remained within the framework of the constitution. As Hugenberg had predicted, Hitler dismissed the idea of a conservative coalition out of hand. Moreover, he insisted on dictatorial authority. As Hitler had said repeatedly, if the president wanted Hitler's support, he needed to entrust Hitler with the same powers that Papen and Schleicher had had in setting up presidial cabinets. Beyond the chancellorship, Hitler demanded the Interior Ministry be given to a National Socialist, as well as two key positions at the state level for Prussia, the *Reichskommissar* and the state's minister of the interior, effectively handing him control over two-thirds of the country, along with the Prussian state police, which, after the Reichswehr, represented the largest official security force in the country. The Prussian police were equipped with military-style units, including their own armored vehicles. Papen told Hitler that Hindenburg had reserved the position of *Reichskommissar* for him in his role as vice chancellor. Hitler complained that Prussia had been controlled by Social Democrats for a decade. He wanted personally to clean things up. Papen was taken aback by Hitler's demands. He asked Hitler, with evident sarcasm, if he had any other requests. Hitler did, in fact. He insisted that any minister chosen by Hindenburg agree to serve in the cabinet on a nonpartisan basis. Hitler wanted to avoid partisan wrangling in his cabinet.

Papen knew that Hindenburg would never agree to all of Hitler's demands, but he played nice. He thanked Hitler. He said he would provide the Reich president with a full report on their deliberations. Papen then met with Fritz Schäffer, head of the Bavarian People's Party, one of the largest conservative factions in the Reichstag. Schäffer's position was simple: his party could be persuaded to support a Hitler cabinet. Support for a Papen cabinet was out of the question. After the meetings, Papen called Krosigk for advice.

As Krosigk saw it, Papen had two options. There was the Papen-Hugenberg cabinet, which would certainly meet with protests, both in the street and in the Reichstag, but possibly with approval by the Reich president. This *"Kampfkabinett,"* or a combat cabinet, as Krosigk called it, could prevail with Hindenburg's backing. The second option was a Hitler-Papen-Hugenberg cabinet, which had the chance of securing majority support of the Reichstag on the strength of the number of National Socialist and German Nationalist delegates, with support from other conservative parties. Krosigk told Papen that this was "the only viable option." He personally would be no part of a *Kampfkabinett.* Which left only Hitler.

Harry Kessler had called on his friend Marie von Hindenburg that afternoon. "Tell me, what's happening? Have all the people gone mad?" she asked Kessler. He said the situation was beyond rational explanation. "The whole thing is a jumble of corruption, backroom dealings, and kickbacks that remind one of the worst times of absolute monarchy," Kessler reflected afterward. It was astonishing to him how all these "poison mushrooms" had suddenly sprung up in the shadow of imminent dictatorship. There was only one thing of which Kessler was certain: when the next chancellorship collapsed, whether it be Papen's or Hitler's or anyone else's, it was taking Marie's uncle, the Reich president, with it.

*

The Press Ball took place in the elegant Festival Hall of the Zoological Garden, opposite the Kaiser Wilhelm Memorial Church, at the terminus of the fashionable Kurfürstendamm. Among the more distinguished guests attending Presseball 1933 were the playwright Carl Zuckmayer and the composer Arnold Schoenberg, along with the conductor Wilhelm Furtwängler and the renowned Hungarian soprano Gitta Alpár, who was taking a star turn in the operetta *Ball at the Savoy*. The ambassadors from France, Britain, and Austria were there, but more notable than those in attendance were those who were not. The popular Berlin daily *B.Z. am Mittag* reported, "Herr von Schleicher and his wife were indisposed. Neither Herr von Papen, Herr Hitler, or Herr Hugenberg were yet authorized [to be chancellor] and as a result this Press Ball had a new and especially timely nuance: the absence of a Reich chancellor." The popular a cappella ensemble Comedian Harmonists, which was preparing for a European tour that would include recording sessions in Paris—eventually one with Josephine Baker—set the tone for the evening. The *Vossische Zeitung* reported, "The Rumba is all the fashion in Calumba, where there is no talk of politics." In fact, politics was all anyone was talking about.

The news that Papen was once again wandering the halls of power, apparently testing the waters for his own reappointment, was cause for consternation and dismay. "It makes me want to vomit to think that we might be ruled again by this notorious muttonhead and gambler," Kessler wrote in his diary. The *Vossische Zeitung* alleged that Papen had revealed his true Machiavellian nature. "[Schleicher] let his predecessor use his official residence and now, if it all works out, will spare his 'good comrade' from the 3rd Guards Regiment the effort of moving."

Like Marie von Hindenburg, Bella Fromm saw the Schleicher demission and, even more so, the potential Papen reappointment as proof of Hindenburg's senility. Quaatz thought that it was his leader, Hugenberg, who had given Schleicher's chancellorship "the death blow." Brüning blamed Papen. "Papen was in daily contact with the son of the Reich president, which was facilitated by the fact that the garden of his official residence, which he had decided not to vacate, was adjacent to the garden of the Reich president's palace," Brüning said.

Krosigk thought that the dismissal had resulted from an accumulation of Hindenburg's frustrations and irritations with his former protégé, including Schleicher's deprecating remark that Oskar owed his career to his connection to *Haus Hindenburg*. One rumor held that Hindenburg had dismissed Schleicher for failing to quash the increasingly awkward *Osthilfe* revelations. "If you aren't strong enough to put a stop [to this scandal] once and for all, then I shall not empower you to dissolve the Reichstag, but ask you to resign instead," Hindenburg roared, according to one account, allegedly pounding the floor with his cane. Schleicher was said to have turned "pale as death and tendered his resignation." Brüning was also thought to have lost his chancellorship over the East Prussian estates. When Brüning had proposed parceling the properties to lesser landed farmers, he had been denounced as an "agrarian Bolshevik" and dismissed. Wheeler-Bennett thought that Schleicher's personality, "attuned" as it was "to intrigue rather than leadership," had ultimately alienated Hindenburg, with Schleicher's own replacement of Papen as chancellor as the final straw. "Rarely had a chancellor [Schleicher] been appointed with such cold hostility and never had one retired [Papen] with such manifestations of affection from the president," he recalled.

The one man who knew more than anyone that evening said nothing. "The only guest in the official box who seemed to feel at ease was Meissner," Fromm observed. "He glowed with the conceited affability of a man who has achieved his work."

Across town, Hitler was taking evening tea with Viktoria von Dirksen, the widowed patron, in the subdued elegance of the Hotel Kaiserhof, chatting amiably and making caustic remarks about the privileged aristocracy and the myriad woes of the Weimar Republic. Goebbels, who had been speaking in Rostock earlier that day, eventually joined them. When Dirksen departed, Hitler and Goebbels turned to the business at hand. Hitler reported on the Schleicher demission, then talked about Papen's claim that Hindenburg was suddenly willing to entertain the idea of a Hitler appointment to the chancellorship. Hitler was "skeptical and suspicious." Papen had offered the same assurance in August, only for the meeting to end in fiasco. Papen had arranged for the "secret meeting" in Cologne for all the world to see. Hitler also knew that Papen had been in discussions with Strasser, as well as recently with Hugenberg, all the while seeking to position himself for reappointment as chancellor. "Maybe it would be best if Papen came again, because then the public outrage would become so threatening that things would be impossible," Goebbels observed. Catastrophe would follow. It seemed that everyone except Hitler had had their chance at the chancellorship, Goebbels complained. Concerned that he was being set up for a third public humiliation with Hindenburg over the Reich chancellorship, Hitler thought it perhaps best to return to Munich.

*

Toward ten o'clock that evening, Papen arrived at the back door to the presidential palace for a late-night meeting with Hindenburg to report on the progress of his negotiations. As Papen reviewed the competing demands of Hugenberg and Hitler, most likely avoiding mention of the two men's tangled relationship and competing political agendas, it became clear just how far the governing crisis was from a resolution. Meissner later said that by that Saturday evening, "the possibility of forming a new government was as distant as it had been fourteen days earlier."

Papen had barely departed when Kurt von Hammerstein came calling, accompanied by Stülpnagel. "What brings you here at such a late hour?" Hindenburg asked. He did not offer the generals a seat. Speaking "on behalf of the Reichswehr," Hammerstein said that he "respectfully" wanted to inform Herr Field Marshal about certain concerns within the officer corps as well as among the troops. "The departure of the Reich chancellor and defense minister [Schleicher] is unbearable for the army," Hammerstein said. "I would like to request, most obediently, that these measures . . ." Hindenburg stiffened. He slammed his walking stick on the floor. "What is tolerable for the Reichswehr is for me to decide," Hindenburg said. "I must request my officers to refrain from any instruction in these matters." Hammerstein and Stülpnagel stood at attention, waiting to be dismissed. But Hindenburg was not yet through: "It would truly be better if the gentlemen worried less about politics and more about the training of their troops." With that, Hindenburg turned and walked to the door that led to his private quarters. Hammerstein and Stülpnagel placed their hands on their daggers, clicked their heels, and offered a stiff bow. Hindenburg paused. He turned. He looked at Hammerstein. "Your hunting venture on the Oder River, Herr von Hammerstein," Hindenburg said, then repeated the phrase for emphasis: "your recent hunting venture on the Oder River did not please me at all."

*

As one might expect, the Sunday morning headlines were cut from the whole cloth of the Schleicher demission, then stitched together with scraps of rumor and Press Ball gossip, and tailored to the shape and size of the corresponding political fashion. Not surprisingly, *Vorwärts* ran a shrill headline trumpeting a *"Staatsstreich,"* or a coup d'état, and an imminent "Papen-Hitler" cabinet. *Der Funke* foresaw a "Hitler-Hugenberg" coalition. The *Vossische Zeitung* traced the Schleicher dismissal all the way back to the awkward sighting on the steps of the Schröder villa in Cologne, when Papen and Hitler began planning his downfall. One commentator wondered how any self-respecting political leader could negotiate with a man who telegraphed his support to the bestial killers of Potempa. One article suggested that Hindenburg had dismissed Schleicher with the intention of solidifying absolutist rule, saying he planned to exercise his Article 53 powers to appoint himself chancellor while retaining the presidency. The headline announced, *"Reichskanzler Hindenburg!" Die Weltbühne* suggested that with the turnover rate of chancellors in the Wilhelmstrasse, a brief fifty-six days for Schleicher, the day was not far off when "every German will have a chance to be Reich chancellor!"

Hindenburg did not appear in the office until ten o'clock on Sunday morning, which was unusually late for him. He told Meissner that he had had a restless night and wished Meissner had been there to talk. Hindenburg said that he had dismissed Papen over concern that Papen's demand for dictatorial power would have precipitated civil war. He had replaced Papen with Schleicher only to have Schleicher make the same demand, and now he was without a Reich chancellor. Hindenburg was still troubled by the article in the *Tägliche Rundschau*. And also by the late-night visit by Hammerstein and Stülpnagel. He wondered whether Schleicher had instigated it. Though Hindenburg did not say it, he must have calculated the possibility of a military coup. Hindenburg now told Meissner to telegraph Geneva. He wanted Blomberg back in Berlin immediately.

*

In those same Sunday morning hours, Hitler was a gravel-pathway walk away in Papen's Wilhelmstrasse apartment. He had initially intended to return to Munich but had reversed himself. As Goebbels reported in his diary, a second Papen chancellorship would end in disaster, perhaps with the impeachment of Hindenburg himself. Hitler was now the only solution—assuming, of course, that Strasser did not step into the breach or Schleicher launch a military coup, as had been rumored. To Papen's relief, Hitler showed a flexibility this Sunday morning that had been absent Saturday afternoon. He was now willing to forgo the post of *Reichskommissar* for Prussia as well as the state Interior Ministry, and would content himself with the chancellorship and two seats in the cabinet for Göring and Frick—as well, he added, as something else. If the Reich president was unwilling to accord him the same presidial powers that he had so easily granted his two previous chancellors, Hitler wanted Hindenburg to permit his new chancellor to dissolve the Reichstag and schedule new elections. He argued that given the gains the party made in Lippe, he was certain that a new round of Reichstag elections would secure the National Socialists the majority needed to grant him the presidial powers within the framework of the constitution.

Papen had a deal. Hitler had "swallowed" the disappointment of the *Reichskommissar* position "with barely contained resentment," Papen recalled later, but was nevertheless willing to accept the chancellorship with restrictions. There was no August bluster about one-party rule, no *"Alles oder nichts"* intransigence. Papen said that he would discuss Hitler's terms with Hindenburg, then set off on his tree-lined path to the Reich president. Now Papen just needed to get Hugenberg on board.

Hugenberg was summoned to Papen's apartment that afternoon. He arrived in the company of Theodor Duesterberg and Franz Seldte, the two key German Nationalists who headed the Steel Helmets. Papen had news. Hitler had acquiesced on key points, and Hindenburg had approved. Hitler was now to be Reich chancellor, with Papen as vice chancellor as well as *Reichskommissar* for Prussia, with two cabinet seats reserved for Frick and Göring, and with Seldte serving as labor minister. The coalition government involving the National Socialists and the German Nationalists represented a resurrection of the Harzburg Front. Most important, Papen told his guests, the Reich president wanted to appoint Hugenberg as minister responsible for developing a comprehensive financial plan for the country, essentially functioning as economic dictator, a position that Papen hoped might satisfy Hugenberg's seemingly insatiable ego. Hugenberg liked the idea. "So, we box Hitler in," he said. Duesterberg and Seldte were not so certain. Hitler was a fanatic. He could not be trusted. Papen pushed back. "What more do you want? Hindenburg trusts me," Papen said. "In two months, we will have pressed Hitler into a corner so tight that he'll squeak." Papen did not mention the potential new Reichstag elections.

Papen's talks were confidential. The results were not. With articles based on a well-informed source, Hugenberg's Telegraph Union mainstreamed Papen's deliberations into its sixteen hundred affiliated news sources and onto the pages of some of the most belligerently liberal newspapers. According to the Telegraph Union's insider, almost certainly Hugenberg, Papen's efforts to build a government were moving along "much quicker" than anticipated, so much so "that perhaps on Monday a new cabinet can be proposed to the Reich president." The coalition government would be headed by Hitler as chancellor, "in cooperation with the Harzburg Front," and with toleration of the Center Party. The main focus of the new government would be the reduction of unemployment and the revival of the economy. The convening of the Reichstag would be postponed until a comprehensive economic plan was completed. There would be no need for new elections since, as had been repeatedly demonstrated, "constantly holding new elections did nothing but cause public disturbance while always delivering exactly the same election results."

*

That afternoon, the streets roiled. Communist demonstrations had been banned for fear of violence, sending Ernst Thälmann and his colleagues underground to arm themselves for an insurrection. Following Schleicher's demission, 10,000 soldiers from the Iron Front, the militarized wing of the Social Democratic Party, had assembled in Mannheim in preparation for action as the country moved from political trench warfare into open battle. At two-thirty on Sunday afternoon, a further 20,000 Iron Front members, fully armed and ready for a fight, converged on the Lustgarten, across from the former royal palace and beside the Berlin Cathedral, on Unter den Linden. The previous April, Tom Delmer had watched "120,000 fanatical Berliners" welcome Hitler. Now, despite alternating sleet and rain, 80,000 Social Democrats joined the Iron Front in a show of support for the republic. Kessler was there that afternoon. He saw a sea of placards and banners. One banner read, "Nazi Victory Will Lead Germany into Civil War." Another hung across the palace façade and proclaimed, "Berlin Remains Red," though with not a Communist in sight; according to Kessler, it was the red of a distinctly Social Democratic tint.

Franz Künstler, leader of the Berlin Social Democrats, took to the podium. He reminded the crowd that the Iron Front had rallied the Social Democrats in the 1932 presidential campaign and helped defeat Hitler in the first and second election rounds. "The Iron Front saved the republic twice before," Künstler said. "Perhaps it will be necessary to rescue it again. We will permit neither the Nazis nor the monarchists to destroy the house that we have toiled so hard to build." There were cheers. Kessler was heartened. He saw it as a sign that the people would rise to save the republic. Meanwhile, Schleicher sat in the Bendlerstrasse, contemplating his next move. On returning from his meeting with Hindenburg, Schleicher told Hammerstein, "I shall not allow myself to be plucked to pieces." Hammerstein responded that the time had come for a coup d'état to restore order to the country. The Potsdam garrison, only twenty miles away, had been reinforced with four fresh regiments. Stülpnagel was convinced that the men could be mobilized in support of Schleicher. "In Potsdam, a splendid spirit reigns," one Bendlerstrasse colleague observed. "The men are ready for anything. Now everything depends on Schleicher, if he will push the button at the right moment."

Schleicher may no longer have been chancellor, but he was still defense minister. The army would listen. On Friday, a day before his dismissal, Schleicher had rejected the idea of a military coup when it had been raised by Günther Gereke, a member of the Schleicher cabinet. Schleicher told Gereke, "Bitter as I might be over the Old Man's [Hindenburg] plotting with Papen and the Nazis, my oath would forbid me from ever even thinking of doing such a thing."

What Schleicher had told Gereke on Friday, he had repeated to Hammerstein on Saturday. After all, for Schleicher, politics had always been war by other means. That afternoon, Schleicher met with the leaders of the Socialist and Catholic trade unions to explore the potential for organizing a general strike against a prospective Hitler or Papen government, with the support of the Reichswehr. Bartering ensued. There were trade union demands and the need for certain guarantees, then questions about the constitutionality of the action. "Leipart, the representative of the red trade unions, had scruples," one meeting participant recalled. "Schleicher's plan of action meant beyond doubt a break with the constitution." The issues were not only political but also legal, with clear implications for the legitimacy of a successor government. Union participation in a mass strike was not ruled out but required further consultation and deliberation. Only there was no time. "Tomorrow, early, Schleicher and I journey to Potsdam to consult with the officers of the regiment," an unnamed Bendlerstrasse colleague noted that evening. For all his scheming and intriguing, Schleicher was at heart a military man, trained in the Prussian tradition, who understood indeed that when all other options had been exhausted, war, in the best Clausewitz tradition, became an extension of politics.

*

Sunday evening at seven o'clock, there was a knock at Goebbels's door. Werner von Alvensleben wanted to speak with Hitler. Goebbels was nonplussed. Hitler and Göring were dining with Goebbels to strategize in advance of the Monday morning audience with Hindenburg. It was unsettling for Goebbels that Alvensleben knew where to find Hitler. More unsettling still was the news he had come to deliver. Goebbels took his unexpected visitor into a separate room. Alvensleben wanted to update Hitler on several developments. First, Alvensleben knew that Papen had no intention of offering Hitler the chancellorship. "Papen only wanted to make it impossible for Hitler to be appointed," Alvensleben said. This would force Hindenburg to reappoint Papen as chancellor. Alvensleben said he knew something else: Schleicher and Hammerstein were preparing the Potsdam garrison for a military coup and wanted to install Hitler as chancellor. "Schleicher is convinced that it won't work without Hitler," Alvensleben said. "Therefore, the new government has to be securely in place, and Schleicher wants to take over the Ministry of Defense."* Hindenburg would need to be "elimi-

---

* When Hindenburg accepted Schleicher's resignation as chancellor, the cabinet was formally dissolved. Schleicher assumed that he was retaining the position of minister of defense, which was not the case.

nated or sidelined," Alvensleben said. "Schleicher is ready to mobilize the Potsdam garrison and possibly intervene."

Hitler had met with Hammerstein a few hours before in the Bechstein villa. When he asked Hammerstein "whether he thought the negotiations in the Reich presidential palace about assuming power were genuine or just for show," Hammerstein said that he would use the army in Hitler's favor to convince Hindenburg, as long as Schleicher remained minister of defense. Now Alvensleben was knocking. "If the folks on the Wilhelmstrasse are only pretending to negotiate with you," he said, "then the Reich defense minister and the army chief of staff would have to alert the garrison in Potsdam and sweep the entire pigsty clean."

It was hard to discern Alvensleben's intentions. Was he betraying Schleicher? Serving as his emissary to offer Hitler the chancellorship? Or was Alvensleben playing his own game, betraying Schleicher and testing Hitler? Was it a threat or an offer? Was Alvensleben working for Hitler or for Schleicher? Hitler suspected that Hindenburg was actually planning to appoint a Papen-Hugenberg cabinet, which was certain to result in a military coup.

Goebbels panicked. "Hindenburg blind and unfit. His son is supposed to be arrested tomorrow," he wrote in his diary that evening. "Hindenburg shipped to Neudeck. So, a coup d'état." Göring called Helldorff and told him to place the SA and the SS on high alert. He called Papen. He called on Meissner but learned that he was at the races. Göring rushed to the races and found Meissner sitting in his box. Meissner seemed little concerned. He also seemed annoyed that Göring was bothering him. Meissner took the news in stride, as did Hindenburg. "The field marshal seemed hardly concerned," Papen recalled. Goebbels, Hitler, and Göring sat in Goebbels's Charlottenburg apartment until five a.m.

planning, trying to make sense of the mixed signals, and wondering about the military coup. "Threat. Serious. Kid's stuff?" Goebbels wrote in his diary. He did not believe that Schleicher had the guts to launch a coup d'état, he said, adding, "But Hammerstein does."

CHAPTER 22

JANUARY 30, 1933

Except for beer, which few Germans consider alcoholic, Adolf Hitler touches no alcoholic tipple. Neither does he smoke. Hot water he calls "effeminate." Last week, on the biggest morning of his life, this pudgy, stoop-shouldered, tooth-brush-mustached but magnetic little man bounded out of bed after four hours sleep, soaped his soft flesh with cold water, shaved with cold water, put on his always neat but never smart clothes and braced himself for the third of his historic encounters with Paul von Beneckendorf und von Hindenburg, Der Reichspräsident.

—*Time* MAGAZINE, FEBRUARY 6, 1933

On the last Monday in January, Berliners awoke to clearing skies, rising temperatures, and chaos of apocalyptic proportions. As the dead grip of winter gave way to a springlike thaw, water released from ice-cracked water mains surged into the streets and squares, flooding entire neighborhoods. Fire brigades careened through the city to pump out businesses, residences, and basements. There was talk of worse to come. "There is fear that the city's huge underground pipeline is also affected by the abnormal temperatures," threatening to overwhelm the capital in a near-biblical deluge, *Vorwärts* reported. The alarming floodwaters were accompanied by a deadly wave of influenza that closed schools and overwhelmed hospitals. Ambulance services were hobbled by manpower shortages.

Political confusion compounded the climate chaos. The Potsdam garrison was rumored to be mobilizing for a military coup. Left-wing newspapers ran headlines warning of an imminent Hitler chancellorship. State Secretary Erwin Planck called Lutz Graf Schwerin von Krosigk with the news that Hitler had broken off negotiations and was on his way back to Munich and that Hindenburg now planned to reappoint Papen, along with Hugenberg, as a "two-man" leadership team, a Teutonic duumvirate. Moments later, Krosigk received another call, this one from Meissner. The Reich president wanted to see Krosigk at the presidential palace at eleven o'clock that morning. Krosigk was to be reappointed as finance minister. There was no mention of who was to be chancellor. Krosigk called Neurath, who had learned that he was to be reappointed foreign minister. Despite the confusion, both men agreed on one thing: they would refuse to serve in another Papen cabinet.

The Monday morning confusion was even greater for Werner von Blomberg. Blomberg had received a telegram on Sunday ordering his immediate return to Berlin. For Blomberg, who had been in Geneva since the spring, the diplomatic assignment had come as a blessing personally as well as professionally. Blomberg had been freed from his demotion and reassignment to East Prussia, following the *Grenzschutz* scandal three years earlier. As head of the German delegation in Geneva, the disgraced general was now in direct communication with Hindenburg, allowing him to avoid dealing with nemesis Defense Minister Schleicher, who had betrayed him, and Chief of Staff Hammerstein, who had replaced him. On a more personal level, the reassignment to Geneva helped distance Blomberg from the grief that had followed his wife's death that May, from cancer, after twenty-eight years of marriage. Brüning was still chancellor at the time and traveled to Geneva as part of the negotiations. He found Blomberg "confused and distracted."

Blomberg experienced a different sort of confusion when he received the urgent summons from Berlin without any clarification. The weather made road and air travel hazardous, so he booked a sleeper car on the overnight train. The general's confusion only deepened Monday morning as the train pulled into Berlin's Anhalter train station.

Major Adolf-Friedrich Kuntzen, a Hammerstein adjutant, stood on the platform with instructions to escort Blomberg to the Bendlerstrasse. Suddenly, Oskar von Hindenburg, in suit and tie, came rushing down the platform with orders from his father to bring Blomberg to the Wilhelmstrasse. Blomberg hesitated only briefly. As Reich president, Hindenburg took precedence. Blomberg was whisked away in a waiting car, leaving the Hammerstein adjutant with his mission incomplete. Within minutes, Blomberg stood in Hindenburg's office. Hindenburg received the fellow aristocrat with warm familiarity. Blomberg had been a regular visitor to Neudeck following his demotion and reassignment to East Prussia. Hindenburg had come to appreciate the handsome general, with his erect bearing and serious demeanor, who had borne the indignities and degradations visited on him by Schleicher with cool restraint, and had appointed him to be envoy to the armament talks in Geneva.

Hindenburg reviewed for Blomberg the weekend's developments, his dismissal of Schleicher, his concern over street violence, even "civil war" as outlined in the *Kriegsspiel Ott* war game, and possibly an impending military putsch. Hindenburg wanted to avert, at all costs, the possibility of German soldiers shooting German citizens in the streets of German cities. "My assignment for you is to keep the Reichswehr out of the political squabbling," Hindenburg told Blomberg. "The Reichswehr belongs to all the people." An oath was sworn to uphold and protect the constitution, with Meissner and Oskar as witnesses. By nine a.m., Blomberg was the new minister of defense. Hindenburg requested that Blomberg return at eleven a.m. for the investiture of the remaining ministers. He did not say who would be the new Reich chancellor. As Blomberg prepared to depart for the Bendlerstrasse, Oskar warned him of the coup d'état. "You'll be arrested," he said. Blomberg went to his hotel instead.

When Schleicher discovered that Blomberg had been intercepted and delivered to the Wilhelmstrasse, he called Meissner. He informed Meissner that the appointment of ministers could come only on the "recommendation of a chancellor." The Blomberg appointment was unconstitutional, he said. Meissner countered that the Reich president was, in the absence of a government, exercising his constitutionally mandated emergency powers. Hindenburg had replaced Schleicher with Blomberg as minister of defense.

Sitting in his Bendlerstrasse office that Monday morning at a desk absent of dossiers, occupied only by his glass menagerie, Schleicher found himself without portfolio or power. As Goebbels had suspected, Hammerstein urged Schleicher to mobilize the Potsdam garrison, but Schleicher knew the game was up. There was no coup d'état, no public accusations, no headlines, no raids, no arrests. Hindenburg had swatted away any hint of a coup like a late-night nuisance.

*

Hitler had spent the night at Goebbels's apartment, with his host and Göring, protected by squads of storm troopers and SS men, awaiting the Schleicher coup that never came. He returned to the Kaiserhof around five o'clock Monday morning to rest, shave, and dress for what *Time* magazine was to call "the biggest morning of his life." Hitler appeared in the hotel lobby at nine-thirty, dressed in a dark double-breasted suit with a swastika pin in his lapel. In a final effort, Goebbels pressed him to hold firm against compromise. Six months earlier, Goebbels had been contemplating a cabinet position for himself with a portfolio large enough "to fill a lifetime." Now he stood in a hotel lobby watching Hitler prepare to walk out the door with Göring and Frick, with the vague assurance that there would eventually be a place for him in the cabinet. Ernst Röhm, who had accompanied Hitler in audiences with Hindenburg and Schleicher, was relegated to sitting at his hotel room window, with a telescope trained on the Reich Chancellery entrance, so he could read Hitler's expression the minute he emerged from his meeting with Hindenburg. Röhm's army of storm troopers waited, for the third time in less than six months, to know whether they were there to parade or putsch.

Hitler knew his situation had never been more promising, nor more perilous, with the press, with his followers, with his financiers. He had twice walked into the Reich president's office with the expectation that he would be appointed chancellor only to emerge chastened, rejected, disparaged, even, some would say, humiliated. It was not certain that his political movement could survive a third debacle. His closest lieutenants had grown increasingly divided. Göring understood that this was his one and perhaps only chance to secure a cabinet post. Goebbels saw nothing but peril in compromise. In August, Hitler had demanded "total power," as he had in November. But now he had accepted the slate of Papen candidates, with room for only Frick, Göring, and himself. He had acquiesced on the *Reichskommissar* post for Prussia. He had agreed, yet again, to cooperate with Hugenberg. But he knew he no longer had a choice. He could not walk out of Hindenburg's office a third time without the chancellorship.

At twenty minutes to ten, with Goebbels still pressing him—"*Alles oder nichts!*"—Hitler turned abruptly and, without a word, strode through the lobby to the hotel entrance, where his Mercedes waited. Goebbels had reason to be insistent and perhaps nervous. Hanfstaengl knew Hitler as intimately as anyone in the inner circle. Hitler was godfather to Hanfstaengl's son, Egon. He was smitten by Hanfstaengl's wife, Helene, and a regular guest in the Hanfstaengl home. But in the first weeks of 1933, Hanfstaengl sensed a shift in sentiment. "The closer Hitler came to power, the more effort he took to create a distance between himself and his immediate associates," Hanfstaengl recalled. Hanfstaengl heard a "sharpness," an "astringency" in Hitler's voice. "He now spoke down at people, as from a superior height, as if he wanted to put everyone in their place."

Hitler was greeted at the hotel entrance by a throng of supporters. As his Mercedes departed, they chanted, "*Heil! Heil! Heil!*" Instructions had been given to avoid "*Sieg heil!*," or "Hail victory!" The car slowly circled the Wilhelmplatz, which swarmed with onlookers, turning right onto the Wilhelmstrasse, and drove through the gated Reichstag entrance. From there, Hitler, Göring, and Frick were escorted to Papen's private quarters for final deliberations before the eleven a.m. audience with Hindenburg. Duesterberg arrived at the same moment. The Steel Helmet leader was taken aback. Ignoring Hitler, Göring, and Frick, Duesterberg then walked straight up to Papen and drew him aside. Göring reminded Hitler of the bitter presidential election campaign and the damaging revelations about Duesterberg's Jewish heritage. Hitler sensed danger instantly. He walked over to Duesterberg and clasped his hand. "I truly regret the hateful insults you suffered because of my press," Hitler said. "I swear to you on my word that I had nothing to do with it." Göring was soon at Hitler's side, extending his hand to Duesterberg. "Now it is vital that we stick firmly together," Göring said.

In that same moment, Blomberg was shown into the room. Papen welcomed the general and was surprised to learn that Hindenburg had already sworn him in as the new defense minister. With a flourish, Papen introduced "Defense Minister Blomberg" to "Reich Chancellor Hitler." Blomberg explained that he had been in Geneva and had been urgently summoned back to Berlin, where he'd unexpectedly found himself suddenly named minister of defense. He explained that he had intended to go directly to the Bendlerstrasse to see Hammerstein after his meeting with Hindenburg, but the Reich president's son had advised against it. Blomberg repeated Oskar's cautionary words: "You'll be arrested." Papen nodded in affirmation, then noted the time. It was ten forty-five a.m. He suggested they proceed to Meissner's office, in order to be punctual for the meeting with the Reich president. Although Duestersberg had no seat in the planned cabinet, Papen suggested that he come along.

The men exited via the rear entrance into the garden, heels crunching on the snow-covered gravel path to Meissner's office, where Hugenberg was already waiting. It was ten minutes to eleven. Hitler had been polite and charming until that moment. On seeing Hugenberg, Hitler reverted, according to Meissner, "to his old tactics." He went on the offensive. Suddenly, he reminded Papen that he represented the largest political party in the country and yet had not been accorded the position of *Reichskommissar* for Prussia. Papen tried to assuage him. He explained that Hitler could always be appointed to the position once he had gained the full trust of the Reich president. But Hitler grew only more belligerent, raising his voice so the others could hear. Since his powers were so limited, Hitler said, he was going to insist on holding new elections. He said that if "Field Marshal Hindenburg" had so little trust in him, he would be forced to turn to the people. He would let the voters provide the proof of trust. "It was a lively discussion," Papen recalled. "Hugenberg firmly dismissed any suggestion of holding new elections."

Hugenberg instructed Meissner that he should inform the Reich president that they would need to delay the swearing-in ceremony for a few minutes. Certain matters required clarification. Meissner looked at the clock. The gentlemen still had a few minutes. Pulling Hitler and Papen into a window niche, Hugenberg said that it was his understanding that a decision had been taken not to hold new Reichstag elections. He reminded Papen that he had made that fact explicitly clear in their previous meeting. The voters were exhausted, Hugenberg continued. The last thing they needed was another Reichstag election. The November results, tabulated on the Smith Premier, were as definitive as they were incontrovertible. Hugenberg said that he would never agree to new elections. Papen grew nervous. "The discussion became so heated that I began to fear that at the last minute the collective understanding that had been reached through so much effort would suddenly fall apart," Papen recalled. It was easy for Hugenberg. He was one of the richest men in the country. For Papen, the most unpopular chancellor in history, this represented perhaps his final bid for power.

Suddenly, Hitler came to the rescue. Instead of his usual belligerence, he assured Hugenberg, "with almost solemn gestures," that regardless of any election outcome, Hugenberg's seat in the cabinet was guaranteed. Hitler said that he would never abandon his current set of ministers. He repeated that any election would have no impact on the composition of the cabinet. He waved his hand. It was a minor matter. For Hugenberg, though, it was not. Quaatz had warned Hugenberg just days earlier. "If we go with Hitler, we have to restrain him; otherwise we are done for, both when he seizes power and when he fails," Quaatz advised. Hugenberg had forced Papen's accommodation and won Hindenburg's trust, just at the time when Hitler's National Socialists were in crisis politically, ideologically, financially. Without the German Nationalists' fifty-one Reichstag delegates it was impossible for Hitler to form a coalition government. Hugenberg had everything on his side: money, votes, trust, time, power. His position would never be stronger. "It is a game with five balls. Luckily we hold all of them," Quaatz told Hugenberg. "*Qui vivra, verra.*" Whoever survives will see.

All attention was now on Hugenberg. Neurath and Krosigk, along with the other candidate ministers, saw no problem with scheduling new elections. Hugenberg refused to budge. His response was simple and adamant: "*Nein!*"

Hitler did not rage. He pleaded: "Herr Hugenberg, I hereby give you my word of honor that I will never break with any of the gentlemen assembled here, regardless of the results of any election." Hugenberg absorbed the promise and paused to reflect on Hitler's attempted appeasement, which echoed previous assurances by Hitler, during their "Liberty Law" referendum, during the Harzburg Front, during their discussions over presidential candidates. Hugenberg's expression hardened. He looked at Hitler and shook his head and, for what must have been the tenth time, snapped, *"Nein!"*

This was the moment *Die Weltbühne* had been waiting for: when Hitler tripped and stumbled in his tangle of endless lies, deceits, and hollow promises, when his iron-fisted rule, his *"Alles oder nichts"* strategy, cracked and fractured and the nimbus of invincibility evaporated, and his movement began disintegrating around him, with tens of millions in party loans and debts, along with 400,000 RM in back taxes, came due, when his brinkmanship broke, and Hitler was forced to walk out of a meeting with Hindenburg for the third and final time, his political career in shambles, after which "Gregor the Great," patiently waiting in the wings, would finally step to the fore.

Meissner now interrupted. He appeared nervous. "Gentlemen, we are five minutes late. The Reich president doesn't like to be kept waiting." But Hugenberg would not budge. Papen pleaded: "But, Herr Hugenberg, do you really want to risk ruining the nationalist coalition that we have all spent so much time negotiating?" He underscored Hitler's assurances. "You mean to tell me that you cannot trust the solemn, sworn word of a German?" Papen asked. Hugenberg did not say that he did not care about how much effort had gone into the negotiations, that Hitler could in fact not be trusted, that Hitler's "word of honor" was worthless, as had been demonstrated on countless occasions. He simply barked, yet again, *"Nein!"* Ignoring the ticking clock on Meissner's mantelpiece, Hugenberg recounted once again all the reasons against holding new elections, without mentioning, of course, the main reason: as a businessman, he calculated he had nothing to gain and everything to lose.

In the meantime, Hindenburg had Meissner summoned

upstairs to his office. He wondered why the gentlemen had already kept him waiting for a quarter of an hour. Once, when Bella Fromm was scheduled for a photo shoot with Hindenburg in the park behind the presidential palace, Hindenburg received her with a rebuke: "You should try to be more punctual." Fromm prided herself on her punctuality. She responded, "I've never been late in my life." "That's just it," Hindenburg replied with a smile. "You were three minutes ahead of time." Hindenburg was not smiling now. He did not want to hear excuses or explanations. Papen had assured him just last night that everything was in order, convinced him against his every instinct to appoint Hitler as chancellor, and now, when Hindenburg had finally been persuaded to take the step, the "Bohemian corporal" was keeping the Prussian field marshal waiting? "They need to decide whether or not they want to form a government," Hindenburg grumbled. "They had plenty of time in advance for negotiating."

Meissner rushed down the stairs to warn the men of the Reich president's growing impatience, only to find Hitler and Hugenberg locked in battle. Hugenberg's cheeks were red with rage. Hitler was shouting. Hugenberg was shouting back. He had never agreed to new elections. He was not agreeing now. Hugenberg barked, yet again, "*Nein!*"

In desperation, Meissner turned to Papen. "The Reich president asks that he not be kept waiting any longer," Meissner said. "It is now eleven-fifteen. The Old Man can decide to leave at any point." Hugenberg heard the warning but didn't care. He was willing, it seemed to Meissner, to withdraw his German Nationalist support from the coalition and let the whole cabinet collapse. Sensing the peril, Göring intervened, seeking to support Hitler and Papen against the "intransigence" of Hugenberg. The other prospective cabinet members, Krosigk and Neurath, stood there "not knowing what to do," according to Meissner. Meissner shrugged. He knew Hindenburg. He had worked for him for the past seven years. At this point, it would not have surprised Meissner if Hindenburg simply refused to receive the delegation.

Hitler now proposed to Hugenberg that after the new elections, he would seek to engage the Center Party and even the Bavarian People's Party in building a broad majority in the Reichstag. Hitler saw Hugenberg soften at the suggestion. Hitler proposed that it should be left to Hindenburg to decide whether or not to dissolve the Reichstag and call for new elections. Hugenberg fell silent.

"Everything is fine now!" Göring proclaimed. "Now we can go upstairs!" Hitler broke from the group, before Hugenberg could reconsider, and bounded up the staircase, hoping to forestall Hindenburg's departure, with the others following in his wake, leaving Hugenberg as the last, struggling and out of breath.

They arrived to find the reception hall empty. A noticeable awkwardness stirred the silence. After a few minutes, the chief of protocol opened the double doors and Hindenburg, dressed in a frock coat and supported with his walking stick, entered the hall. Papen approached the Reich president and introduced the cabinet. Hindenburg made no response. He simply began to read the formal oath that the new chancellor and the ministers were to repeat.

Hitler was first. He raised his hand. "I swear: I will devote all my strength to the good of the German people, will respect the constitution and laws of the German people, will fulfill responsibly my assigned duties, and will conduct my affairs in a nonpartisan manner that is just for every person."

Meissner then presented the formal appointment letter for signature. Hindenburg took the fountain pen and exercised his Article 53 constitutional authority, placing his signature across the bottom of the page in an elegant swath of black ink with the *H* towering above the "von," at an imposing height, with the final *g* buttressing this fortress of a name, as complete and self-contained as the man and the life he had lived. Hitler scratched his name, as a clerk might initial a receipt, a barely legible "Adolf" unraveling from the *A*, followed by his surname, once again with the initial capital *H* rendered in full form, and the rest of the letters unspooling in a thread of indecipherable scrawl.

Hitler was followed by Papen, then the other ministers except for Blomberg, who had been sworn in two hours earlier. Hitler then took the floor, though protocol called for the president to speak, and offered his first remarks as chancellor. He repeated his sworn oath to serve the German people and return the government to majority rule. Hindenburg listened patiently, then dispensed with his traditional welcome remarks to the new government and invoked a phrase with which he had once launched major offensives during the Great War: "And now, Gentlemen, forward with God!"

Film footage shows the newly appointed ministers assembling that afternoon for the traditional cabinet portrait. Hitler and Göring, both in suits, both smiling, stand before a row of vacant chairs, looking right beyond the frame. Hitler holds a dossier in his left hand. Suddenly, Göring points and Papen arrives, looking as poised and dapper as ever. The new Reich chancellor greets his vice chancellor, taking him by the arm and leading him to the empty chairs. As Hitler seats himself and gestures for Papen to join him, Papen hesitates. He looks up. He points. He smiles. Hitler, already seated, looks over his shoulder. His expression darkens. Hugenberg enters. Papen welcomes the new arrival with a smile. Hitler remains seated, stone-faced, expressionless, his eyes fixed on Hugenberg as Papen gestures for him to take the vacant seat beside

Hitler. Hugenberg declines, gently presses Papen to take the seat, and positions himself behind the vice chancellor. Hitler ignores Hugenberg and turns away, still grim-faced, to speak to Göring, seated to his right. Hugenberg adjusts his spectacles then stares, equally grim-faced, into the camera. Hugenberg told a friend the next day, "I just made the biggest mistake of my life."

POSTSCRIPT

... the laws are thine, not mine.

—WILLIAM SHAKESPEARE, *King Lear*, ACT 5, SCENE 3

In June 1934, Harry Kessler was renting a villa with a garden and a view of the sea just outside Palma de Mallorca when he learned that Kurt von Schleicher was dead. Schleicher had been on the telephone with a friend around ten o'clock in the evening when there was a knock at the door. Schleicher set the phone down. The friend heard Schleicher open the door and say, *"Jawohl, ich bin General von Schleicher."* Gunshots followed. Schleicher's wife rushed into the foyer. She was gunned down. In those same hours, Gregor Strasser was taken into custody, placed in a jail cell, shot in the neck, and left to bleed to death. Ernst Röhm was handed a pistol and ordered to shoot himself. "If I'm to be killed, let Adolf do it himself," Röhm replied. He was shot dead on the spot.

"Murder of Röhm, Schleicher and his wife, Gregor Strasser, along with many other Hitler opponents," Kessler noted in his diary. "Shot by the SS. Allegedly to prevent a coup." The weekend bloodbath, known as the Night of the

Long Knives, was precipitated, according to John Wheeler-Bennett, by a final and colossally misconceived Schleicher intrigue. Schleicher had allegedly approached Röhm about reconstituting the Hitler cabinet with Schleicher as vice chancellor and Röhm as defense minister. Brüning and Strasser were to be foreign and economic minister, respectively. Papen, Göring, and Neurath were to be dismissed. André François-Poncet was said to have assured French approval. By spring 1934, lists of Schleicher's "shadow cabinet" were circulating in Berlin with a "lack of discretion" that Wheeler-Bennett found nothing short of "terrifying." The former British diplomat recalled being handed a typewritten list at a Berlin bar whose staff were known to include National Socialist informants. "The preparation of the list was in all probability the work of his more devoted though irresponsible followers," Wheeler-Bennett recalled. He mentioned the former Schleicher protégé, Ferdinand von Bredow, by name. Bredow was having tea with friends in the lounge of the Hotel Adlon when he learned Schleicher and his wife were dead. Bredow refused to go into hiding. "I am going home," he said. "They have killed my chief. What is left for me?" Bredow was at home that evening when his doorbell rang. He opened the door and was shot dead.

By June 1934, Kessler had been resident on Mallorca since late autumn. Kessler had celebrated New Year's Eve 1932 at his house in Weimar, returning to Berlin on January 2. He spent the next day in bed with a cold and high fever. Kessler dined in the Hotel Kaiserhof the day Hitler was appointed chancellor. He recalled hearing the "sounds of boots and songs" as tens of thousands of storm troopers paraded through the Brandenburg Gate and down the Wilhelmstrasse in a torchlight parade, past the presidential palace and the Reich Chancellery and the Hotel Kaiserhof,

where the lobby was flooded with jubilant brown-shirt strag-
glers. The next morning, Kessler received a call from Hugo
Simon, a Hamburg banking friend. Simon was heartened by
the Hitler chancellorship. "If he ever tries to extract himself
from the government, his reputation will be ruined," Simon
told Kessler. "If he stays in, he will be crushed between the
anti-socialist measures and the large landholder interests."
Hitler had, it seemed, walked haplessly again into a political
trap. "The 'poor chap' [Hitler] isn't very bright; he is now
bound hand and foot and delivered to the cunning schem-
ers, Papen and Hugenberg," Simon said. That afternoon, a
reporter from *The New York Times* appeared to confirm Hitler's compromised position in an article headlined "Hitler
Puts Aside Aim to Be Dictator." One observer noted dryly,
"No Third Reich, not even a 2½."

Kessler generally spent the winter months in France,
away from the grim, penetrating Berlin weather, but postponed his travels to vote in the upcoming Reichstag elections
on March 5 that Hitler had announced on his first day as
chancellor. Hitler said he was finally positioned to secure a
Reichstag majority and, with it, a legal claim to dictatorial
power. Kessler was a committed Social Democrat who knew
every vote mattered. He would wait until after the election
to travel. On the evening of February 27, Kessler was dining
at Lauer, a fashionable restaurant on the Kurfürstendamm,
when the owner approached his table with news that the
Reichstag was on fire. "The planned assassination took place
today, though not against Hitler but instead against the
Reichstag," Kessler wrote facetiously in his diary that evening. Observing that a twenty-year-old Dutch Communist
had been arrested and charged in the attack, Kessler marveled that one person was capable of setting thirty fires, that
the alleged arsonist had stripped almost naked and stood in a

window of the blazing building waving a torch to ensure his arrest by the police. In brief, Kessler was certain it was the work of the Nazis. He noted that Göring's overblown statements about a Communist plot sounded like the "lady doth protest too much."

Hitler could have suspended the March Reichstag elections, but he was determined to secure his Reichstag majority. In advance of the voting, a reporter for *The New York Times* wrote: "No stranger election has perhaps ever been held in a civilized country." A reporter noted, "In a campaign marked by forceful repression of the opposition, Chancellor Hitler has forbidden both Communist and Socialist election activity and put heavy limitations on the electioneering of the other Left parties." If Hitler did not secure a majority vote, it would represent "an immense popular disapproval of his party."

Kessler was in Frankfurt for election day. He cheered the results. "The Nazis now have 288 mandates, or 43.9 percent of the Reichstag," he wrote, not even close to Hitler's aspirational 51 percent. Meanwhile, the Social Democrats, "despite massive oppression," had lost a mere one hundred thousand votes.

The next day, Kessler left for Paris, to make the rounds of the spring garden parties. A week after his arrival, he received a letter from Roland de Margerie, the son of a former French ambassador to Berlin. Roland had spoken to a mutual friend in Berlin with close contacts to a senior SA man, who'd informed him that Kessler's name was on a "list." Roland recommended that Kessler not return to Berlin *"pour éviter des violences possibles."* Kessler showed the letter to a friend of his, the author André Gide, who was "deeply shocked," and cautioned Kessler against returning to Germany. Kessler also received a call from Roland's father, who underscored the seriousness of the threat.

Finding himself on a Hitler hit list, faced with the threat of an SA or SS murder detail, Kessler was compelled to abandon friends and properties in Berlin and Weimar, possibly for years, maybe for the rest of his life. He did what he always did when conditions, whether political or climatic, became uncomfortable: he looked for an agreeable setting with agreeable weather.

Kessler spent the summer in Paris, where he dined with Vladimir Nabokov and visited the sculptor Aristide Maillol, then traveled to London, where he saw a wax figure of Hitler at Madame Tussauds, doused in red paint and hung with a sign that read, "Mass Murderer." Kessler returned to Paris, made a brief trip to Switzerland, then traveled south to Marseille before departing by boat for Mallorca, where he disembarked on November 11.

Kessler returned occasionally to the continent. On one visit to Paris, on July 20, 1935, he crossed paths with Heinrich Brüning in a bookstore in the rue Vignon. As with Schleicher, there had been a late-night knock at Brüning's door. Instead of answering, Brüning rushed out the back, jumped a fence, and fled. Now he was passing through Paris, incognito. The two men dined that evening at the apartment of a mutual friend. Brüning spoke about attempts to restore the monarchy, which he seemed to suggest would have been the best solution for the country. "But you cannot make an omelet without an egg," he said. Brüning went on at length about his nemesis, Kurt von Schleicher. He recalled one confidential meeting that Schleicher had gotten wind of. "It was supposed to be secret, but Schleicher leaked it at a press conference the next day," Brüning told Kessler. "The whole thing went up in smoke." Brüning was equally disparaging of Hindenburg, the man whose reelection campaign he had championed and who had abruptly dismissed him amid further Schleicher machinations. The old field marshal had always waffled, Brüning said, even during the war. Hindenburg was "terrorized" by his son. And then there was Hindenburg's Neudeck neighbor, Elard von Oldenburg.

Brüning departed Paris the next day, eventually traveling to the United States, where he was given a teaching position at Harvard University. Kessler returned to Mallorca, suddenly impoverished by the confiscations of his German properties.

By then, Alfred Hugenberg had lost his seat in the cabinet and control over his media empire. Fritz Thyssen had been sent to Dachau. Bella Fromm had fled to America. Werner von Blomberg remarried and was appointed commander in chief of the armed forces, but he was forced to resign when Göring and Himmler revealed that his new wife had posed for pornographic photos.

Others survived and thrived. Riefenstahl became a successful documentary filmmaker. Papen, who had always cut a fine figure in representational roles, went on to serve as German ambassador to Turkey. Ribbentrop stepped from the shade of his Dahlem villa into the global spotlight, signing a treaty with Vyacheslav Molotov that precipitated a second world war. Himmler oversaw thirty-eight Waffen-SS divisions, as well as a security service, the Gestapo, which appears never to have detected Schleicher's Brown House mole, Franz von Hörauf, a closet monarchist and Strasser admirer. Hörauf had run National Socialist training schools from his Brown House office. Goebbels managed the Third Reich propaganda machine by day and continued to make daily entries in his diary by night. Göring, the World War I flying ace who had arranged a state-of-the-art Lufthansa aircraft rental for Hitler, went on to command one of the largest air armadas in the world. Hans Frank was appointed governor-general of occupied Polish territories, where he became complicit in the implementation of National Socialist racial policies that led to the extermination of six million European Jews. Frank was eventually hanged in Nürnberg, as were Ribbentrop, Rosenberg, Frick, and six other Nazi leaders. Göring committed suicide shortly before his scheduled execution. Goebbels and Hitler had already killed themselves, in April 1945, in the bunker complex beneath the Reich Chancellery, fulfilling Goebbels's August 1932 vow that they would have to be dragged out of the Reich Chancellery as corpses.

*

It has been said that the Weimar Republic died twice. It was murdered, and it committed suicide. There is little mystery to the murder. Hitler vowed to destroy democracy through the democratic process, and he did. An act of state suicide is more complicated, especially when it involves a democratic republic with a full complement of constitutional protections—civil liberties, due process, press freedom, public referendum. Which leaves one wondering whether any democracy could have withstood an assault on its structures and processes by a demagogue as fiercely determined as Hitler. Might a better designed constitution have been less susceptible to dictatorial instrumentalization? A less polarized electorate more resilient to partisan manipulation? Could a political leadership more committed to democratic values have provided a bulwark against more extremist tendencies? Or would a younger, less world-weary head of state have been able to guide the nation through the political and economic turmoil of the day to more stable times?

As it was, less than three weeks after the March 1933 elections, the Reichstag passed an enabling law—*Ermächtigungsgesetz*—that empowered Hitler and his cabinet to pass and enforce laws, essentially establishing the Hitler government as a legal dictatorship. The following year, in August 1934, Hindenburg passed away peacefully at Neudeck. That same day, Hitler merged the presidency and the chancellorship, establishing himself as head of state and government, a final act that made good on his promise to dismantle the democratic system, though leaving the Weimar constitution, which he had disparaged so vociferously for thirteen long years, untouched. It remained a testament to the durability but also the fragility of the rule of law, with its Article 1 serving as a cautionary reminder: "The political power emanates from the people."

Acknowledgments

In the 1980s, I served as a graduate teaching assistant in a course on Weimar and Nazi Germany taught by Dr. Richard M. Hunt, a faculty member and senior administrator at Harvard University. For Rick, the collapse of the Weimar Republic was as much a moral conundrum as it was an historical event. He wondered, in particular, to what degree the average German was complicit in the destruction of the country's democratic system. Rick spoke of gradations of responsibility and culpability, of moral and ethical dilemmas. Earlier generations of Harvard undergraduates referred to his course as "krauts and doubts," much to Rick's bemusement.

When I visited Rick in a retirement community outside Boston in autumn 2019, he was asking similar questions about political fragmentation and polarization in America. He wondered whether Weimar Germany might serve as a cautionary tale even as he warned against drawing false parallels or tenuous conclusions. He invoked an old adage: History never repeats itself, but the events of past and present can rhyme. With this caveat in mind, I have let the historic facts speak for themselves. Rick did not live to see *Takeover* completed, but I like to think of it as my final writing assignment for a man who was teacher, mentor, and friend over the course of nearly four decades.

I would also like to acknowledge Robert Littell, who provided encouragement and guidance, as did Mike Poulton. Appreciation also goes to Michael Dean at Andrew Nurnberg Associates in London, who is always there for me. Most important, Jonathan Segal, vice president at Knopf, who has now edited three of my books, recognized the potential in this project, championed it in its early development, and helped bring it to final form with patience, wisdom, and a flawless editorial eye.

Early drafts were critiqued by Eva Segura and François Delpla, both of whom contributed important insights and additional details that enhanced the narrative. A number of others were also helpful in locating specific resources, namely Angela Betz, Manfred Griffthaler, Olaf Guercke, Regina Gülicher, Oxana Khazanova, Rainer Lotz, Meredith Mann, David Seubert, and Monique VanLandingham. Several friends were supportive in offering feedback, encouragement, and assistance: David Goldman, Anne de Henning, David Hunt, Linnea Pedersen, Luke Pontifell, Russell Riley, Alexandra Schmidt-Rieche, and Berel Rodal. I owe particular thanks to my friend and colleague Florian Beierl, who has generously shared his expertise and rich trove of documentation of the Obersalzberg with me for more than twenty-five years. I would also like to acknowledge Gabriella Lazzoni, who has helped in uncountable ways, not least of all in providing a "place of inspiration" in the heart of Paris.

Special thanks also to Isabel Frey Ribeiro, Sarah Perrin, Andrea Monagle, Bonnie Thompson, and other members of the Knopf team for all their patience, help, and support.

Finally, appreciation to my children, Katrina, Audrey, Brendan, and my daughter-in-law, Birgitta, for their forbearance as I completed, once again, my "last book" on the Nazi era. I continue to welcome, as always, the support and prayers of my mother, ninety-seven as I write this. And, of course, appreciation beyond words to my best friend, collaborator, and companion of many, many decades, Marie-Louise, with love.

A Note on Sources

There were several institutions whose work and resources have been central to the research and writing of this book. First and foremost, the Institute for Contemporary History (IfZ), in Munich, which continues to publish landmark editions of works, ranging from Hitler's speeches to the two-volume annotated edition of *Mein Kampf*, along with countless books and monographs dating back to the 1950s. The Berlin State Library provided digitized editions of dozens of newspapers from the 1930s, as well as other online resources. Similarly, the Friedrich Ebert Foundation has an extensive online collection of newspapers, including *Vorwärts*. I might also mention Zeitpunkt NRW, a project funded by the German federal state of Westphalia, to which dozens of archives, universities, and libraries in the region contributed. The collection has digitized twenty million pages from newspapers published between 1801 and 1945. The German Newspaper Portal, Deutsches Zeitungsportal, is a project of the German National Library that provides online access to millions more pages of German newspapers. The photo collections at the Prussian Heritage Image Archive (BPK) and the Bavarian State Library (BSB) contain a trove of primary source materials important to the writing of this book. The German Federal Archives have generously placed one hundred thousand historical photographs from their collection into the public domain.

The United States Holocaust Memorial Museum and the National Archives and Records Administration (NARA) contributed documents as well as images. I would like to mention other U.S.-based institutions important for the research and writing of this book: New York Public Library; New-York Historical Society; Hoover Institution at Stanford University; Hesburgh Libraries at the University of Notre Dame; the sound archive at the University of California Santa Barbara; and Thornwillow Press in Newburgh, New York.

The digital lending library Archive.org was another important resource, not only for the easy access it permitted to books, but also because the digital formats made the editions searchable. This was also the case with the online transcripts of the Nuremberg International Military Tribunal, and the digitized resources at the Yad Vashem Holocaust History Museum, in Israel. An invaluable source for audio recordings of speeches by Hitler, Hindenburg, and others, collected by the German discographer Rainer Lotz, is available in the Zeitgeschichte Collection at the University of Santa Barbara in California.

The German Historical Institute Paris, funded by the German Federal Ministry of Education and Research, was a welcome resource not only for authoritative editions of speeches, diaries, memoirs, but also an extensive collection of scholarly works, as well as relatively obscure works, such as the collected *Der Angriff* essays of Joseph Goebbels, the memoirs of Hitler press spokesman Otto Dietrich and Brown House manager Philipp Bouhler.

All these institutions have provided many of the primary sources that I relied on for the research and writing of this book. I have turned to secondary works only for occasional orientation or details, since my main objective was to recount the last six months of Hitler's ascent to power as it was reported and perceived at the time. To this end, I took a phased approach to structuring and layering the source material. Newspapers served their traditional role as the "first draft of history," informing the overall structure and contour of the narrative. Official protocols, meeting notes, internal reports, correspondence, diary entries, and the like were used to deepen and detail particular moments, and also offered insights and perspectives.

Finally, postwar memoirs, interviews, and courtroom testimonies provided color, commentary, and additional details. I drew on scholarly works sparingly but gratefully when it seemed prudent to do so. Needless to say, each of these sources has strengths and weaknesses. Among them I found not only a diversity of opinions and perspectives, including contradictory information and perceptions, but also intentional obfuscations and accidental errors. I have included these, sometimes with commentary and additional information in the Notes, to help the reader experience those months in all their uncertainty, promise, and threat.

While there were dozens of news sources from which to choose, I decided to focus on a representative selection of newspapers, from the far right to the radical left, with the foreign press providing an outside perspective. The National Socialist *Völkischer Beobachter* and *Der Angriff* anchored the fascist right. The Communist newspaper *Die Rote Fahne* and the Social Democratic *Vorwärts* presented the perspectives from the left. The venerable *Vossische Zeitung* was always intelligent, insightful, and centrist, though with a noticeable liberal tilt. Hindenburg told Bella Fromm that the *Vossische*, also known as "Tante Voss" ("Auntie Voss"), was his favorite newspaper mainly because it was the only one to print his birth announcement. I also relied frequently on *The New York Times*, not only because it was the newspaper of record but also because it occasionally got things so remarkably wrong, repeatedly predicting Hitler's political demise, even after January 30, 1933.

The published minutes from cabinet meetings of the Brüning, Papen, and Schleicher governments, which include extensive annotation, allow the reader to experience firsthand the behind-the-scenes deliberations to headline-making events. Similarly, Hitler's speeches from 1932, more than a thousand pages of text meticulously transcribed and diligently annotated for the IfZ, offer insights into the major issues that occupied his attention on an almost daily basis. Diaries provide a similar service but in a more personal and intimate manner.

The daily entries of Joseph Goebbels's diary not only trace his personal reaction to the events of the day but frequently record Hitler's own thoughts and feelings. The entries are a complicated and occasionally contradictory source of information since they have appeared in various editions. Goebbels himself published select diary entries from January 1, 1932, to May 1, 1933, in a 1934 volume titled *Vom Kaiserhof zur Reichskanzlei: Eine historische Darstellung in Tagebuchblättern*. This version has some additional material, and occasionally deleted or misleading information, such as references to Hitler's family life. The fourteen-volume edition published by the IfZ between 1998 and 2006, under the title *Die Tagebücher von Joseph Goebbels: Im Auftrag des Institut für Zeitgeschichte*, edited by Elke Fröhlich, is based on the original handwritten diary entries preserved by Goebbels on microfiche glass plates. Originally found in Potsdam in 1945, they were sent to the Moscow State Archives.

An earlier four-volume version, *Die Tagebücher von Joseph Goebbels Sämtliche Fragmente 1924–1941*, also edited by Elke Fröhlich for the IfZ, was published by the Saur Verlag in 1987. An annotated source, *Joseph Goebbels Tagebücher 1924–1945*, edited by Ralf Georg Reuth (Munich: Piper Verlag, 1992), is a compilation of the 1987 Elke Fröhlich *Sämtliche Fragmente* edition and the Goebbels *Vom Kaiserhof* diary entries. Reuth indicated the latter next to the date with *Kaiserhof* in parenthesis. Annotations include references to Goebbels's speeches, and historical details providing context.

The diary of Reinhold Quaatz provides a similar mirror into Alfred Hugenberg, as does the journal of Kurt von Hammerstein into Kurt von Schleicher. Questions have been raised about the provenance of an anonymous diary of a defense ministry general, edited by Helmut Klotz. "The book is obviously the work of a group of insiders," John Chamberlain wrote in a review for *The New York Times*, on June 14, 1934. I have therefore used only those entries that I could corroborate with alternate sources. There has been similar speculation about the Bella Fromm diary, with evidence suggesting that she wrote it after immigrating to America. Again, I used only what I could verify. There is no question about the authenticity of Count Harry Kessler's diary, which provides a perfect barometric reading of the political, social, and economic pressures of the times, a reflection of the inner life of the outside world.

Like diaries, memoirs offer personal perspectives on the events of the day, but filtered through hindsight, often with the intent of shaping historical memory and perception after the fact. This tendency is perhaps most evident in the two memoirs written by Franz von Papen, one published in 1953 and the other in 1968, in which he seeks to shape our understanding of his role in facilitating Hitler's rise to power. The memoirs of Heinrich Brüning were similarly self-serving, so much so that their publication was withheld until after his death. To my mind, one of the most insightful and balanced memoirs was provided by State Secretary Otto Meissner; it offers the ultimate insider account of events in the Reich Chancellery and the president's office. Meissner served two Reich presidents, Friedrich Ebert and Paul von Hindenburg, and one Reich chancellor, Adolf Hitler. The memoirs of Hitler associates Ernst Röhm, Hans Frank, Otto Dietrich, Ernst Hanfstaengl, Hermann Rauschning, Hans Baur, Otto Strasser, and Leni Riefenstahl, to name a few, provided nuance, insight, and detail but were read with a critical eye to potential distortions and invention. I applied the same caution to a four-hundred-page family memoir compiled and written by Hitler's older half brother and sister-in-law. Needless to say, Hitler's own autobiography, *Mein Kampf,* published in an annotated edition in 2016 by the IfZ, was an indispensable resource.

There is, of course, a vast secondary literature that has been accumulating for nearly a century. Two readings I continue to recommend from my years as a graduate student are *Weimar Culture,* by Peter Gay, and *The Politics of Cultural Despair,* by Fritz Stern, as well as, of course, the landmark works of Henry Ashby Turner, who parsed the role of industrialists in Hitler's rise to power much more deeply than I have here. Turner would certainly have taken issue with my stance on the Schleicher strategy to split the Nazi Party, but I hope he would have appreciated the devils' dance I describe among Hitler, Papen, Hugenberg, Schleicher, and, ultimately, Hindenburg. Scholars of the era may have wished to see a fuller treatment of certain issues, such as the tensions between state and federal authorities, especially regarding the dissolution of the state government of Prussia, in July 1932, and perhaps the ever-present potential restoration of the monarchy, but I do make certain they are at least in evidence.

I would like to mention a few secondary sources that I found particularly helpful. These include the excellent, annotated four-volume work *Hitler: Das Itinerar: Aufenthaltsorte und Reisen von 1889 bis 1945*, published in 2016 by Harold Sandner, which chronicles virtually every day of Hitler's whereabouts. Mostly corroborated with other sources, *Das Itinerar* is an excellent resource to follow Hitler in his many travels, although not without some contradictions from other sources.

Other scrupulously researched works include the biography *Hindenburg: Herrschaft zwischen Hohenzollern und Hitler*, by Wolfram Pyta, and *Gregor Strasser und die NSDAP*, by Udo Kissenkötter, as well as a most helpful biography, *Alfred Hugenberg: The Radical Nationalist Campaign Against the Weimar Republic*, by John Leopold. *Werner von Blomberg: Hitlers erster Feldmarschall*, by Kirstin Anne Schäfer, should also be mentioned. There are, of course, many excellent Hitler biographies, some recent, like that by Volker Ullrich, and those from the recent past, including the landmark volumes by Ian Kershaw and Joachim Fest, but also some early works, like those by John Toland and Konrad Heiden. I would also like to mention several books for the details they provided, in particular, James Pool and Suzanne Pool's *Who Financed Hitler: The Secret Funding of Hitler's Rise to Power, 1919–1933* and Daniel Siemens's *Stormtroopers: A New History of Hitler's Brownshirts,* as well as *Die Totengräber: Der letzte Winter der Weimarer Republik*, by Rüdiger Barth and Hauke Friederichs. *Die Machtergreifung: 30. Januar 1933*, by Hans Otto Meissner deserves special mention, as does *Hitler—30 janvier 1933—La Véritable Histoire*, by François Delpla.

A major challenge was balancing the occasionally contradictory information found in primary sources with details in the secondary literature, as in the case with the dating of Eva Braun's suicide attempt and subsequent hospitalization. The medical records have vanished. In his memoirs, Heinrich Hoffmann placed the suicide attempt and Hitler's visit on November 1, which has led most accounts to use this date. Heike B. Görtemaker, who has written an authoritative account of Eva Braun, *Eva Braun: Leben mit Hitler* (Munich: Verlag C.H. Beck, 2010), situates Braun's suicide attempt in August, a dating that I have used, and that is consistent with Hitler's itinerary. Given that Hitler held a series of rallies on November 1, 2, and 3 in Karlsruhe, Berlin, and Hannover, respectively, it would have made it impossible for him to have visited Eva Braun in the hospital at that time.

There were similarly conflicting accounts of Hitler's exact location following his August meeting with Hindenburg. Goebbels notes, in his original diary entry, that Hitler planned to return to the Goebbels country house in Caputh, while his published diary entry has Hitler returning to the Obersalzberg. Otto Dietrich claimed that Hitler departed Berlin for Munich, where he worked "in the midnight hour at the Brown House," an account supported by Ernst Hanfstaengl in his memoirs. The most recent scholarship has hardly clarified matters. *Das Itinerar* reports Hitler staying overnight at the Hotel Kaiserhof. Volker Ullrich writes that Hitler departed directly for the Obersalzberg. I have tried to navigate these contradictions by selecting the version that seems best supported by evidence, generally citing contradictory accounts in the notes.

The photographic documentation posed its own set of complexities. There was the occasional manipulation of an image, as with the photograph of Hitler and Hugenberg together during the Harzburger Front meeting. Hitler has obviously been "photoshopped" into the scene, as evidenced by his awkward stance, and by his absence in the original photograph. (Despite the manipulation, the image conveys the two men's abiding and mutual disdain.) In some cases, the exact date or even year is difficult to determine. A photograph of Hitler casting his ballot at a polling station has been variously attributed to the presidential election in spring 1932 or one of the subsequent Reichstag elections, in November 1932 or March 1933. The curators in the NARA photographic collection, where the original is held, have marked the image tentatively "March 1933 (?)."

NARA places a photograph of Hitler addressing "107 Reichstag delegates" at September 1930, while the German Federal Archives dates it at December 8, 1932. The Polish National Archives indicates it at August 13, 1932, as does *Das Itinerar.* In each case, I have sought to weigh the existing evidence and prevailing academic opinion to select the most logical date. For example, in this latter case, I chose August 13 over August 10, because we know from multiple sources, including press accounts and Goebbels's diary entries, that on August 10, Hitler was on the Obersalzberg. In cases of continuing doubt, as with the photograph of Hitler voting, I have captioned the image, without specific attribution to date, simply as an example of him exercising his democratic right to vote.

Finally, a note on the translations. I have generally sought to transpose rather than directly translate the German text into English, not only for the sake of the narrative flow but also to make certain words or passages more comprehensible to the reader. For example, when Goebbels expresses frustration at Hindenburg's resistance to appointing Hitler chancellor, he writes, *"Hitler muss heran,"* which might be translated literally as "Hitler has to come." I have translated this as "It has to be Hitler." At times, I have left the original German, as with Hugenberg's initial response to joining a Hitler cabinet: *"Nein! Nein! Nein!"* In some cases, there were nuanced differences in the languages that I have sought to convey. I have translated *Reichstagfraktion* as Reichstag "faction," rather than "fraction," since in English the term "fraction" can refer to a splinter grouping within a parliamentary faction, thus, one could speak of a potential Strasser fraction within the National Socialist Reichstag faction.

Notes

CHAPTER 1 STARGAZING

3 "The world's greatest": Frederick T. Birchall, "Hitler Is Expected to Be Chancellor in Cabinet Shake-up," *New York Times*, August 11, 1932.

3 "Death Descends": "Der Tod aus den Wolken," *Vorwärts*, August 6, 1932 (morning). *Vossische Zeitung* ("Unwetter an der Mosel," August 5, 1932), and *Der Funke* ("Schwere Wetter Katastrophen," August 9, 1932) all reported various weather catastrophes in the first two weeks of August.

3 "With Hitler on the Obersalzberg": Goebbels diary entry, August 7, 1932. *Joseph Goebbels Tagebücher 1924–1945*, ed. Ralf Georg Reuth (Munich: Piper Verlag, 1992). Citations from this work take the following form: Goebbels, *Tagebücher*, and date of entry.

4 "We have won": "Nationalsozialisten! Nationalsozialisten!," *Hitler Reden, Schriften und Anordnungen: Februar 1925 bis Januar 1933* (Munich: K. G. Saur, 1995), vol. 5, part 1, doc. 163, July 31–August 1, 1932.

4 "I am getting": Goebbels, *Tagebücher*, August 9, 1932.

4 "My father refused": Adolf Hitler, *Mein Kampf: Eine kritische Edition*, ed. C. Hartmann, T. Vordermayer, O. Plöckinger, and R. Töppelth (Munich: Institut für Zeitgeschichte, 2022), vol. 1, p. 7.

4 "Father beat me": Ibid.

4 "Hitler had almost": Goebbels, *Tagebücher*, August 9, 1932.

5 *The New York Times* announced: "Hitler to Contest Validity of Election," *New York Times*, April 30, 1932.

5 the disparity was "so significant": "Wahl gültig erklärt," *Vorwärts*, May 4, 1932 (morning).

5 "That is a feat": "Interview mit dem Daily Express," in *Hitler Reden, Schriften, Anordnungen,* vol. 5, part 1, doc. 33, April 10, 1932.

6 "individual against individual": "Propagandaschallplatte" in *Hitler Reden* vol. 5, part 1, doc. 109, July 15, 1932. An original copy of the two-disk shellac recording is available in the Rainer Lotz Collection at the University of California Santa Barbara, listed as *"Die Braune Platte: Hitlers Appell an die Nation,"* Parts 1 and 2. Call number: 990045547400203776. The recording is unusual, though not singular, in that it is a recording of Hitler holding an address rather than speaking at a rally with the usual attendant ambient sounds of the audience.

6 What made Hitler: Harry Graf Kessler, *Das Tagebuch, 1926–1937,* eds. Sabine Gruger and Ulrich Ott (Stuttgart: Cotta, 2010), vol. IX, April 12, 1936.

7 "They keep thinking": "Uber den Nationalsozialismus bei Hans Prinzhorn," *Der Ring,* Year 5, vol. 46, 1932: 2, cited in André Postert, "Der Anziehungskraft von Adolf Hitler 1930–1932," blogpost, Hannah-Arendt-Institut, TU Dresden, November 25, 2020.

7 "Hitler knows his": Bella Fromm, *Blood and Banquets: A Berlin Social Diary 1930–1938* (New York: Birch Lane, 1990), August 30, 1932.

8 "The Almighty who": "Propagandaschallplatte," *Hitler Reden,* vol. 5, part 1, doc. 109, July 15, 1932.

9 *"maître de l'intrigue":* André François-Poncet, *Souvenirs d'une ambassade à Berlin, Septembre 1931–Octobre 1938* (Paris: Flammarion, 1946), 48.

9 "everything which seems": Frederick T. Birchall, "German Legend Raises a New Iron Man," *New York Times Magazine,* August 28, 1932.

9 "He kept moving them": Gottfried Reinhold Treviranus, *Das Ende von Weimar: Heinrich Brüning und seine Zeit* (Düsseldorf: Econ-Verlag, 1968), 248–85.

10 *"Wirrkopf":* Hans Magnus Enzensberger, *Hammerstein oder Der Eigensinn: Eine deutsche Geschichte* (Frankfurt am Main: Suhrkamp Verlag, 2008), 9.

11 "What am I to do": Ibid., 11.

11 "Junker clique": Fromm, *Blood and Banquets,* December 25, 1930.

11 Papen's head: Thilo Vogelsang, *Kurt von Schleicher. Ein General als Politiker* (Göttingen: Musterschmidt, 1965), 71.

11 *"Fränzchen":* Lutz Graf Schwerin von Krosigk, *Memoiren* (Stuttgart: Seewald Verlag, 1977), 141.

11 "Papen is isolated!": Otto Wagener, *Hitler aus nächster Nähe: Aufzeich-nungen eines Vertrauten 1929–1932*, ed. H. A. Turner Jr. (Frankfurt am Main: Ullstein Verlag, 1978), 474.

12 "Difficult decisions": Goebbels, *Tagebücher*, August 3, 1932.

12 "Consulted briefly": Ibid.

13 heard that the meeting: Frederick T. Birchall, "Reich Will Enforce Curb on Riots Today: Nazi Coup Rumored," *New York Times*, August 10, 1932.

13 town of Kyritz: "Intime Vorbesprechungen," *Vorwärts*, August 9, 1932 (evening).

13 "He was a man of thirty-one": Otto Strasser, *Hitler and I*, trans. Gwenda David and Eric Mosbacher (Boston: Houghton Mifflin, 1940), 4.

14 "The visionary genius": Wagener, *Hitler aus nächster Nähe*, 127.

14 "Germany, Germany, and only Germany!": Gregor Strasser, radio speech, June 14, 1932, in *Kampf um Deutschland: Reden und Aufsätze eines Nationalsozialisten* (Munich: Franz Eher Verlag, 1932), 387.

15 "It is curious": Goebbels, *Tagebücher*, May 10, 1932.

15 "a pale aesthete unfit": Ibid., July 8, 1932.

15 "a weakling": Ibid., June 14, 1932.

15 "If God wanted": "Rede auf NSDAP-Gautag in Nürnberg," *Hitler Reden*, vol. 5, part 1, doc. 180, September 4, 1932.

15 "to gradually lure": Goebbels, *Tagebücher*, April 26, 1932.

16 "modest, orderly man": Otto-Ernst Schüddekopf, *Das Heer und die Republik, Quellen zur Politik: Der Reichswehrführung, 1918 bis 1933* (Hannover: Norddeutsche Verlagsanstalt O. Goedel, 1955), 329.

16 "malicious lies": Schleicher letter to Ernst Röhm, November 4, 1931, in Schüddekopf, *Das Heer und die Republik*, 328.

16 "between Scylla and Charybdis": Peter Hayes, "'A Question Mark with Epaulettes'? Kurt von Schleicher and Weimar Politics," *Journal of Modern History* 52, no. 1 (March 1980): 46.

16 "Hitler stated that": *Bundesarchiv: Akten der Reichskanzlei Weimarer Republik, Das Kabinett von Papen, June 1–September 1932*, vol. 1, no. 99 (August 10, 1932): 379–80n7. The files of the Reich Chancellery in the Bundesarchiv are also online: www.bundesarchiv.de. Hereafter listed as "RKA" (for Reichskanzlei archive), along with the cabinet of the chancellor.

17 "could be done without difficulty": Hans-Otto Meissner, *Die Machtergreifung: 30–Januar 1933* (Munich: Herbig Verlag, 1983), 120.
17 "Here the memorable": John W. Wheeler-Bennett, *Hindenburg: The Wooden Titan* (London: Macmillan and Company, 1936), 406.
17 "The Hitlerites believe": Frederick T. Birchall, "Hitler Is Expected to Be Chancellor in Cabinet Shake-up," *New York Times*, August 11, 1932.
17 "I have friends": Kessler, *Das Tagebuch*, September 1, 1932.
18 "Slowly we got": Hitler, *Mein Kampf*, 2:242.
18 "We were all proud": Hans Frank, "Adolf Hitler: Eine 'Gestalt-Gestaltung' aus Erlebnis und Erkenntnis," written by Frank during his trial at Nuremberg. Yad Vashem Archives, item ID 3726995, record group 0.23, G. Gilbert, Nuremberg Collection, 8/3/1946–9/25/1946, p. 91.
19 "Excuse me!": Ibid.
19 "We have the line": Goebbels, *Tagebücher*, March 3, 1932.
19 SA headquarters: The abbreviation "SA" derives from *Sturmabteilung*, or "storm detachment," and "SS" from *Schutzstaffel*, or "protection squads," originally designed as Hitler's personal security service.
19 "The police searched": Adolf Dresler, *Das Braune Haus und die Verwaltungsgebäude der NSDAP* (Munich: Franz Eher Verlag: 1939), 15.
19 "The occupation lasted": Philipp Bouhler, *Kampf um Deutschland* (Berlin: Franz Eher Verlag, 1942), 82.
20 "It was here": *Adolf Hitler: Monologe im Führerhauptquartier, 1941–1944*, ed. Werner Jochmann (Munich: Orbis Verlag, 2000), 207.
20 "After meals": Otto Dietrich, *Mit Hitler in die Macht: Persönliche Erlebnisse mit meinem Führer* (Munich: Franz Eher Verlag, 1934), 125.
21 "I found this an excellent": Frank, "Adolf Hitler: Eine 'Gestalt-Gestaltung,'" 116.
21 "We have won a pittance": Goebbels, *Tagebücher*, August 1, 1932.
22 "Wonderful evening": Ibid., August 11, 1932.

CHAPTER 2 VICTIMS OF DEMOCRACY

23 "an act of state suicide": "Ministerbesprechung vom 9 August 1932," RKA, Papen, vol. 1, no. 98.
24 left six wounded: "Fifteen Killed in Week-End Clashes in Reich: Reds Shoot at Nazis from Roofs in Altona," *New York Times*, July 18, 1932.

24 "Reds Shoot": Ibid.

24 "For Germany, it would be a blessing": "Hitler im Anmarsch!," *Der Funke*, August 14, 1932.

24 "With that I do not mean": Ibid.

24 "If, within twenty-four hours": "Drohung mit Bewaffnung," *Vossische Zeitung*, July 16, 1932 (evening).

25 "When the hour": Camill Hoffmann, "Berliner Tagebuch, 1932–1934: Aufzeichnungen des tschechoslowakischen Diplomaten Camill Hoffmann," *Vierteljahrshefte für Zeitgeschichte* 36, no. 1 (1988): August 13, 1932. The original lyric is *"Wer hat, Dich, Du schöner Wald, aufgebaut so hoch da droben?"* ("Who put you, you beautiful forest, so high up there?") The German corruption of the lyrics read: *"Kommt einst die Stunde der Vergeltung, Sind wir zu jedem Massenmord bereit."*

25 The Steel Helmets, or Stahlhelm: The Eiserne Front (Iron Front) was represented primarily by the Reichsbanner, or Bearers of the Banner of the Reich. The Roter Frontkämpferbund, or Red Front Fighters' League, also known as the Antifaschistische Aktion, or Antifa, sought to overthrow the republic. The Stahlhelm (Steel Helmets) was officially known as the *Bund der Frontsoldaten* (League of Frontline Soldiers); their official symbol was the distinctive "coal scuttle helmet" used by German soldiers during the First World War.

25 "casualty lists": "Bilanz des Bürgerkrieges," *Vossische Zeitung*, August 11, 1932.

26 "The smuggling": "Menschenschmuggel über die grüne Grenze," *Vossische Zeitung*, January 29, 1933.

27 "Adolf Hitler gave": "Three Against Hitler," *Time*, December 21, 1931.

27 number 479,709: Wikipedia, "Liste von NSDAP-Parteimitgliedsnummern," https://de.wikipedia.org/wiki/Liste_von_NSDAP-Partei mitgliedsnummern. Based on information in the Bundesarchiv Lichtenberg: R 9361-VIII Kartei.

27 "Hitler made his appearance": Magnus Brechtken, *Albert Speer: Eine deutsche Karriere* (Munich: Siedler Verlag, 2017), 31.

27 "But now Hitler": Ibid.

27 Article 88 of the Treaty of Versailles: Treaty of Peace with Germany (Treaty of Versailles), https://www.census.gov/history/pdf/treaty_of _versailles-112018.pdf.

28 "where 22,800 residents": "Abstimmungsergebnis," *Vossische Zeitung*, March 21, 1921.

28 "It is reported": "Polish Advance Continues," *New York Times*, May 9, 1921.

29 "secret sympathy": Ibid.

29 "Of course there have been losses": "Abstimmungsergebnis," *Vossische Zeitung*, March 21, 1921.

29 "In order to prevent": "Zweierlei Mass in Oberschlesien," *Danziger Volksstimme*, May 23, 1921.

29 vote of 52 percent: "Abstimmungsergebnis," *Vossische Zeitung*, March 21, 1921.

30 "Take Upper Silesia away": "Staatsmänner oder Nationalverbrecher," *Völkischer Beobachter*, March 15, 1921; text also in E. Jäckel and A. Kuhn, *Hitler: Sämtliche Aufzeichnungen, 1905–1924* (Stuttgart: Deutsche Verlags-Anstalt, 1980), doc. 209, March 15, 1921.

30 "Heil Moscow!": "Kommunistenmörder vor Gericht!," *Der Funke*, August 21, 1932.

31 "The day will come": "Die NSDAP droht und verlässt das Parlament 9.2.1931," in "Der Reichstag vor Hitler: Parlamentsdebatten 1931 bis 1933," SWR2 Archivradio, February 15, 2021. Six-minute sound recording segment of the session, as well as a written description of the event; https://www.swr.de.

31 "Does one recall": "Frei Feld," *Vossische Zeitung*, February 10, 1931 (evening).

32 "Street Terror": *Nationalsozialistische Parteikorrespondenz*, August 9, 1932. The article, reprinted in local newspapers across the country, including the *Berchtesgadener Anzeiger*, was part of a National Socialist disinformation campaign to provide an alibi for the National Socialists' own terror bombings. Article 118 of the Weimar constitution, guaranteeing freedom of the press, permitted fake news to proliferate.

32 "extremist organization": The size of the Reichswehr was limited by the Treaty of Versailles: Articles 160 and 163.

32 Their ages ranged: For information about the individuals and details of the event, see Paul Kluke, "Der Fall Potempa," *Vierteljahrshefte für Zeitgeschichte* no. 5 (1957): 279–97. Testimonies can be found in "Kommunistenmöder vor Gericht!," *Der Funke*, August 21, 1932; *Potempa: Die Ermordung des Airbeiters Pietzuch* (Berlin: Ernst

Schneller, 1932); and "Verfehlte Entlastungsversuche in Beuthen," *Vossische Zeitung*, August 19, 1932.

32 "If you're going to do it": "Kommunistenmörder vor Gericht!," *Der Funke*, August 21, 1932. Several versions were given during court testimonies, but the generally accepted version is "*Halbe Arbeit ist keine ganze Arbeit*" ("If you are going to do something, do it right").

CHAPTER 3 TRANQUILITY

35 "Acts of political murder": "Verordnung des Reichspräsidenten gegen politischen Terror," *Reichsgesetzblatt* Part I 1932, no. 54, Berlin, August 9, 1932.

35 "The German Cabinet": Frederick T. Birchall, "Reich Will Enforce Curb on Riots Today," *New York Times*, August 10, 1932. Birchall noted that in the penitentiary, punishment was administered for even mild cases of rioting and breaking the peace, as well as "the invasion of domestic premises from political motives."

35 Couriers shuttled confidential: Brüning, *Memoiren, 1918–1934*, 594.

36 when several carriages: "Foreign News: Corridor," *Time*, Monday, May 11, 1925.

36 "Polish management": Ibid.

36 "The journey [from Neudeck] was": François-Poncet, *Souvenirs*, 27.

36 "He often interrupts": "A Day's Work for President Hindenburg," *New York Times*, March 27, 1932.

37 "Hindenburg's gigantic": Daniel A. Binchy, "Paul von Hindenburg," *Studies: An Irish Quarterly Review* 26, no. 102 (June 1937): 223.

37 "a man of service": Wheeler-Bennett, *Hindenburg: The Wooden Titan*, xi–x. For the footnote regarding the stab-in-the-back anecdote, see Wheeler-Bennett, "Ludendorff: The Soldier and the Politician," *The Virginia Quarterly Review* 14, no. 2 (Spring 1938): 187–202.

38 "with its old-fashioned": Bernhard von Hindenburg, *Paul von Hindenburg: Ein Lebensbild* (Berlin: Schuster & Loeffler, 1915), 48.

39 "slow, unheated trains": Paul von Hindenburg, *Generalfeldmarschall von Hindenburg: Aus meinem Leben* (Leipzig: Verlag Hirzel, 1920), 12.

39 "In this way, it may be said": Ibid., 7.

39 "conservative country squire": Richard von Kuehlmann, "Heinrich Bruening: A Character Study of the German Chancellor," *New York Times*, February 14, 1932.

39 When asked what: Elard von Oldenburg-Januschau, *Erinnerungen* (Leipzig: Verlag Koehler & Amelang, 1936), 222.

39 "Since the field marshal": Ibid.

39 "entirely to the benefit": "Vorbereitungen für die Feier des 80 Geburtstages des Reichspräsidenten," RKA, Marx III and IV, vol. 1, part 3, no. 240 (May 20, 1927).

40 "so that we were able": Oldenburg-Januschau, *Erinnerungen*, 222.

40 "The young Hindenburgs": Fromm, *Blood and Banquets*, February 10, 1926.

40 "incompetent militarily": Kessler, *Das Tagebuch*, July 20, 1935.

40 Schleicher credited: Krosigk, *Memoiren*, 156.

40 "ein seltenes Abbild": Goebbels, *Tagebücher*, January 25, 1933.

40 "Oskar Hindenburg wants": Helmut Klotz, ed., *The Berlin Diaries: The Private Journals of a General in the German 1934 War Ministry Revealing the Secret Intrigue and Political Barratry of 1932–33* (London: Jarrods, 1934), July 2, 1932.

41 "just as true": Binchy, "Paul von Hindenburg," 232.

41 "Last night, there were eleven": "Schluss mit Terror!," *Vorwärts*, August 10, 1932, 2.

41 "energetic defense": Ibid.

41 "white cloaks": Hindenburg, *Aus meinem Leben*, 23–24.

42 "Whereas the Reichstag": "Hindenburgs Eidesleistung," *Vossische Zeitung*, May 12, 1925 (evening).

43 "the Almighty, All-Knowing God": Article 42 of the constitution stipulates the oath to read: "I swear to devote my energies to the well-being of the German people, to further their interests, to protect them from injury, to keep the Constitution and the laws of the Reich, to fulfill my duties conscientiously and to maintain justice for all." Available online: Constitution of the German Reich, August 11, 1919, Translation of Document 2050-PS, Office of U.S. Chief of Counsel; https://digital.library.cornell.edu.

43 The preamble: Die Verfassung des Deutschen Reiches ("Weimarer Reichsverfassung"), August 11, 1919. English translation: German Historical Institute, German History in Documents and Images, vol. 6; https://ghdi.ghi-dc.org/docpage.cfm?docpage_id=4860&language=english.

43 "that Bohemian corporal": "Aufzeichnung des Staatssekretärs Meissner über eine Besprechung des Reichspräsidenten mit Adolf Hitler am 13 August 1932," RKA, Papen, vol. 1, no. 101, note 5.

43 "When I was asked": "Hindenburg stellt sich zur Wahl," *Vossische Zeitung*, February 15, 1932 (evening). The speech was recorded and is available on internetarchive.org: Hindenburg Kanditatur Rede 1932, "1932—Paul von Hindenburg—Rede über die zweite Kanditatur als Reichspräsident."

44 "speak to his single": Ibid.

45 "The recent acts of terror": "Politische Lage," RKA, Papen, vol. 1, no. 99.2 (August 10, 1932).

45 "For those who injure": "Ministerbesprechung: Wiederherstellung der öffentlichen Sicherheit," RKA, Papen, vol. 1, no. 95.2 (August 4, 1932).

46 "The current situation": Ibid.

46 "anyone who commits": *Reichsgesetzblatt*, part 1, no. 54 (August 9, 1932).

46 "Do people really believe": "Die Todes-Notverordnung," *Vorwärts*, August 10, 1932 (morning).

47 "beginning to the annihilation": *Völkischer Beobachter* quoted in *Vorwärts*, "Die Todes-Notverordnung," August 10, 1932.

47 "One would expect": Ibid.

47 "immediate arrest and conviction": Ibid.

47 "The SA conducted": "Telegramm an Wilhelm Freiherr von Gayl" in *Hitler Reden*, vol. 5, part 1, doc. 119, July 17, 1932.

48 *"eine innere Liebe zur Waffe"*: "Zeugenaussage vor dem IV Strafsenat des Reichsgericht in Leipzig" in *Hitler Reden*, vol. 3, part 3, doc. 123, September 25, 1930.

48 "Even if I could order": Ibid.

48 "Subtly [the judge's] soul": Emil J. Gumbel, *Vier Jahre politischer Mord* (Berlin-Fichtenau: Verlag der Neuen Gesellschaft, 1922), 149.

49 "honest efforts": Bernd Steger, "Der Hitlerprozess und Bayerns Verhältnis zum Reich 1923/1924" in *Vierteljahrshefte für Zeitgeschichte* 25 (1977) v. 4: 465.

CHAPTER 4   THE HITLER GAMBIT

50 "Schleicher advocates": Kessler, *Das Tagebuch*, August 6, 1932, note 1.

51 "Hitler wants to rule": "Hitler Will Regieren!," *Vorwärts*, August 10, 1932 (evening).

51 "The appointment of Hitler": Ibid.

51 Unlike Hitler's anti-Semitism: Hitler claims in *Mein Kampf* that his first exposure to anti-Semitic writings was as a teenager in Vienna (*"Ich kaufte mir damals um wenige Heller die ersten antisemitischen Broschüren meines Lebens,"* vol. 1, p. 56). The initial evidence of his anti-Semitism is found in a letter, dated September 1919, when he was thirty years old and associating with Dietrich Eckart, a playwright who was virulently anti-Semitic and served as an early mentor and supporter of Hitler's. See: Letter to Adolf Gemlich, Munich, September 16, 1919, *Hitler: Sämtliche Aufzeichnungen, 1905–1924,* ed. Eberhard Jäckel and Axel Kuhn (Stuttgart: Deutsche Verlags-Anstalt, 1980), doc. 6:88.

51 "Is it really": *Hitler Reden,* vol. 5, part 1, doc. 161, July 30, 1932.

51 "Parliament can take": *Mein Kampf,* 2:77.

51 "Law is worthless": *Der Hitler-Prozess 1924: Wortlaut der Hauptverhandlung vor dem Volksgericht München I, Part IV* (Munich: K. G. Saur Verlag, 1999), 1574.

52 "How was Bismarck": Ibid.

52 "The legalization of": Ibid., 1575.

52 He had expressed this same: "Hitler to Testify in Army Case Today," *New York Times,* September 25, 1930.

52 Hitler reminded the judges: For the text to the Weimar consitution (1919), see: German History in Documents and Images: https://ghdi .ghi-dc.org/docpage.cfm?docpage_id=4860.

52 "The constitution only": "Zeugenaussage vor dem IV Strafsenat des Reichsgericht in Leipzig" in *Hitler Reden,* vol. 3, part 3, doc. 123, September 25, 1930. Hitler appeared before the Constitutional Court in Leipzig, on September 25, 1930, as a witness in the *Ulmer Reichswehrprozess,* the trial of three Reichswehr officers accused of planning an insurrection in collusion with the National Socialist German Workers' Party. Hitler used the occasion to distance his movement from the plot and to state publicly his commitment to respecting the constitution, in a statement known as Hitler's *Legalitätseid,* or legality oath, which the National Socialists exploited for electioneering purposes.

53 "The National Socialist movement will achieve": Harold Callender, "Herr Hitler Replies to Some Fundamental Questions," *New York Times,* December 20, 1931.

53 "In the course of the day": Kessler, *Das Tagebuch,* August 10, 1932.

53 "The people are already": Ibid.

53 Goebbels noted in his: Goebbels, *Tagebücher*, August 11, 1932. Reference to the diary entry is also made in "Ministerbesprechung," RKA, Papen, vol. 1, no. 104, "1. Politische Lage," note 6 (August 15, 1932).

54 "Hitler is as furious": Goebbels, *Tagebücher*, January 31, 1930.

54 "jubilation beyond": Ibid., June 23, 1930.

54 "He is so clear-headed": Ibid., April 6, 1931.

54 "Departure from Obersalzberg": Ibid., August 11, 1932.

54 "The old man is resisting": Ibid., August 12, 1932.

55 "Warning! Those Who Play": "Warnung! Wer mit dem Faschismus spielt, der spielt mit Deutschlands Untergang!," *Vorwärts*, August 7, 1932.

55 "*unberechenbar*": Goebbels, *Tagebücher*, January 29, 1933.

55 "terrified by the idea": Kessler, *Das Tagebuch*, August 20, 1932.

55 "Goebbels and Strasser": Ibid.

56 "In any event, we": Ibid.

56 "man with a funny": John Toland, *Adolf Hitler* (New York: Doubleday, 1976), 248.

56 "I saw Hitler surrounded": *I Was Hitler's Pilot: The Memoirs of Hans Baur* (Barnsley, UK: Frontline Books, 2013), 32.

56 "As a matter of fact": Ibid.

57 Hitler's private life: From the outset, Hitler sought to keep his older half siblings, Alois and Angela, and his kid sister, Paula, away from public attention. He devotes the first chapters of *Mein Kampf* to his childhood without mentioning his three siblings.

57 When Hitler called: Ernst Hanfstaengl, *Zwischen Weissem und Braunem Haus: Erinnerungen eines politischen Aussenseiters* (Munich: Piper Verlag, 1982), 239.

57 "In the driving mirror": Toland, *Adolf Hitler*, 266–67.

58 "Dr. Dresler had just": Hanfstaengl, *Zwischen Weissem und Braunem Haus*, 239.

58 "A mysterious": "Selbstmord im Hause Hitler," *Vorwärts*, September 21, 1931 (evening).

58 "Officially she has lived": Ibid.

58 "In the luxuriously": "Onkel und Nichte: Eine seltsame Parallele," *Vorwärts*, September 21, 1931 (evening).

59 "Dear Herr Hitler": Toland, *Adolf Hitler*, 266.

59 "Yes, yes, that is": Hanfstaengl, *Zwischen Weissem und Braunem Haus*, 241.

59 "Do you think that Fräulein": Toland, *Adolf Hitler*, 287.

60 "Bestial Murder in": "Viehischer Mord in Oberschlesien," *Vorwärts*, August 11, 1932 (morning).

60 "I have the SA": Cartoon, *Vorwärts*, August 8, 1932 (evening).

60 "I had an honest": Ernst Röhm, *Memoirs of Ernst Röhm*, trans. Geoffrey Brooks (Yorkshire: Frontline Books, 2012), 219. Originally published under the title *Röhm: Die Geschichte eines Hochverräters* (Munich: Franz Eher Verlag, 1928).

60 "machine guns poked": Röhm, *Memoirs*, 150.

61 "The artillery brought up": Ibid.

61 "When he took": Louis P. Lochner, *What About Germany?* (New York: Dodd, Mead, 1942), 126.

61 "Hindenburg was a figurehead": Röhm, *Memoirs*, 229.

61 "It was the old story": Ibid., 219.

62 "I most respectfully": Ibid., 237.

62 "to wear a top hat": Ibid., 220.

62 "Every adjournment": K. L. Gerstoff, "Spaltungstendenzen bei den Nazis," in *Die Weltbühne: Vollständige Nachdruck der Jahrgänge, 1918–1953*, vol. 26, *1930* (Königstein/Ts: Athenäum Verlag, 1978), 384.

63 "To revolt or negotiate": "Putsch oder Kuhhandel," *Vorwärts*, August 8, 1932.

63 They were instructed: Goebbels, *Tagebücher*, August 12, 1932.

63 "They all smell the prey": Ibid.

63 "It is hardest": Goebbels, *Tagebücher*, August 13, 1932.

63 "The Führer stands before": Goebbels, *Tagebücher*, August 12, 1932.

CHAPTER 5 SATURDAY THE THIRTEENTH

65 "There are few days": Dietrich, *Mit Hitler in die Macht*, 115.

65 "Looking back": "Denkschrift des Bayerischen Ministerpräsident Held zur Verfassungs- und Reichsreform," RKA, Papen, vol. 1, no. 108, note 4 (August 20, 1932).

66 "It is not the guilt": "Busspredigt zur Verfassung," *Vorwärts*, August 11, 1932 (evening).

66 "The stronger these moral": Ibid.

66 "Last Constitution Day ever": Goebbels, *Tagebücher*, August 11, 1932.

66 "He said that he found it": "Politische Lage," RKA, Papen, vol. 1, no. 99.2, note 4 (August 10, 1932).

67 Sitting in the diplomatic loge: Camill Hoffmann, "Berliner Tagebuch, 1932–1934," 150.

67 "behind the chairman's": Frederick T. Birchall, "Republic Is Ignored
   on Reich Fete Day: Hitler Strikes Snag," New York Times, August 12,
   1932.

68 "I saw Frau Meissner": Fromm, Blood and Banquets, August 13,
   1932.

69 He had every right to the chancellorship: The Weimar Constitution
   gave the president the right to allow chancellors to set up a "Präsidi-
   alkabinett" (presidial cabinet), whose authority was based exclusively
   on presidential emergency decrees that gave them the right to govern
   without consent of the Reichstag.

69 "Hitler was staggered": Wheeler-Bennett, Hindenburg: The Wooden
   Titan, 408.

69 "fire and sword": "Ministerbesprechung," RKA, Papen, vol. 1,
   no. 104, "1. Politische Lage," note 1 (August 15, 1932).

69 "They try to": Goebbels, Tagebücher, August 13, 1932.

70 "If the decision": Ibid.

70 "same-sex inclinations": Helmut Klotz, "Der Fall Röhm" (Berlin:
   Georg Koenig, 1932), 8. Klotz published Röhm's letters to Dr. Heimsoth in this ten-page booklet. The first four pages chronicle the history of the letters, Hitler's statement that he stood by Röhm, and
   Röhm's letters to his friend Karl-Heinz Heimsoth in which he writes
   about his homosexuality.

71 "dirtiest and most disgusting": Ibid., 1.

71 "Hitler yelled for": Hanfstaengl, Zwischen Weissem und Braunem Haus,
   341–42.

71 Rumors held that: Hubert Renfo Knickerbocker, Is Tomorrow Hitler's?
   200 Questions on the Battle of Mankind (New York: Reynal & Hitch-
   cock, 1941), 34. Lothar Machtan examines Hitler's alleged homosexuality in Hitlers Geheimnis. Das Doppelleben eines Diktators (Berlin: A.
   Fest Verlag, 2001).

71 Hindenburg expressed to Meissner: "Aufzeichnung des Staatssekretärs Meissner über eine Besprechung des Reichspräsidenten
   mit Adolf Hitler am 13. August 1932," RKA, Papen, vol. 1, no. 101,
   note 5.

71 "a veritable monument": Hans-Otto Meissner, Die Machtergreifung,
   135.

71 "Herr Hitler, I called": "Aufzeichnung des Staatssekretärs Meissner über eine Besprechung des Reichspräsidenten mit Adolf Hitler am 13. August 1932," RKA, Papen, vol. 1, no. 101, note 5.

72 "the Herr Reich President": Ibid.

72 "I kept my promises": "Adolf Hitler an den Reichswehrminister, Staatssekretär Meissner und Staatssekretär Planck," RKA, Papen, vol. 1, no. 102 (August 13, 1932).

72 "bestial murder": "Viehischer Mord in Oberschlesien," *Vorwärts*, August 11, 1932 (morning).

72 "intolerant, undisciplined": Otto Meissner, *Staatssekretär unter Ebert, Hindenburg, Hitler: Der Schicksalsweg des deutschen Volkes von 1918–1945, wie ich ihn erlebte* (Hamburg: Hoffmann und Campe Verlag, 1950), 240.

72 "have a bit of understanding": Ibid.

72 "God, his conscience": Aufzeichnung des Staatssekretärs Meissner über eine Besprechung des Reichspräsidenten mit Adolf Hitler am 13. August 1932," RKA, Papen, vol. 1, no. 101. In the autumn of 1918, Hindenburg availed himself of a similar self-exploration when recommending an armistice, but this time he invoked "the Kaiser, the Fatherland and my conscience."

73 "Herr Hitler stated": Ibid.

74 "Herr Reich President wishes": "Vermerk des Staatssekretärs Planck über Telefongespräche mit Ministerialdirigent Doehle," RKA, Papen, vol. 1, no. 105 (August 16, 1932).

74 "no thought of exchanging": Wheeler-Bennett, *Hindenburg: The Wooden Titan*, 407.

74 "Uncle Hindenburg": Kessler, *Das Tagebuch*, May 20, 1932.

74 "grotesque nonsense": Goebbels, *Tagebücher*, August 14, 1932.

74 "for immediate attack": "Ministerbesprechung," RKA, Papen, vol. 1, no. 104, "1. Politische Lage," note 1 (August 15, 1932).

75 "The entire German nation": Konrad Heiden, *Adolf Hitler: Das Zeitalter der Verantwortungslosigkeit. Eine Biographie.* (Zürich: Europa Verlag, 1936), 300.

75 "I would rather besiege": Dietrich, *Mit Hitler in die Macht*, 129.

75 "Hardly had the Führer": Ibid., 118.

75 "Hitler Demands Full": "Hindenburgs Nein," *Vorwärts*, August 14, 1932 (morning).

75 "so he can lick": "Hitler höchstens Postminister!," *Vorwärts*, August 12, 1932 (morning). The story allegedly came into circulation

through an American press report and was picked up by numerous newspapers, including *Der Angriff,* which denounced the story as a "lie spread by an American correspondent."

75 The French newspaper: "Hitlers Gesundheitszustand," *Vorwärts,* August 27, 1932 (evening).

76 "It is untrue": "Nazis Map Policy in the Reichstag," *New York Times,* August 27, 1932.

76 "Herr Hitler, if you achieve power legally": Karl Dietrich Bracher, *Die Auflösung der Weimarer Republik* (Stuttgart: Ring Verlag, 1955), 264n121. See also Alfred Rosenberg, *Letzte Aufzeichnungen: Ideale und Idole der Nationalsozialistischen Revolution* (Göttingen: Plesse Verlag, 1955), 226.

76 "I can sleep easily": Enzensberger, *Hammerstein oder Der Eigensinn,* 109.

76 "What now? Civil war": Kessler, *Das Tagebuch,* August 14, 1932.

CHAPTER 6 MAJORITY RULES

77 "My plan is now": "Interview mit Universal Service," in *Hitler Reden,* vol. 5, part 1, doc. 192, August 18, 1932.

77 "I must flatly": Ibid.

77 "Dean of American": "H. V. Kaltenborn," Radio Hall of Fame, https://www.radiohalloffame.com/hv-kaltenborn.

78 "compensated for": Hans V. Kaltenborn, "An Interview with Hitler, August 17, 1932," *Wisconsin Magazine of History* 50, no. 4 (Summer 1967): 283.

78 "He rose from": Harold Callender, "Hitler Replies to Some Fundamental Questions," *New York Times,* December 20, 1931.

78 "simply intolerable": "Der Vorsitzender der Staatsparteilichen Fraktionsgemeinschaft im Reichstag Weber an den Reichskanzler," RKA, Brüning, vol. 3, no. 595, note 3 (December 7, 1931).

78 when the German postmaster: "Rundfunkrede," RKA, Brüning, vol. 3, no. 91, note 1 (December 11, 1931).

79 "Adolf Hitler sat": "Three Against Hitler," *Time,* December 21, 1931.

79 "*les tribulations héroï-comiques*": "Rundfunkrede," RKA, Brüning, vol. 3, no. 91, note 2 (December 11, 1931).

79 "The official communication": "Adolf Hitler an den Reichswehrminister, Staatssekretär Meissner und Staatssekretär Planck," RKA, Papen, vol. 1, no. 102, "Anlage" (August 13, 1932).

80 "Oh, the Reichstag": Ibid.

80 "I consider the involvement": "Erklärungen Adolf Hitlers," *Rheinisch-Westfälische Zeitung*, in *Hitler Reden*, vol. 5, part 1, doc. 169, August 16, 1932.

80 "Politics is no longer": Ibid.

80 "If you tell a lie": The full quote commonly attributed to Goebbels is: "If you tell a lie big enough and keep repeating it, people will eventually come to believe it. The lie can be maintained only for such time as the State can shield the people from the political, economic and/or military consequences of the lie. It thus becomes vitally important for the State to use all of its powers to repress dissent, for the truth is the mortal enemy of the lie, and thus by extension, the truth is the greatest enemy of the State." However, there is no evidence to support attribution to Goebbels. In *Mein Kampf*, Hitler wrote, "One could conclude based on the clearly logical principle that a big lie must necessarily contain a certain level of credibility." He added that the broad masses, due to the "primitive simplicity of their nature," succumb "more easily to a big lie than a small one." *Mein Kampf*, vol. 1, chapter X, "Ursachen des Zusammenbruchs," 252.

81 "Our press could not": Dietrich, *Mit Hitler in die Macht*, 118.

81 "Hitler fell into": Goebbels, *Tagebücher*, August 14, 1932.

81 "strangely distorted head": Fromm, *Blood and Banquets*, March 17, 1933.

81 "the very prototype": Dorothy Thompson, *"I Saw Hitler!"* (New York: Farrar and Rinehart, 1932), 13.

81 "Don't ever bring": Hanfstaengl, *Zwischen Weissem und Braunem Haus*, 249.

82 "Judging by the way": "Interview mit Associated Press," in *Hitler Reden*, vol. 4, part 2, doc. 88, December 6, 1931.

82 Kaltenborn recalled: Kaltenborn, "An Interview with Hitler, August 17, 1932," 284.

82 "one of the most interesting": Karl von Wiegand interview with Adolf Hitler in November 1922. Excerpts of Wiegand's November 2022, August 17, 1932, and June 14, 1940, interviews with Hitler are reprinted in World War II on Deadline: Mark Lancaster, "An Interview with Adolf Hitler," June 14, 2020, https://ww2ondeadline.com/2020/06/14/adolf-hitler-interview-karl-von-wiegand-paris-nazis.

82 "On a number of occasions": Excerpt from Wiegand's August 17, 1932, interview, "An Interview with Adolf Hitler."

83 "That man is hopeless": Kaltenborn, "An Interview with Hitler, August 17, 1932," 285.

83 "In your antagonism": Ibid., 286.

83 "we demand the right": Ibid.

83 "Did you promise": "Interview mit Associated Press," in *Hitler Reden*, vol. 5, part 1, doc. 173, August 18, 1932.

84 "No, I only": Ibid.

84 "It is reported in the German press": Kaltenborn, "An Interview with Hitler, August 17, 1932," 287.

85 "Europe cannot maintain": Ibid., 288.

85 "best disciplined": "Interview mit Associated Press," in *Hitler Reden*, vol. 5, part 1, doc. 173, August 18, 1932.

85 "I don't have to": Kaltenborn, "An Interview with Hitler, August 17, 1932," 287.

86 "Do you expect": Ibid., 289.

86 "High up": "Hitler Now Claims 75% of Cabinet Jobs," *New York Times*, August 19, 1932.

CHAPTER 7 BOYS OF BEUTHEN

87 "I had been hit": "Kommunistenmörder vor Gericht!," *Der Funke*, August 21, 1932.

87 "This is how": "Wie Hitlers Sturmführer," *Rote Fahne*, August 20, 1932.

88 "pick mushrooms": "Die Mordnacht von Potempa," *Vorwärts*, August 20, 1932 (evening).

88 "I thought I would": Ibid.

88 "Bestial Killing": "Viehischer Mord in Oberschlesien," *Vorwärts*, August 11, 1932 (morning).

88 *Die Rote Fahne*: "Wie Hitlers Sturmführer," *Die Rote Fahne*, August 20, 1932.

88 François-Poncet recalled: François-Poncet, *Souvenirs*, 57.

88 "scandal that": *Völkischer Beobachter* quoted in "Hitler im Anmarsch," *Der Funke*, August 14, 1932.

88 "formal equality": Statement by Alfred Rosenberg in *Völkischer Beobachter*, cited in "Killing Not Murder," *Manchester Guardian*, August 27, 1932.

89 "I see it as": "Dank für SA Verbrechen," *Vorwärts*, August 18, 1932.

89 "The defendants aren't guilty": The *Ostfront* statement is quoted in "Schamlosigkeit und freche Drohung," *Vorwärts*, August 20, 1932 (morning).

89 "His opponents always": Hans Frank, "Adolf Hitler. Eine 'Gestalt-Gestaltung,'" 68–69.

90 As it was, Walter Luetgebrune: The SA Rechtsabteilung (legal department) was responsible for the legal affairs of the SA as well as the SS—in particular, criminal defense. Hans Frank was responsible for the overall legal affairs of the National Socialist movement, as well as Hitler's private legal matters. In 1928, Frank had founded the Bund Nationalsozialistischer Deutscher Juristen, a professional organization that experienced the same exponential growth as the party, with 90 members in 1929, 701 by the end of 1931, and 1,374 by the end of 1932.

90 League for Human Rights: The Bund für Menschenrecht had an estimated 50,000 members and was the leading organization in the Weimar Republic for promoting and protecting the rights of gay, lesbian, and trans persons. For discussion of Röhm's sexual identity, see: Eleanor Hancock, "'Only the Real, the True, the Masculine Held Its Value': Ernst Röhm, Masculinity, and Male Homosexuality," *Journal of the History of Sexuality* 8, no. 4 (April 1998): 616–41.

90 "You went heavily": "Wie Hitlers Sturmführer Arbeiter abschlachten lassen," *Die Rote Fahne*, August 20, 1932.

91 "I was drunk": "Die Mordnacht von Potempa," *Vorwärts*, August 20, 1932 (evening).

91 "We could see": Ibid.

91 "The National Socialists": Ibid.

91 "Did he jump": "Kommunistenmörder vor Gericht!," *Der Funke*, August 21, 1932.

91 "I didn't see that": Ibid.

92 "The intruders kept": "Wie Hitlers Sturmführer Arbeiter abschlachten lassen," *Die Rote Fahne*, August 20, 1932.

92 "Children, what will": "Der Mordprozess Potempa," *Vossische Zeitung*, August 20, 1932.

92 "The corpse was": Ibid.

93 "latent self-defense": "Sondergerichtsverhandlungen in Krieg und Beuthen," *Senftenberger Anzeiger*, August 20, 1932.

93 "an accumulation of unfortunate circumstances": "Todesstrafen in Beuthen beantragt," *Vossische Zeitung*, August 22, 1932.

94 "This verdict": Goebbels, *Tagebücher*, August 22, 1932.

94 "Inconsolably embittered": "Göring drahtet nach Beuthen," *Vorwärts*, August 24, 1932 (morning).

94 "Stay strong!": Ibid.

94 "Doesn't Herr Göring": Ibid.

94 "lambasted the court's": Hermann Rauschning, *Gespräche mit Hitler* (New York: Europa Verlag, 1940), 20.

95 "But a miscarriage": Ibid.

95 "Papen will have to": Ibid., 21.

95 "My comrades!": "Telegramm an August Früpner, Reinhold Köttisch, Paul Lachmann, Hellmuth Josef Müller und Ruffin Wolnitza," in *Der Angriff*, August 23, 1932. See *Hitler Reden*, vol. 5, part 1, doc. 174, August 22, 1932.

95 "More than 300 [National Socialists] massacred": "Ein Aufruf des Führers," *Der Angriff*, August 23, 1932.

96 "Then Edmund": Frederick T. Birchall, "Nazis Riot in Court as 5 Are Condemned," *New York Times*, August 23, 1932.

96 "The death sentence": Kessler, *Das Tagebuch*, August 23, 1932.

CHAPTER 8 DETERRENT EFFECT

97 "Personally, I am inclined": "Niederschrift des Staatssekretärs Meissner über eine Besprechung beim Reichspräsidenten in Neudeck am 30. August 1932," RKA, Papen, vol. 1, no. 120.

98 *"höhere Instanz"*: Interview with Günther Gaus, RBB Interview Archive, October 30, 1963.

99 "The royal crown": "Hindenburg Urges Fatherland Before Party When Steel Helmet Students Visit His Home," *New York Times*, August 28, 1932. (The bracketed phrase appears in the article.)

99 "Dear young men": Ibid.

100 "For the most part": Oldenburg-Januschau, *Erinnerungen*, 218.

100 Between December 1930: Otto Meissner, *Staatssekretär*, 210.

100 *Time* magazine dryly observed: "Three Against Hitler," *Time*, December 21, 1932.

101 "Be still": Oldenburg-Januschau, *Erinnerungen*, 219.

101 "Even if there were a parliamentary": "Niederschrift des Staatssekretärs Meissner über eine Besprechung beim Reichspräsidenten in Neudeck am 30 August 1932," RKA, Papen, vol. 1, no. 120.

102 "somewhat calmer opinions": Ibid.

104 "As far as the present": Ibid.

104 "deterring effect": Franz von Papen, *Der Wahrheit eine Gasse* (Munich: Paul List Verlag, 1952), 227.

105 *The New York Times* anticipated disruptions: Frederick T. Birchall, "Papen to Open Fight with Recovery Plan," *New York Times*, August 28, 1932.

105 "The principal feature": Clara Zetkin, *Reminiscences of Lenin (January 1924)*, pamphlet (International Publishers, 1934). Transcribed October 2012 by Martin Fahlgren for the Marxists Internet Archive; https://www.marxists.org/archive/zetkin/1924/reminiscences-of -lenin.htm.

105 "No party, no class": The slogan in German reads: *"Keine Partei, keine Klasse, Keine Interessengruppe—das ganze Deutschland soll es sein, dem wir dienen."* RKA, Papen, no. 104, note 8 (August 15, 1932).

105 "Both sides demand": Frederick T. Birchall, "12-Month Program to Rescue Germany Offered by Papen," *New York Times*, August 29, 1932.

106 "When one declares": Heinrich Brüning, excerpt from radio address, December 8, 1931; available as "1931-12-08—Heinrich Brüning über Hitler" on Internet Archive.

106 "searching eyes": Richard von Kuehlmann, "Heinrich Bruening: A Character Study of the German Chancellor," *New York Times*, February 14, 1932.

106 "fighting speech": Frederick T. Birchall, "12-Month Program to Rescue Germany Offered by Papen," *New York Times*, August 29, 1932.

106 "contained enough dynamite": Ibid.

CHAPTER 9   ARSENAL OF DEMOCRACY

107 "It is a rule": Clara Zetkin, "Rede als Alterspräsidentin bei der Eröffnung des Reichstags (30. August 1932)," available on the Marxists Internet Archive; www.marxists.org/deutsch/archiv/zetkin/1932/08 /alterspraes.html.

107 "hoarse and weak": Frederick T. Birchall, "Reichstag Is Calm: Will Ask Hindenburg to Let It Continue," *New York Times*, August 31, 1932.

108 "murder and annihilation": Clara Zetkin, "Rede als Alterspräsidentin."

108 Zetkin spoke for nearly: Camill Hoffmann, "Berliner Tagebuch, 1932–1934," 152.

108 "Back in the years": Oldenburg-Januschau, *Erinnerungen*, 224.

108 "traitor to the country": "Parlamentsouvertüre!," *Volksblatt*, August 31, 1932.

109 "I open the Reichstag": Clara Zetkin, "Rede als Alterspräsidentin."

110 "The big joke": Joseph Goebbels, "Die Dummheit der Demokratie," in *Der Angriff: Aufsätze aus der Kampfzeit* (Munich: Franz Eher Verlag, 1936), 71.

110 "proportional representation": Candidates ran on a "list" rather than as individuals; each list was given a numerical ranking based on the size of the electorate it commanded. Thus, the National Socialists were List 9 in the 1928 Reichstag elections. By 1930, they were List 3, and after the July 1932 election, they were List 1. It should also be noted that since voters cast their ballots for political parties rather than candidates, election speeches focused on the party platforms rather than the personal characteristics of the individual candidates.

110 "Wiener schnitzel and pork chops": Goebbels, "Die Dummheit der Demokratie," 63.

110 "We enter the Reichstag": Ibid., 71.

111 "Overnight the little heap": Joseph Goebbels, *Vom Kaiserhof zur Reichskanzlei: Eine historische Darstellung in Tagebuchblättern* (Munich: Franz Eher Verlag, 1937), entry September 21, 1930.

111 "A dark day": Kessler, *Das Tagebuch*, September 15, 1930.

112 "strutted around": Fromm, *Blood and Banquets*, August 30, 1932.

112 "He crossed the lobby": Ibid.

112 "The Kaiserhof has once again": Goebbels, *Tagebücher*, August 29, 1932.

113 "Shortly before Munich": Brüning, *Memoiren, 1918–1934*, 622.

113 "that in the end": Ibid., 623.

114 "Hitler appeared to agree": Ibid.

114 "It's all talk": Goebbels, *Tagebücher*, August 29, 1932. Brüning did come away with one terrifying realization: if Hindenburg was impeached, as Clara Zetkin was proposing, then Hitler would be elected Reich president. Brüning knew that impeachment needed to be blocked at all costs.

114 "crucial moment": Frederick T. Birchall, "Papen Uses Decree to End Reichstag as It 'Ousts' Him," *New York Times*, September 13, 1932.

115 "a vote of no confidence": "Dramatische Reichstags-Auflösung," *Vossische Zeitung*, September 13, 1932 (morning).

116 "Of the 550": Ibid.

117 Göring claimed afterward: "Neuer Verfassungskonflikt," *Vorwärts*, September 13, 1932 (evening).

117 "Each election costs": "Papen Uses Decree to End Reichstag as It 'Ousts' Him," *New York Times*, September 13, 1932.

117 "government without people": "Novemberstürme," *Vorwärts*, November 11, 1932 (morning).

118 "*Das Volk wird*": *Hitler Reden*, vol. 5, part 1, doc. 187, September 15, 1932.

120 "The Führer has driven": Goebbels wrote on Monday, September 19, 1932, that Hitler would be visiting the grave. However, Harald Sandner in *Hitler: Das Itinerar*, notes that the visit took place on Sunday, September 18, and that Hitler was back on the Obersalzberg on the Monday. The itinerary listing the route on the eighteenth would support the timing.

120 "We sat": Hubert Renfro Knickerbocker, *Can Europe Recover?* (London: John Lane, 1932), 249.

120 "When businessmen": Ibid., 260.

120 "bread and work": "Reichstag Rede May 10, 1932," in Gregor Strasser, *Kampf um Deutschland: Reden und Aufsätze eines Nationalsozialisten* (Munich: Franz Eher Verlag, 1932), 345.

121 "We recognize": Knickerbocker, *Can Europe Recover?*, 261.

121 "When Hitler comes to power": Ibid., 261–62.

CHAPTER 10   EMPIRE OF LIES

123 "They were five": Arthur Koestler, *Arrow in the Blue: The First Volume of an Autobiography, 1905–1931* (London: Macmillan and Company, 1969), 215.

123 *Vorwärts* attributed: "Durcheinander um Hindenburg," *Vorwärts*, January 13, 1932 (morning).

124 "No politician": Otto Kriegk, *Hugenberg* (Leipzig: R. Kittler Verlag, 1932), 13. The biography appeared in a series, *Männer und Mächte* ("Men and Power"), that includes Hindenburg, Hitler, Mussolini, Stalin, and Pope Pius XI, among others. Kriegk was a star reporter within the Hugenberg media group.

124 *"Heil Hugenberg!"*: "Nicht Mehr 'Heil Hugenberg,'" *Vossische Zeitung*, October 7, 1932 (morning).

124 "Today there is": "Der Führer der NSDAP," *Bochumer Tageblatt*, December 18, 1929.

124 through *Führerbefehl*: Kriegk, *Hugenberg*, 89.

125 "Two hours before": "Weshalb blitzt Hitler ab?," *Vorwärts*, August 20, 1932 (evening).

125 "as funny a sight": Fromm, *Blood and Banquets*, December 19, 1932.

125 "Sturdy Alfred": Ibid.

125 *Vorwärts* caricatured him: "Der aufgeblasene Frosch," *Vorwärts*, November 9, 1932 (morning).

125 "woof woof": Hitler Rede auf NSDAP-Versammlung in München," *Hitler Reden*, vol. 3, part 1, doc. 93, February 24, 1929.

125 "gold-rimmed spectacles": François-Poncet, *Souvenirs*, 30.

127 "The press must refrain": "Was ist Aufpeitschung?," *Vossische Zeitung*, August 11, 1932 (evening).

127 "Blown to Bits": The statement in *Der Angriff* was reported in the article "Der Schamlosigkeit die Krone!," *Vorwärts*, August 10, 1932 (morning).

127 "We opened": "Was ist Aufpeitschung?," *Vossische Zeitung*, August 11, 1932 (evening).

128 "law against the enslavement": "Entwurf eines Aufrufs gegen das Volksbegehren zum Young-Plan," RKA, Müller 2, vol. 2, no. 317 (October 10, 1929).

128 "We do not see": "Zeugenaussage vor dem IV Strafsenat des Reichsgericht in Leipzig," in *Hitler Reden*, vol. 3, part 3, doc. 123, September 25, 1930.

128 "Hitler Would Scrap": Guido Enderis, "Hitler Would Scrap Versailles Treaty and Use Guillotine," *New York Times*, September 26, 1930.

129 "that they be hanged": Verhandlungen des Deutschen Reichstags, Reichstagsprotokolle, Session 104, November 29, 1929. The minutes of the Reichstag meetings can be found on www.reichstagsprotokolle .de.

130 "The Defensive Battle": "Der Front-Abwehrkampf eingeleitet," *Lippische Tages-Zeitung*, September 29, 1929.

130 "annual governmental review": "Die Sklavenlüge," *Vossische Zeitung*, October 16, 1929 (evening).

130 In a joint statement: "Gegen das Sklaverei-Begehren," *Vossische Zeitung*, October 16, 1929 (morning).

130 "Ladies and gentlemen": *Hitler Reden*, vol. 3, part 2, doc. 50, July 9, 1929.

131 fake war guilt: The *Dolchstosslegende*, or the "stab in the back myth," was advanced primarily by Paul von Hindenburg in public statements and in his memoirs. "An English general rightly said that the German army was stabbed in the back," Hindenburg told a government committee on November 19, 1919. He offered a more maudlin version in his memoirs, when he wrote, "Just as Siegfried fell to the treacherous spear of terrible Hagen, so did our exhausted front line collapse." Paul von Hindenburg, *Aus meinem Leben* (Leipzig: S. Hirzel Verlag, 1920), 403. Erich Ludendorff also credits a British general with the remark in his memoirs; he writes that General Neill Malcolm allegedly said to him, "Do you want to tell me, General, that you were stabbed in the back?" John Wheeler-Bennett, "Ludendorf: The Soldier and the Politician," *The Virginia Quarterly Review* 14, no. 2 (Spring 1938): 187–202. The assertion that the frontline soldiers were undefeated in battle but betrayed on the home front by Social Democrats and Communists who fomented strikes was instrumentalized by Hitler and others for political purposes, frequently with anti-Semitic overtones and iconography.

131 "There must come a time": "Rede auf Kundgebung des Reichausschusses für das deutsche Volksbegehren in Berlin," in *Hitler Reden*, vol. 3, part 2, doc. 50, July 9, 1929.

131 "The main player": Goebbels, *Tagebücher*, July 12, 1929.

131 "Hugenberg has had": Ibid.

132 "with all means possible": "Rede auf NSDAP-Versammlung in München," in *Hitler Reden*, vol. 3, part 2, doc. 116, December 21, 1929.

132 Of 42 million registered voters: "Volksbegehren und Volksentscheid zum Young-Plan reichsweit und in den Wahlkreisen," Wahlen in Deutschland; https://www.wahlen-in-deutschland.de/wvbveYoungplan.htm.

132 "pathetic political bankruptcy": "Klägliche Pleite Hugenberg," *Vorwärts*, December 23, 1929 (evening).

132 A cartoon in *Vorwärts* depicted: "Die Freiheitssonne des Volksentscheid ging auf," *Vorwärts*, December 23, 1929 (evening).

133 "The claim is untrue": "Erklärung" in *Hitler Reden*, vol. 3, part 2, doc. 68, August 19, 1929.

133 "Hitler was in the library": Hanfstaengl, *Zwischen Weissem und Braunem Haus*, 283.

133 "deception": "Schreiben an Alfred Hugenberg," in *Hitler Reden*, vol. 4, part 2, doc. 27, September 7, 1931.

133 "I now solemnly": Ibid.

134 "in your own party": Hugenberg's reply on September 9, 1931, and his subsequent letter on September 11 are noted in footnote 17 of "Schreiben an Alfred Hugenberg," in *Hitler Reden*, vol. 4, part 2, doc. 27, September 7, 1931.

134 "They have been deliberating": "Hitler und Hugenberg in der Zwickmühle," *Danziger Volksstimme*, January 11, 1932.

135 "If you accept": Ibid.

136 "that I earned": Manfred Overesch, "Die Einbürgerung Hitlers 1930," *Vierteljahrshefte für Zeitgeschichte* 40, no. 4 (1992): 558.

136 "I immediately realized": Ibid., 557.

136 "more merriment": "Hitler Aide Faces Indictment in Plot," *New York Times*, February 5, 1932.

136 "bottomless slop pail": Goebbels, *Tagebücher*, February 4, 1932.

136 "There is no justification": Overesch, "Die Einbürgerung Hitlers 1930," 550. The legal opinion was issued by the ministerial adviser Georg Kaisenberg, from the department of constitutional affairs of the interior ministry. For further information, see also Ulrich Menzel, "Professor oder Regierungsrat?: Hitlers Einbürgerung in Braunschweig zwischen Provinzposse und Weichenstellung zur 'Machtergreifung,'" Institut für Sozialwissenschaften, University of Braunschweig, November 2013.

137 "diligently perform": "Regierungsrat Hitler," *Vorwärts*, February 26, 1932 (evening).

137 "effective immediately": "Der Partei-Buch Beamte," *Vorwärts*, February 27, 1932 (evening).

137 "We can already see": "Herr Regierungsrat Adolf Hitler," *Vorwärts*, February 26, 1932 (morning).

138 "appearing on the world stage": Overesch, "Die Einbürgerung Hitlers 1930," 556.

138 "constitutional comedy": Ibid., 551.

138 Hitler entered: "Wahltermin: 13 März," *Vorwärts*, February 27, 1932.

138 "We once served": "Tritte zur Seite, Hindenburg!," *Vossische Zeitung,* February 28, 1932.

138 "Were President von Hindenburg": Richard von Kuehlmann, "Heinrich Bruening: A Character Study of the German Chancellor," *New York Times,* February 14, 1932.

139 "golden rain": "Reden auf der NSDAP-Versammlung in Breslau," in *Hitler Reden,* vol. 5, part 2, doc. 25, October 19, 1932.

CHAPTER 11 "GOLDEN RAIN"

140 "Let the battle begin": "Rede auf Reichspropagandatagung der NSDAP in München," in *Hitler Reden,* vol. 5, part 2, doc. 5, October 6, 1932.

140 "Tomorrow morning": Sefton Delmer, "Hitler Air Tour," *Daily Express,* April 5, 1932.

140 "But both of these": Ibid.

141 "The next morning at nine": Baur, *I Was Hitler's Pilot,* 30.

141 "The speech disappointed": "Hitler im Fluge," *Vossische Zeitung,* April 5, 1932 (morning).

141 *"Hitlers dümmste Lüge!":* Headline in *Vorwärts,* April 5, 1932 (morning).

141 Hitler flew to Würzburg: "Die Hohenzollern und die Nazis," *Main Post,* November 21, 2021.

141 "Hitler usually sat": Hanfstaengl, *Zwischen Weissem und Braunem Haus,* 264.

141 "That's the North Sea": Ibid., 265.

142 *Hitler über Deutschland:* Alfons Brümmer served as cameraman with Luitpold Nusser as assistant. An accompanying book of still photographs by Heinrich Hoffmann and Josef Bechthold was published by Franz Eher Verlag in a printing of 500,000 copies. Surviving clips of the film in eight segments can be viewed online at www.net-film.ru/en/film-65564.

142 Hitler logged: Dietrich, *Mit Hitler in die Macht,* 70.

143 "Autumn flying": Baur, *I Was Hitler's Pilot,* 34.

144 "I know that those": "Rede auf NSDAP-Versammlung," in *Hitler Reden,* vol. 5, part 2, doc. 10, October 13, 1932.

144 "Here one Polish": "Geleitwort [in Coburg]," in *Hitler Reden,* vol. 5, part 2, doc. 52, October 1932.

145 "Of the 51 percent": "Die politische Lage Rede auf NSDAP-

Versammlung in München," in *Hitler Reden*, vol. 5, part 1, doc. 183, September 7, 1932.

145 "When Mr. Hugenberg": "Rede auf NSDAP-Versammlung in Breslau," in *Hitler Reden*, vol. 5, part 2, doc. 25, October 19, 1932.

146 "Don't worry": Ibid.

147 "storms of applause": "Rede auf NSDAP-Versammlung in Berlin," in *Hitler Reden*, vol. 5, part 2, doc. 55, November 2, 1932.

147 "For thirteen years": Ibid.

148 "That, Mr. von Papen": Ibid.

148 "He spoke without": Leni Riefenstahl, *A Memoir* (New York: St. Martin's, 1993), 123.

149 "The storm of enthusiasm": "Die falschen Propheten," *Vorwärts*, November 7, 1932 (evening).

149 A transit strike: "Nur mangelhafter Teilverkehr," *Vorwärts*, November 6, 1932 (supplement).

149 "Everything is calm": Goebbels, *Tagebücher*, November 5, 1932.

150 "This counter-maneuver": Ibid.

150 Meanwhile, election officials: "Die Jagd nach den Zahlen," *Vorwärts*, November 7, 1932 (evening).

150 When Hitler had challenged: "Wahl gültig erklärt," *Vorwärts*, May 4, 1932 (morning).

150 "irregularities and fraud": "Über 300,000 Stimmscheine!" *Vorwärts*, August 1, 1932 (morning).

151 "Every update": Goebbels, *Tagebücher*, November 6, 1932.

151 "If 12,000 farmers": "Zwei Tage nach der Hitler-Rede," *Vossische Zeitung*, October 17, 1932 (evening).

151 "The country is getting": Frederick T. Birchall, "New Deadlock Seen in Reich Poll Today," *New York Times*, November 6, 1932.

151 "Der Führer hat verspielt": The entire quote reads: "Hitler hat im letzten Augenblick verspielt" ("Hitler misplayed his cards at the last moment"). Frank, "Adolf Hitler: 'Eine Gestalt-Gestaltung,'" 112.

CHAPTER 12   TRIUMPH OF THE SHRILL

152 "Hitler is a man": Curzio Malaparte, *Coup d'état: The Technique of Revolution* (New York: E. P. Dutton, 1932), 29.

152 "CRUSHING DEFEAT": "Hitler Schwer Geschlagen!," *Vorwärts*, November 7, 1932 (morning).

152 "The most important result": Ibid.

152 *"Donquichoterie"*: Ibid.

153 A front-page political cartoon: "Enttäuschung," *Vorwärts*, November 7, 1932.

153 "NSDAP Decline": "Hitler Verliert—Papen Will Bleiben," *Vossische Zeitung*, November 7, 1932 (evening).

153 "Miserable mood": Goebbels, *Tagebücher*, November 8, 1932.

153 "Our expectations": Dietrich, *Mit Hitler in die Macht*, 60.

153 Hitler sat in stunned: Hanfstaengl, *Zwischen Weissem und Braunem Haus*, 271.

153 "bleeding to death": Dietrich, *Mit Hitler in die Macht*, 61.

154 "We must renew": Ibid., 62.

154 "Well, we'll see": Hanfstaengl, *Zwischen Weissem und Braunem Haus*, 271.

154 "a classic example": Ibid.

154 "The most difficult": "Nationalsozialisten! Nationalsozialisten! Parteigenossen! Aufruf," in *Hitler Reden*, vol. 5, part 2, doc. 61, November 6, 1932.

154 "A massive attack": Ibid.

155 "Hitler spoke as if": Riefenstahl, *A Memoir*, 184.

156 "The commander who throws": Ryback interview with Traudl Junge, Munich, July 2001. The quote is also referenced in her memoirs, *Bis zur letzten Stunde: Hitlers Sekretärin erzählt ihr Leben* (Munich: Claassen, 2002): 176.

156 in the Kreuzberg: "Die Wahlen in Berlin," *Vorwärts*, November 7, 1932 (supplement).

156 "mercenaries": "Das Endresultat," *Vorwärts*, November 7, 1932 (morning).

156 "I know exactly why": Hanfstaengl, *Zwischen Weissem und Braunem Haus*, 263.

157 "[The address] was the last": Frank, "Adolf Hitler: Eine 'Gestalt-Gestaltung,'" 111.

157 "Only the weak": Riefenstahl: *A Memoir*, 127.

158 "Until the first": Quietus [Walther Karsch], "Hitlers Finanzen," in *Die Weltbühne* (I. Halbjahr, 1932), 583.

158 "It's no longer": Ibid.

158 Adolf Müller, a Munich printer: James Pool and Suzanne Pool, *Who Financed Hitler: The Secret Funding of Hitler's Rise to Power, 1919–1933* (New York: Simon & Schuster, 1978), 413.

159 "My most tragic": Ibid.

159 John Wheeler-Bennett heard: Wheeler-Bennett, *Hindenburg: The Wooden Titan*, 425.

159 "Even the smallest": "Aufruf zum Hilfswerk für die Opfer aus den Reihen der S.A.," in *Hitler Reden*, vol. 5, part 2, doc. 12, October 14, 1932.

159 "Accordingly in my case": Oron James Hale, "Hitler as Taxpayer," *American Historical Review* 60, no. 4 (July 1955): 830.

160 His declared income: Hale, "Hitler as Taxpayer," 832.

160 11,000 and 15,000 RM: For the conversion, see Harold Marcuse, "Historical Dollar-to-Marks. His table at https://www.measuringworth.com/datasets/exchangeglobal/ indicates that in 1932, $1 = 4,2110 RM. The value today is calculated here: "Currency Conversion Page," https://marcuse.faculty.history.ucsb.edu/projects/currency.htm.

160 "It's a fact": "Vermerk des Staatssekretärs Pünder über die Finanzierung der NSDAP," RKA, Brüning II, vol. 3, no. 722 (April 16, 1932).

160 Over the past twelve months: Ibid.

161 "The primary donor": Ibid.

161 "My contributions": Fritz Thyssen, *I Paid Hitler* (London: Hodder and Stoughton, 1941), 134.

161 "Aside from this": Ibid., 133.

161 For a time: Ibid., 134.

161 "The speech made": Thyssen, *I Paid Hitler*, 132.

162 "They gave the money": Ibid., 134.

162 60 million RM: "Vermerk des Staatssekretärs Pünder über die Finanzierung der NSDAP," RKA, Brüning II, vol. 3, no. 722 (April 16, 1932).

162 His final contribution: Thyssen, *I Paid Hitler*, 132.

162 "Just waves": Goebbels, *Tagebücher*, November 11, 1932.

162 90 million reichsmarks: Poole and Poole, *Who Financed Hitler*, 385.

162 "The ancient Romans": Hale, "Hitler as Taxpayer," 842.

163 "It's too expensive": Baur, *I Was Hitler's Pilot*, 34.

164 "When the Reich president": "Adolf Hitler an den Reichskanzler," RKA, Papen, vol. 2, doc. 214, note 2 (November 16, 1932).

164 "welcomed the idea": Ibid.

165 "We must try": Ibid.

165 "I have endured": "Schreiben an Franz von Papen," in *Hitler Reden*, vol. 5, part 2, doc. 65, November 16, 1932.

165 "The discussions that have taken place": Ibid.

166 "Göring will probably": "Hitlers Träume," *Vorwärts*, November 18, 1932 (evening).

166 Harry Kessler heard: Kessler, *Das Tagebuch*, November 18, 1932.

166 "The Reich president saw": Otto Meissner, *Staatssekretär*, 247.

167 "I am not taking": "Aufzeichnung des Staatssekretärs Meissner über den Empfang des Vorsitzenden der DNVP Hugenberg beim Reichspräsidenten am 18 November 1932," RKA, Papen, vol. 2, no. 217.

168 "In principle": Ibid.

168 The *Vossische Zeitung* observed: "Hitler soll verhandeln," *Vossische Zeitung*, November 19, 1932 (evening).

168 "In place of": Guido Enderis, "Hitler Gets Chance to Combine Parties," *New York Times*, November 20, 1932.

169 "There he is again": "Da ist er wieder," *Vorwärts*, November 19, 1932 (evening).

169 "I tried to establish": "Aufzeichnung des Staatssekretärs Meissner über eine Besprechung des Reichspräsidenten mit dem Führer der NSDAP Hitler," RKA, Papen, vol. 2, doc. 222, note 3 (November 19, 1932).

171 "like a schoolboy": Hans-Otto Meissner, *Die Machtergreifung*, 160.

171 "I do not intend": "Aufzeichnung des Staatssekretärs Meissner über eine Besprechung des Reichspräsidenten mit dem Führer der NSDAP Hitler," RKA, Papen, vol. 2, doc. 222 (November 19, 1932).

172 "*Millionenbewegung*": Hans-Otto Meissner, *Die Machtergreifung*, 168.

173 "It is impossible": Goebbels, *Tagebücher*, November 19, 1932.

173 "love letters": "Die 'Führer' sind hilflos," *Vorwärts*, November 23, 1932 (morning).

173 hand-delivered a letter: "Nicht angenommen, aber . . . ," *Vorwärts*, November 22, 1932 (morning).

173 "The Reich president fears": Otto Meissner, *Staatssekretär*, 249.

173 "Hitler had been knocking": "Zum Trommler geboren," *Vossische Zeitung*, November 25, 1932 (morning).

174 "prevalent view": "Reich Will Return to Presidial Rule," *New York Times*, November 26, 1932.

174 "It was most amusing": "Round Robins from Berlin: Louis Lochner's Letter to His Children, 1932–1941," *Wisconsin Magazine of History Archives* 50, no. 4 (Summer 1967): 293.

174 "One cannot shake": Goebbels, *Tagebücher*, November 20, 1932.

174 "In calling me": "Aufruf," in *Hitler Reden*, vol. 5, part 2, doc. 71, November 25, 1932.

CHAPTER 14   CLUELESS

175 "You cannot rule": Sefton "Tom" Delmer's interview with Hitler, "Interview mit dem *Daily Express*," in *Hitler Reden*, vol. 5, part 2, doc. 73, November 27, 1932. Sefton Delmer, a British subject, born in Berlin, was a freelance journalist for the *Daily Mail* and bureau chief for the *Daily Express* in Berlin.

175 "These young Germans": "Lord Rothermere and Herr Hitler," *Spectator*, September 27, 1930.

175 "campaign of terrorism": Sefton "Tom" Delmer, "Hitler Air Tour," *Daily Mail*, April 5, 1932.

176 "In the evening": Goebbels, *Tagebücher*, November 27, 1932.

176 "Never once": "Interview mit dem *Daily Express*" in *Hitler Reden*.

176 "Look, I have been told": Ibid.

177 "Hitler's reputation": Ibid.

178 A front-page cartoon: "Die starken Männer," *Vorwärts*, November 28, 1932 (evening).

178 Strasser knew that: Otto Meissner, *Staatssekretär*, 251.

178 In a commentary: "Schach oder matt?," *Vossische Zeitung*, December 10, 1932 (morning).

179 "There were already reports": "Strasser sagt ab," *Vossische Zeitung*, November 29, 1932 (morning).

179 "he did not have": Ibid.

179 "The result of this": Otto Strasser, *Hitler and I*, 94.

179 "I think it would be": Thyssen, *I Paid Hitler*, 133.

179 "Adolf Hitler, I love": Goebbels, *Tagebücher*, April 19, 1926.

180 "In response to Gregor": "Hitler heute bei Schleicher," *Vossische Zeitung*, November 30, 1932 (morning).

180 Werner von Zengen: Udo Kissenkötter, *Gregor Strasser und die NSDAP*, Schriftenreihe der Vierteljahrshefte für Zeitgeschichte, vol. 37 (Stuttgart: Deutsche Verlagsanstalt, 1978), 167.

180 "Hitler should arrive": "Hitler kommt zu Schleicher," *Vorwärts*, November 30, 1932 (morning).

181 "After several tense": "Der Aufenthalt in Weimar," *Vossische Zeitung*, December 1, 1932 (evening).

181 "Furious, Strasser and": "Eine aufregende Nacht," *Vorwärts*, December 1, 1932 (morning).

181 By late afternoon: Kissenkötter, *Gregor Strasser und die NSDAP*, 167. Kissenkötter suggests that Hitler's decision to deboard in Jena had been made at the last minute in the Munich train station. Hitler had initially boarded the D-25 overnight train, which was scheduled to depart at 9:15 but did not stop in Jena. At the last minute, Hitler deboarded the train and instead took the D-49, with a scheduled stop in Jena, which left five minutes later than the D-25.

181 "It is not exactly": "Der Aufenthalt in Weimar," *Vossische Zeitung*, December 1, 1932 (evening).

182 "Hitler as you've never": Heinrich Hoffmann, "Hitler wie ihn keiner kennt," Broschüre (Berlin 1932), in the Obersalzberg Institute collection.

182 "It is not true": "Der Aufenthalt in Weimar," *Vossische Zeitung*, December 1, 1932 (evening).

182 The incident inspired: "Nächtliches Abendteuer," *Vorwärts*, December 1, 1932 (evening). The original rhyme reads: "Mit dem Kanzlerposten ist es wasser / Platzen sollen jetzt Frick und Strasser."

182 "with whom we also": "Was soll werden?," *Der Funke*, August 16, 1932.

182 "There was one single": "Machtkämpfe in der NSDAP," *Vorwärts*, August 17, 1932.

183 "clueless only because": "Hitler zieht Notlinie," *Vorwärts*, November 30, 1932 (evening).

183 "Move it, Hitler": "Der Führer" cartoon, *Vorwärts*, December 2, 1932.

183 "pack of lies": "Der Aufenthalt in Weimar," *Vossische Zeitung*, December 1, 1932.

184 "Strasser is for coalition": Goebbels, *Tagebücher*, December 1, 1932.

184 "Since I have already": "Schreiben an Otto Meissner," in *Hitler Reden*, vol. 5, part 2, doc. 74, November 30, 1932.

184 "Schleicher's move blocked": Goebbels, *Tagebücher*, December 1, 1932.

184 "We've got the upper": Ibid., December 2, 1932.

185 "In order to approximate": Klotz, *The Berlin Diaries*, September 23, 1932.

185 "in a hunting blind": Hans-Otto Meissner, *Die Machtergreifung*, 258.

185 "The old field marshal": Ibid.

185 "Anyone who is both": Enzensberger, *Hammerstein oder Der Eigensinn*, 77–78.

186 "The excellent presentation": "Tagebuchaufzeichnung des Reichsfinanzministers über den Verlauf der Ministerbesprechung," RKA, Papen, vol. 2, no. 239 (December 2, 1932).

186 "I am declining": "Rede auf NSDAP-Versammlung in Greiz," in *Hitler Reden*, vol. 5, part 2, doc. 76, December 1, 1932.

186 The newspaper *Nationalsozialist*: Ibid., note 1.

187 "a golden lock": "Rede auf der NSDAP Versammlung in Altenburg," in *Hitler Reden*, vol. 5, part 2, doc. 77, December 1, 1932.

187 "not as citizen": "Rede auf NSDAP Versammlung Eisfeld," in *Hitler Reden*, vol. 5, part 2, doc. 80, December 3, 1932.

187 "dull, listless speech": "Rede auf NSDAP Versammlung in Altenburg," in *Hitler Reden*, vol. 5, part 2, doc. 77, note 1, December 1, 1932.

187 In Altenburg: Ibid.

187 "The Führer spoke today": "Hitlers Verluste in Thüringen," *Vossische Zeitung*, December 5, 1932; reprinted from the December 4 *Völkischer Beobachter* about Saturday.

188 25 percent drop: "Die Naziniederlage," *Vorwärts*, December 6, 1932 (evening).

188 from 1,843 votes to 894: "Von 1843 auf 894: Gewaltige Verluste der Nationalsozialisten," *Vossische Zeitung*, November 28, 1932.

188 "the majority of the student": "Es dämmert," *Vorwärts*, December 2, 1932 (morning).

188 "The situation in": Goebbels, *Tagebücher*, December 6, 1932.

188 *Vorwärts* reported a: "Die Wahl als Wahrzeichen," *Vorwärts*, December 5, 1932 (evening).

188 "The nimbus of the inexorable": "Hitlers Verluste in Thüringen," *Vossische Zeitung*, December 5, 1932.

CHAPTER 15   BETRAYAL

189 "Tell your boss": Ernst Hanfstaengl: *Zwischen Weisem und Braunem Haus* (Munich: R. Piper & Co., 1970), 282.

190 "man who tirelessly": Gregor Strasser, *Kampf um Deutschland: Reden und Aufsätzen eines Nationalsozialisten* (Munich: Franz Eher Verlag, 1932).

190 "I have eight": Otto Strasser, *Hitler and I*, 97.

190 "in eternal loyalty": Philipp Gassert and Daniel S. Mattern, eds., *The Hitler Library: A Bibliography* (Westport, CT: Greenwood, 2001).

190 "Thank God, we didn't lose": Alfred Rosenberg, *Letzte Aufzeichnungen*, 112.

190 "like a brother": Ibid.

190 "I fought as a Hitler man": Ibid., 111.

191 "For the first time, he": Goebbels, *Tagebücher*, August 31, 1932.

191 "I had a long talk": Ibid., September 3, 1932.

191 "nothing less than the worst betrayal": Ibid., December 5, 1932.

192 "Gregor Strasser considers": Konrad Heiden, commentary in *Vossische Zeitung*, December 10, 1932.

192 "No great movement": "Rede vor der Reichstagsfraktion der NSDAP in Berlin," in *Hitler Reden*, vol. 5, part 2, doc. 84, December 5, 1932.

192 "It is not true": Ibid.

193 "the honor and prestige": Goebbels, *Tagebücher*, December 5, 1932.

193 "no internal disagreements": Hitler, *Mein Kampf*, 2:234.

193 "If the party collapses": Goebbels, *Tagebücher*, December 9, 1932.

193 "Those traitors": Riefenstahl, *A Memoir*, 186.

194 "We're going to keep": Ibid.

194 Reading from prepared remarks: "Eröffnung des Reichstages," *Vorwärts*, December 7, 1932 (morning).

195 "notetaker": "Die Schriftführerwahl," *Vorwärts*, December 8, 1932.

195 "president of a dictatorship": "Prügelszenen im Reichstag," *Vorwärts*, December 8, 1932 (morning).

196 "a wild fracas": Ibid.

196 "Heavy injuries": Ibid.

196 "WILD NAZI-RED FIGHT": "Wild Nazi-Red Fight Halts the Reichstag," *New York Times*, December 8, 1932.

197 "If one individual": Volker Ullrich, *Hitler: Die Jahre des Aufstiegs*, vol. 1 (Frankfurt a/M: S. Fischer Verlag, 2013), 343–44.

198 "Dr. Ley is an idiot": Goebbels, *Tagebücher*, September 30, 1925.

198 "Is Ley perhaps": Ibid., August 10, 1928.

199 "I refuse to go down": Ullrich, *Hitler*, 343.

200 Lohse found Hitler: Ian Kershaw, *Hitler: 1889–1936 Hubris* (New York: W. W. Norton & Company, 1999), 401.

200 "First it was Strasser": Heiden, *Hitler*, vol. 1, 305.

201 "clueless, indecisive": Ernst Hanfstaengl, *Zwischen Weissem und Braunem Haus: Erinnerungen eines politischen Aussenseiters*, 281.

201 "Hitler's nature": Hermann Rauschning, *Hitler Speaks* (London: Eyre & Spottiswoode, 1940), 165.

201 "'Gregor the Great'": Heinz Pol, "Gregor der Grosse" in *Die Weltbühne, Vollständige Nachdruck der Jahrgänge 1918–1953* (Köngisstein/Ts: Athenäum Verlag, 1978), vol. 26, 1930: 566. The sentence has been translated in abbreviated form.

201 "Party comrade Gregor": "Konflikt Hitler–Strasser," *Vossische Zeitung*, December 9, 1932.

201 "Hitler's approved illness": "Krach in der Hitler-Partei," *Vorwärts*, December 9, 1932.

202 "Strasser's Declaration of War Against Hitler": Quoted in "Die Rebellion," *Vorwärts*, Decembers 9, 1932 (evening).

202 "Strasser as the great man": Goebbels, *Tagebücher*, December 9, 1932.

202 "general dissatisfaction": "Die Rebellion," *Vorwärts*, December 9, 1932 (evening).

202 "After I heard": Hitler, *Mein Kampf*, 1:232.

203 "disaster for the nation": "Die Rebellion," *Vorwärts*, December 9, 1932 (evening).

203 "the smoldering conflict": "Hitler Takes over Strasser's Duties," *New York Times*, December 11, 1932.

203 "They Lie! They Lie!": "Die Rebellion," *Vorwärts*, December 9, 1932 (evening).

203 "card system": Louis Lochner, *What About Germany?*, 26–27.

204 *"divide et impera"*: Heinrich Brüning, *Memoiren 1918–1934* (Stuttgart: Deutsches Verlagsanstalt, 1970), 609.

204 "master of counterintelligence": Ibid., 282.

205 "I was never": Kirstin A. Schäfer, *Werner von Blomberg: Hitlers erster Feldmarshall* (Padeborn: Ferdinand Schöningh, 2006), 81.

205 "You can no longer": Goebbels, *Tagebücher*, August 26, 1932.

205 "He considers Strasser": "General a.D. von Hörauf an Wilhelm von Preussen," RKA, Schleicher, no. 35 (December 21, 1932).

205 "Kurt and Willi": Wolfram Pyta and Rainer Orth, *Gutachten über die politische Haltung und das politische Verhalten von Wilhelm Prinz von Preussen (1882–1951), letzter Kronprinz des deutschen Reiches und von Preussen, in den Jarhen 1923–1945* (Stuttgart, June 25, 2016), 17. This expert opinion was prepared as part of a legal dispute over Hohenzollern family claims to former properties and to determine their potential culpability in Hitler's rise to power.

206 "With heartfelt greetings": "Wilhelm von Preussen an den Reichskanzler," RKA, Schleicher, no. 54 (January 13, 1933).

206 "Schleicher's plans": Otto Strasser, *Hitler and I*, 138.

206 "The idea was": Ernst Hanfstaengl, *The Unknown Hitler* (London: Gibson Square Books, 2005), 204.

206 Schleicher received a phone call: "Aufzeichnung des Staatssekretärs des Auswärtigen Amtes von Bülow, 12 Dez 1932," in *Akten zur deutschen auswätigen Politik, 1918–1945: Serie B, 1925–1933*, vol. 21 (Göttingen: Vandenhoeck & Ruprecht, 1983), doc. 218.

206 "shift in sentiment": Neurath telegram, morning of December 10, 1932, in *Akten zur deutschen auswärtigen Politik, 1918–1945: Serie B, 1925–1933*, 21:451.

207 "willingness of the American": "Der Botschaft in Washington: von Prittwitz und Gaffron an das Auswärtige Amt," sent December 14, 1932; arrived December 23, 1932, in *Akten zur deutschen auswätigen Politik, 1918–1945: Serie B, 1925–1933*, 21:470.

207 "'dead as a doornail'": Krosigk, *Memoiren*, 148.

207 "The Government remits": Knickerbocker, *Can Europe Recover?*, 238–39.

207 the first time since 1920: "Reichstag Grants Schleicher a Truce," *New York Times*, December 10, 1932.

208 "in a quiet and even": "Schleicher Pledges More Jobs in Reich," *New York Times*, December 16, 1932.

208 "My policy is one of steadying": Lochner, *What About Germany?*, 39–40.

CHAPTER 16   GHOST OF CHRISTMAS PRESENT

209 *"Vorwärts, Frankfurter Zeitung,* and other": "Erklärung," in *Hitler Reden,* vol. 5, part 2, doc. 104, December 19, 1932.

210 "that many people": "Hitlers Gesundheitszustand," *Vorwärts,* August 27, 1932 (evening).

211 "It shows how deep": "Prügelei in Hitler-Versammlung," *Vorwärts,* December 18, 1932 (morning).

211 "Strasser's exit was just": "Wilhelm von Preussen an den Reichskanzler," RKA, Schleicher, no. 54 (January 13, 1933).

211 mutinied in Kassel: "Geld für die Uniformen Fehlt," *Vossische Zeitung,* December 19, 1932.

211 "The hatred is directed": Weiss and Hoser, *Aus den Tagebüchern von Reinhold Quaatz,* December 21, 1932.

211 "The financial collapse": Klotz, *The Berlin Diaries,* January 3, 1933.

211 Three Hitler Youth leaders: "Ihrem 'Führer' den Fensterscheiben eingeworfen," *Vossische Zeitung,* December 31, 1932.

211 A fight between: "Tumulte innerhalb der SA," *Der Funke,* January 4, 1932.

212 Goebbels dismissed the killing: Goebbels, *Tagebücher,* December 30, 1932.

212 "Those can't be SA": Frank, "Adolf Hitler: Eine 'Gestalt-Gestaltung,'" 84.

212 "In Potempa the National": "Bangende Mütter," *Vorwärts,* December 29, 1932 (morning).

213 *Der Funke* ran an exposé: "Aus dem Nazifeme-Sumpf," *Der Funke,* December 31, 1932.

213 The *Bayerische Staatszeitung:* "Strassers Forderungen," *Vossische Zeitung,* December 27, 1932.

213 "If Strasser were to return": Ibid.

214 "I am surrounded": "Hitler Family Chronicle," unpublished manuscript, Obersalzberg Archive, a private archive in Berchtesgaden. The nephew, William Patrick Hitler, was the son of Hitler's older half brother, Alois, and a full-blood sibling to Angela. Alois Hitler lived in Hamburg and eventually moved to Berlin, after Hitler's appointment as chancellor. He opened a restaurant on the Wittenbergplatz, just beside the elegant KaDeWe department store. Originally named Café Alois Hitler, it was changed simply to "Café Alois" at Hitler's insistence. National Socialists were advised to avoid it on all accounts.

215 "In loyalty that is so deeply": The page was inscribed in Houston Stewart Chamberlain, *Immanuel Kant: Die Persönlichkeit als Einführung in das Werk*, 4th ed.; it was published in 1921 by her husband's publishing house, F. Bruckmann, in Munich. The Chamberlain book is referenced with the inscription in Philipp Gassert and Daniel S. Mattern, eds., *The Hitler Library: A Bibliography*.

215 "deep concern": "Ministerbesprechung," RKA, Schleicher, doc. 56, "Politische Lage," note 9 (January 16, 1933).

215 "This time, he did not": Weiss and Hoser, *Aus den Tagebüchern von Reinhold Quaatz*, December 24, 1932.

216 "distancing himself": Ibid.

216 "History will find": "Ministerbesprechung," RKA, Schleicher, vol. 1, no. 56, "Politische Lage," note 9 (January 16, 1933).

217 "The Strassers have inflicted": Goebbels, *Tagebücher*, December 30, 1932.

217 "Hitler has been dictating": Ibid.

217 "One day, the year": "Adolf Hitlers Neujahrsbotschaft," in *Hitler Reden*, vol. 5, part 2, doc. 107, December 31, 1932.

218 "Either the German people": Ullrich, *Hitler*, 330.

218 "revolts and insurrections": "Adolf Hitlers Neujahrsbotschaft," in *Hitler Reden*, December 31, 1932.

219 "No reconciliation!": Goebbels, *Tagebücher*, December 31, 1932.

219 "This has been the greatest": "Adolf Hitlers Neujahrsbotschaft," in *Hitler Reden*, December 31, 1932.

220 "Hitler's decline began": "Ein Jahr Kampf um die Macht," *Vossische Zeitung*, January 1, 1933. This article was the first of a three-part series.

220 "the turning point": "Ein Jahr Kampf um die Macht," *Vossische Zeitung*, January 3, 1933 (morning).

220 "A decline on such": "Der Weg eines Jahres: Hitlers Aufstieg und Niedergang," *Vorwärts*, January 1, 1933 (morning). The article quotes statements in the *Frankfurter Zeitung* and the headline in *Volkssktimme*.

220 "Dieses 'Führers' Zeit ist um": *Simplicissimus* 37, no. 41 (January 8, 1933): 486.

220 "a man with a great": Kurt Erich Suckert, a.k.a., Curzio Malaparte, *Coup d'état: The Technique of Revolution* (New York: E. P. Dutton, 1932), 29.

220 "The year 1932": Goebbels, *Tagebücher*, December 24, 1932.

CHAPTER 17 HITLER IN LIPPERLAND

221 January 1933 was as cold: *Vorwärts* ran several stories highlighting the frigid temperatures, including "Berlin im Eispanzer"(January 25, 1933, evening); "Eiszeit über Deutschland" (January 26, 1933, morning); and "Ëisnotdienst der Lufthansa" (January 27, 1933, evening).

221 "bone-chilling cold": Goebbels, *Tagebücher,* January 26, 1933.

222 "She was an attractive": Hanfstaengl, *Zwischen Weissem und Braunem Haus,* 287.

222 "This year belongs": Ibid.

222 "Someone has to manage": Wagener, *Hitler aus nächster Nähe,* 133.

222 "Department fumigated": Goebbels, *Tagebücher,* December 13, 1932.

222 *Blut und Boden:* Walther Darré, *Neuadel aus Blut und Boden* (Munich: Lehmann Verlag, 1930), 129.

223 "Just like the farmer": "Rede auf argrarpolitischer Tagung der NSDAP in München," in *Hitler Reden,* vol. 5, part 2, doc. 112, January 3, 1933.

223 "The Führer had given us": Dietrich, *Mit Hitler in die Macht,* 170.

224 Hitler had a defamation: "Strasser bei Schleicher," *Vorwärts,* January 5, 1933 (evening).

224 "Hitler, Papen and I": "Eidesstattliche Erklärung des Freiherrn Kurt von Schroeder vor der amerikanischen Untersuchungsbehörde des Internationalen Militärgerichtshofes in Nürnberg zu den Verhandlungen in seinem Hause in Köln mit Hitler am 4. Januar 1933" ["Sworn Statement by Kurt Baron von Schroeder to the American Investigatory Committee of the International Military Tribunal in Nuremberg on the Negotiations with Hitler at Schroeder's House in Cologne on January 4, 1933"], reprinted in Reinhard Kühnl, *Der deutsche Faschismus in Quellen und Dokumenten* (Düsseldorf: Paul-Rugenstein Verlag, 1977), 172–75, cited in German History in Documents and Images, https://ghdi.ghi-dc.org.

224 "Hitler raked me": Papen, *Der Wahrheit eine Gasse,* 255–56.

225 "Papen went on": "Eidesstattliche Erklärung des Freiherrn Kurt von Schroeder vor der amerikanischen Untersuchungsbehörde des Internationalen Militärgerichtshofes in Nürnberg zu den Verhandlungen in seinem Hause in Köln mit Hitler am 4 Januar 1933," reprinted in Reinhard Kühnl, *Der deutsche Faschismus in Quellen und Dokumenten* (Düsseldorf: Paul-Rugenstein Verlag, 1977), 172–75.

225 The supposed secret meeting: *Tägliche Rundschau* cited in "Strasser bei Schleicher," *Vorwärts,* January 5, 1933 (evening).

226 "Adolf and Little Franz": "Adolf und Fränzchen," *Rheinische Zeitung*, January 7–8, 1933.

226 "most awkward moment": Papen, *Der Wahrheit eine Gasse*, 260.

226 John Wheeler-Bennett surmised: Wheeler-Bennett, *Hindenburg: The Wooden Titan*, 425.

226 "Schleicher's intelligence services": Dietrich, *Mit Hitler in die Macht*, 172.

226 "If he is sitting": "Strasser bei Schleicher," *Vorwärts*, January 5, 1933 (evening).

226 *Vorwärts* dryly observed: "Hitlers Unehrlichkeit am Pranger," *Vorwärts*, January 7, 1933 (morning).

227 "a Jewish banker": Klotz, *The Berlin Diaries*, January 5, 1933.

227 "Swedish Money Pump": "Hitler's Schweden Pump," *Vorwärts*, January 14, 1933 (evening).

227 Carl Wallenberg: Papen, *Der Wahrheit eine Gasse*, 258.

227 The most sensational: The rumor about the Warburg connection was an invention of Jean Gustave Schoup, who, under the pseudonym Sidney Warburg, published a book in the Netherlands titled *De geldbronnen van het nationaal-socialisme, 3 gesprekken met Hitler*. An English version translated from German is titled *Hitler's Secret Backers*, available from Ethos publishing house in Singapore.

227 "I don't know what": Papen, *Der Wahrheit eine Gasse*, 259.

227 "In recent days": "Hitlers Geldquellen," *Vossische Zeitung*, January 14, 1933 (morning).

228 Marcus Wallenberg, for his part: "Wallenberg Dementier," *Vossische Zeitung*, January 15, 1933 (morning).

228 "Hitler could breathe": Treviranus, *Das Ende von Weimar*, 356.

228 "Finances have suddenly": Goebbels, *Tagebücher*, January 18, 1933.

228 "mini-parliament": François-Poncet, *Von Versailles bis Potsdam*, 229.

229 "The election results show": "Hitlers Verluste in Thuringia," *Vossische Zeitung*, December 5, 1932.

229 "Each evening around": Dietrich, *Mit Hitler in die Macht*, 176.

230 "When Hitler arrived": "Rede auf NSDAP-Versammlung in Bösingfeld," in *Hitler Reden*, vol. 5, part 2, doc. 114, note 2, January 4, 1933.

230 "If given the choice": "Rede auf NSDAP-Versammlung in Detmold," in *Hitler Reden*, vol. 5, part 2, doc. 115, January 4–5, 1933.

231 "From this historic": "Rede auf NSDAP-Versammlung in Leopoldshöhe," in *Hitler Reden*, vol. 5, part 2, doc. 177, January 5, 1933.

231 "Hitler Hits the Villages!": "Hitler geht auf die Dörfer!" *Niederrheinisches Tageblatt,* January 6, 1933.

231 "A Triumphant Victory March": "Triumphaler Siegeszug durch Lipperland," in *Hitler Reden,* vol. 5, part 2, doc. 177, January 5, 1933.

231 "Oracle of Lippe": "Hinter den Kulissen," *Vossische Zeitung,* January 5, 1933 (evening).

232 "There have been discussions": "Schleicher Verhandelt," *Vossische Zeitung,* January 14, 1933.

232 "I ran into Strasser": Alfred Rosenberg, *Letzte Aufzeichnung: Ideale und Idole der Nationalsozialistischen Revolution* (Göttingen: Pleese Verlag, 1955), 113.

232 Brüning heard that Strasser: Brüning, *Memoiren 1918–1934,* 635.

232 "However things": "Strasser's Freunde," *Vossische Zeitung,* December 10, 1932 (evening).

232 "Gregor Strasser is also": Ibid.

233 "I am a Hitlerman": "Hitler und Papen erklären," *Vossische Zeitung,* January 7, 1933 (morning).

233 "deeply wounded": Krosigk, *Memoiren,* 155.

233 "the most confident": Frank, "Adolf Hitler: Eine 'Gestalt-Gestaltung,'" 113.

233 "Hitler seems to me": Ibid., 114.

233 "inaccurate interpretations": "Der Krach um Hitler," *Vorwärts,* December 10, 1932 (morning).

234 *Battle Against High Finance:* Gottfried Feder, *Kampf gegen die Hochfinanz* (Munich: Franz Eher Nechfolger, 1933). Hitler's inscribed copy can be viewed in the Rare Books and Manuscripts Division of the Library of Congress. The inscription is transcribed in Gassert and Mattern, *The Hitler Library: A Bibliography.*

234 Hitler acquiesced: Heiden, *Adolf Hitler,* 306.

234 "[Hitler had] triumphed": Kershaw, *Hitler,* 401.

235 Hanfstaengl thought: Hanfstaengl, *Zwischen Weissem und Braunem Haus,* 281.

235 "The first round": "Hitler setzt Strasser ab," *Vossische Zeitung,* December 10, 1932 (evening).

235 "For a whole month": Fromm, *Blood and Banquets,* January 19, 1932.

235 "is clever but not loyal": Brüning, *Memoiren 1918–1934,* 640.

235 "The aim of the discussion": "Wilhelm von Preussen an den Reichs-kanzler," RKA, Schleicher, no. 54 (January 13, 1933).

236 "Germany, only Germany": Gregor Strasser, radio speech, June 14, 1932, in *Kampf um Deutschland: Reden und Aufsätze eines Nationalsozia-listen* (Munich: Franz Eher Verlag, 1932), 387.

237 "The German people are protesting": Ibid.

237 "The Reich president had the wish": "Gregor Strasser bei Hinden-burg," *Vorwärts,* January 12, 1933 (morning).

237 "Even the Reich president": Otto Meissner: *Staatsekretär,* 251–52. Meissner places the meeting with Hindenburg in January 1933 but references the meeting in the deliberations from early December.

238 One "optimistic" estimate: "Politische Hellseherei," *Vorwärts,* January 3, 1933 (morning).

238 "in a positive direction": Ibid.

239 "a gradual change": "Ministerbesprechung," RKA, Schleicher, no. 56 "Politische Lage" (January 16, 1933).

240 "I consider it a mistake": Ibid., note 13.

240 "Apparently he had my phone": Papen, *Der Wahrheit eine Gasse,* 260.

240 *"Fränzchen hat Sie verraten":* Gottfried Reinhold Treviranus, *Das Ende Von Weimar: Heinrich Brüning und seine Zeit* (Düsseldorf: Econ-Verlag, 1968), 355.

241 "false assumptions": "Erklärung," in *Hitler Reden,* vol. 5, part 2, doc. 116, January 5, 1933.

CHAPTER 19 VISITATIONS

242 "Papen visits": Christopher Isherwood, *Christopher and His Kind, 1929–1939* (New York: Avon, 1977), 117.

242 "I recall with particular": Joachim von Ribbentrop, *Zwischen London und Moskau: Erinnerungen und letzte Aufzeichnung,* ed. Annelies von Ribbentrop (Leoni am Starnberger See: Druffel Verlag, 1953), 36.

242 "She was never": Fromm, *Blood and Banquets,* June 12, 1933.

243 "Helldorff did so": Joachim von Ribbentrop testimony, International Military Tribunal, Nuremberg, March 26, 1946.

243 "A Prussian general": Joachim von Ribbentrop, *Zwischen London und Moskau,* 36.

243 "When Father": *My Father Joachim von Ribbentrop: Hitler's Foreign Minister, Experiences and Memories* (Pen & Sword Military; 2019), 31.

243 "A few days after": Ibid., 32.

244 "Papen strongly opposed": Goebbels, *Tagebücher,* January 10, 1933.

245 "all these attempts": Krosigk's January 29, 1933, entry in his *Memoiren* is cited in "Tagebuchaufzeichnung des Reichsfinanzministers über Vorgänge in Berlin zwischen dem 23 und 28 Januar 1933 und den Rücktritt des Kabinetts von Schleicher," RKA, Schleicher, no. 77.

245 *Vorwärts* reported: "Kommt Strasser?," *Vorwärts,* January 14, 1933 (evening).

245 "Hugenberg was cunningly": Brüning, *Memoiren, 1918–1934,* 635.

245 "Strasser will join": "Kommt Strasser?," *Vorwärts,* January 14, 1933 (evening).

246 "He was an educated": Thyssen, *I Paid Hitler,* 132–33.

246 "Strasser is really": Hanfstaengl, *Zwischen Weissem und Braunem Haus,* 268.

246 "election campaign battle": "Gespräche hinter den Kulissen," *Vossische Zeitung,* January 5, 1933 (evening), and "Riesenwahlkampf um Lippe-Detmold," *Vossische Zeitung,* January 4, 1933 (evening).

246 "Traitor!": Goebbels, *Tagebücher,* January 15, 1933.

246 "Hitler falls far": "Sozialdemokratischer Erfolg in Lippe," *Vorwärts,* January 16, 1933 (evening).

247 with 38,844 votes: Ibid.

247 "beaming like": Frank, "Adolf Hitler: Eine 'Gestalt-Gestaltung,'" 117.

248 "Just like a field marshal": "Rede auf Amtsanwalter-Versammlung des Gaues Thüringen der NSDAP in Weimar," in *Hitler Reden,* vol. 5, part 2, doc. 138, January 15, 1933.

248 "Poor Gregor!": Goebbels, *Tagebücher,* January 17, 1933.

248 "Hitler demands": J. Ribbentrop, *Zwischen London und Moskau,* 39.

248 "Such a demand": Ibid.

249 "impervious to poking": Kessler, *Das Tagebuch,* January 29, 1933.

249 "I have to be": Weiss and Hoser, *Aus den Tagebüchern von Reinhold Quaatz,* January 17, 1932.

250 "If Hitler sits in the saddle": Ibid.

250 "He [Hitler] was with Hugenberg": Goebbels, *Tagebücher,* January 18, 1933.

251 "When Hitler asked how": Papen, *Der Wahrheit eine Gasse,* 265.

251 "Once Hitler is in power": Rüdiger Barth and Hauke Friederichs, *Die*

Totengräber: Der letzte Winter der Weimarer Republik (Frankfurt am Main: Fischer Verlag, 2019), 321.

252 "a glittering elaborate": Fromm, *Blood and Banquets*, January 17, 1933.

252 "He seems to have": Ibid.

252 "Gregor, that shrewd": Goebbels, *Tagebücher*, January 20, 1933.

252 "It's characteristic": Fromm, *Blood and Banquets*, January 19, 1932.

253 "People are slowly": Ibid., January 23, 1932.

254 "ungracious reception": Klotz, *The Berlin Diaries*, January 6, 1933.

254 "subjugate": "Ministerbesprechung," RKA, Schleicher, no. 56, "Politische Lage," note 13 (January 16, 1933).

254 "He sees the chancellor": Ibid.

CHAPTER 20   HINDENBURG WHISPERERS

255 "He doesn't want": Goebbels, *Tagebücher*, January 18, 1933. The German original reads: *"Er will nicht. Quatsch. Seine Einbläser wollen nicht."* I have translated *"Einbläser"* as "advisers," although this fails to convey the nuance of the German original, which could be rendered as "those who blow into the ear."

255 "They understand now": Fromm, *Blood and Banquets*, January 22, 1932.

255 "Previously, Oskar never had": Kessler, *Das Tagebuch*, January 28, 1933.

256 "sentimental memories": Ibid., July 20, 1935.

256 "jovial manner": Binchy, "Paul von Hindenburg," 240.

256 political vocabulary: Weiss and Hoser, *Aus den Tagebüchern von Reinhold Quaatz*, January 17, 1933.

256 "neither a mental": Otto Meissner, *Staatssekretär*, 214.

256 "Afterward, he quickly": Ibid.

257 "Yet this flood": Hindenburg, *Aus meinem Leben*, 442.

257 "against which the constitution": "Vermerk des Ministerialrats Neumann zur Frage der rechtlichen Beurteilung einer vom Reichspräsidenten einzuleitenden Abänderung der Reichsverfassung," RKA, Schleicher, no. 60 (January 17, 1933).

258 "the great benefactor": Kessler, *Das Tagebuch*, November 13, 1932.

258 "I don't believe": Goebbels, *Tagebücher*, January 22, 1933.

259 "would not change the situation": "Niederschrift aus dem Büro des Reichspräsident über den Empfang des Reichskanzlers durch den Reichspräsident," RKA, Schleicher, no. 65 (January 23, 1933).

260 "the loss of trust": Krosigk, *Memoiren,* 136.

260 "On the second": RKA, Schleicher, no. 65 (January 23, 1933).

260 "Under such circumstances": Papen, *Der Wahrheit eine Gasse,* 266.

262 "But along with": Klotz, *The Berlin Diaries,* June 8, 1932.

262 "not to the Old": Ibid.

262 "in the usual manner": "Kavalierkrach um Gut Neudeck," *Vorwärts,* January 3, 1933 (evening).

262 "none of the": Otto Meissner, *Staatssekretär,* 265.

263 "The army would then": Enzensberger, *Hammerstein oder der Eigensinnhu,* 102.

263 "Hindenburg was extremely sensitive": Ibid.

263 "Today Hitler insists": "Das Spiel Hinter den Kulissen," *Vossische Zeitung,* January 26, 1933.

264 "The New Hamlet": Cartoon, *Vorwärts,* January 24, 1933 (evening).

CHAPTER 21   FATEFUL WEEKEND

265 "States have changed": "Berliner Presseball 1933," *Vossische Zeitung,* January 30, 1933.

265 "Crisis in Wilhelmstrasse": "Es kriselt in der Wilhelmstrasse—Hitler und Papen als Kanzlerkandidaten—Schleicher wackelt," *Vorwärts,* January 29, 1933.

266 "ice sheet of isolation": "Kanzlersturz und dann?," *Vossische Zeitung,* January 29, 1933 (morning).

266 Less clear: "Schleicher zurückgetreten: Verhandlungs-Auftrag an Papen," *Vossische Zeitung,* January 28, 1933.

266 "If Hitler wants to": Otto Meissner, *Staatssekretär,* 247.

266 "People who cannot sleep at night": Brüning, *Memoiren 1918–1934,* 624.

266 "Don't worry so much": Fromm, *Blood and Banquets,* January 28, 1932.

267 "Trevi, you are": Treviranus, *Das Ende von Weimar,* 285.

267 John Wheeler-Bennett recalled: Wheeler-Bennett, *Hindenburg: The Wooden Titan,* 427.

267 If anyone had that chance: "Ministerbesprechung," RKA, Schleicher, no. 71 (January 28, 1933).

268 "Unfortunately, [a majority]": Ibid.

269 "I have something": Hans-Otto Meissner, *Die Machtergreifung,* 101.

269 "Look, Little Franz": Ibid., 156.

269 "I wish to reserve": Ibid.

269 "I know it sounds strange": Brüning, *Memoiren 1918–1934*, 579.

270 "crisis for the Reich president": Hans-Otto Meissner, *Die Machtergreifung*, 254.

270 Hindenburg asked Meissner: Ibid.

271 "You mean to tell me I have": Ibid., 255.

271 "It was quite unusual": Nuremberg Trial Proceedings Volume 16, One Hundred Fifty-Sixth Day, Monday, June 17, 1946, The Avalon Project, Yale Law School.

272 "I have never seen": J. Ribbentrop, *Zwischen London und Moskau*, 40.

272 Hitler wanted presidial: Hans-Otto Meissner, *Die Machtergreifung*, 255.

272 "A Papen dictatorial cabinet": Papen, *Der Wahrheit eine Gasse*, 268.

273 "Hitler will do his utmost": Ibid.

273 if the president wanted: Ibid., 270.

274 *"Kampfkabinett"*: Krosigk, *Memoiren*, 156.

274 "the only viable": Ibid.

274 "Tell me, what's happening?": Kessler, *Das Tagebuch*, January 28, 1933.

275 "Herr von Schleicher": "Berliner Chronik der Machtergreifung," *Tagesspiegel*, January 29, 1933. The article, posted by Stephan Wiehler on January 26, 2013, quotes the *B.Z. am Mittag*. See https://www.tagesspiegel.de/berlin/sally-rehfisch-ist-tot-2547349.html.

275 "The Rumba": "Berliner Presse Ball 1933," *Vossische Zeitung*, January 30, 1933. The actual song title was "Der Onkel Bumba aus Kalumba tanzt nur Rumba."

275 "It makes me want": Kessler, *Das Tagebuch*, January 28, 1933.

276 "[Schleicher] let his": "Kanzlersturz—und dann?," *Vossische Zeitung*, January 29, 1933 (morning).

276 "Papen was in daily": Brüning, *Memoiren 1918–1934*, 639.

276 Krosigk thought that: Krosigk, *Memoiren*, 156.

276 "If you aren't": Klotz, *The Berlin Diaries*, January 28, 1933.

277 "Rarely had a chancellor": Wheeler-Bennett, *Hindenburg: The Wooden Titan*, 422.

277 "The only guest": Fromm, *Blood and Banquets*, January 29, 1933.

277 "Maybe it would be best": Goebbels, *Tagebücher*, January 29, 1932.

278 "the possibility of forming": Hans-Otto Meissner, *Die Machtergreifung*, 256.

278 "What brings you here": Ibid., 257.

279 "every German will have": Barth and Friederichs, *Die Totengräber*, 358.

280 wished Meissner had been there: Hans-Otto Meissner, *Die Machtergreifung*, 259.

281 "with barely contained resentment": Franz von Papen, *Vom Scheitern einer Demokratie 1930–1933* (Mainz: v. Hase & Koehler Verlag, 1968), 381.

282 "In two months": Barth and Friederichs, *Die Totengräber*, 259.

282 "much quicker": "Hitler Kanzler?," *Vorwärts*, January 29, 1933.

282 "constantly holding new elections": Ibid.

283 "The Iron Front saved": Barth and Friederichs, *Die Totengräber*, 356.

283 "I shall not allow myself": John W. Wheeler-Bennett, *The Nemesis of Power: The German Army in Politics 1918–1945* (London: Macmillan and Company, 1953), 281.

284 "In Potsdam, a splendid": Klotz, *Berlin Diaries*, January 29, 1933.

284 "Bitter as I might be": Barth and Friederichs, *Die Totengräber*, 344.

284 That afternoon, Schleicher met: Klotz, *The Berlin Diaries*, January 28, 1933.

284 "Leipart, the representative": Ibid.

284 "Tomorrow, early, Schleicher": Ibid.

285 "Papen only wanted": Goebbels, *Tagebücher*, January 30, 1933.

286 "If the folks": Ullrich, *Hitler*, 367.

286 Hitler suspected that Hindenburg: Ibid.

286 "Hindenburg blind and unfit": Goebbels, *Tagebücher*, January 30, 1933.

286 "The field marshal seemed": Papen, *Der Wahrheit eine Gasse*, 273.

287 "Threat. Serious": Goebbels, *Tagebücher*, January 30, 1933.

CHAPTER 22 JANUARY 30, 1933

288 "There is fear": "Wasserrohrbrüche," *Vorwärts*, January 29, 1933 (morning).

289 "two-man" leadership team: Hans-Otto Meissner, *Die Machtergreifung*, 262.

289 Krosigk received another call: Barth and Friederichs, *Die Totengräber*, 367.

290 "confused and distracted": Schäfer, *Werner von Blomberg*, 97.

291 "My assignment for you": Hans-Otto Meissner, *Die Machtergreifung*, 268.

291 "You'll be arrested": Ibid., 271.

292 sitting at his hotel room window: Ibid.

293 Hitler turned abruptly: Ibid., 269.

293 "The closer Hitler": Hanfstaengl, *Zwischen Weissem und Braunem Haus*, 269.

294 "I truly regret": Ibid.

294 Blomberg repeated Oskar's: Ibid., 271.

295 "Hugenberg firmly dismissed": Papen, *Der Wahrheit eine Gasse*, 275.

295 "The discussion became so heated": Ibid., 276.

296 "If we go with Hitler": Weiss and Hoser, *Aus den Tagebüchern von Reinhold Quaatz*, January 29, 1933.

296 "It is a game": Ibid.

296 *"Nein!"*: Hans-Otto Meissner, *Die Machtergreifung*, 273.

296 "Herr Hugenberg, I hereby": Ibid., 272.

297 "Gentlemen, we are five minutes": Ibid., 273.

298 "You should try": Fromm, *Blood and Banquets*, March 11, 1932.

298 "They need to decide": Hans-Otto Meissner, *Die Machtergreifung*, 273.

299 "I swear: I will devote": Ibid., 275.

300 Film footage shows: Volker Heise, "Berlin 1933: Tagebuch einer Grossstadt," part 1, 15:35, first broadcast on ARTE, 8:15 p.m., January 24, 2023.

301 "I just made": Hugenberg is widely known to have said this to Carl Goerdeler, the mayor of Leipzig. The original reads: *"Ich habe gestern die größte Dummheit meines Lebens gemacht; ich habe mich mit dem größten Demagogen der Weltgeschichte verbündet."* See Heinz Höhne, "Warten auf Hitler," *Der Spiegel* 6 (1983). See also Larry Eugene Jones, "'The Greatest Stupidity of My Life': Alfred Hugenberg and the Formation of the Hitler Cabinet, January 1933," *Journal of Contemporary History* 27, no. 1 (January 1992): 63–87.

POSTSCRIPT

303 *"Jawohl, ich bin"*: Wheeler-Bennett, *Nemesis*, 323.

303 "If I'm to": William Shirer, *Rise and Fall of the Third Reich* (New York: Simon & Schuster, 1960), 221.

303 "Murder of Röhm": Kessler, *Das Tagebuch*, June 30, 1934. The entry for this date was inserted by Kessler into his diary on October 9,

1934, along with several other entries describing events from spring and summer 1934.

304 "lack of discretion": Wheeler-Bennett, *Nemesis*, 316.

304 "The preparation of": Ibid., 318.

304 "I am going home": Ibid., 324.

305 "If he ever tries to extract": Kessler, *Das Tagebuch*, January 31, 1933.

305 "No Third Reich, not even a 2½": Johann Wilhelm Brügel and Norbert Frei, eds., "Aufzeichnungen des tschechoslowakischen Diplomaten Camill Hoffmann," *Vierteljahrshefte für Zeitgeschichte* 36 (1988): 159.

305 "The planned assassination": Kessler, *Das Tagebuch*, February 27, 1933.

306 "No stranger election": Edwin L. James, "Germany Voting Today in Weirdest Election," *New York Times*, March 5, 1933.

307 "But you cannot make": Kessler, *Das Tagebuch*, July 20, 1935.

Index

1. *Time* magazine cover, December 31, 1931: New York Historical Society
2. Hitler speaking in the Lustgarten: Bayerische Staatsbibiliothek München/ Bildarchiv
3. Hindenburg running for president, 1932: Creative Commons: Bundesarchiv 102-13227 CC-BY-SA 3.0`
4. Campaigners for the July 31 Reichstag election: Creative Commons: Bundesarchiv 102-03497A CC-BY-SA 3.0
5. Hitler in the front passenger seat: Bayerische Staatsbibliothek München / Bildarchiv
6. Harry Kessler: public domain
7. Eva Braun: Bayerische Staatsbibliothek München/Bildarchiv
8. Postman Hitler: Bibliothek im Archiv der Sozialen Demokratie der Friedrich-Ebert-Stiftung; reprinted courtesy of Princeton University Library
9. Franz von Papen: Bundesarchiv, Bild 183-1988-0113-500 / CC-BY-SA 3.0
10. Kurt von Schleicher: public domain
11. Otto Meissner: Bayerische Staatsbibliothek München/Bildarchiv
12. Neudeck terrace meeting: Bayerische Staatsbibliothek München/Bildarchiv
13. Hitler and Hugenberg: Bundesarchiv, Bild 102-12403 / CC-BY-SA 3.0
14. Gregor Strasser; National Archives and Records Administration, College Park, Maryland
15. Reichstag, August 30, 1932: Bundesarchiv, Bild 102-13801 / CC-BY-SA 3.0
16. Lufthansa poster: Bayerische Staatsbibliothek München/Bildarchiv
17. Leni Riefenstahl: Aafa/Ross Verlag, publicity photo, public domain
18. Hitler voting: United States Holocaust Memorial Museum / public domain
19. Brown House interior: National Archives and Records Administration, Public Domain, College Park, Maryland
20. Hitler and NSDAP delegates: National Archives and Records Administration, College Park, Maryland

21. Hitler, Goebbels, Dietrich: Bayersiche Staatsbibliothek München/Bildarchiv
22. Campaign truck in Lipperland: Landesarchiv Nordrhein-Westfalen
23. Hitler as Hamlet: Bibliothek im Archiv der Sozialen Demokratie der Friedrich-Ebert-Stiftung
24. Hitler cabinet: Bayerische Staatsbibliothek München/Bildarchiv

Timothy W. Ryback is the author of *The Last Survivor, Hitler's Private Library*, and *Hitler's First Victims*. His books have appeared in more than forty editions around the world. *The Last Survivor* was a *New York Times* Notable Book, *Hitler's Private Library* a *Washington Post* Notable Book. Ryback has written for *The Atlantic Monthly*, the *Financial Times*, *The New Yorker*, *The New York Times*, and *The Wall Street Journal* and has appeared in numerous television documentaries. Ryback has served as director of the Institute for Historical Justice and Reconciliation, in The Hague; deputy secretary-general of the Académie Diplomatique Internationale, in Paris; vice president and resident director of Salzburg Global Seminar, in Salzburg; and lecturer in the Concentration of History and Literature at Harvard University. Ryback and his wife divide their time between Europe and the United States.

A NOTE ON THE TYPE

This book was set in Janson, a typeface long thought to have been made
by the Dutchman Anton Janson, who was a practicing typefounder in
Leipzig during the years 1668–1687. However, it has been conclusively
demonstrated that these types are actually the work of Nicholas Kis
(1650–1702), a Hungarian, who most probably learned his trade from
the master Dutch typefounder Dirk Voskens. The type is an excellent example of the influential and sturdy Dutch types that prevailed
in England up to the time William Caslon (1692–1766) developed his
own incomparable designs from them.

Composed by North Market Street Graphics,
Lancaster, Pennsylvania

Printed and bound by Berryville Graphics,
Berryville, Virginia

Designed by Soonyoung Kwon